Preface

This book is a guide to remediating learning and behavioral problems, intended for special and regular classroom teachers in training or in service. In our experience, nearly all teachers can be successful if they have instruction and guidance.

This third edition reflects the rapid educational changes during the thirteen years since the first edition was published. Most significant, this text has two new chapters on cognitive strategy training and study skills. We thought it crucial to show the implications of recent research on effective teaching. We incorporated visual-motor information in other chapters, added information on the use of microcomputers throughout the book, and cover more teaching and management activities for older students with learning and behavioral problems. In addition, we have included the most current references, curriculum materials, and assessment techniques. We believe that these changes will allow teachers to keep pace with the continuing emphasis on teaching students with all types of handicaps in the mainstream of public education.

Part One is a practical approach to remediation. We define learning problems in terms of specific behavioral deficits (not by traditional labels). We use down-to-earth language to describe principles of behavior management and academic remediation and illustrate these ideas with examples drawn from the classroom. Teaching competencies that apply across curriculum areas are also presented. We show that early detection and good teaching can positively impact the prevention of learning and behavioral problems.

Part Two details how to assess and remediate problems in social behavior, spoken language, reading, written language, mathematics, and study skills. The beginning teacher will find many proven teaching suggestions, and the more experienced teacher will find the suggested activities adaptable to particularly difficult problems.

We appreciate the continued support and assistance of many individuals in completing this book. We would like to thank our reviewers: Dr. Jim Krause, Bowling Green State University; Dr. Maurice Miller, Indiana State University; and Dr. Ann Ryan, College of St. Thomas, Minnesota. We are grateful to Carlyn Fujimoto, Denise Green, Donna Murphy, Patty Pullen, and Patty Whitfield for their help in library research, proofreading, and preparing test questions for the testbank. We are especially appreciative of the patience and forebearance of our own children, Tim and Missy Kauffman and Chris and T. J. Wallace, and the students and parents whose photographs appear throughout the book.

Gerald Wallace
James M. Kauffman

TEACHING STUDENTS WITH LEARNING AND BEHAVIOR PROBLEMS

Third Edition

Gerald Wallace

University of Virginia

James M. Kauffman

University of Virginia

Merrill Publishing Company
A Bell & Howell Company
Columbus Toronto London Sydney

Published by Merrill Publishing Co.
A Bell & Howell Company
Columbus, Ohio 43216

This book was set in Bookman.
Cover Design Coordination: Cathy Watterson
Text Design and Production Coordination: Jeffrey Putnam

Cover photographs by James M. Kauffman and James Hogg.

Photos: All photographs by James Kauffman, except page 163, which is by Myron
Cunningham.

Library of Congress Catalog Card Number: 85–43448
International Standard Book Number: 0–675–20534–4
Printed in the United States of America
1 2 3 4 5 6 7 8 9—91 90 89 88 87 86

Contents

PART TWO
A Guide to Instructional Activities, 163

for Marti

PART ONE

A Practical Approach
To Remediation

Most students in American schools do not experience major learning problems. Their academic achievement is within the expected range for their age and abilities, and their behavior is generally acceptable to their teachers. A significant percentage of students, however, do exhibit academic difficulties or social-behavioral problems. Students with learning and behavior problems are becoming easier to recognize as educational technology, pressure for excellence, and the requirements of Public Law 94–142 (the Education for All Handicapped Children Act) shape American education.

Efforts to meet the educational needs of all students with learning and behavior problems have not been entirely successful to date. The preparation of special teachers and the enactment of P.L. 94–142 have not yet resulted in adequate educational opportunities for all students. The proliferation of school personnel designated as "resource," "crisis," "prescriptive," or "consultant" teachers has not resolved the problem of appropriate education for all students. Increasingly, educators recognize that if the educational needs of all students are to be met, all teachers must become skillful in the instruction of students with learning and behavior problems.

All teachers know the pleasure of teaching students who learn quickly and easily. Likewise, all teachers share the frustration and anxiety associated with students who learn slowly and with great difficulty. But frustration, anxiety, depression, and anger can be replaced with joy and satisfaction for both teacher and student when learning and behavior problems are managed successfully. Unfortunately, teachers often fail unknowingly to help students with learning and behavior problems because they lack technical skill. Consequently, our emphasis here is on the knowledge and application of sound learning principles and instructional strategies. A working knowledge of the principles presented in part one of this text will increase the probability of developing the technical skill necessary to remediate learning and behavior problems successfully.

Affective aspects of education—self-awareness, self-actualization, and sensitivity to the needs of students—are prerequisites for good teaching, but they must be accompanied by technical knowledge and skill if students are to be helped. Just as awareness and personal concern for patients can enhance but cannot replace the competent physician's technical knowledge and skill in the practice of medicine, so sensitivity and humanistic goals can supplement but cannot supplant the understanding and application of learning principles in teaching. Technical mastery allows the educational practioner to give form and substance to human values.

Part one provides a foundation for the development of specific teaching techniques. Chapter 1 is an overview of the characteristics and etiologies of and the educational services for students with learning and behavior problems. Chapter 2 introduces basic principles of behavior management from a behavior modification point of view. Chapter 3 presents principles of remediating academic deficits, which apply to all curriculum areas. Chapter 4 summarizes recently developed teaching procedures involving cognitive strategies. Chapter 5 outlines the competencies teachers must have to be effective instructors and to evaluate their instruction. Chapter 6 points the way to prevention of learning and behavior problems through early identification.

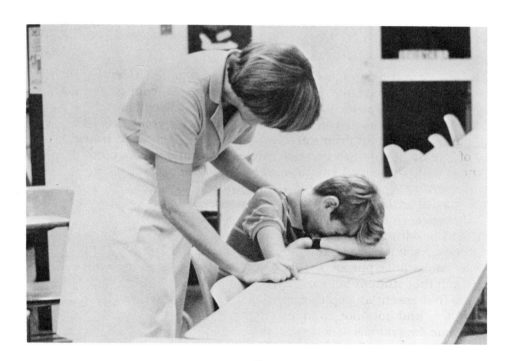

1

Dimensions of Learning Problems

Public education in America has undergone significant changes and shifts in focus during the past decade. The federal government has mandated special education and related services for all handicapped children under P.L. 94–142. Commissions and study groups have called for a return to basics and an emphasis on excellence. Professional associations, state education agencies, and local school boards have debated merit pay plans for teachers, weighed the merits of voucher systems and tax credits as funding mechanisms for education, and considered the advisability of competency testing for teachers. Through all these proposals run two currents that are the simultaneous goals of American public education: equal educational opportunity and educational excellence. This book is concerned with improving the educational opportunities of students who have become known as school failures. Our intent is to contribute to excellence in their remedial and special education.

The pragmatic spirit of the United States is reflected in public education designed to meet the needs of most students. But for a significant percentage of the nation's elementary and secondary students, education designed for the average learner leads to personal confusion, academic failure, feelings of inadequacy, disparagement by teachers and peers, and finally despair or disgust for school. These students, commonly designated as having learning problems at school, have been identified by a wide variety of labels, all of which carry negative connotations: *learning disabled, emotionally disturbed, mentally retarded, educationally handicapped, disadvantaged, slow learning, perceptually handicapped, dyslexic, minimally brain-damaged,* and many more.

Our concern in this book is not with labels by which students can be called but with the specific learning difficulties preventing the students' success in school. We assume that the way a student is labeled or defined for administrative purposes makes very little difference in determining how to teach that student but that a precise definition of his learning problem is the first essential step in remediation. Specifically, it is what the student does and does not do in response to an educational program that is our focus. Individuals defy meaningful classification, but the problems they experience do not. The history of systems of classification shows that attempting to fit people into neat psychological or educational categories is

---

BEAU

Beau is a 14-year-old-ninth grader who had been receiving special assistance from the high school resource room teacher. Beau is well liked by his classmates and his teachers report that he is well groomed, polite, and quite personable.

Although Beau has above-average intellectual capacity, he continues to experience severe written language problems. He still prints almost all written work because he is completely confused by cursive writing, and his printing is marked by many erasures and incorrectly formed letters. While copying assignments from the chalkboard, Beau must refer back to the board after writing just a few letters. His sentence and paragraph writing is marked by many misspelled, jumbled, and incoherent word combinations. Although Beau does make an effort to use capitalization and punctuation, his work is almost completely void of paragraphing and logical development. In contrast, during spoken language periods Beau uses complete sentences and an appropriate ordering of details.

During a recent school conference regarding Beau's placement, his teachers suggested that the written language problems were contributing to his frustration and poorer grades in other academic subjects. Beau's parents reported that he had recently begun to fight more often with his two younger siblings. For now, Beau has been recommended for additional time with the resource room teacher.

futile (see Hobbs, 1975). On the other hand, precise definition of the individual's learning abilities and difficulties is feasible and points toward specific remedial procedures. The dimensions of learning necessary for school progress provide the most logical framework for defining learning problems.

ACADEMIC LEARNING

The curricular focus within almost all public schools in the United States is on academic skills. Basic language arts and math skills are emphasized in the elementary grades; secondary schools usually stress academic achievement in various content areas. This concentration serves as a constant reminder to all students that the key to success is effective academic performance. Few realize this more than the student with academic difficulties. The frustration and agony of school failure are only too familiar to the pupil with difficulty learning to read, write, or calculate.

The academic characteristics of students with learning problems vary widely. Wallace and Larsen (1986) point out that many of these students encounter difficulties in one specific area (e.g., mathematics), whereas others experience problems in a number of academic subjects. To a large extent, these problems involve the understanding or use of spoken or written language and reveal themselves in difficulty with reading, thinking,

---

ELIZABETH

Ten-year-old Elizabeth was referred for help because she was functioning 2 years below grade level in all academic areas. She is the youngest of four children in a single-parent family. Her older siblings perform near or above average grade level in school. In addition to her academic deficiencies, Elizabeth is approximately 30 pounds overweight. Her obesity is a source of continual teasing from her classmates.

Assessment results suggest that Elizabeth is functioning in the high normal range of intelligence. The test examiner reported that Elizabeth was concerned about incorrect responses. She often asked, "Is that right?" and many times responded, "I don't know," rather than guess an answer.

Among her many academic problems, math seems to be an area that is particularly troublesome for Elizabeth. She has some understanding of numbers and functions; however, she is confused by place value. Consequently, regrouping is a difficult operation for her. She accomplishes addition and subtraction by counting on her fingers. However, she has great difficulty keeping numbers in the correct columns. She cannot tell time or count money. In fact, she does not know the value of coins greater than a dime.

Elizabeth's teacher notes that she seems to know various math skills one day and then completely forgets them the following day. During these times Elizabeth becomes frustrated and often starts misbehaving in the classroom.

talking, listening, writing, spelling, or doing math (Hammill & Bartel, 1982).

In addition to extending across academic tasks, learning problems are further complicated by varying degrees of severity. Academic skill deficiencies range from mild to severe with the vast majority in the mild to moderate range. Wallace and McLoughlin (1979) note that the complexity of the learning problem is often dependent on the chronological age of the student. Younger pupils exhibit difficulties that are often easily categorized. As the individual matures, however, the once-clear difficulties pervade other academic areas and become quite complex. Thus, students with academic learning problems may have very different types and degrees of difficulty.

SOCIAL-BEHAVIORAL LEARNING

When children enter school, their progress depends not only on their learning academic responses but also on their displaying adequate social-interpersonal behavior. They must adopt behavior patterns that indicate self-acceptance as well as self-realization. The student most likely to succeed in school is one who is both productive (i.e., achieving academically) and happy—reflecting confidence, organization, initiative, persistence in learning desirable skills, self-control, and pride in accomplishment. The successful student also relates well to others. Among peers she is usually outgoing, friendly, popular, and able to take a leadership role. Her relationship to adult authority figures is characterized by confidence, respect, and cooperation (see Kauffman, 1985).

A wide variety of maladaptive behaviors contribute to student problems at school (Cullinan, Epstein, & Kauffman, 1984; Epstein, Kauffman, & Cullinan, 1985). Those behavioral characteristics likely to attract the negative attention of teachers and peers include aggression, impulsiveness, disruptiveness, social withdrawal, and immaturity (see Kauffman, 1985). An individual student who is having significant problems progressing through school often exhibits multiple social-behavioral problems. However, his problems can typically be described as primarily externalized or internalized, as acting out against others or withdrawing into oneself (Achenbach & Edelbrock, 1983; Edelbrock & Achenbach, 1984). Thomas and Glenda illustrate these two types of social-behavioral learning problems.

CAUSES OF SCHOOL LEARNING PROBLEMS

The causes of learning and behavior problems are many and complex. Seldom, if ever, is a single cause of difficulty unequivocally identified. Some causal factors, such as genetics, operate over a long period of time and may *predispose* an individual to have problems. A predisposing factor does not cause a learning or behavior problem directly, but it increases the probabili-

---

THOMAS

Thomas is a 9-year-old third grader who seems constantly to be in trouble. His teacher says he is more "street-wise" than other boys in his class. During unstructured time he is particularly likely to be out of the teacher's sight causing a disruption. He frequently lies and is known by his peers as someone who steals. He receives little supervision at home and has, since the age of 5, been free to roam the neighborhood at will. Few days go by without conflict between Thomas and someone at school. Reports for the last 3 school days have been characteristic: Monday—sent to the principal's office for playing with his food in the cafeteria; Tuesday—sent back to his homeroom teacher for hitting another student in music class; Wednesday—sent to the principal for choking another child on the bus. Thomas has the intelligence to do grade level academic work, but his grades are consistently *D*s and *F*s. He seems almost never to be on task and seldom completes an assignment.

---

ty that an individual will develop such a problem. Other factors, such as a traumatic event or inadequate teaching, are more immediate in their effects and may *precipitate* a learning or behavioral difficulty. A precipitating factor may be relatively innocuous yet trigger a problem in someone predisposed to have difficulty; a major trauma or prolonged exposure to poor teaching may lead to a problem in a student who is not predisposed, or "at risk," to experience problems. Most learning and behavior problems appear to be caused by an interaction of several predisposing and precipitating factors (Hallahan, Kauffman, & Lloyd, 1985; Kauffman, 1985; Wallace & McLoughlin, 1979).

GLENDA

Glenda is a slender, plain-looking 14-year-old. She is in the top 20% of her eighth grade class in achievement, although she is not an academic star. Few of her peers know anything about her, other than her first name. She causes no problems in class and always turns in neat, accurate work. She is never singled out for negative attention by teachers and almost never receives special attention for her achievements. In short, she is close to a social nonentity among her peers and the school personnel. She seldom smiles and seems not to enjoy the things her classmates enjoy. Her English teacher has become concerned about her because of her apparent anxiety, shyness, and lack of self-confidence. They day before she was to give an oral report in class, Glenda complained of feeling nauseous. She eventually confided in her English teacher that she had not been sleeping through the night for months and had begun a pattern of overeating, then vomiting.

Not only do the causes of school learning problems interact and overlap, but the problems they cause also interact and overlap. That is, causal factors seldom operate in isolation; likewise, the resulting problems. Figure 1-1 illustrates the interrelation of extrinsic and intrinsic causes and the categories of resulting learning problems. The figure suggests that the causes are unknown in a significant number of cases.

Figure 1-1.   Causal factors related to learning disabilities and other disorders.

Any one of several extrinsic, intrinsic, or unknown factors can cause a child to be learning disabled (LD), mentally retarded (MR), or emotionally disturbed (ED). Typically, the causal factors in a given case cannot be pinpointed. The causal factors tend to be interrelated, as do the disabilities.

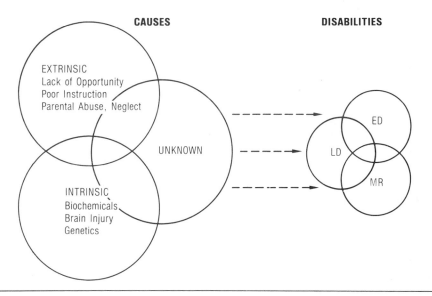

SOURCE: From *Introduction to Learning Disabilities* (2nd ed.,) p. 17 by D. P. Hallahan, J. M. Kauffman, and J. W. Lloyd, 1985, Englewood Cliffs, NJ: Prentice-Hall. Copyright 1985 by Prentice-Hall. Reprinted by permission.

The importance of identifying the causes of a student's problem can easily be overemphasized. Even if an exhaustive catalog of specific causes of learning and behavior problems could be compiled, the list would be instructive only if each cause implied a specific and available remedy. At present, few specific remedies are implied by known or suspected causes of learning difficulties, and fewer still are usable by educators (see Kauffman & Hallahan, 1974; Hallahan, Kauffman, & Lloyd, 1985; Reeve & Kauffman, in press). Nevertheless, educators may find it useful to be aware of the possible causes of school learning problems so that proper referral can be made when remediation by other professionals is appropriate. Often suspected, and sometimes identified are biophysical, sociocultural, psychodevelopmental, and educational factors.

Biophysical Factors

Among the biophysical factors thought to cause learning and behavior problems are genetics, brain injury, missing biochemicals, allergens, and toxic substances such as lead. Biophysical factors are most frequently suggested for problems related to hyperactivity and learning disabilities. No convincing evidence, however, links hyperactivity or learning disabilities to specific biological factors (Hallahan, Kauffman, & Lloyd, 1985; Kauffman & Hallahan, 1979; Whalen, 1983).

A child's genetic endowment and physical status obviously have a profound effect on her behavior patterns (Cravioto & DeLicardie, 1975; Scarr-Salapatek, 1975). Birth trauma, oxygen deprivation, infectious disease, drug intoxication, malnutrition, environmental pollutions, and congenital defects are only a few of the biological events that may predispose a child toward learning and behavior problems. Moreover, children are apparently born with a temperament or behavioral style. Temperament can change over time from the effects of the child's environment, but temperament remains a biologically based pattern of behavior that can affect both behavioral and cognitive development (Pullis & Cadwell, 1982; Thomas & Chess, 1984; Thomas, Chess, & Korn, 1982). In addition, teachers exhibit temperaments, which can affect teacher-student interaction (Osborne, 1985).

Attempts to pinpoint specific biological correlates of individual learning problems have not often been productive. Certainly the teacher must be aware of the biophysical factors that may have contributed to the development of a school learning problem, and they should refer students to medical personnel for evaluation whenever appropriate. However, most medical diagnoses have few implications for educational remediation.

Sociocultural Factors

The social and cultural contexts in which children live undoubtedly shape their learning and behavior. Family relationships, social class discrimination, sex role stereotyping, and the expectations of subcultural groups are all known to affect children's development. Clearly, family disintegration, poverty, racial discrimination, and other negative social and cultural factors can give rise to learning and behavior problems (Dornbusch et al., 1985; Elder, Nguyen, & Caspi, 1985; Gesten, Scher, & Cowen, 1978; Patterson, 1982). Seldom, however, is one able to state confidently that one of these influences is the sole or primary cause of a particular difficulty.

Teachers should be concerned with the social and cultural conditions that may contribute to students' learning and behavior problems. They should have a multicultural perspective and should not confuse cultural difference with social deviance, but they cannot make sociocultural in-tervention the focus of their professional activity. As Engelmann (1969) points out, teachers are primarily responsible for their students' academic competence, not for social policy.

Psychodevelopmental Factors

Learning and behavior problems are often said to stem from an underly-ing psychological disturbance or developmental delay (Berkowitz & Rothman, 1960; Bettelheim, 1961; Scharfman, 1978; Tuma & Sobotka, 1983). Certainly, growing up, being separated from one's parents, establishing one's own identity, experiencing traumatic events, learning to express emotions appropriately, building trusting relationships, and many other developmental tasks and psychological processes are related to school learning. There is no reason to doubt that removal of emotional problems makes the remediation of learning and behavioral difficulties easier. As in the case of biophysical factors, however, psychological diagnoses seldom give a teacher guidance for remedial teaching.

Educational Factors

It is axiomatic that learning and behavior problems may occur because of inadequate or inappropriate teaching—the student may have difficulty learning because the teacher does not provide adequate or appropriate in-struction. The specific teaching deficits that account for a student's failure to learn can be identified; it is then the teacher's responsibility to correct them because she is trained to control the instructional variables that govern learning—the learning of *all* students. This responsibility does not mean that the teacher who has failed to teach a given student has failed as a person or as a professional. It does mean that the teacher must be con-cerned primarily with educational reasons for learning and behavior prob-lems and must continue to examine and improve teaching techniques rather than blame the student or some other causal factor (Engelmann, 1969; Englemann & Carnine, 1982).

Kauffman (1985) has suggested six ways in which educational factors can contribute to learning and behavior problems. Note that affective, behavioral, and instructional aspects of teaching all may be involved.

1. *Insensitivity to the student as an individual.* In a school environment that is conducive to academic and social development, students are allowed to demonstrate their individuality in appropriate ways. Demands for strict uniformity for its own sake, regimentation, and in-tolerance of the legitimate expression of individual differences tend to increase anxiety, frustration, and resistance to learning.

2. *Expectations that are too high or too low.* Skillful teachers adjust their expectations to fit the student's ability to perform so that the student is challenged but also experiences a high level of success. Expectations

that are not appropriate may lead to feelings of inadequacy and failure or to boredom and a lack of motivation.

3. *Inconsistency in behavior management.* Good school and classroom environments are carefully structured so that expectations and consequences are clear to students and are highly predictable (i.e., consistent). When students are not certain what they are to do, how they are to behave, or what the consequences will be, they are much more likely to exhibit academic and social-behavioral problems.

4. *Instructional tasks unimportant to the student.* Students are much more likely to demonstrate achievement and desirable conduct when they feel that what they are being taught is interesting and valuable. Instruction in skills for which students see little purpose and tasks that do not capture student interest are almost certain to result in low performance and undesirable behavior.

5. *Reinforcement of undesirable behavior.* Competent teachers make sure that social rewards such as praise, attention, and privileges (and extrinsic rewards such as stars, awards, trinkets, and food when necessary) follow desirable behavior; undesirable behavior is not rewarded. Unfortunately, students in many classrooms receive attention more often for inappropriate conduct, an arrangement certain to foster failure and misbehavior.

6. *Undesirable models of behavior.* In the best schools and classrooms, students learn much about how to perform academically and how to behave socially by observing and imitating their peers and teachers. When students observe these individuals behaving inappropriately, especially if that inappropriate behavior is being rewarded, they tend to learn patterns of misbehavior and failure.

EDUCATIONAL PROVISIONS FOR SCHOOL LEARNING PROBLEMS

Educational provisions for students with learning and behavioral difficulties have traditionally been the assignment of educators operating outside the regular classroom. These support personnel, teaching in special classes or resource rooms, have had the major responsibility for ameliorating problems. During the past decade, however, it has been widely suggested that working within the regular classroom and allowing regular classroom teachers the opportunity to remediate learning and behavioral difficulties may provide an alternative (Hallahan & Kauffman, 1986). In a short period of time, this approach has proven to be feasible and effective in remediating the learning problems of many students (Heron, 1978). During this same period of time, special education provisions have been widely expanded and considerably modified. Some of the advantages and disadvantages of the various educational provisions are summarized in Table 1–1.

Table 1-1
Advantages and Disadvantages of Educational Service Models for the Learning Handicapped

Educational Provision	Advantages	Disadvantages
Regular classroom	Least restrictive setting provides for interaction of handicapped with nonhandicapped peers. Prevents needless labelling.	Instructional factors may compound learning problems. Large number in class population. Teacher not specifically trained.
Consultant teacher	Able to reach more teachers. Can supply specific instructional methods, programs, and materials. Can serve more children. Influence environmental learning variables. Coordinates comprehensive services for the child.	Consultant may not be considered a member of the teaching staff. Lacks firsthand knowledge of child that comes from teaching. Possible separation of assessment and instruction.
Resource room	Reduces stigmatization. Supplements regular classroom instruction. Separates handicapped learner from nonhandicapped peers for limited periods of the school day. Specially trained teacher provides individualized instruction in problem areas. Teacher may serve as a consultant to the child's regular teachers. Goal is to mainstream the child. Regular classroom teacher remains responsible for student's instructional program.	Scheduling problems. Overenrollment. Misunderstanding of teacher role. Role conflicts. Little time to assess, plan, and consult.

Table 1-1 (continued)

Educational Provision	Advantages	Disadvantages
Itinerant teacher	Aids in screening and diagnosis. Consulting help. Part-time services. Covers needs of children in different schools or areas. Economical ways to serve mild problems.	More involved students need consistent support. Lack of identification with staff. Difficulty in transporting materials. Lack of continuity of program. Lack of regular follow-up.
Special class	Least restrictive setting for severe cases. Individual or small-group instruction. Maintenance of self-esteem. Social acceptance of the student. Full-time attention of one teacher. Provides full-time, highly specialized learning conditions.	Socially segregates. Stigmatizing. Danger of misplacement. Placement may become inappropriately permanent. Very restrictive for mild and moderate cases. Possible modeling of inappropriate behavior by others. Danger of low teacher expectations.

SOURCE: From *Learning Disabilities: Concepts and Characteristics* 2nd ed., (p. 373) by G. Wallace and J. A. McLoughlin, 1979, Columbus, OH: Charles E. Merrill. Copyright 1979 by Bell & Howell Company. Adapted by permission.

Regular Classroom

Hallahan and Kauffman (1986) point out that, nationwide, over two-thirds of all handicapped children and youth are served primarily in regular classes. However, most of these students receive special instruction for part of the school day from special education resource teachers.

We believe that the current trend in American education toward more personalized instruction has provided a means for handling some types of learning and behavioral problems in the regular classroom. Teachers and administrators alike have become more aware of individual differences among students, and particular attention has been given to the means of accommodating these differences. Teachers' aides, team teaching, departmentalization, and lay volunteers have provided classroom teachers with both the time and the resources to meet the instructional goals for students with individual learning needs. The teacher with 25 students, for example, now may have the opportunity to work with individual students or small groups while another person works with the larger group. The wide availability of personalized instructional tools—programmed materials, individual study carrels, microcomputer software—also makes it possible to remediate academic problems in the regular class.

All these changes have helped to make it possible for all teachers to teach all students in their classes. Nothing, however, has been of more help than many educators' recognition of the necessity of planning for individual instructional needs. This has given strong impetus to working with all types of learning problems within the confines of the regular classroom. However, it is probably unrealistic to suppose that students with severe academic or behavioral problems can be managed in the regular classroom. Wallace and McLoughlin (1979) suggest that the regular classroom can best be expected to serve mild learning and behavioral problems.

Consultant Teacher

The consultant teacher model is another increasingly popular provision for serving students with learning and behavior problems. The consultant teacher usually serves as a resource and support for the regular classroom teacher, other school staff, and parents of the learning handicapped student. Wallace and McLoughlin (1979) list the following functions of the consultant teacher: assessment, program design, development and adaptation of materials, demonstration of methods, and program evaluation. Usually, the consultant teacher does not directly instruct the student on a regular basis. According to Lerner (1985), a new set of skills is required for the teacher consultant: this individual needs skills in analysis, synthesis, and problem-solving strategies and a high aptitude for human relations and communication. We feel that open and clear communication between the regular classroom teacher and the consultant teacher is probably the most important and crucial aspect of the consultant teacher model. Without it misunderstandings and obvious dissatisfaction develop. We also believe that the lack of ongoing and direct teaching experience with the student can give the consultant teacher an inaccurate idea of the pupil's learning difficulties.

Resource Room

In this educational arrangement students are enrolled with their peers in a regular classroom. Depending on the nature of their difficulty, students are provided instructional services by a specially trained teacher. Some pupils may be seen individually by the resource teacher for 45 to 60 minutes daily; others may be seen in small groups for 30 minutes each day. The extent of the contact with the resource teacher depends largely on the severity of the student's learning difficulty.

Normally, the resource teacher is housed in a classroom specially furnished with materials and equipment suited to the needs of students with learning and/or behavior problems. In addition to teaching, the resource teacher is usually involved in assessing, screening, and observing students recommended for special education placement. The resource teacher also

supports the regular classroom teachers by supplying activities for the identified population and by maximizing the transfer of skills to the regular
classroom (Wallace & McLoughlin, 1979).

We believe that resource teachers must be highly skilled and personable
individuals. Regular teaching experience is a prerequisite that later helps
the resource teacher make realistic and accurate teaching suggestions to
regular classroom teachers. No less important, however, is the ability to
establish strong personal and professional relationships with other
educators in the school.

The most realistic expectation for this educational arrangement is to provide appropriate service for the mildly to moderately learning handicapped
student. Pupils with severe learning problems may have educational objectives too complex to be adequately handled in the resource room.
Although the resource room model has been widely adopted throughout
the United States for academically handicapped and behaviorally disordered students, little empirical evidence is available to support the effectiveness of the model. Nonetheless, until further research suggests
otherwise, Mercer and Mercer (1985) believe that the resource room will
continue to be the predominant model for service to mildly handicapped
learners.

Itinerant Teacher

The itinerant teacher model is very similar in many respects to the resource
teacher program. Itinerant teachers, however, travel to several schools.
This model is often used in rural areas, where learning handicapped
students are scattered over a wide geographical area. Most speech-language
pathologists and many teachers of the visually handicapped have utilized
the itinerant model for many years.

In addition to instructing students on a limited basis, itinerant teachers
are usually expected to provide the regular teaching staff with suggestions
for follow-up activities. Consequently, the willingness of the regular school
staff to implement teaching plans is an important component of this model.
The major teaching responsibility for the student remains with the regular
classroom teacher.

Among the limitations of the itinerant teacher model, in our experience,
is the unwise use of this type of program as a catch-all for various types
of handicapped students. In addition, we have found that most learning
handicapped students require more consistent support than that provided
by the itinerant teacher model.

Special Class

One of the oldest special education arrangements is the self-contained
special class for specific types of handicapped students. In terms of actual
numbers, classes for the mentally retarded have been most common; but
the number of special classes for the learning disabled and behaviorally

disordered have increased substantially during the last decade (Larsen, 1978). Students enrolled in special classes usually spend the entire day in the segregated class with other similarly handicapped students. In some cases students may be integrated with nonhandicapped children during part of the day. Because the maximum enrollment per class is usually dictated by state law, the special class often serves fewer students than does the regular classroom.

Most critics of special classes argue that their segregated nature detrimentally affects the overall development of children (see Hallahan & Kauffman, 1986). Isolation from normal peers and poor academic achievement are often cited as disadvantages of special class placement (Hammill & Bartel, 1982; Houck, 1984). On the other hand, the increased social and emotional adjustment achieved by special class pupils provides an argument for their use (Ribner, 1978; Smith, 1983). Currently, legal questions threaten the existence of many special classes (Hallahan & Kauffman, 1986).

A PRESCRIPTION FOR CHANGE

The principles of remedial and special education discussed in the next five chapters are intended to provide all teachers with a practical guide to teaching students with learning and behavioral problems. Such a guide is important both to regular classroom teachers, who are becoming one of the most crucial components of the remediation process, and to special education teachers, who can profit from carefully reexamining their teaching procedures and techniques. The principles and techniques that follow can be used in any type of administrative arrangement. Successful remediation of learning and behavioral problems is not dependent on types of service models, appropriate labels for children, or detailed studies of hypothetical causes of academic failure and misbehavior. The competent teacher is the key to effective remediation.

REFERENCES

Achenbach, T. M., & Edelbrock, C. S. (1983). Taxonomic issues in child psychopathology. In T. H. Ollendick & M. Hersen (Eds.), *Handbook of child psychopathology.* New York: Plenum.

Berkowitz, P. H., & Rothman, E. P. (1960). *The disturbed child.* New York: New York University Press.

Bettelheim, B. (1961). The decision to fail. *The School Review, 69,* 389–412.

Cravioto, J., & DeLicardie, E. R. (1975). Environmental and learning deprivation in children with learning disabilities. In W. M. Cruickshank & D. P. Hallahan (Eds.), *Perceptual and learning disabilities in children: Vol. 2. Research and theory.* Syracuse, NY: Syracuse University Press.

Cullinan, D., Epstein, M. H., & Kauffman, J. M. (1984). Teachers' ratings of students' behaviors: What constitutes behavior disorder in school? *Behavioral Disorders, 10*, 9–19.

Dornbusch, S. M., Carlsmith, J. M., Bushwall, S. J., Ritter, P. L., Leiderman, H., Hastorf, A. H., & Gross, R. T. (1985). Single parents, extended households, and the control of adolescents. *Child Development, 56*, 326–341.

Edelbrock, C. S., & Achenbach, T. M. (1984). The teacher version of the child behavior profile: I. Boys aged 6–11. *Journal of Consulting and Clinical Psychology, 52*, 207–217.

Elder, G. H., Nguyen, T. V., & Caspi, A. (1985). Linking family hardship to children's lives. *Child Development, 56*, 361–375.

Engelmann, S. (1969). *Preventing failure in the primary grades.* Chicago: Science Research Associates.

Engelmann, S., & Carnine, D. (1982). *Theory of instruction: Principles and applications.* New York: Irvington.

Epstein, M. H., Kauffman, J. M., & Cullinan, D. (1985). Patterns of maladjustment among the behaviorally disordered. II: Boys aged 6–11, boys aged 12–18, girls aged 6–11, and girls aged 12–18. *Behavioral Disorders, 10*, 125–135.

Gesten, E. L., Scher, K., & Cowen, E. L. (1978). Judged school problems and competencies of referred children with varying family background characteristics. *Journal of Abnormal Child Psychology, 6*, 247–255.

Hallahan, D. P., & Kauffman, J. M. (1986). *Exceptional children: Introduction to special education* (3rd ed.). Englewood Cliffs, NJ: Prentice-Hall.

Hallahan, D. P., Kauffman, J. M., & Lloyd, J. W. (1985). *Introduction to learning disabilities* (2nd ed.). Englewood Cliffs, NJ: Prentice-Hall.

Hammill, D. D., & Bartel, N. R. (1982). *Teaching children with learning and behavior problems* (3rd ed.). Boston: Allyn & Bacon.

Heron, T. (1978). Maintaining the mainstreamed child in the regular classroom: The decision-making process. *Journal of Learning Disabilities, 11*, 50–55.

Hobbs, N. (1975). *The futures of children.* San Francisco: Jossey-Bass.

Houck, C. K. (1984). *Learning disabilities: Understanding concepts, characteristics, and issues.* Englewood Cliffs, NJ: Prentice-Hall.

Kauffman, J. M. (1985). *Characteristics of children's behavior disorders* (3rd ed.). Columbus, OH: Charles E. Merrill.

Kauffman, J. M., & Hallahan, D. P. (1974). The medical model and the science of special education. *Exceptional Children, 41*, 97–102.

_____ (1979). Learning disability and hyperactivity (with comments on minimal brain dysfunction). In B. B. Lahey & A. E. Kazdin (Eds.), *Advances in clinical child psychology* (Vol. 2). New York: Plenum.

Larsen, S. (1978). Learning disabilities and the professional educator. *Learning Disability Quarterly, 1,* 5–12.

Lerner, J. (1985). *Children with learning disabilities: Theories, diagnosis, and teaching strategies* (4th ed.). Boston: Houghton-Mifflin.

Mercer, C. D., & Mercer, A. R. (1985). *Teaching students with learning problems* (2nd ed.). Columbus, OH: Charles E. Merrill.

Osborne, S. (1985). Effects of teacher experience and selected temperament variables on coping strategies used with distractible children. *American Educational Research Journal, 22,* 79–86.

Patterson, G. R. (1982). *Coercive family process.* Eugene, OR: Castalia.

Pullis, M., & Cadwell, J. (1982). The influence of children's temperament characteristics on teachers' decision strategies. *American Educational Research Journal, 19,* 165–181.

Reeve, R. E., & Kauffman, J. M. (in press). Learning disability. In V. Van Hasselt, P. S. Strain, & M. Hersen (Eds.), *Handbook of physical and developmental disabilities.* New York: Pergamon Press.

Ribner, S. (1978). The effects of special class placement on the self-concept of exceptional children. *Exceptional Children, 45,* 319–323.

Scarr-Salapatek, S. (1975). Genetics and the development of intelligence. In F. D. Horowitz (Ed.), *Review of child development research* (Vol. 4). Chicago: University of Chicago Press.

Scharfman, M. A. (1978). Psychoanalytic treatment. In B. B. Wolman (Ed.), *Handbook of treatment of mental disorders in childhood and adolescence.* Englewood Cliffs, NJ: Prentice-Hall.

Smith, C. (1983). *Learning disabilities: The interaction of learner, task, and setting.* Boston: Little, Brown.

Thomas, A., & Chess, S. (1984). Genesis and evolution of behavioral disorders: From infancy to early adult life. *American Journal of Psychiatry, 141,* 1–9.

Thomas, A., Chess, S., & Korn, S. J. (1982). The reality of difficult temperament. *Merrill Palmer Quarterly, 28,* 1–20.

Tuma, J. M., & Sobotka, K. R. (1983). Traditional therapies with children. In T. H. Ollendick & M. Hersen (Eds.), *Handbook of child psychopathology.* New York: Plenum.

Wallace G. (in press). *Assessment: Evaluating students with learning and behavior problems.* Austin, TX: Pro-Ed.

Wallace, G., & McLoughlin, J. (1979). *Learning disabilities: Concepts and characteristics* (2nd ed.). Columbus, OH: Charles E. Merrill.

Whalen, C. K. (1983). Hyperactivity, learning problems, and the attention deficit disorders. In T. H. Ollendick & M. Hersen (Eds.), *Handbook of child psychopathology.* New York: Plenum.

2

Behavior Management

All teachers face the task of managing problem behavior in the classroom. Students who have learning problems typically make behavior management a more difficult task, and behavior management problems add to the difficulty of remediating academic deficits. School failure and misbehavior feed into each other—each compounds the problems presented by the other. Teachers are unlikely to be successful in remediating academic deficits unless they are skillful in the management of classroom behavior problems. Consequently, we have devoted this entire chapter to the principles of behavior management.

Many different approaches to behavior management have been suggested by psychologists and educators over the years (see Kauffman, 1985, for a history of approaches to managing the behavior of emotionally disturbed children). We have chosen a *behavior modification* approach because it is supported by more reliable, empirical research than any of the alternatives (see Cullinan, Epstein, & Kauffman, 1982; Gelfand & Hartmann, 1984; Kazdin, 1978; Kerr & Nelson, 1983; Morris, 1985; Nelson, 1981). Behavior modification has another advantage for educators—it keeps the focus clearly on teaching and learning. A major assumption underlying this approach is that both desirable and undesirable behavior is learned. Therefore, problem behavior is viewed as a learning problem with which the teacher can deal directly, rather than a manifestation of psychological problems requiring solution by mental health professionals. Undoubtedly, other approaches have contributed to our understanding of students' behavior, and the services of mental health professionals are sometimes helpful in dealing with students' problems. Our considered opinion, nevertheless, is that teachers can benefit most by adopting a behavioral approach to classroom management because (1) it has been shown by extensive research to be effective, (2) it emphasizes the teaching-learning process that is the stock-in-trade of educators, and (3) it is understandable and practical for classroom applications.

Behavioral scientists today have available a wide variety of techniques for changing behavior. Most of these techniques were derived from the operant conditioning principles researched and described by B. F. Skinner (Skinner, 1953) and other behavioral psychologists. Researchers, clinical psychologists, and educators have applied these principles to the solution of nearly every type of behavior problem a teacher might face in the classroom (Gelfand & Hartmann, 1984; Kazdin, 1984; Kerr & Nelson, 1983; Morris, 1985). Not every behavior problem has a tidy, immediate solution if the teacher uses behavior modification techniques; however, applied behavioral research has been reported for just about every imaginable difficulty a teacher might face. Whether or not a behavior modification strategy will work in a given situation depends to a large extent on the experience, creativity, sensitivity, skill, and intelligence of the teacher who employs it. Behavior modification, like every other approach to managing behavior, is not a magic solution or a panacea. It is a tool—a powerful but not a limitless one—to be used in solving management problems.

BEHAVIOR MODIFICATION DEFINED

Behavior modification refers to any systematic arrangement of environmental events to produce specific changes in observable behavior. This definition emphasizes systematic procedures and observable behavioral change that can be attributed to specific teaching techniques. The elements of a behavior management strategy are diagrammed in Table 2–1. As indicated by the table, we are concerned not only with what the student does, but also with what happens immediately before and after the student's action. The antecedents and consequences of the student's response can be controlled to modify behavior. Thus, the approach to a behavior management problem entails an ABC analysis—antecedents, behavior, consequences.

Table 2-1
The Essential Elements of Behavior Management Strategy

Program	Stimulus	Behavior	Arrangement	Consequence
The system that programs the presentation of the cue or task; the daily sequence of activities	*Antecedent event:* What happens just before student's behavior; the cue or task presented to the student; the setting in which the behavior is likely to occur	*Action:* What the student does that can be observed, counted, and repeated; a response	The system that arranges the consequence of the student's behavior; the contingency of reinforcement	*Subsequent event:* What happens just afterward; what the student's activity produces; a reinforcing or punishing event
Example: During daily arithmetic period 9:00–9:30	Teacher gives student 10 arithmetic problems to work.	Student writes answers to 10 problems.	When all answers are written correctly	Student may engage in quiet activity of his choice for remainder of arithmetic period.
Example: During weekly P.E. instruction 1:00–1:15	Teacher asks student to do jumping jacks with class.	Student runs crying from P.E. area.	Whenever student runs crying from P.E. area	Teacher leaves class, runs after student, and returns him to the classroom.
Example: At any time during school day	Teacher gives student seatwork.	Student leaves desk and walks around room.	Occasionally when student is walking around room during seatwork	Teacher or peer reminds student to sit down and do his work.

SOURCE: Basic elements from "Direct Measurement and Prosthesis of Retarded Behavior" by Ogden R. Lindsley, 1964, *Journal of Education, 147,* pp. 62–81.

DEFINING AND MEASURING BEHAVIOR

Definition and measurement are the foundation of any applied science—including applied behavior analysis, the applied behavioral science often referred to as behavior modification. Scientific principles—for example, the principles of learning—operate whether or not measurement is employed by the person who applies them. A student's behavior can be improved by arranging appropriate consequences to follow her behavior even though the behavior was never defined or measured. However, if someone wants to know when, how much, and why a student's behavior has been changed, precise definition and measurement are absolutely indispensable. Definition and measurement are important concerns with students who do not behave the way their teachers and parents want them to behave; the adults who are responsible for them perceive them as having or making trouble in the classroom. Under such circumstances it is important to find out when, how much, and why students' behavior changes; not to measure their responses would be, in our opinion, close to educational malpractice. Sound educational practice *demands* the objective, reliable definition and measurement of behavior when it is so disturbing that adults are seriously concerned. To deal effectively and competently with students who have learning problems, a teacher must go beyond subjective impressions and employ the techniques of applied behavioral science.

Defining Behavior

In applied behavioral science the behavior of concern—the *target behavior*—must be defined so that it can be measured reliably. And it must be defined objectively enough that independent observers can agree about its occurrence or nonoccurrence. For example, being out of one's seat and talking out are behaviors that, with practice, observers can count reliably. Likewise, hitting another student, kicking the wastebasket, giving "the finger," throwing books on the floor, smiling, saying thank you, completing arithmetic problems, completing arithmetic problems correctly, and writing words are observable behaviors. Poor self-concept, rage, hyperactivity, and humiliation, however, are not directly observable. They are interpretations of behavior that may vary considerably from one observer to another. Behavior modification starts with a definition of the problem that allows direct measurement of the problem behavior. Any other definition is simply not adequate. Behavior modification proponents often refer to the process of defining the problem behavior as *pinpointing*. Pinpointing is a way of saying, "This is exactly what the student does (or does not do) that is a problem, and it is this behavior that we will measure to find out whether the problem is getting worse or the student is improving."

In recent years behavioral scientists have expanded behavior modification procedures to include covert behaviors—thoughts and feelings that are not directly observable except to the person in whom they occur

(Bandura, 1977, 1978; Meichenbaum, 1977, 1979). The term *cognitive behavior modification* is generally applied to procedures in which covert behaviors are included. In many such procedures an individual is trained to use a *cognitive strategy* to modify his own behavior. This advance in behavior modification is important enough that we deal with cognitive strategy training in a separate chapter. Even though covert responses are often included in behavior modification programs now, behavioral scientists have not abandoned measurement of overt behavior as the primary focus of their efforts.

At least three important points must be kept in mind regarding the definition of behavior. First, students with learning problems often exhibit many problem behaviors, and it is tempting to try to modify all of them at once. However, it is important to choose only the one or two most critical problems and work on those first. Trying to change all of a student's faults at once is unrealistic and is almost always an invitation to failure. On the other hand, if the most worrisome behavior is tackled first and is successfully modified, some of the other problems often take care of themselves or become easier to change. A good rule of thumb is, First things first, one at a time.

Second, it is at least as important—perhaps even more important—to consider what behavior to increase. Unfortunately, when teachers think of behavior modification, they typically think first of the undesirable behaviors they want to stop. But behavior modification principles are just as applicable to the learning of appropriate behavior. A good approach is to ask, How would I like this student to behave? and try to frame the answer in positive rather than negative terms (e.g., He should stay in his seat during reading, rather than He should not get out of his seat during reading). This point cannot be stressed too much: unless the teacher can state how she wants the student to act, a behavior modification program is probably going to be unsuccessful.

Third, important aspects of teaching and learning do not lend themselves to precise behavioral definition. Affective states and thoughts that accompany the educational process are vitally important, though very difficult (and sometimes impossible), to define and measure precisely. A focus on precise definition and measurement of overt behavior is critically important in effective behavior management, but it does not negate concern for subjective matters.

Measuring Behavior

Behavior modification typically involves *direct measurement* of behavior. Direct measuremment means that the behavior itself, not a sample of apparently related phenomena, will be measured. For example, if a teacher is concerned about aggression, he should measure specific aggressive behaviors (e.g., hitting another student) rather than relying on a student's responses to a projective test or an interview (from which he might hypothe-size something about the student's aggressive traits). If a teacher is inter-ested in reading ability, he should measure the student's rate of correct reading, using instructional materials (see Lovitt, 1970, 1977, 1981; Shinn & Marston, 1985).

Behavior modification ordinarily involves *daily measurement* of be-havior. Measuring behavior daily (or at least very frequently) is superior to using standardized achievement tests—in terms of making decisions about instruction and management, communicating information about a student's progress to parents and other teachers, and evaluating the stu-dent's learning (Eaton & Lovitt, 1972; Lovitt, 1981; Kerr & Nelson, 1983; Morris, 1985; Wesson, Skiba, Sevcik, King, & Deno, 1984). Daily measure-ment provides a more accurate, reliable picture of the student's capacity to perform and a more sensitive indicator of the effects of teaching and man-agement techniques.

Behavior can be measured and recorded by any one of several methods, which must be chosen to fit the target behavior and the situation. Behavior must be recorded immediately after it is observed so that accuracy is main-tained. Furthermore, a second observer (e.g., a teacher aide or another teacher) should occasionally record the target behavior to check the re-liability of the teacher's observation. Observation is reliable to the extent that two independent observers' records agree on the occurrence and non-occurrence of the target behavior.

In some cases the target behavior can be observed and recorded con-tinuously during the entire school day. In other cases this is simply not feasible, and the teacher must take a sample (or samples) of the target be-havior sometime during the school day. For example, if talking out with-out permission is the target behavior, the teacher might record talk-outs during the first hour of the day or during two 15-minute periods, one in the morning during math seatwork and one in the afternoon during spell-ing. If the target behavior is being out of one's seat without permission, then the teacher might glance at the student every 5 minutes during 2 hours of the school day and record whether or not the student was out of her seat at that moment. The target behavior should be recorded at the time and/or in the setting in which it is the greatest problem. The length and type of the samples and the time of day they are taken should be con-sistent from day to day, and the samples should be taken over a long enough period to provide an accurate picture of how often the behavior occurs (i.e., the more frequently the behavior occurs, the shorter the sam-ple can be). The goal of observing and recording is to capture a sample of behavior that accurately represents its occurrence.

Target behaviors can be recorded according to many factors: frequency, rate, duration, latency, percent of intervals in which they are observed, percent completed or correct, percent of students present who are engaging in the behavior, or number of acts or products produced by a group of individuals. *Frequency* is simply a count of the number of times the target behavior occurred during observation. *Rate* is the frequency divided by the amount of time observed (e.g., if the 15 talk-outs occur during 30 minutes of observation, the talk-out rate is 15/30, or 0.5 times per minute). *Duration* is a measure of how long the target behavior lasts (e.g., a student may be observed thumb-sucking for a cumulative total of 15 minutes during a 30-minute observation period). *Latency* is a measure of the amount of time elapsing before a student engages in the target behavior (e.g., a student may, on a given day, be in class 42 minutes before falling asleep). Interval recording requires that the teacher observe and record behavior at regular intervals and then compute the *percent of intervals* during which the student has engaged in the target behavior. *Percent of behavior completed or correct* is an obvious measure that is dependent upon the student's opportunity to respond (e.g., the number of questions that can be answered is controlled directly by how many questions the teacher asks; the number of arithmetic problems that can be completed depends on the number of problems the teacher assigns). *Percent of students engaging in the target behavior* is a useful measure when the teacher is interested in a group's performance (e.g., members of the class coming in on time from recess or students handing in completed homework). When the teacher is interested in the aggregate performance of a group, *the number of acts or products of the group* can be measured without regard to the individual responsible (e.g., the number of aggressive acts on the playground, the amount of trash left on the floor of the classroom, or the number of trays left unscraped in the cafeteria might be recorded without concern for which students are performing the target behavior).

The teacher using behavior modification techniques should record behavior immediately after it occurs, and the observational data should be accumulated systematically on a record form. A sample record form is shown in Table 2–2. For any given behavior only those parts of the form appropriate for the recording technique should be used.

When behavior is measured directly and daily, it is usually most efficient and understandable to display the results in the form of a line graph. The graph quickly indicates the level, variability, and trend in the student's behavior. In addition, the graph shows at a glance what change, if any, has occurred in response to a teaching or management strategy.

Ordinarily, behavioral data are plotted for many days, spanning several distinct phases. Usually, a *baseline* phase precedes any attempt to change the target behavior; the baseline phase indicates just how problematic the behavior is. Sometimes in the process of defining the behavior and recording baseline data, one discovers that what seemed to be a problem actually is not a problem after all or that the problem is being resolved. Baseline data also provide an objective basis for judging the effects of any *inter-*

Table 2-2
Record Form for Accumulating Behavioral Data

Behavior recorded: _____   Name of student: _____

Day	Date	Time behavior recorded	Tot. time behavior recorded	# of behaviors observed	Rate per min.	Duration in min. or sec.	Behavior recorded each ___ min. for intervals		% completed	% correct	% of students
							# of times behavior observed	% of intervals behavior observed			
1.		— to —									
2.		— to —									
3.		— to —									
4.		— to —									
5.		— to —									
6.		— to —									
7.		— to —									
8.		— to —									
9.		— to —									
10.		— to —									

(Continue in this manner)

vention, that is, any special teaching or management technique that is implemented. If the intervention is effective, the graph will show a noticeable change when the procedure is instituted. (Behavior modification research typically includes alternating intervention and nonintervention phases; staggered introduction of the intervention across individuals, behaviors, or settings; or other experimental designs to test the causal relationship between intervention and behavioral change.) Sometimes a *follow-up* phase is also included, which provides an objective indication of the permanence of any behavioral change observed during intervention. Measurement of behavior is continued during follow-up to assess the extent to which further teaching or intervention is necessary.

The details of measurement and graphing techniques and the research and evaluation designs employed in behavior modification are beyond our scope here (see Hersen & Barlow, 1976; Kazdin, 1984; Morris, 1985, for further discussion). In short, measurement should yield a reliable and representative sample of the target behavior. The length and sequence of the baseline and other phases are determined by the stability of the behavior over time (day-to-day variability and trends) and the importance of demon-

---

DECREASING SAMMY'S CRYING

Sammy, a third grader, had frequent crying spells each day. The teacher's usual strategy was to ask Sammy why he was crying and to try to comfort him. One of his spells could last anywhere from 5 minutes to 2 hours, and during these spells the class was disrupted by his extremely loud wailing. In fact, his crying was so loud that it could be heard in other classrooms, and other children in the school were beginning to tease and taunt him. The teacher recorded each crying spell as one occurrence (regardless of the length of the spell) and tallied the spells on a sheet of paper she kept handy for that purpose. Each day she plotted the number of crying spells on a graph. As shown in Figure 2–1, Sammy had an average of about 17 crying spells per day during the baseline phase. Beginning on the 11th day, the teacher tried ignoring all crying, a strategy that she could see was not working after 5 days. On the 16th day the teacher began a new intervention. She held a class discussion in which everyone, including Sammy, agreed that he would be called by his "grown-up" (and highly preferred) name, Sam, as long as he was not crying. If he cried, however, everyone in the class would ignore him. If he did not cry for 3 days, everyone in the class would get a special treat. Sammy would record his crying by making the tally marks on the teacher's recording sheet. Figure 2–1 shows the results of this intervention; a special treat was earned on the 3rd day of no crying. Sam seldom cried again, and his improved behavior continued even though no more treats were given. During the follow-up phase his improved behavior was maintained by occasional praise from the teacher and the self-recording technique.

Figure 2-1. Sammy's Crying

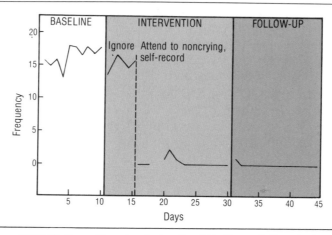

SOURCE: From *Managing Instructional Problems: A Case Study Workbook* (p. 189) by J. Worell and C. M. Nelson, 1974, New York: McGraw-Hill. Copyright 1974 by McGraw-Hill. Reprinted by permission.

INCREASING WRITTEN COMPOSITION RATES

Students are often resistant to teachers' efforts to get them to write compositions. Van Houten, Morrison, Jarvis, and McDonald (1974) experimented with a simple method of increasing the speed with which fifth graders wrote compositions. They recorded the rate (words per minute) of the fifth graders' writing during 10-minute sessions each school day. During baseline sessions the students were merely given a topic and told to write a composition on that topic; after 10 minutes they were told to stop. They were not told they were being timed, and they were not given feedback on their rate. During intervention they were told they would be timed with a stopwatch and were given feedback on their previous day's rate, which they were encouraged to exceed. Figure 2–2 shows the results (averaged for all children in the class) for two classes (Section A and Section B). The delay of 3 days in starting the intervention for Section B was a research strategy (technically, a multiple baseline across subjects) used to assess whether the increase in composition rate could be attributed to something other than the intervention. Because the rate changed for both sections only when the intervention was introduced, we can assume that the increase was probably due to the intervention. Results for individual students (A.M. and S.G. in Section A, M.A. and B.V. in Section B) are shown in Figure 2–3. Clearly, timing and feedback increased these students' writing rates when they were writing compositions on assigned topics. Other data presented by Van Houten et al. indicated improvement in the quality of the compositions and in attitudes toward writing during the timing and feedback intervention.

strating experimentally that any behavior change was a result of the intervention. The principles of behavioral definition, direct daily measurement, graphing, and behavioral analysis are illustrated by the following case descriptions. Some of the observation and recording procedures described are feasible for classroom teachers, whereas others would have to be adapted or simplified for classroom use.

The data regarding Sammy's behavior illustrate a nonexperimental case study approach that any teacher could employ. The behavioral definition and recording procedure was simple but effective; the graphing technique was uncomplicated but clearly displayed the level of behavior during each phase.

The behavioral definition, recording procedure, and graphing technique used in this study are clearly within the capability of all classroom teachers. Most teachers will find it helpful to take systematic samples of students' academic performance rates and evaluate the effects of various instructional or motivational procedures.

Figure 2-2. The Mean Response Rate in Words per Minute for Both Grade 5 Classes in Each Daily Session

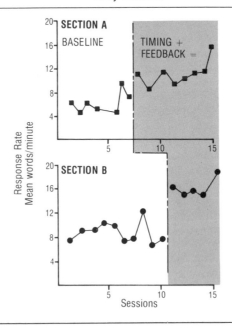

SOURCE: From "The Effects of Explicit Timing and Feedback on Compositional Response Rate in Elementary School Children" by R. Van Houten, E. Morrison, R. Jarvis, and M. McDonald, 1974, *Journal of Applied Behavior Analysis*, 7, 552. Copyright 1974 by *Journal of Applied Behavior Analysis*. Reprinted by permission.

Figure 2-3. The Individual Response Rate in Words per Minute of Four Children from the Two Grade 5 Classes in Each Daily Session

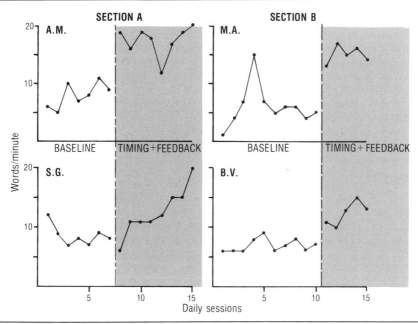

SOURCE: From "The Effects of Explicit Timing and Feedback on Compositional Response Rate in Elementary School Children" by R. Van Houten, E. Morrison, R. Jarvis, and M. McDonald, 1974, *Journal of Applied Behavior Analysis*, 7, 552. Copyright 1974 by *Journal of Applied Behavior Analysis*. Reprinted by permission.

REDUCING PLAYGROUND AGGRESSION

Murphy, Hutchison, and Bailey (1983) were faced with the problem of aggressive, inappropriate behavior on the school playground by children who arrived before the opening of school. The school served over 300 children in kindergarten through second grade. Problems frequently observed included striking, slapping, tripping, kicking, or pushing others; throwing books and lunches; throwing objects at passing or parked cars; breaking pencils and pens; taking the belongings of others; resisting or talking back to adults; and playing dangerously on playground equipment. Murphy and his colleagues devised an observation system for measuring aggressive playground incidents that was implemented by several college students. Baseline observations showed that aggressive incidents during the 20 minutes prior to the beginning of the school day averaged over 200 per day (see Figure 2–4).

The intervention devised by Murphy et al. emphasized antecedent conditions designed to reduce the likelihood of aggression rather than negative consequences for aggressive acts. Playground monitors organized foot races and rope jumping during the intervention phase. Children who persisted in particularly unruly behavior were given a brief time out (they had to sit quietly on a bench for 2 minutes). As shown in Figure 2–4, aggressive incidents were reduced during the intervention to about half the baseline level. Murphy et al. tested the reliability of the effect of organized games by returning to baseline conditions (no games) for 4 days, then reinstituting the intervention (technically, an ABAB or reversal design). Because the number of aggressive incidents changed dramatically with the introduction of the intervention and the change was replicated in the second baseline and intervention phases, we can assume that the intervention was the likely cause of the improved behavior.

Most teachers would find it difficult or impossible to use the observational procedures described in this study without special training and assistance. However, any teacher could arrive at an objective definition of aggressive acts and keep a systematic tally of the number of such acts observed at a specified time and place each day, thus obtaining a useful measure of behavior. The intervention is the type of procedure that is easy and natural for school personnel to try.

Figure 2-4. Frequency of Incidents Recorded During 20-Minute Morning Observation Periods on the Playground

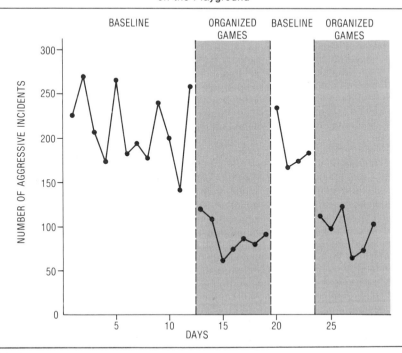

SOURCE: From ''Behavioral School Psychology Goes Outdoors: The Effect of Organized Games on Playground Aggression'' by H.A. Murphy, J.M. Hutchison, and J.S. Bailey, 1983, *Journal of Applied Behavior Analysis, 16*, p. 33. Copyright 1983 by *Journal of Applied Behavior Analysis*. Reprinted by permission.

INCREASING MATTHEW'S INTERACTIONS

Matthew was a 5-year-old enrolled in a nursery school serving about 15 children 3 to 6 years of age. He had been variously diagnosed as autistic-like, learning disabled, and minimally brain damaged. He exhibited a variety of peculiar and inappropriate behaviors that resulted in his being avoided by other children. He did not like to be touched by anyone and typically resisted the approach of other children with statements such as "I hate you," "Get away from me," and "Don't look." He was videotaped for 15 minutes during 30-minute free-play periods several times per week; the videotapes were later reviewed and scored to measure the percentage of time he spent in interaction with his peers. During baseline observation sessions Matthew was found to be interacting with his peers only about 15% of the time, as shown in Figure 2–5. An intervention involving group affection activities was designed to increase his social interaction; it was conducted for 10 minutes each day. "The group affection activities consisted of progressively more intimate and extended physical contact between Matthew and his peers" (Twardosz, Nordquist, Simon, & Botkin, 1983, p. 317). Matthew, nine other children, and two teachers participated; children were encouraged but not required to participate. The activities began with shaking hands and saying hello and progressed to clasping arms, hugging, and tickling. As shown in Figure 2–5, the affection training had a marked effect on Matthew's interaction with his peers. During the reversal phase the affection activities were discontinued, and peer interaction declined; later they were reintroduced, and again they produced increased interaction.

Figure 2-5. Matthew's Percentage of Peer Interaction for Baseline and Intervention Conditions

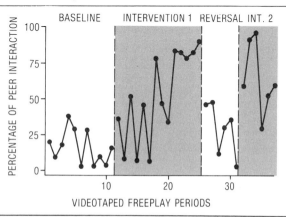

SOURCE: From "The Effect of Group Affection Activities on the Interaction of Socially Isolate Children" by S. Twardosz, V.M. Nordquist, R. Simon, and D. Botkin, 1983, *Analysis and Intervention in Developmental Disabilities, 3,* 318. Copyright 1983 by *Analysis and Intervention in Developmental Disabilities.* Reprinted by permission.

Relatively few teachers are able, without special assistance, to videotape and record peer interaction as was done in this study. However, most teachers can define peer interaction with sufficient clarity that they or an aide could devise a reliable means of sampling such behavior. For example, an aide or the teacher might set aside 10 minutes to observe a child's interaction during a given activity each day. The observer could glance at the target child every 30 seconds and record whether or not he was engaged in peer interaction at that moment, yielding a percentage of time the child was interacting with peers. An intervention similar to the one described in this study could be easily implemented by most teachers, with modifications suitable for the particular child and the community's standard of appropriate physical contact between preschoolers.

OVERCOMING ADOLESCENT SHYNESS

Franco, Christoff, Crimmins, and Kelly (1983) worked with a 14-year-old boy who was referred to a clinic by his parents because they were concerned about his shyness and his lack of peer relationships. Norbert, as we shall call him, associated primarily with children 5 to 8 years younger than he, spent a great deal of time alone in his bedroom, and seldom talked to anyone at all. At school he had few friends and was often teased by peers, who referred to him as a "dope," "nerd," and so on. He did not seem to be particularly anxious but "appeared to be a somewhat depressed young person with minimal conversational skills, no friends, and a longstanding socially isolated lifestyle" (Franco et al., 1983, p. 570). Franco and his colleagues set up a series of videotaped 10-minute sessions involving conversations between Norbert and conversational partners who were teenagers or young adults. The videotapes were scored to assess Norbert's interactional skills along four dimensions that are important in social relationships: asking conversational questions, making verbal acknowledgments of and giving verbal reinforcers for what one's conversational partner says, making eye contact during conversation, and showing affective warmth. After five baseline sessions Norbert was given training in each of the four conversational skills in succession (technically, a multiple baseline across behaviors) so that the experimenters could assess whether the training was, in fact, the cause of improvement. Because improvement was observed for each component behavior only when training was introduced, as shown in Figure 2–6, we can assume that the training probably produced the improvement. Training consisted of 20 to 30 minutes of discussion of the importance of the particular conversational skill, modeling of the skill by the trainer, and guided rehearsal of the skill by Norbert. Other information obtained by Franco et al. indicated that Norbert's skills generalized to situations outside the training sessions. In fact, follow-up data obtained 16 months after the end of intervention indicated that Norbert's social relationships remained improved: Norbert "now had classmates visit the house, had begun to date, and was trying out for a school athletic team" (Franco et al., 1983, p. 574).

Figure 2-6. Frequency of Skill Behaviors During 10-Minute Unstructured Conversations with Novel Partners

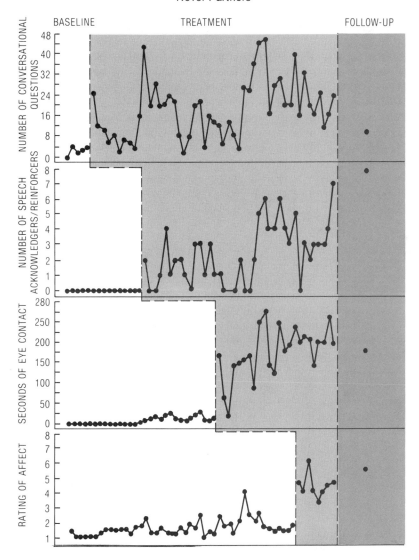

SOURCE: From ''Social Skills Training for an Extremely Shy Young Adolescent: An Empirical Case Study'' by D. P. Franco, K. A. Christoff, D. B. Crimmins, and J. A. Kelly, 1983, *Behavior Therapy, 14,* p. 573. Copyright 1983 by *Behavior Therapy.* Reprinted by permission.

Clearly, few classroom teachers can carry out the procedures used in this study. However, most teachers can pinpoint social skills (e.g., asking questions, establishing eye contact) that they could record systematically during certain school activities. Most teachers can provide reinforcing consequences for specific social skills, and most can provide explicit instruction and modeling in how to exhibit appropriate social behaviors. Moreover, teachers can often have students help to improve the social skills of socially inept classmates.

THE CONTROLLING FUNCTION OF CONSEQUENCES

All behaviors are followed by environmental events of one kind or another. Some of these subsequent events have a profound effect on future behavior. Behavioral scientists have demonstrated that much of our behavior is controlled to a large degree by its immediate consequences. For example, when a student receives attention from adults or peers following a particular behavior, she is much more likely to perform that behavior again. Ordinarily, the experience of a painful consequence decreases an individual's tendency to repeat the behavior that resulted in that consequence (e.g., burning one's mouth on hot soup decreases the future probability of taking a spoonful without testing the temperature).

A *reinforcer* is an event that changes the future probability of a behavior. Reinforcers can be positive (things a person will try to get or retain) or negative (things a person will try to escape or avoid). Reinforcers can be used to increase (reinforce) or decrease (punish) a behavior. A reinforcer can be either presented or withdrawn to influence behavior. Thus, there are four distinct methods of changing a behavior—by presenting or withdrawing positive or negative reinforcers—as shown in Table 2–3. The process of reinforcement always results in an increase in the rate, strength, or probability of a behavior—the behavior is reinforced. Punishment results in a decrease in or weakening of behavior. Note that negative reinforcement—withdrawing something unpleasant, or aversive, after a behavior occurs—increases, strengthens, or accelerates the behavior it follows. Punishment—withdrawing something pleasant or presenting something unpleasant after a behavior—has the opposite effect on the behavior it follows.

A nearly infinite number of environmental events occur subsequent to any given behavior, but not all subsequent events have a controlling function. In many cases it is difficult to identify precisely the events that do control a specific behavior. In the classroom positive reinforcers for maladaptive behavior often go unidentified because someone makes an inappropriate assumption about the reinforcers. A reinforcer is defined by its effect on the behavior it follows, not by the way one thinks it should function. Although it is possible to make some generalizations regarding the classification of events, the reinforcing property of a subsequent event can vary from individual to individual, group to group, and circumstance to circumstance. Teachers often assume that their reprimands and "desist" signals are negative reinforcers, that is, that their presentation following undesirable behavior will weaken such behavior. Unfortunately, a reprimand may serve to strengthen rather than weaken the undesirable behavior if, for example, attracting the teacher's attention is a positive reinforcer for a student (Kazdin, 1984; Kerr & Nelson, 1983; Morris, 1985).

Table 2-3
Methods of Influencing Behavior by Using Consequences

	Positive Reinforcer	Negative Reinforcer
Present Reinforcer	*Positive reinforcement* increases or strengthens behavior that produces reinforcer, accelerates behavior. *Example* Behavior: Student begins assigned seatwork. Consequence: Teacher smiles at student and remarks, "Good, I see you've started!" If the student's initial effort to do assigned work is consistently given immediate attention and praise by the teacher, the promptness with which he begins his work will likely increase.	*Punishment* decreases or weakens behavior that produces reinforcer, decelerates behavior. *Example* Behavior: Student destroys paper of another student. Consequence: Teacher points at student and shouts, "No!" If the teacher is generally positive, controlled, and soft-spoken in interaction with the student but consistently points at student and shouts, "No!" when she begins to destroy another student's paper, the destruction of papers will likely decrease.
Withdraw Reinforcer	*Punishment* decreases or weakens behavior that results in loss of reinforcer, decelerates behavior. *Example* Behavior: Student tattles to teacher. Consequence: Teacher turns away from student (withdraws attention completely). If the teacher consistently and totally withdraws attention from the student immediately after the student begins to tattle, tattling will likely decrease.	*Negative reinforcement* increases or strengthens behavior that avoids or escapes the reinforcer, accelerates behavior. *Example* Behavior: Student throws tantrum when given seatwork. Consequence: Teacher does not require student to finish work. If the student can avoid the task by throwing a tantrum, it is likely tantrums will recur when the teacher gives seatwork.

Positive Consequences: The Key to Behavioral Improvement

Students learn appropriate behavior primarily because of positive consequences. If a student exhibits little appropriate conduct at school, it may be because the consequences for his appropriate behavior are relatively few, whereas the consequences for his misbehavior are numerous. Successful behavior management requires that the teacher focus on positive consequences for desirable performance rather than on negative consequences for undesirable performance. Punishment of misconduct has a legitimate place in behavior management, but the first concern of the teacher must be positive reinforcement. Because of the primacy of positive reinforcement in bringing about behavioral improvement, our discussion of the controlling function of consequences does not include punishment.

Individual Choice of Consequences

The effective use of consequences to control classroom behavior must be individualized for the student, teacher, and situation. Since a reinforcer is defined by its effect on behavior, a consequence that is reinforcing for one student may not be for another. The teacher's task is to find and use those events or consequences that are reinforcing for the student under consideration. This can be accomplished by (1) observing what the student does or seems to enjoy when given a free choice, (2) asking the student what she would like to work to obtain, or (3) arranging consequences for the student and observing their effects on behavior (Gelfand & Hartmann, 1984; Morris, 1985). For example, if the student spends most of her free time looking at fashion magazines, then it is highly probable that extra time to look at fashion magazines will be a reinforcer for her. Furthermore, it is a simple matter to ask a student to list several things that she would like to do after finishing an assignment and use her responses in selecting trial consequences.

The Premack Principle

A practical consequence selection principle was formulated by Premack (1959). The Premack Principle states that whatever a student likes to do more can be used as a reinforcer for any other behavior that the student likes to do less: preferred activities are reinforcers for nonpreferred activities. Thus, by observing a student's preferences for certain activities, the teacher can choose powerful reinforcers. The greater the difference in preference between two activities, the more powerful the preferred activity will be in reinforcing the nonpreferred activity. Examples of the application of the Premack Principle are given in Table 2–4. Remember that the preferred activity is a reinforcer for a specific behavior (the nonpreferred activity), not for just any behavior the teacher may want to strengthen. What serves as a reinforcer varies from individual to individual, and a reinforcer is sometimes specific to one particular behavior.

The Premack Principle works only if the relationship between the preferred and nonpreferred activities is *contingent*. A contingency is a rule or arrangement between events. The contingency for reinforcement must be this: do the nonpreferred activity first; then you may engage in the preferred activity. If the relationship between preferred and nonpreferred activity is not governed in this manner, reinforcement will not occur.

Table 2-4
Application of the Premack Principle

Student's Preference	Reinforcement Arrangement
Student prefers drawing to reading.	Make drawing contingent upon reading.
Helping the teacher is preferred to going outside for recess.	Allow going outside for recess to earn the privilege of helping the teacher.
Student likes to eat candy kisses more than he likes to do arithmetic.	Make eating candy kisses contingent upon doing arithmetic.
Given the choice of writing or reading, the student always reads.	Require writing just before allowing reading.
Writing on the chalkboard is something the student relishes; writing on paper is something he detests.	Allow writing on the chalkboard only after a writing assignment on paper has been satisfactorily completed.
Student would rather put together a model than spell words.	Let correctly written spelling words earn permission to work on a model.
Student spends every spare moment reading but rarely speaks to anyone.	Make access to reading material contingent upon a specific amount of verbal interaction.

Reinforcer Menus and Token Reinforcers

Reinforcement is often made more effective by giving the student a choice of reinforcers. Contingencies can be arranged so that a student who has performed the target behavior can select a reinforcer from a list or menu. The choice of reinforcing activities often increases motivation.

In many situations behavior management transactions or contingencies can be arranged so that reinforcing events follow appropriate behavior immediately (a matter of great importance that we will discuss later). In other situations it is impractical to provide the reinforcer immediately; practical considerations may dictate that the student be allowed to engage in the reinforcing activity only at a specified time, which may follow performance of the target behavior by hours, days, or weeks. For example, the teacher may be able to arrange the following contingencies: a grade of C or higher on a science test will be followed by a Ping-Pong game with the school principal; a student will earn the privilege of working with the school custodian for 2 hours by completing all math problems assigned on a given day; a student will be allowed to help the cooks in the school cafeteria for 2 days if she brings in all her homework for 1 week. The logistics of making reinforcing events or activities contingent upon specific behaviors and allowing them to occur immediately after the appropriate behavior can be difficult. One method for solving the logistics and timing problems is to establish a token system of reinforcement. In a token system the student earns points (or some tangible, exchangeable commodity) that can be saved and later exchanged for the reinforcer. Tokens are a medium of exchange—like money—that can be used to buy reinforcing events. The possible benefits of a token system are many, but the pitfalls are numerous, too. The possible problems encountered in token reinforcement include those of any monetary system: theft, extortion, oversupply, inflation, and so on (see Kazdin & Bootin, 1972; O'Leary & Drabman, 1971).

Contingency Contracting

Contingencies of reinforcement can be stated in the form of an agreement or contract. Students often benefit from an explicit, written statement of the relationship between their behavior and its consequences. Negotiating a contingency contract involves reaching an agreement that the teacher will provide something the student wants after the student has done something the teacher wants him to do. An effective contingency contract must meet the requirements of any good business contract; that is, it must be fair to both parties, be clear in its statement of terms, offer a positive incentive, and require systematic and honest adherence (Homme, 1969; Kazdin, 1985). Contracts must be written with the age and intelligence of the student in mind. Figures 2–7 and 2–8 give examples of contingency contracts for primary and secondary level students.

Group Contingencies

Classroom teachers often find advantages in managing contingencies for groups of students as well as for individual students. The teacher who excuses rows of students only when each student in the row is seated quietly is employing a group contingency. In this example each member of the group must exhibit appropriate behavior before any individual in the group can obtain the reinforcing consequence (being excused). When such a contingency is applied, there is considerable group pressure to conform to the teacher's expectation. It is also possible to make a reinforcing event for the entire class dependent on the behavior of a single individual. For example, a special treat for each member of the class could be made contingent on a single student's completing her work or staying in her seat. In this case there is also likely to be group pressure; peers may encourage the student whose behavior regulates their own reward. When using this type of group contingency, the teacher must be sure that the task for the target student is well within her ability. Moreover, the target student's performance must result in an extra reward for the class, never in punishment; negative peer interactions will almost certainly follow if the target student's misbehavior results in others' punishment. Finally, contingent rewards can be arranged

Figure 2-7. Contract for a Primary School Student

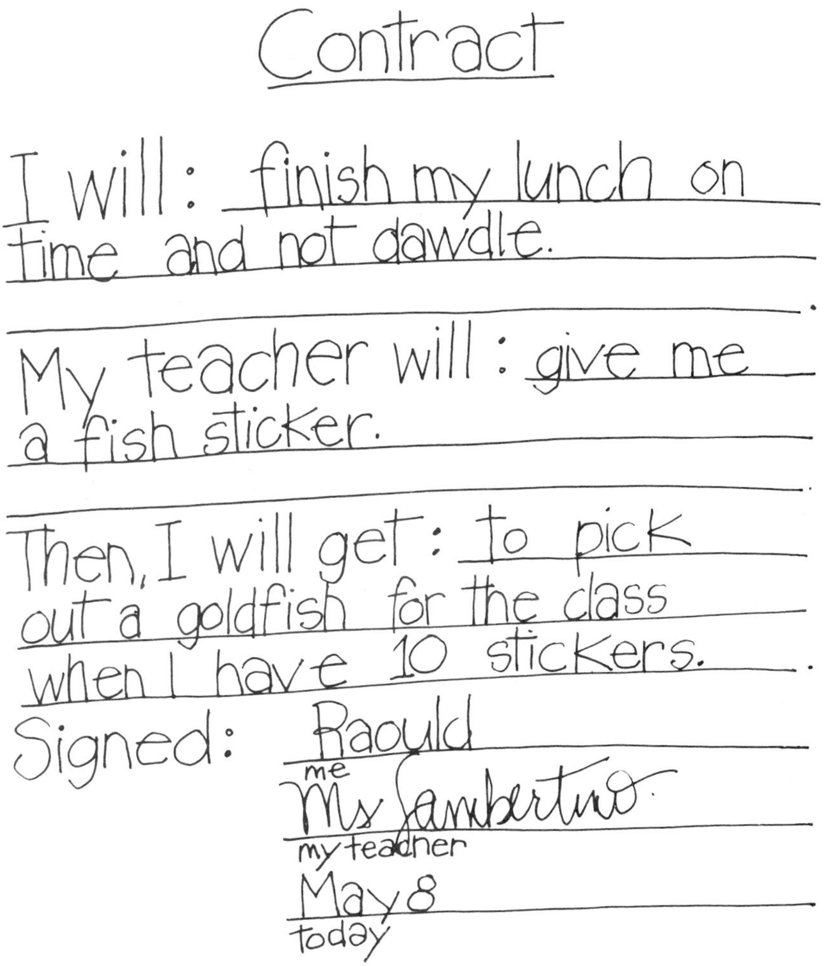

Contract

I will: finish my lunch on time and not dawdle.

My teacher will: give me a fish sticker.

Then, I will get: to pick out a goldfish for the class when I have 10 stickers.

Signed: Raould
me

Ms Lambertino.
my teacher

May 8
today

SOURCE: From *Strategies for Managing Behavior Problems in the Classroom* (p. 123) by M. M. Kerr and C. M. Nelson, 1983, Columbus, OH: Charles E. Merrill. Copyright 1983 by Bell and Howell Company. Reprinted by permission.

so that the same contingency applies to all members of the class, but each member earns them individually. For example, any member of the class completing an assignment might be allowed to go to recess 2 minutes early. With this type of group contingency group pressure does not operate.

Additional Considerations

Consequences are chosen by individual teachers. Some teachers find it difficult or impossible to administer consequences that other teachers consider appropriate. Some teachers willingly offer visits to their homes, special

Figure 2-8. Contract for a Secondary School Student

I, *Rebecca* agree to accept the following responsibilities within the
(student)
specified time periods:
1. *Decrease out of seat behavior*
from 50 times a day to 20.

by *10/8/80*
2. *Record my out of seat behavior.*

by *Daily*

In return, I wish to receive the following privileges at school:
Typing activity with Mr. Sanson at
the end of the week.
to be received *Friday at 1:30*

to be received _____

I, *Mrs. Jamieson* agree to provide the designated privileges in
(teacher)
accordance with the schedule stated. We have read and reviewed the terms of
this contract. We will re-evaluate the
contract on *10/8/80* .

Signed: *Rebecca Gumentz* *E. Jamieson*
(student)   (teacher)
Witness: *Deborah Carlson* Date: *10/1/80*

activities after school, small toys, or treats, whereas others feel that some or all of these rewards are inappropriate. However, unless the teacher is willing to provide some meaningful reward for students (either social or material) on a contingent basis, classroom management will be ineffective.

Other variables affecting the selection of consequences include the constraints of school administrators, parents, and other teachers; even the physical limitations of the school building may prohibit the use of certain consequences. Unsympathetic principals, parents who demand strict adherence to traditional methods, cynical fellow teachers, and poorly designed school buildings pose problems for many teachers. However, principals, parents, and colleagues are often invaluable allies in successful modification of students' inappropriate behavior; and the negative features of school buildings can provide unusual opportunities for innovation. The assessment of situational variables demands no less attention than the consideration of one's own feelings and the careful evaluation of the individual student. In behavior management, as in other aspects of teaching, the creativity and perseverance of the teacher are keys to success.

Timing of Consequences

As we have already suggested, reinforcers are most effective when they follow desired behavior immediately. Adults can often work for distant rewards; children and youth, particularly those who have learning problems, usually work diligently only for more immediate consequences. Praise given immediately after performance of a desirable behavior is more likely to have the desired effect than a delayed compliment. Some students respond to grade contingencies but only if they are given grades daily; the consequences of grades every 6 to 8 weeks are far too long delayed. As a student's behavior improves, he may gradually begin to work for rewards or reinforcers that are longer delayed; but the temptation to move too quickly to delayed reinforcement must be resisted. In the analysis of many behavior management problems, we find that immediate rather than delayed consequences control behavior. When immediate, positive consequences for desirable behavior are provided, a student's performance usually improves.

Shaping Behavior

In teaching students to behave appropriately, the teacher must carefully define terminal and immediate goals. The teacher must describe in objective and measurable terms how students are to behave after they are taught and also how students presently behave. This presentation requires analyzing the behavioral goal in relation to present behavior and describing a sequence of ordered steps or tasks to attain the goal. The teacher must begin by reinforcing a behavior that the student already exhibits and must then gradually increase the requirement for reinforcement. The sequence of steps arranged by the teacher must be *successive approximations* of the ultimate goal. If the approximations involve steps that are too large, the student is unlikely to learn the behavior or may learn it inefficiently. Further, the teacher who fails to reward increments of improvement in behavior is not likely to be successful in using behavior modification techniques (Morris, 1985).

The process of teaching successive approximations is called *shaping.* Several examples of behavior shaping in the classroom are presented in Table 2–5. The size of the steps must be adjusted to the learning char-

Table 2–5
Examples of Behavior Shaping in the Classroom

Behavioral Goal	Successive Approximations
Student will sit at her desk continuously for 20 minutes.	Standing near her desk for a few seconds; touching desk or chair; sitting, leaning, or kneeling on her desk or chair; sitting in her chair for a few seconds; sitting in her chair for 3 minutes; sitting for 5 minutes . . .
Student will complete seatwork assignments.	Looking at assignment, picking up pencil, putting pencil on paper, completing 1 answer, completing 2 answers . . .
Student will participate fully with class in softball game.	Watching game from a distance, standing behind backstop, keeping score, serving as bat girl, playing a position for ½ inning, playing a full inning . . .
Student will be able to print the letter *H.*	Making a vertical line, making another vertical line, making a horizontal line to combine the two lines.
Student will be able to color within the lines.	Holding a crayon, coloring large areas, gradually decreasing the size of the area until the student colors the desired figure.
Student will be able to name his body parts.	Knowing parts making up the body, naming gross features of a stick figure, naming and relating stick figure features to her own body, gradually learning specific features of human figures and relating them to his own body.

acteristics of the individual student. Highly gifted students may be able to make great leaps in learning, omitting some steps. Students with learning problems, on the other hand, may need additional steps. The more severe the student's learning problem, the smaller the difference between successive approximations must be.

Schedules of Reinforcement

A contingency of reinforcement always involves a schedule, either explicitly stated or implicit in the sequence of events. The schedule of reinforcement defines the relationship between behavior and a reinforcing consequence; it can be continuous or intermittent.

Under a *continuous reinforcement* schedule every target behavior receives reinforcement. It is advantageous to use a continuous schedule when a behavior is first being taught. After a response is learned, however, other schedules are more efficient and effective in maintaining the behavior. For example, when a student is being taught a new computational skill, the teacher should attempt to reward every correct response. When the student has mastered the new skill, continued reinforcement of every correct response is unnecessary, inefficient, and impractical. In addition, if continuous reinforcement is maintained, the student may lose interest in the reward and begin to perform poorly. Instead, continued interest and a high rate of response can be sustained with intermittent reinforcement.

Under an *intermittent reinforcement* schedule only a fraction of the student's appropriate responses receive reinforcement. Reinforcement can be based on the total number of responses performed (a ratio schedule) or on the number of responses performed after the passage of a given amount of time (an interval schedule). When a change is made from continuous to intermittent reinforcement, the requirement for reinforcement must not be increased too quickly. A gradual increase in the requirement will ensure a smooth transition without loss of the newly acquired behavior.

In actual classroom practice teachers usually employ approximations of the basic schedules of reinforcement described in Table 2–6. That is, a teacher often provides intermittent reinforcement that does not fulfill the exact requirements of a particular schedule; reinforcement may be given on a variable schedule that depends on an unspecified amount of time having elapsed and an unspecified number of appropriate behaviors having been exhibited. Likewise, in everyday life there are not many true or pure schedules of reinforcement. However, certain characteristics must be taken into account to give intermittent reinforcement its maximum effect. As a rule, variable schedules produce a higher rate of appropriate behavior than fixed schedules. That is, reinforcement that is dependent on an average but unpredictable factor is typically more powerful. If the teacher can arrange a variable ratio schedule or a close approximation, the effect on behavior is likely to be optimal (see Kauffman, Cullinan, Scranton, & Wallace, 1972).

Table 2-6
An Outline of Basic Schedules of Reinforcement

I. Continuous reinforcement

Every time the behavior occurs, it is reinforced.

Example: Each time the student completes an arithmetic problem correctly, he is given a point for his progress chart.

II. Intermittent reinforcement

A. Ratio schedules

Reinforcement is given for every *n*th behavior and depends on the number of behaviors performed, regardless of time.

1. Fixed ratio

A fixed number of behaviors must occur for each reinforcement. *Example:* Every 10th sight word read correctly is rewarded with a piece of candy.

2. Variable ratio

An approximate number of behaviors must occur for each reinforcement. The number of behaviors required varies around a mean.

Example: On the average the student is called on by the teacher every 5th time he raises his hand. The actual number of times varies.

B. Interval schedules

Reinforcement depends on the passage of time and the occurrence of a behavior.

1. Fixed interval

A fixed amount of time must pass, after which the next appropriate behavior will be reinforced.

Example: Every 3 minutes during recess the teacher observes the student to see whether he is talking to another student. The next time he approaches another student and speaks to her, the teacher pats him on the shoulder and praises him for being friendly.

2. Variable interval

A variable amount of time must pass, after which the next correct response will result in reinforcement. The amount of time required varies around a mean.

Example: On the average every 5 minutes the teacher observes whether the student is writing a correct answer to a question on the geography lesson. When he answers the next question correctly, the teacher draws a happy face on his paper. The actual number of minutes that elapse before the teacher checks the student's behavior varies.

A wide variety of complex schedules of reinforcement are described in the professional literature. Many are combinations of the schedules outlined in Table 2–6; several others are particularly useful to teachers—the DRL, DRO, DRA, DRI, and DRH schedules. A DRL schedule—differential reinforcement of low rate—specifies that reinforcement is provided only if the rate of behavior stays below a certain level. A DRL schedule is useful for maintaining a manageable level of behavior when too frequent occurrence of the behavior is the basic problem (see Deitz & Repp, 1983). Behaviors related to biological functions (e.g., eating, toileting) are likely to be appropriate targets for this technique. When DRL is implemented, the contingency explicitly states the maximum number of target behaviors that can be performed during a specified interval of time if reinforcement is to be delivered. For example, the contingency for a student who bolts his food may grant a reward if he finishes his lunch in no less than 15 minutes or if he takes fewer than six bites per minute.

A DRO schedule—differential reinforcement of other behavior—specifies that reinforcement is given only if a certain behavior has not occurred during an interval of time. Thus, a student may be offered reinforcement only if she has not screamed, talked out, or performed some other specified undesirable behavior for a period of time (which may be a fixed or variable interval). A DRA schedule—differential reinforcement of alternative behavior—and DRI—differential reinforcement of incompatible behavior specify that some particular behavior other than the target response will be reinforced. DRO, DRA, and DRI schedules are obviously intended to reduce the strength of a target behavior in a positive way, by offering rewards for omission or performance of a behavior (see Dietz & Repp, 1983).

For speeding up the rate of a response that is being made too slowly, a teacher can employ a DRH schedule—differential reinforcement of high rate. In DRH the student can earn reinforcement only by making more than a specified number of responses during a specific interval of time. For example, Lovitt and Esveldt (1970) set up a schedule in which working math problems faster resulted in the student's earning additional reinforcers.

THE CONTROLLING FUNCTION OF ANTECEDENT EVENTS

Thus far, we have stressed the use of subsequent events or consequences in classroom management. Although behavior is shaped and maintained only if it is followed by effective reinforcers, teaching also involves setting the stage for behavior. The teacher must establish appropriate instructional goals, acquire instructional materials, provide a model for the student, schedule a sequence of activities, and give unambiguous signals that behavior should occur. Each of these classes of antecedent events has a significant controlling function in classroom management.

Antecedent events or stimuli increase the likelihood that a specific behavior will occur. For example, when a second grader is presented with the stimulus $2 + 2 = \underline{\hspace{1cm}}$, it is what occurs after the response is given that provides reinforcement. If the teacher informs the student that his answer is correct or offers some other reward, the probability is increased that the student will give the response 4 the next time the same stimulus is presented. When reinforcement is consistently paired with a stimulus, the stimulus signals that reinforcement is likely to occur. Similar responses that lead to the same consequences will also increase in probability. Thus, the student may respond to 2 + 2 = _____ by writing 4, saying "four," tapping four times with a pencil, or pointing to the numeral 4. This tendency, in the presence of a stimulus, to give similar but not identical responses, all of which lead to reinforcement, is called *response generalization* and is a part of concept formation. It is often necessary to teach response generalizations. Students who have been successful learners tend to be able to respond appropriately in many different ways to an instructional task (i.e., to learn concepts quickly). Those with learning problems, on the other hand, may need to be taught a variety of appropriate responses.

When stimuli differ perceptibly along a significant dimension or combination of features, a similar response is not considered appropriate and is not reinforced. The task 2 + 2 = _____ calls for a completely different response from that of 2 × 2 = _____ or 2 + _____ = 4. The process of learning to respond differentially to different stimuli is called *stimulus discrimination* and is also a part of concept learning. When a student consistently makes a differential response to a stimulus (e.g., when she consistently says "cat" for *c-a-t*), she has learned a discrimination. A basic problem in remedial education is teaching appropriate discriminations (Engelmann & Carmine, 1982). Learning to read and do simple arithmetic computations involves learning many discriminations. Learning to behave appropriately in the classroom means that the student must learn to discriminate the stimuli that signal reinforcement for sitting down, listening, following directions, and performing other behaviors that facilitate academic learning. Discriminations are learned only when behavior is differentially reinforced in the presence of *specific* stimuli. For example, the student will learn not to talk out if she is consistently ignored for doing so and reinforced for talking when appropriate.

Determination of Tasks: Goals, Rules, and Instructions

The teacher can determine specific instructional tasks for a student only after formulating a behavioral goal. The behavior desired must first be defined in observable terms. In addition, the conditions under which the student should perform the behavior and the criterion for satisfactory performance must then be stated. When adequate goals have been established, instructional tasks then logically follow (see chapter 5). It is essential that each task be clearly stated in terms of beginning and ending points; the student must know what he is to do and what constitutes completion of the task. The directive "Study your spelling" does not specify exactly what the student is to do, nor does the task have an unambiguous beginning or ending. "Write each of your spelling words five times," on the other hand, specifies the behavior that the student is to perform.

Clarity in the presentation of tasks allows both the student and the teacher to discriminate the occasions for reinforcement. If the student does not know what to do to obtain reinforcement, she is likely to exhibit maladaptive behavior. Analysis of many behavior-management problems suggests that the student is uncertain about what specific behavior the teacher considers desirable at the moment. On the other hand, if the teacher does not know exactly what the student is to do, the teacher will not be able to determine when to provide a reinforcer for appropriate behavior.

There is often ambiguity concerning desired behavior during nonacademic activities and during the transition between academic tasks. At these times the teacher must set clear expectations. The explicit statement of positive rules for behavior is an essential feature of efficient classroom control (Madsen, Becker, & Thomas, 1968). To avoid confusion, the number of rules should be kept small. To be effective, the rules must be stated positively and should specify behaviors that are incompatible with misconduct. Rules stating what a student should *not* do invite pupils to demand additional rules to cover each example of misconduct. Such rules are not a guide to reinforcement for students or teachers. "Work quietly at your desk," is preferable to "Don't bother others" because it specifies how students are expected to behave and tells the teacher what behavior to reinforce. Positive and explicit rules also simplify communication with students concerning their behavior.

Instructions, when they are effective, are the simplest, most efficient way of changing behavior. Yet instructions have been studied less than any other behavior modification technique (cf. Berman, 1973; Lovitt, 1977). Research evidence indicates that students will often do what the teacher wants them to do if they are simply told exactly what that is (Lovitt, 1977; Lovitt & Smith, 1972). Simple, clear, firm instructions about how to behave or how to perform an academic task may solve an apparent learning or behavior problem.

Use of Models

Stated goals, rules, and instructions are methods of communicating with students. In addition, students constantly observe the behavior of the teacher and their peers, and that behavior provides a model or example for them to follow. Watching the reinforcement of others who are behaving appropriately tends to induce similar behavior in the observer. Modeling and vicarious reinforcement can significantly decrease the amount of time required for a student to learn desirable behavior (see Bandura, 1969; Cullinan, Kauffman, & LaFleur, 1975).

Modeling or demonstration of appropriate behavior is commonly used by teachers in presenting academic tasks (Smith & Lovitt, 1975). Teachers characteristically demonstrate how to solve an arithmetic problem before expecting the student to solve a similar problem. It is less common, however, for teachers to provide models and vicarious reinforcement for nonacademic behavior. Ignoring the misbehaving student and focusing praise and attention on those who are behaving well can be an effective management technique (Birnbrauer, Hopkins, & Kauffman, 1981).

Furthermore, the teacher who sets a poor behavioral model will be less effective in controlling misbehavior than the teacher whose behavior should be emulated. Teachers can also provide an academic model for students. Reading for pleasure, searching for information, writing, and applying computational skills to the solution of everyday problems are behaviors every teacher can model in the classroom.

Providing Cues for Behavior

Teachers must give students signals that indicate *when* they are to perform a behavior. Hand signals, special visual or auditory stimuli, facial expressions, touching, and single words can be used to cue performance. To help students learn to discriminate specific behaviors, cues must be systematically followed by consequences. To be effective, cues must be made especially clear and consistent.

Teachers tend to emphasize cues that signal a student to stop a maladaptive behavior. Nearly every teacher has a well-developed repertoire of "desist" signals—finger snapping, bell ringing, ruler tapping, frowning, ear tugging, finger pointing, shushing, or "boys and girls!" These signals are used after students have begun to exhibit undesirable behaviors. They are often either ineffective or only temporary because (1) they are mildly aversive actions that students can easily cut short by temporarily behaving well and (2) the attention of the teacher, although intended as punishment, reinforces the students' disturbing behavior. Although desist cues can be used effectively and should be part of every teacher's repertoire, their effectiveness will deteriorate if they constitute a majority of the teacher's behavior cues.

Few teachers have developed an extensive set of cues to signal that desired behaviors should occur. Learning to use such signals, however, is an important skill in behavior management. When teachers emphasize cues for desired behavior rather than desist signals, they are likely to observe an increase in reinforceable behavior. For example, cueing students to speak in a discussion is more likely to achieve the desired result than reprimanding those who speak out of turn.

Programs of Activities

Relatively little attention has been given to the controlling function of programs or schedules of antecedent events. The controlling effects of specific antecedent events themselves have not been studied in classroom situations in great detail, yet the program of tasks presented may significantly affect academic and social behavior. Because many students with learning problems have experienced inconsistent and unpredictable environments, it is helpful to follow an invariant daily schedule of activities. Students should be able to predict from day to day the sequence of tasks that will be presented. As academic and social responses improve, the routine can be made more flexible, and students can take a greater part in determining their work schedules.

Generally, the daily schedule should consist of a series of short work periods followed by brief periods of reward. As behavior improves, reward periods can be decreased in length and frequency. Work that can be done individually and without movement about the classroom should be emphasized until appropriate patterns of response are established. Subsequently, academic activities requiring social interaction, free movement about the classroom, and small group participation can be increased gradually. The student's least preferred work should be scheduled early in the day and the most preferred work, late in the day. A student should not be allowed to go on to the next activity until he has successfully completed the task preceding it. Both the first and last activities of the day should be easily accomplished tasks that are pleasant for the student and will encourage him to return to school. These programming suggestions are based on the observation that arrangement of antecedent events builds reinforcement into the schedule and makes the occurrence of reinforceable behavior more likely.

GENERAL BEHAVIOR-MANAGEMENT TECHNIQUES

The behavior principles discussed in this chapter have led to the development of thousands of specific techniques for the management of individuals and groups. The principles can be applied to the unique requirements of each problem situation. Classroom teachers and researchers are constantly devising new techniques for behavior-management problems. A number of specific procedures that have been found useful in resolving common behavior problems are listed in chapter 7. Teachers may find some of the techniques listed in part two directly applicable to their classrooms, but knowledge of the general principles of behavior will give important flexibility in improvising specific management methods that are most effective for particular pupils.

Over the years behavior principles have led to the development of a number of general methods and procedures. These procedures emphasize a highly structured environment in which clear directions, firm expectations of performance, and consistent follow-through are of primary importance. Teacher interaction with students is kept task centered, and students are given many success experiences through individualized assignments and behavioral expectations. Unnecessary verbalizations to students are kept at a minimum. Academic work is evaluated immediately to provide feedback on performance. Improvement in behavior indicates that teaching has been successful, whereas lack of improvement is a signal to try different procedures. Punishment is deemphasized as a behavior control technique, and shaping appropriate responses by successive approximations is stressed. Emotions are evaluated as by-products of behavior rather than causes of behavior; and it is assumed that as behavior improves students' feelings about themselves and their attitudes toward others will also improve. This structured, directive approach to behavior management has a long and successful history (see Kaufman, 1985), and its 20th century proponents have provided ample description of its value (e.g., Cruickshank, Bentzen, Ratzeburg, & Tannhauser, 1961; Haring & Phillips, 1962; Phillips, 1967).

Newer techniques of behavior management, which have been tested empirically in the classroom, provide even more powerful and positive methods of controlling behavior problems (see Kerr & Nelson, 1983; Morris, 1985). There is no guarantee that teachers using these techniques will be successful in their first attempts to change behavior. As in the acquisition of any set of skills or the solution of problems in any field of human endeavor, repeated trials may be necessary. The teacher who at first is not successful must try to determine the reasons for failure and try again. After all, teachers expect no less from their students.

General Techniques for Decreasing Unwanted Behavior

The most common classroom management problems involve talking without permission, getting out of one's seat without permission, refusing academic work, failing to complete assignments, hitting other students, having tantrums, and crying. Although the management problem may involve the entire class, one or two pupils frequently account for most of the troublesome behavior.

As we suggested earlier, it is self-defeating for the teacher to try to change many troublesome behaviors at once. Concentrating on the one or two most serious problems is much more likely to be successful. When the targets for behavior change have been selected, it is helpful to collect baseline data so that a valid assessment of change can be made. Then, one or more of several general procedures can be used to decrease the unwanted behavior.

Extinction. As a procedure, *extinction* refers to preventing a behavior from being reinforced. As a process, it means that behavior that is not reinforced will decrease in strength and eventually cease. When observing maladaptive behavior, the teacher must also observe what happens immediately after the behavior occurs to reinforce it. If the reinforcer can be withheld, the behavior will eventually be extinguished. A very common reinforcer for inappropriate behavior is the attention of another person. Often the student's misbehavior prompts attention from the teacher or other students, usually in the form of reprimands or reminders to behave appropriately. Misbehavior is often followed by attention on an intermittent schedule, which has the effect of maintaining unwanted responses at a high rate. When using an extinction procedure, *all* reinforcers must be consistently withheld from the undesirable response so that there is no reinforcement.

Most troublesome classroom behavior does not result in permanent damage to persons or property and, consequently, can be ignored. Ignoring misbehavior completely can be an effective extinction procedure. However, extinction will not be maximally effective unless other, more appropriate behaviors are strengthened.

When using an extinction procedure, the teacher must be prepared for a temporary increase in the behavior before its strength begins to drop. When the usual reinforcer for a response is not forthcoming, the child will at first attempt to produce the expected consequence by escalating the misbehavior. During extinction the teacher may also notice a spontaneous recovery—temporary resurgence of the behavior before it dies out completely.

Reinforcing Incompatible Behaviors. Incompatible behaviors are behaviors that cannot occur at the same time. Sitting is incompatible with walking about the room. Reading is incompatible with sleeping. But sitting in a chair is not incompatible with talking, nor is writing incompatible with standing. A more powerful procedure than merely withholding the reinforcer (extinction) is reinforcing a behavior incompatible with the inappropriate response. For example, a student may not only be ignored whenever she is out of her seat without permission, but may also be reinforced for sitting. In fact, extinction alone is a dead-end procedure. Reinforcement of desirable conduct is a key factor in decreasing inappropriate behavior. Consequently, the teacher always needs to consider what type of differential reinforcement schedule to employ in dealing with misbehavior (see Dietz & Repp, 1983).

Changing Antecedent Events. Maladaptive behavior sometimes occurs primarily in certain settings that predispose the student to misbehave. A change in the situation in which the behavior is likely to occur may produce marked improvement. For example, being in close proximity to a certain classmate may be the setting in which a student tends to make distracting noises. Changing the seating arrangement so that the two pupils are away from each other may decrease the inappropriate behavior significantly. Likewise, keeping objects such as dolls, balls, or small rubber animals in their desks may provide the occasion for desk searching, unwanted noise making, or arguments. Removal of these objects from students' desks may resolve the management problem.

Some academic responses can be greatly improved by simple changes in the way tasks are presented. Presenting fewer problems per worksheet, presenting single pages cut from a workbook, presenting tasks at a faster pace, heightening the stimulus value of the materials with color cues, amplification, or tactile stimuli—all of these strategies can accelerate response rate and decrease dawdling, daydreaming, and other behaviors that interfere with instruction.

The effectiveness of reinforcers is determined in part by events antecedent to the behaviors they follow. The probability that a behavior will occur—and its power as a reinforcing event for other behaviors—is constantly changing. One factor affecting these changes is the passage of time. For example, immediately after a full meal eating food is a less powerful reinforcing event than it is after several hours with no food. The pupil who has been deprived of candy is more likely to work to obtain candy as a reward than one who has continuous access to sweets. Thus, the probability that a behavior will occur can sometimes be decreased by allowing it to occur freely or requiring that it occur frequently, a technique that produces *satiation.* Children's tendency to tire quickly of a prohibited activity as soon as restrictions are removed is well known.

However, forcing a student to behave in a given manner usually produces unpleasant emotional responses. Allowing the behavior to occur freely is usually preferable to forcing repetition of the undesirable response. For example, the student prone to write socially unacceptable four-letter words on the walls may be permitted (not forced) to write them freely on a special sheet of paper. (Some prudent restaurant owners control the defacement of their restroom walls by providing chalkboards for graffiti.)

Punishment.   American public education has historically emphasized the use of punishment to suppress undesirable behavior. Today, corporal punishment is more frequently administered to mildly handicapped students than is commonly realized (Rose, 1983). A behavior modification approach to discipline focuses on positive rather than punitive control (Kerr & Nelson, 1983; Morris, 1985; Smith, 1984; Skinner, 1971). Most classroom behavior problems can be resolved without the use of punishment. Except when maladaptive behavior is a serious threat to health or safety, positive means of reducing behavior problems should always be tried first. In the few cases in which punishment is necessary, mild, minimally restrictive methods should be employed (Barton, Brulle, & Repp, 1983). Moreover, teachers should realize that "punishment is not synonymous with physical pain or bodily harm and does not necessarily result in emotional responses" (Hall et al., 1971, p. 25). Teachers are urged to consult the professional literature regarding the use of punishment before instituting such procedures (see Axelrod & Apsche, 1983; Polsgrove, 1983).

As we have already noted, punishment is defined as the systematic use of consequences to decrease the strength of a behavior. Punishment may involve presenting an aversive consequence or withdrawing a rewarding consequence contingent upon behavior. Thus, the contingent removal of teacher attention may be a mild punishing consequence for many students, especially young children. The contingent removal of earned rewards or token reinforcers, restriction of activity, or removal of privileges may also be punishing consequences. Other punishing consequences that do not involve inflicting physical pain may require a student to expend extra effort in practicing appropriate behavior or making restitution for a misdeed. Aversive stimuli of a wide variety can be presented—shouts, slaps, spanks—but these are seldom justified as a means of dealing with misbehavior. Physically painful punishment is justified only in the most extreme cases of self-injury or dangerous aggression, if then, and we will not discuss such methods further (see Axelrod & Apsche, 1983; Barton et al., 1983; Wood & Braaten, 1983).

Punishment is perhaps the most controversial topic in behavior modification and school discipline. No doubt, punishment can be used humanely and effectively; punishment in some form may, in fact, be an indispensable tool of the effective teacher. "Great care is necessary in the use of punishment, however, for ill-timed, vengeful, and capricious punishment without incentives for appropriate behavior—punishment as it is typically measured out by parents and teachers of aggressive children—will only provide a vicious model for the child" (Kauffman, 1985, p. 234). Certain general guidelines should be followed whenever punishment is necessary (see Wood & Braaten, 1983, for further guidelines).

1. Use punishment only after positive methods, such as rewarding incompatible behavior, have been given a fair trial and have failed. Reserve punishment for cases in which the continuing behavior would result in more suffering than the punishment would cause.

2. Allow punishment to be administered only by persons who are warm and loving toward students when their conduct is acceptable, that is, by persons who give ample positive reinforcement for appropriate behavior.

3. Administer punishment matter-of-factly, without anger, threats, or moralizing.

4. Administer punishment fairly, consistently, and immediately for specific behavior that the student knew was punishable.

5. Make punishment reasonable in intensity; more serious offenses should result in more severe punishment, but punishment should never be cruel or involve ridicule, humiliation, or unnecessary pain.

6. Relate the type of punishment to the misdeed whenever possible. For example, if the student damages or destroys something, punishment might involve repairing or replacing it; if an item is stolen, punishment should involve restitution.

7. Use loss of rewards, privileges, attention, or points rather than aversive stimuli whenever possible. Withdrawing positive reinforcers tends to produce better long-term results than presenting painful or highly aversive consequences.

8. When punishment is necessary, implement it early. If the student is allowed to continue or complete misbehavior before the punishment is applied, the effectiveness of the punishment will be lessened.

9. Try the mildest form of punishment first; use more severe forms of punishment only after milder forms have been given a fair trial and have failed.

10. Teach self-control strategies (e.g., self-monitoring, self-evaluation, self-application of consequences—see chapter 4) in conjunction with punishment.

Teachers are often mystified by student behavior that seems to persist in the face of punishment, sometimes even severe punishment. Punishment often is ineffective because it is paired with reinforcement—the student engages in the inappropriate behavior, then receives reinforcement as well as punishment. In fact, punishing consequences often contain an unfortunate and destructive reinforcing component. For example, if the teacher gets emotionally upset while administering punishment, the emotional reaction may be highly reinforcing for the student. If the misbehavior gets attention from classmates before or while the punishment is applied, the student is obtaining reinforcement before punishment. Teachers faced with a punished-but-still-misbehaving student must analyze the situation carefully and try to be certain that (1) the punishment does not include features that are reinforcing to the student and (2) reinforcement does not immediately precede punishment.

Discussion of the details of punishing consequences are beyond our scope here. However, we will briefly describe three procedures commonly employed in classrooms: response cost, overcorrection, and time out. Before implementing any of these procedures, however, the teacher should consult the professional literature for guidance in using the procedure effectively, humanely, and with minimum risk of criticism or legal action.

Response Cost. Reponse cost (RC) is punishment in which rewards (usually points or tokens) are withdrawn, contingent upon specific undesirable behavior. RC cannot be implemented properly unless it is tied to an ongoing reinforcement system and the procedure has been carefully explained to the student(s) involved. If used with care, it is a mild form of punishment that can be highly efficient and effective for a wide range of classroom behavior (Lloyd, Kauffman, & Weygant, 1982; Walker, 1983). The interested teacher should consult Axelrod and Apsche (1983) and Walker (1983) for discussion of specific guidelines for using RC.

Overcorrection. Overcorrection (OC) can be of two types: positive practice or restitutional. Positive practice requires that an individual who exhibits a maladaptive behavior practice a more appropriate response repeatedly for a specific number of trials or period of time. For example, a student who disrupts the class by getting out of his seat at inappropriate times might be required to practice requesting permission (Azrin & Powers, 1975). Restitutional OC involves restoring a situation to its prior condition and improving it further. For example, a student who defaces a desk might be required to clean or repair the one defaced and several others as well. OC has been applied with success to a wide variety of behavior problems, including severe self-stimulation and other maladaptive behaviors of the severely handicapped. However, the procedures have limitations and can easily be misused or abused. Interested teachers should consult Foxx and Bechtel (1983) for further information and guidance.

Time Out. Time out (TO) refers to a time when reinforcement is not available. It does not mean merely time out of the classroom or out of the teacher's sight. The teacher will not be able to use TO effectively unless the classroom is a place in which the student receives frequent reinforcement. TO can be implemented on at least four different levels: contingent omission, contingent observation, exclusion, or seclusion. Contingent omission means that the teacher simply ignores the student and omits reinforcement for a brief period of time. Sometimes the student or the student's desk is marked for omission (e.g., a ribbon or band is placed on the student, or a card is placed on her desk to remind the teacher that the student is not to be reinforced until the TO is over. Contingent observation requires the student to sit out of the group briefly but to observe others participating and earning reinforcement. Exclusion TO involves removing the student completely from the environment in which she has been earning reinforcement. This may mean removing the student from the classroom, but exclusion does not entail complete social isolation. Seclusion TO, on the other hand, means that the student is placed in an isolation room or cubicle that makes any social interaction impossible.

Seclusion TO is among the most controversial (and frequently misused and abused) forms of punishment, and it should never be implemented without thorough consideraton of all alternative consequences and the ramifications of its use (Nelson & Rutherford, 1983; Wood & Braaten, 1983). TO at any level, but particularly when exclusion and seclusion are involved, involves administrative, legal, and political as well as professional concerns. Moreover, many details of the implementation of TO—how it is explained, how the student is placed in the TO condition, and how the student is released from TO—can make a great difference in its effectiveness. The interested teacher is advised to consult the literature before using the procedures (see Axelrod & Apsche, 1983; Kerr & Nelson, 1983; Morris, 1985; Nelson & Rutherford, 1983). Regardless of the level of TO employed, TO of long duration (more than a few minutes) is almost never justified; the purpose of education is to keep the student actively engaged in learning and to offer frequent reinforcement for appropriate performance.

General Techniques for Increasing Good Behavior

Teachers must establish priorities for good behavior as well as for reducing behavior problems. After teachers have determined the most important things for their students to learn, they must select effective methods for teaching those skills. At least five general techniques for increasing desirable behavior are available to every teacher.

Giving Rules and Praise, Ignoring, and Reprimanding. Efficient behavior management in the classroom seems to consist of at least three basic techniques that must be used in combination to be most effective (Madsen et al., 1968). Rules for conduct in the classroom must be clearly and positively stated. Students must know how they are to behave. It may be helpful to post rules in a conspicuous place in the classroom and review them periodically. Rules alone, however, are not likely to produce appropriate behavior. They are antecedent events that are of little value without the systematic application of consequences for related behavior.

Teacher attention and praise for rule-following behavior are powerful positive consequences for most students. The teacher must seek out those displaying appropriate behavior and praise them. In this way the teacher calls attention to appropriate models and offers vicarious reinforcement for other class members. Teacher attention can consist of nearness or proximity to the pupil, a touch on the shoulder, assistance with academic work, a wink, or any other sign of recognition. Praise can be given with a smile, a nod of approval, a happy face drawn on the child's paper, other nonverbal signals of approval, and a variety of verbal statements. When verbal praise is given, the teacher should indicate specifically what the student is doing that is praiseworthy. "I'm glad you've started your work already" is preferable to "You're being a good boy this morning," or "Agnes, you're a doll."

In addition to establishing rules and "catching them being good," ignoring most inappropriate behavior will probably increase classroom control. The fallacy of attempting to control misbehavior primarily by criticism or "talking it through" has already been discussed. The more skillful the teacher becomes at totally withdrawing attention from misbehaving students, the more likely he is to achieve efficient classroom management.

Criticizing, nagging, rebuking, and punishing are more tiring than positive interactions such as praising, complimenting, approving, and thanking—whether one is the giver or the receiver of the transaction. Nonetheless, negative interactions seem more likely to occur when an individual's energy is depleted. Consequently, teachers who do not waste their energy and the energy of their students by attending to minor misbehavior may successfully avoid a dangerous spiral of unpleasant behavior.

Certainly, some behavior is too disruptive to ignore; the teacher must intervene to stop it. In this case the offending student should be given a verbal reprimand in as private a manner as possible. Reprimands are most effective if they are used infrequently (the focus should be on desirable conduct). In giving a reprimand, the teacher should go to the student, grasp the student firmly, establish eye contact, use a facial expression showing displeasure, and quietly tell the student in a direct and commanding way to stop the misbehavior. To the extent possible, the offense should be a matter confined to the teacher and the offending individual (Kazdin, 1984).

Rewarding Approximations. Few complex behaviors are learned in a day. Acquisition of a complex skill requires repeated trials over a period of days, weeks, months, or even years. The student whose expectation turns to disappointment when she does not learn to read a book the first day of school does not know how learning takes place. The teacher who expects a disruptive student to become a model of perfection immediately has lost sight of the principle of behavior shaping and will be disappointed. Looking for and rewarding small improvements in behavior is one key to successful teaching. The teacher who waits for perfection will probably never have an opportunity to reinforce student behavior. The teacher who identifies and reinforces successive approximations of the behavior goal will likely see gradual but steady improvements. Before embarking on a behavior management program, the teacher should be able to state what actions of the student will constitute improvement.

Strengthening Reinforcers. Individuals vary greatly in their behavioral responsiveness to reinforcers. Traditional social reinforcers, such as attention and praise, are sufficient to control the classroom behavior of most students. For others it is necessary to provide more powerful consequences—perhaps food, money, toys, personal care items, special privileges, or special activities (see chapter 7, page 168) for a list of possible reinforcers). The strength of reinforcers can be determined by observing what students prefer, asking them what they would like to work for, or providing a consequence for behavior and observing its effect. A subsequent event that is not a reinforcer is of no value in teaching appropriate behavior. It is essential that the teacher find what *each* student will work for and employ those things as reinforcers. Consequences that are more natural are always preferable to those that are more contrived or artificial. However, when the teacher must employ more extrinsic or primitive rewards, little is to be gained by appealing to a love of learning, lamenting a lack of maturity, or disparaging the student's acquisitiveness. Whenever a teacher is unsuccessful in obtaining the desired response, an increase in the strength of the reward should be considered. In addition to strengthening the reinforcers themselves, it is often helpful to make the consequences of behavior more explicit by using a contingency contract or establishing a system of token reinforcement.

Deprivation of reinforcers, the inverse of satiation, can also be used to increase the reinforcing potential of consequences for good behavior. Someone who has been deprived of a reinforcer for a period of time is more likely to work to obtain it. For example, a pupil is more likely to work for the privilege of writing on the chalkboard when he has not had that opportunity for several hours. Reinforcement should be offered frequently but in relatively small amounts so that the student does not become satiated.

Making Reinforcement More Immediate. Delayed rewards are effective only for individuals who have a high level of self-control. Students with learning problems seldom have learned the self-control necessary to work for distant reinforcers. Until the complex task of self-control is taught, their behavior will remain almost exclusively under the control of immediate environmental consequences. One technique for increasing appropriate behavior is to move the reinforcers closer in time to the occurrence of the behavior. In general, the sooner a student is allowed to have a reward after behaving appropriately, the more successful the teacher will be. A token reinforcement system helps to reduce the tactical problem of delivering immediate rewards; tokens can be given immediately after an appropriate behavior without interrupting classroom routine.

Varying the Schedule of Reinforcement. Schedules of reinforcement may be as important in behavioral change as the reinforcers themselves. The schedule according to which a reinforcer is administered often determines its power. Although some target behaviors are apparently acquired with intermittent reinforcment, learning is more likely to occur when every response is reinforced. Continuous reinforcement, however, is not an efficient schedule for maintaining behavior; and change to an intermittent schedule may produce marked acceleration in response rates. With intermittent reinforcement a variable ratio or variable interval schedule will maintain a steadier rate of behavior than a fixed ratio or fixed interval. Consequently, the teacher must always choose a schedule of reinforcement that fits the teaching objectives and the student's level of learning. When the student is not responding to a behavior modification procedure, an appropriate change in the schedule of reinforcement may produce the desired results. It is not uncommon to find that learning has not been acquired because reinforcement has been too infrequent or that learning has not been maintained because of failure to shift gradually to an intermittent schedule.

Changing Antecedent Events. Antecedent events that can be modified to produce behavioral change include rules, tasks, cues, models, and setting events. Establishing positive rules for behavior has already been discussed. The tasks presented to students must be carefully prepared and presented if other elements of behavior management are to be effective (see chapter 5). For students with learning problems, teachers may need an individualized instructional program. Chapter 3 provides principles of academic remediation.

Cues and models can be presented for social-emotional as well as academic behavior. The performance of many behaviors can be regulated by appropriate prompts or cues. Adults program cues for their own behavior by using watches, notes, hand signals, grocery lists, flashing lights, metronomes, bells, and a wide variety of other devices. Student behavior and academic performance often fall short of teacher expectations because the students have no clear cues indicating how, when, or where they are to behave. Students who talk out may do so because the teacher has not developed clear, consistent signals for permission to speak. Students with auditory learning difficulties may have trouble understanding the verbal prompts of the teacher, especially if the teacher ververbalizes instructions. Sometimes students have difficulty reading the teacher's cues because the postural, gestural, intonational, and verbal signals are not consistent. For example, a teacher may call a student's name, indicating that he is to make a verbal response, but fail to look at the student or turn away. For the student with a history of acting-out behavior or learning deficits, the teacher may need to use more dramatic and abbreviated prompts. Withdrawn students, on the other hand, may respond more readily to subtle prompts.

A behavioral model is invaluable in teaching. In attempting to help a pupil acquire a new skill, a teacher must provide many demonstrations of the final performance or risk inefficient teaching and needless attention to detail in shaping behavior (see Cullinan et al., 1975). However, the student who consistently hears a good language model is much more easily taught appropriate language patterns than one who is exposed frequently to models of poor language.

Changes in antecedent settings and events can be used to decrease unwanted behavior. Providing a quiet and uncluttered place to work, attractive and interesting materials, and individualized tasks at which the student can be highly successful will increase learning. Study booths or "offices" in which someone can work without the distraction of other classroom activity may increase attention to the task at hand.

Changing the program or schedule of antecedent events can be a technique for increasing good behavior. The teacher who would like a student to talk only when called on in class discussions must remember to cue that behavior by calling on the student frequently. Making sure that every student has ample opportunities to respond appropriately is an essential element of behavior management. A student who has completed an academic task can make more responses only when additional tasks are presented.

General Techniques for Maintaining Behavioral Gains

Behaviors learned are not necessarily skills retained. Reinforcement is needed to maintain behavior as well as to acquire it. Teaching a new behavior only to see it forgotten or not applied is both inefficient and disheartening. The ultimate goal of classroom management should be self-controlled, highly motivated learners. When artificial or obvious contingencies of reinforcement are necessary to control behavior, an individual is perceived as lacking self-control; when consequences native to the individual's environment produce appropriate behavior, that person is said to have self-control. When frequent reinforcement is necessary to maintain behavior, a student is thought to lack motivation; when the student continues to behave as desired under contingencies with a low frequency of reinforcement, that pupil is considered highly motivated. Every teacher should try to maintain appropriate behavior by using infrequent reinforcement in the student's natural environment. At least four general techniques for achieving this goal are available (see also Kazdin, 1984).

Gradually Reducing Reinforcement. The frequency and amount of reinforcement can be varied to increase good behavior. After a behavior is learned, reinforcement should be intermittent rather than continuous to make the behavior more resistant to extinction. The shift to intermittent reinforcement must be gradual, and occasional reinforcement of the behavior must continue, or the response may be extinguished. Gradual reduction of the frequency of reinforcement will increase the likelihood that the student will adopt a normal motivational pattern.

Gradually Delaying Reinforcement. Immediate reinforcement is essential for effective modification of behavior. As soon as a student has learned a behavior, delayed reinforcement can be effective for maintenance; but feedback is important regarding progress in earning the reinforcer. A student is not likely to continue working toward a long-term goal without recognition of intermediate accomplishments. Token reinforcement is particularly well-suited to the successful use of delayed reinforcement because the accumulation of tokens is an immediate consequence. As the student is able to work for rewards that are delayed for a longer time, she will more closely approximate the motivational model of the teacher.

Gradually Fading from Artificial to Natural Reinforcers. Natural reinforcers are those that can be viewed as native to the everyday social environment of the individual, assuming that that environment is not pathological. Thus, tokens, toys, money, candy, and other reinforcers contrived for therapeutic ends can be considered artificial because they are not ordinarily used as classroom consequences. Teacher attention, praise, grades, records of progress, and special activities are natural reinforcers since good teachers ordinarily provide such consequences. Natural reinforcers have two distinct advantages over artificial reinforcers: (1) they occur in a wider range of environments, and (2) they are less obvious to the casual observer. As remediation of the student's behavioral deficits progresses, a gradual shift should occur from artificial, material rewards to natural, social rewards. It is important to remember, however, that reinforcers are natural or artificial in terms of specific behaviors and situations. The successful teacher continues in the profession for both material and social rewards. If either is lacking—that is, if the teacher receives no social reinforcement from students or no payment from the school—few will continue to teach. Although material rewards for students' appropriate behavior are sometimes essential, the emphasis should be on social rewards.

Teaching Self-Control Behaviors. Response to natural reinforcers is not the only characteristic of self-control. Haring and Whelan (1965) have suggested the stages through which a student may pass in remediation of maladaptive behaviors. The final stage is one of integration, in which the student not only observes the relationship between behavior and its consequences but also begins to control reinforcers to further improve behavior. Students can be taught to manage their own behavior through systematic development and reinforcement of the behaviors that constitute self-control. The student who self-selects an appropriate task, makes a realistic and positive self-statement, or establishes her own contingency of reinforcement offers the teacher a clear opportunity for reinforcement of self-control. Failure to respond to such behavior with a positive social consequence is costly for everyone concerned with that student's success as a learner.

Recently, behavior modifiers have become increasingly interested in the cognitive aspects of self-control and have begun to teach children with learning and behavior problems to talk to themselves in order to control their responses (see Bornstein & Quevillon, 1976; Mahoney, 1974; Meichenbaum, 1983). We will discuss this topic further in chapter 4.

Extending Control in and Beyond the Classroom.   The teacher does not control all of the consequences for students' behavior. Parents, siblings, other teachers, the school principal, peers, or acquaintances in the community may be able to provide powerful reinforcers (Strain, 1981). Teachers can increase their effectiveness as modifiers of behavior by enlisting the aid of other people who control the student's rewards. The coach, the industrial arts teacher, the principal, the janitor, and the cook often can offer powerful school-related incentives. If these individuals agree to assist in providing contingent rewards, they can contribute significantly to the modification of student behavior.

Beyond the classroom teacher, the principal has the greatest potential to affect behavior in the school. He is responsible for the emotional climate of the school and determines whether it emphasizes punitive control or the positive control of rewards. The principal's support of teacher efforts to establish a climate of positive control can make the difference between success and failure in the implementation of behavior modification techniques. The principal who responds primarily to misbehavior seems doomed to an ever-widening spiral of unpleasant interactions. The teacher who arranges to send students to the principal for compliments rather than criticism, pats on the back rather than spanks, and rewards rather than punishment can help the principal focus on positive control and increase the options for positive consequences.

Behavior modification techniques can also be taught to parents and other persons outside the school environment (Kazdin, 1984; Krumboltz & Krumboltz, 1972; Madsen & Madsen, 1972). However, little empirical evidence indicates that behavioral improvement at school necessarily results in positive changes outside the classroom, or vice versa (Wahler, 1969). Remediation should be a joint effort of parents and teachers. Parental use of behavior modification techniques can contribute significantly to the acquisition and maintenance of learning.

LEVELS OF APPLICATION OF BEHAVIOR PRINCIPLES

Like an artisan selecting tools, the teacher must select techniques for changing behavior. However, just as the tool does not determine the skill of the artisan, the behavior management technique does not make a good teacher. Behavior modification techniques must be viewed as precison instruments—useless in the hands of the incompetent and invaluable in the hands of a master. The behavior principles discussed in this chapter have produced numerous techniques that can be applied with varying degrees of precision and sophistication. At least three levels of application can be defined.

Structured Classroom

Good teachers have used behavior principles for centuries. Experienced teachers sometimes remark about behavior modification, "But I've been doing that for years!" When an experienced teacher is having classroom-management problems despite knowledge of basic principles, it is often because she has not applied them consistently and systematically.

The principles of work before play, contingent rewards for good behavior, consistency, firmness, fairness, clarity of instructions, and individualization of expectations seem to be minimum requirements for successful teaching. When these underlying principles of behavior management are employed systematically, a high degree of structure is introduced into the classroom. This structure, or predictability of the classroom environment, has been found to have a therapeutic effect on children's social-emotional and academic behavior (Cruickshank et al., 1961; Haring & Phillips, 1962; Phillips, 1967; Smith, 1984). The structured classroom makes systematic use of most of the behavior principles discussed in this chapter, but it represents a more intuitive, less technological level of application than methods currently being researched. A major difference between the structured classroom and more sophisticated levels of application is its lack of emphasis on daily recording of specific behaviors.

Behavior Technology

At a second level of application, greater precision is employed in manipulating environmental variables and monitoring behavioral change. The structured classroom concept is extended to include more explicit contingencies of reinforcement and daily recording of behaviors (Haring & Phillips, 1972; Haring & Schiefelbusch, 1976; Kerr & Nelson, 1983; Lovitt, 1977). Teachers applying behavior principles at this level are interested in precise measurement of the effects of their teaching procedures. Although it is possible to use behavior principles successfully at a less sophisticated level, teachers should strive to be as precise as possible in teaching and evaluating learning. The application of behavior principles at this level may not be as simple as it first appears (Birnbrauer, Burchard, & Burchard, 1970), but the competent teacher is not likely to encounter extreme difficulty in learning to use behavior technology.

Research Designs. Some teachers may want to develop skills in the scientific analysis of behavior change. Many teachers are capable of using basic research designs to explore the extent of their control over the variables influencing learning. Research designs allow teachers to know whether their teaching is responsible for changes in pupil behavior. The efficacy of various teaching procedures can also be compared by using research methods. Discussion of specific research designs is beyond the scope of this chapter, but the teacher who has mastered the basic elements of behavior technology may want to use behavior principles more scientifically (see Gelfand & Hartmann, 1984; Kazdin, 1984).

LIMITATIONS OF BEHAVIOR MODIFICATION

Any assertion that a behavior modification approach to classroom management represents a limitless solution to educational problems is presumptuous. On the other hand, the assumption that all intervention approaches to school learning problems are equally valid or useful is naïve. No other approach is supported by as much empirical research as behavior modification. Of the alternatives available to classroom teachers, we believe that a behavior modification strategy is the best point of departure. Certainly, it is important to keep in mind that behavior modification is only a tool that will allow a teacher to serve students' needs more effectively *if* that teacher is sensitively attuned to students as human beings. Behavior modification techniques can be (and sometimes are) used mindlessly to squelch individuality or to teach meaningless or unimportant skills. In addition to competence in the application of behavior principles, teachers need skills in listening and talking to students, knowledge of curriculum, and awareness of how they relate to students as persons.

SUMMARY

Behavior modification involves the systematic manipulation of environmental events to produce specific change in observable behavior. The teacher can control events that occur before, during, and after a problem behavior to modify its occurrence. The teacher with a classroom-management problem must first define the problem behavior as an observable action. An objective and reliable baseline record of occurrences should be obtained and plotted on a graph. After a baseline has been established, a wide variety of intervention techniques can be used. General procedures for decreasing undesirable behavior include extinction, reinforcement of incompatible behaviors, changing stimuli that precede the behavior, and punishment. General techniques for increasing good behavior include stating rules, praising good behavior, ignoring misbehavior, giving private reprimands, rewarding approximations, strengthening reinforcers, making reinforcement more immediate, varying the schedule of reinforcement, and changing the tasks, cues, and models presented. Behavioral gains can be maintained by gradually reducing the frequency of reinforcement, delaying reinforcement, fading from artificial to natural reinforcers, teaching self-control behaviors, and extending control to the home and other settings outside the classroom. Although behavior modification can be misused and is not a panacea, its effectiveness is supported by more scientific research in the laboratory and classroom than any other approach to behavior management.

REFERENCES

Axelrod, S., & Apsche, J. (Eds.). (1983). *The effects of punishment on human behavior.* New York: Academic Press.

Azrin, N. H., & Powers, M. A. (1975). Eliminating classroom disturbances of emotionally disturbed children by positive practice procedures. *Behavior Therapy, 6,* 525–534.

Bandura, A. (1969). *Principles of behavior modification.* New York: Holt, Rinehart & Winston.

———— (1977). *Social learning theory.* Englewood Cliffs, NJ: Prentice-Hall.

———— (1978). The self system in reciprocal determinism. *American Psychologist, 33,* 344–358.

Barton, L. E., Brulle, A. R., & Repp, A. C. (1983). Aversive techniques and the doctrine of least restrictive alternative. *Exceptional Education Quarterly, 3*(4), 1–8.

Berman, M. L. (1973). Instructions and behavior change: A taxonomy. *Exceptional Children, 39,* 644–650.

Birnbrauer, J. S., Burchard, J. D., & Burchard, S. N. (1970). Wanted: Behavior analysts. In R. H. Bradfield (Ed.), *Behavior modification: The human effort.* San Rafael, CA: Dimensions.

Birnbrauer, J. S., Hopkins, N., & Kauffman, J. M. (1981). The effects of vicarious prompting on attentive behavior of children with behavior disorders. *Child Behavior Therapy, 3,* 27–41.

Bornstein, P. H., & Quevillon, R. P. (1976). The effects of a self-instructional package on overactive preschool boys. *Journal of Applied Behavior Analysis, 9,* 179–188.

Cruickshank, W. M., Bentzen, F. A., Ratzeburg, F. H., & Tannhauser, M. T. (1961). *A teaching method for brain-injured and hyperactive children.* Syracuse, NY: Syracuse University Press.

Cullinan, D., Epstein, M. H., & Kauffman, J. M. (1982). The behavioral model and children's behavior disorders. In R. L. McDowell, G. W. Adamson, & F. H. Wood (Eds.), *Teaching emotionally disturbed children.* Boston: Little, Brown.

Cullinan, D., Kauffman, J. M., & LaFleur, N. K. (1975). Modeling: Research with implications for special education. *Journal of Special Education, 9,* 209–221.

Deitz, D. E. D., & Repp, A. C. (1983). Reducing behavior through reinforcement. *Exceptional Education Quarterly, 3*(4), 34–46.

Eaton, M., & Lovitt, T. C. (1972). Achievement tests vs. direct and daily measurement. In G. Semb (Ed.), *Behavior analysis and education.* Lawrence, KS: University of Kansas, Department of Human Development.

Engelmann, S., & Carnine, D. (1982). *Theory of instruction: Principles and applications.* New York: Irvington.

Foxx, R. M., & Bechtel, D. R. (1983). Overcorrection: A review and analysis. In S. Axelrod & J. Apsche (Eds.), *The effects of punishment on human behavior.* New York: Academic Press.

Franco, D. P., Christoff, K. A., Crimmins, D. B., & Kelly, J. A. (1983). Social skills training for an extremely shy young adolescent: An empirical case study. *Behavior Therapy, 14,* 568–575.

Gelfand, D. M., & Hartmann, D. P. (1984). *Child behavior analysis and therapy* (2nd ed.). New York: Pergamon Press.

Hall, R. V., Axelrod, S., Foundopoulos, M., Shellman, J., Campbell, R. A., & Cranston, S. S. (1971). The effective use of punishment to modify behavior in the classroom. *Educational Technology, 11*(4), 24–26.

Haring, N. G., & Phillips, E. L. (1962). *Educating emotionally disturbed children.* New York: McGraw-Hill

‾‾‾‾‾ (1972). *Analysis and modification of classroom behavior.* Englewood Cliffs, NJ: Prentice-Hall.

Haring, N. G., & Schiefelbusch, R. L. (Eds.). (1976). *Teaching special children.* New York: McGraw-Hill.

Haring, N. G., & Whelan, R. J. (1965). Experimental methods in education and management. In N. J. Long, W. C. Morse, & R. G. Newman (Eds.), *Conflict in the classroom.* Belmont, CA: Wadsworth.

Hersen, M., & Barlow, D. H. (1976). *Single-case experimental designs: Strategies for studying behavior change.* New York: Pergamon Press.

Homme, L. E. (1969). *How to use contingency contracting in the classroom.* Champaign, IL: Research Press.

Kauffman, J. M. (1985). *Characteristics of children's behavior disorders* (3rd ed.). Columbus, OH: Charles E. Merrill.

Kauffman, J. M., Cullinan, D., Scranton, T. R., & Wallace, G. (1972). An inexpensive device for programming ratio reinforcement. *Psychological Record, 22,* 543–544.

Kazdin, A. E. (1978). *History of behavior modification: Experimental foundations of contemporary research.* Baltimore: University Park Press.

———— (1984). *Behavior modification in applied settings* (3rd ed.). Homewood, IL: Dorsey Press.

Kazdin, A. E., & Bootzin, R. R. (1972). The token economy: An evaluative review. *Journal of Applied Behavior Analysis, 5,* 343–372.

Kerr, M. M., & Nelson, C. M. (1983). *Strategies for managing behavior problems in the classroom.* Columbus, OH: Charles E. Merrill.

Krumboltz, J. D., & Krumboltz, H. B. (1972). *Changing children's behavior.* Englewood Cliffs, NJ: Prentice-Hall.

Lloyd, J. W., Kauffman, J. M., & Weygant, A. D. (1982). Effects of response cost on thumbsucking and related behaviors in the classroom. *Educational Psychology, 2,* 167–173.

Lovitt, T. C. (1970). Behavior modification: The current scene. *Exceptional Children, 37,* 85–91.

———— (1977). *In spite of my resistance—I've learned from children.* Columbus, OH: Charles E. Merrill.

———— (1981). Charting the academic performances of mildly handicapped youngsters. In J. M. Kauffman & D. P. Hallahan (Eds.), *Handbook of special education.* Englewood Cliffs, NJ: Prentice-Hall.

Lovitt, T. C., & Esveldt, K. A. (1970). The relative effects on math performance of single- versus multiple-ratio schedules: A case study. *Journal of Applied Behavior Analysis, 3,* 175–182.

Lovitt, T. C., & Smith, J. O. (1972). Effects of instructions on an individual's verbal behavior. *Exceptional Children, 38,* 685–693.

Madsen, C. H., Becker, W. C., & Thomas, D. R. (1968). Rules, praise, and ignoring: Elements of elementary classroom control. *Journal of Applied Behavior Analysis, 1,* 139–150.

Madsen, C. K., & Madsen, C. H. (1972). *Parents/children/discipline.* Boston: Allyn & Bacon.

Mahoney, M. J. (1974). *Cognition and behavior modification.* Cambridge, MA: Ballinger.

Meichenbaum, D. (1977). *Cognitive-behavior modification: An integrative approach.* New York: Plenum.

———— (1979). Teaching children self-control. In B. B. Lahey & A. E. Kazdin (Eds.), *Advances in clinical child psychology* (Vol. 2). New York: Plenum.

———— (1983). Teaching thinking: A cognitive-behavioral approach. In *Interdisciplinary voices in learning disabilities and remedial education.* Austin, TX: Pro-Ed.

Morris, R. J. (1985). *Behavior modification with exceptional children.* Glenview, IL: Scott, Foresman.

Murphy, H. A., Hutchinson, J. M., & Bailey, J. S. (1983). Behavioral school psychology goes outdoors: The effect of organized games on playground aggression. *Journal of Applied Behavior Analysis, 16,* 29–35.

Nelson, C. M. (1981). Classroom management. In J. M. Kauffman & D. P. Hallahan (Eds.), *Handbook of special education.* Englewood Cliffs, NJ: Prentice-Hall.

Nelson, C. M., & Rutherford, R. G. (1983). Time-out revisited: Guidelines for its use in special education. *Exceptional Education Quarterly, 3*(4), 56–67.

O'Leary, K. D., & Drabman, R. (1971). Token reinforcement in the classroom: A review. *Psychological Bulletin, 75,* 379–398.

Phillips, E. L. (1967). Problems in educating emotionally disturbed children. In N. G. Haring & R. L. Schiefelbusch (Eds.), *Methods in special education.* New York: McGraw-Hill.

Polsgrove, L. (Ed.). (1983). Aversive control in the classroom. *Exceptional Education Quarterly, 3*(4), special issue.

Premack, D. (1959). Toward empirical behavior laws: I. Positive reinforcement. *Psychological Review, 66,* 219–233.

Rose, T. L. (1983). A survey of corporal punishment of mildly handicapped students. *Exceptional Education Quarterly, 3*(4), 9–19.

Shinn, M., & Marston, D. (1985). Differentiating mildly handicapped, low-achieving, and regular education students: A curriculum-based approach. *Remedial and Special Education, 6*(2), 31–38.

Smith, D. D. (1984). *Effective discipline: A positive approach.* Austin, TX: Pro-Ed.

Smith, D. D., & Lovitt, T. C. (1975). The use of modeling techniques to influence the acquisition of computational arithmetic skills in learning disabled children. In E. Ramp & G. Semb (Eds.), *Behavior analysis: Areas of research and application.* Englewood Cliffs, NJ: Prentice-Hall.

Strain, P. S. (Ed.). (1981). *The utilization of classroom peers as behavior change agents.* New York: Plenum.

Twardosz, S., Nordquist, V. M., Simon, R., & Botkin, D. (1983). The effect of group affection activities on the interaction of socially isolate children. *Analysis and Intervention in Developmental Disabilities, 3,* 311–338.

Van Houten, R., Morrison, E., Jarvis, R., & McDonald, M. (1974). The effects of explicit timing and feedback, public posting, and praise upon academic performance and peer interaction. *Journal of Applied Behavior Analysis, 8,* 449–457.

Wahler, R. G. (1969). Setting generality: Some specific and general effects of child behavior therapy. *Journal of Applied Behavior Analysis, 2,* 239–246.

Walker, H. M. (1983). Applications of response cost in school settings: Outcomes, issues, and recommendations. *Exceptional Education Quarterly, 3*(4), 47–55.

Wesson, C., Skiba, R., Sevcik, B., King, R. P., & Deno, S. (1984). The effects of technically adequate instructional data on achievement. *Remedial and Special Education, 5*(5), 17–22.

Wood, F. H., & Braaten, S. (1983). Developing guidelines for the use of punishing interventions in the schools. *Exceptional Education Quarterly, 3*(4), 68–71.

3

Academic Remediation

$\mathbf{A}$t some time in their careers all teachers are faced with students experiencing academic learning problems. These students often require specialized instruction to overcome their academic difficulties. Successful instruction will depend on a concisely formulated system of remediation. This chapter will present the basic principles that we believe all teachers should consider in designing a program of remediation for students with learning problems.

ASSESSMENT FOR TEACHING

Successful instructional programming for students with learning problems depends on a thorough appraisal of each student's specific learning strengths and weaknesses. Assessment procedures are an essential part of the remedial process; individual circumstances and the type of program affect exactly what is included in the diagnosis, which assessment procedures are used, who will be involved in the process, and when and where the evaluation will take place (Myers & Hammill, 1982).

Unfortunately, the concept of diagnosis has been misunderstood and inappropriately implemented in many schools. Assessment has often been viewed as a highly structured and formal situation where the student is administered a battery of specialized, standardized tests. Generally, these formal evaluations within a school occur in settings other than the regular classroom, and the tests are often administered by an individual other than the person who is actually teaching the student. The assessment data are most often integrated into a written report that is subsequently shared with the classroom teacher and the student's parents.

In contrast to these procedures, we believe that assessment should be an ongoing part of the teaching process, one in which the teacher has a responsible and central role. Testing instruments need not be so highly specialized that teachers are excluded from diagnostic procedures. It seems more reasonable to have teachers play an active assessment role since most teachers are in the best position to appraise a student's educational problems.

Assessment Approaches

We have found that the most efficient measurement process employs a variety of appraisal techniques. The large number of assessment procedures available are listed in Table 3–1.

Standardized Tests. Standardized tests are among the most widely used, commercially prepared assessment techniques in educational settings. A standardized test, according to Bertrand and Cebula (1980), is one that calls for uniformity in administration and interpretation in order to allow comparison among students of the same age or grade level.

Schools are presently among the largest users of tests, and Wallace (in press) believe that educators must carefully consider the merits and weaknesses of each test used. Initially, the selection of a standardized test should involve careful planning. Most importantly, the teacher should know the specific purpose for a test. In addition, the teacher should know how the information obtained from the test will be used. We feel that it is an inefficient use of both the teacher's and the student's time to administer assessment instruments that provide little specific instructional information. Table 3–2 summarizes some of the important advantages and limitations of standardized tests. Although a significant advantage of standardized tests is the ability to compare a student with national or regional normative data, it is nonetheless important that test findings not be overgeneralized. Ekwall and Shanker (1983), for example, point out that many individual placement decisions are made on the basis of group standardized tests even though such test scores often have so little reliability that it is difficult to place any real confidence in them.

When a standardized test is administered, the individual teacher should administer all aspects of the evaluation within her capabilities. Because standardized testing is likely to require one-to-one interaction with the stu-

Table 3-1
Assessment Approaches

I. Objective tests and standardized measures
  A. Standardized tests and measures.
    1. Achievement tests.
    2. Mental and intelligence tests.
    3. Tests of motor skills and abilities.
    4. Aptitude and readiness tests.
    5. Physiological measures and medical examinations.
    6. Personality and adjustment tests.
    7. Interest inventories and attitude scales.
  B. Unstandardized short-answer objective tests.
    1. Simple recall or free response tests.
    2. Completion tests.
    3. Alternate response tests.
    4. Multiple choice tests.
    5. Matching tests.
  C. Improved essay types of tests consisting of questions so formulated that they can be scored on a fairly objective basis.
  D. Scales for analyzing and rating a performance or a product.
  E. Tests involving evaluation of responses using projective methods.

II. Evaluation of behavior by less formal procedures
  A. Problem-situation tests.
    1. Direct experience.
      a. Experiment to be performed.
      b. Actual life situation to be met.
    2. Indirect approach.
      a. Improved essay-type examinations.
      b. Expressing judgments about described situations.
      c. "What would you do?"
  B. Behavior records concerning in and out-of-school activities.
    1. Controlled situations.
      a. Use of checklists, rating scales, score cards, codes for evaluating personality traits, behavior, attitudes, opinions, interests, and so on.
      b. Self-rating devices, "Guess-Who?"
      c. Time studies of attention, activities.
      d. Photographs and motion pictures.
      e. Stenographic reports.
      f. Dictaphone and tape recordings.
    2. Uncontrolled situations.
      a. Log or diary; autobiographical reports.
      b. Anecdotal records; behavior journals.
      c. Records of libraries, police, welfare agencies, and so on.
      d. Still or motion pictures.
      e. Tape recordings.
  C. Inventories and questionnaires of work habits, interests, activities, associates, and the like.

Table 3-1 (Continued)

   D. Interviews, conferences, personal reports.
      1. With the individual learner himself.
      2. With others, such as parents or associates.
   E. Analysis and evaluation of a creative act or product, such as a poem, music, constructions, and so forth.
   F. Sociometric procedures for studying group relationships.
   G. Evaluation of reactions using projective and expressive techniques.
      1. Psychodrama and play technics.
      2. Free-association tests.
      3. Interpretation of reactions to selected pictures and drawings.
      4. Interpretation of free oral and written expression.
      5. Interpretation of artistic and constructive products.

SOURCE: From *The Diagnosis and Treatment of Learning Difficulties* (pp. 8–10) by L. J. Brueckner and G. L. Bond, 1955, Englewood Cliffs, NJ: Prentice-Hall. Copyright 1955 by Prentice-Hall. Reprinted by permission.

dent, the teacher sometimes finds it difficult to schedule the time for it. Consequently, standardized testing is often left to someone else. Despite this tendency, we believe that the teacher should attempt to conduct the evaluation—during a quiet time in the class, before or after school, or during class breaks.

One last note concerns the administration of more exacting tests that require specific training in interpretation and analysis. For these it may be necessary to employ a qualified examiner trained in the areas of per-

Table 3-2
Advantages and Limitations of Standardized Tests

Advantages	Limitations
1. Comparisons to various norm groups	1. Lack of specific teaching information
2. Standard procedures for administration and scoring	2. Overgeneralizations and misuse of findings
3. Measure of continuous growth	3. Some tests may discriminate against various groups within the culture.
4. Interpretation aided by examiner manual	4. Low reliability and validity for some standardized tests
5. Measurement of variability in specific developmental areas	5. Emphasis on total scores rather than on an item analysis

sonality or intelligence testing. When this type of service is warranted, the test results should be considered in conjunction with the data previously obtained by the teacher. Too often teachers do not use the information accumulated by others because its implications for instructional programs are indirect. There should be closer coordination between informal teacher evaluations and formal test results. Individuals working together can evaluate more accurately the specific instructional needs of students experiencing learning problems in school.

Criterion-Referenced Tests. In this method of assessment, each student's performance is evaluated in terms of a specific criterion that has been set for that pupil. Correctly translating 80% of 50 Spanish vocabulary words might be the criterion set for one student; correctly computing 10 out of 12 math word problems might be the criterion set for another student.

Guerin and Maier (1983) point out that the focus of criterion-referenced testing (CRT) is clearly on the student's level of performance—what the student can do and what is needed to reach a level of success. In contrast to norm-referenced testing, the performances of other individuals have little relevance in CRT. A student's performance is interpreted in relation to each item on the test rather than to a national sample of age or grade peers.

Among the many advantages of criterion-referenced testing, Proger and Mann (1973) have included the following: (1) flexibility in addressing various individual requirements; (2) continuous assessment of individual student progress; (3) adaptability to any commercially available curriculum; and, most important for the learning handicapped student, (4) judgment of the student relative to his own strengths and weaknesses rather than to any group performance.

The limitations of CRT include the amount of time and detail that is often required to construct criterion tests, the narrowness of the focus, and the appropriateness of the criterion (Guerin & Maier, 1983). In some cases Wallace and Larsen (1978) note that a student might be unduly struggling with a specific activity because the criterion that was set was too difficult for the student. In addition, Mehrens and Lechmann (1978) point out that many criterion-referenced tests are shorter and therefore not as reliable as many norm-referenced tests.

Criterion-referenced testing has become one of the most prevalent approaches to assessment of the learning handicapped because these tests provide specific information regarding skills in the school curriculum. Furthermore, Wallace (in press) note that since CRT is best adapted for appraising basic skills, teachers can continually note how students are progressing toward mastery of the subskills within a sequence of broader reading or math skills. Also, CRT provides information that enables teachers to design various instructional strategies to help students master the criterion being measured.

Informal Teacher-Made Tests. Informal teacher-constructed tests are also administered to students with learning problems. Informal tests are often administered when specific data are not available from standardized tests or are inadequate. These specific, task-oriented tests often provide evaluative teaching data at least as important as the information obtained through formal testing procedures. According to Wallace (in press), the advantages of informal teacher-made tests include (1) direct teacher involvement, (2) immediate teacher feedback concerning pupil strengths and weaknesses in specific content areas, (3) similarity in content and skills to classroom instructional programs, (4) provision for continuous evaluation, and (5) ease of construction and administration.

Informal tests are not intended to be complicated, expensive, or time-consuming. Most are teacher-made and teacher-administered, and the information obtained is typically intended to provide the teacher with planning data pertinent to the instructional needs of individual students. Informal tests can be adapted from a variety of sources: (1) seatwork exercises emphasizing one specific task, (2) orally administered exercises, (3) informal teaching lessons assessing various skills, and (4) individually administered written assignments. These tests can be used to assess a wide variety of both specific and broad-range skills. For example, a student's knowledge of certain consonant blends can be measured by an informal test. On the other hand, broader skills such as solving math word problems or taking notes can also be evaluated through informal testing. A number of informal tests are described by content areas in part two of this book.

Although we believe that informal teacher-made tests are uniquely suited to the needs of students with learning problems, a number of cautions must be mentioned. The fact that informal tests cannot be constructed with the same degree of reliability and validity that many standardized tests possess must certainly be considered as a serious limitation. In addition, precise planning, administration, and interpretation of informal tests is necessary if the results are to hold any meaning for the teacher. Moreover, informal test results cannot be used to compare a student with individuals in other parts of the country. Regardless of the precision used in constructing, administering, and interpreting informal tests, they can reflect only the progress and skills of the students for whom they are planned (Wallace, in press).

Observation. A large part of the information utilized in planning an instructional program for students with learning problems can be obtained through observation of the students during school activities. Throughout a school day teachers are provided with many different opportunities to observe academic skills. For the elementary teacher oral reading periods provide an excellent time to observe a student's word analysis, word recognition, or reading comprehension skills. Similarly, teachers of older students can observe spoken language skills during a student's conversation with other pupils, question-and-answer sessions, and oral discussion periods.

According to Cartwright and Cartwright (1974) the first step in the process of observation is to determine the purpose for observing a particular student. A teacher might want to determine the types of word analysis techniques a certain student uses; in another case the teacher might be interested in the number of times a student is out of his seat without permission during a specified length of time. As soon as the purpose for observation is determined, Cartwright and Cartwright (1974) suggest other factors to consider.

- □ Who will make the observation?
- □ Who or what will be observed?
- □ Where will the observation take place?
- □ When will the observation occur?
- □ How will the observation be recorded?

Among the many different approaches to observation, anecdotal recordings have probably been the most widely used in the past. Such records usually describe specific behavioral events in some detail. More recently, however, a variety of time-sampling techniques have been used to observe different aspects of behavior. Time-sampling techniques allow the teacher to determine how often a behavior is occurring during a specified time interval. The teacher who is interested in how often a student is talking out of turn during the social studies period, for example, would probably find such a technique quite useful.

Rating scales and checklists can also be used during observation periods to help focus the observer's attention on specific behaviors. Nevertheless, we have found that rating scales and checklists tend to limit the observer to the behaviors included on the list. Furthermore, ratings are somewhat difficult to translate into specific instructional practices.

Although we believe that observational data should be included in the total assessment process, there are a number of limitations related to observation. In particular, the potential for bias on the part of the observer should be strongly considered. Some individuals may look only for what is already in their minds about the student. In addition, observers should be careful in interpreting observational data since most observations are only a sample of a student's behavior. Finally, observations should be made in a variety of situations and time periods to validate the behaviors that are observed.

Continuous Assessment

In planning a program of remediation the initial evaluation of a student should be viewed as only a starting point for continuous evaluation. All of the information required to help the student with learning problems will not be obtained during the initial evaluation (Spache, 1976). Some students will continue to experience specific difficulties as they progress academically, whereas other students will outgrow certain methods and materials. Sometimes teachers will be able to clarify troublesome concepts by improvising a diagnostic teaching procedure. In other cases a more detailed analysis of the situation might be necessary before the student can be successfully taught; standardized tests and other alternatives might be needed.

Continuous assessment is actually the basis upon which clinical or diagnostic teaching is formulated (Wallace & Larsen, 1978). In the process of teach-test-teach-test the teacher is constantly observing the student's behavior, her responses to the approach being used, and the apparent impact on her development (Spache, 1976). The cycle of clinical teaching, as diagrammed in Figure 3–1, requires continual planning and implementation of teaching tasks based on an ongoing program of assessment and evaluation.

We do not view continuous assessment as a series of formal tests that are administered to the student. Rather, continuous assessment involves the many different opportunities that teachers have throughout a school day to evaluate a student's achievement. Written seatwork, for example, can provide a good indication of a student's understanding of a unit of work. Similarly, teachers can evaluate achievement by observing a child during

Figure 3-1. Diagram of the Clinical Teaching Cycle

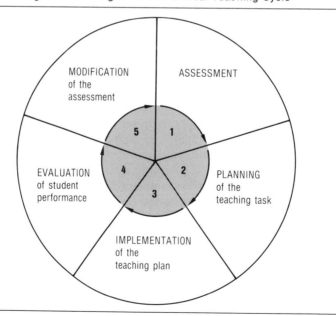

oral reading periods or chalkboard work sessions. As noted by Lerner (1985), continuous assessment actually becomes a part of the entire teaching process as the teacher continually evaluates units of instruction.

Continuous assessment should also involve overall program evaluation. In most cases teachers can informally evaluate the effectiveness of the remedial program through observation and teaching procedures. When a student is not succeeding, it might be necessary for the teacher to change the method, give additional support, or reevaluate the entire remedial process. In the latter case the teacher would need to reassess remedial goals and look for possible explanations of the program's ineffectiveness. When supportive teaching is required, the teacher might present similar amounts of work, change response modes, or provide additional practice time. All of this requires some creativity, originality, and flexibility on the part of the teacher. The teacher must appraise the situation and evaluate the effectiveness of his teaching. Ultimately, the success of the program will depend on this phase of the teaching process.

Applying Assessment Information

In many schools across the country, testing has become an end in itself rather than a means for planning an instructional program. The emphasis on scores (e.g., grade-level scores, age equivalents, percentiles) has contributed to the incorrect usage of test results. Few teachers seem to remember that the purpose of educational assessment is to provide data to develop an instructional program for individual students. The important information that led to the formulation of the grade or age score is often overlooked.

Most assessment approaches, when appropriately analyzed, provide educationally relevant information. Descriptive data obtained from tests can help teachers plan and implement instructional programs. Stephens (1977) points out that, on the basis of test information, teachers can decide *what* needs to be taught and eventually *how* it should be taught. For example, the information pertaining to specific skills that is usually obtained from informal teacher-constructed tests provides the teacher with data about what the student can and cannot do in terms of actual academic behaviors. In most instances the test results require little analysis since the student's performance is easily interpreted; the particular skill was either attained or not attained. Consequently, informal test results are often immediately applicable to the solution of instructional problems (McLoughlin & Lewis, 1986).

Specific skill strengths and weaknesses can also be determined from a selected number of standardized tests (Wallace & Larsen, 1978). Many of the formal tests discussed in part two can provide information of an exact nature. However, teachers must go beyond grade scores and percentiles to the student's actual responses on individual test items. In this way the results can be informally studied and analyzed, and the information obtained can then be applied to instructional strategies and ongoing programs of remediation. This integration of formal test information into instructional practices is illustrated by David's case.

DAVID

David is a 10-year-old youngster experiencing written language problems and reading difficulties. His teacher reported that David was also having great difficulty following directions and paying attention in class. David was administered the Gates-McKillop-Horowitz Reading Diagnostic Test (Gates, McKillop, & Horowitz, 1981) with the following results: David knew all of the letter sounds except the short /o/. With regard to the names of the letters, David identified B as P, i as L, and q as p. He was particularly weak in discriminating final letter sounds, substituting /f/ for /v/, /l/ for /k/, /p/ for /b/, and /n/ for /b/.

On the oral reading subtest he tended to omit and mispronounce words. He read slowly with poor phrasing and emphasis and used a low, often indistinct voice. His word attack appeared to depend mainly on a combination of initial letter sounds and general configuration; he frequently skipped unfamiliar words. Infrequently, he named the letters in attacking a word. On the spelling subtest David usually guessed at the remainder of the word after correctly saying the initial sound.

The results of the Gates-McKillop-Horowitz and informal measures provided the teacher with a basis for initiating an instructional program. The teacher is using a language experience approach to develop sight vocabulary, word analysis skills, and writing ability. Telephone conversations aid in developing David's attending and listening skills. The teacher is also using the Language Master to develop a sight vocabulary and work on medial and final letter combinations.

In addition to the Gates-McKillop-Horowitz other standardized tests can be used if the administrator is willing to analyze the test carefully for the needed instructional information. Often the teacher must translate test information into instructional processes, since most tests provide few guidelines for this particular purpose. However, this requirement does not preclude using test results for planning a program of remediation. The teacher must obtain all the important information.

An important but often overlooked facet of evaluation is the information that points clearly to a student's strengths. What a student *can* do is as important in planning a program as what a student cannot do or cannot do well. Learning strengths exhibited both in the classroom and on informal and formal tests can often provide a teacher with the basis for a teaching program. Spache (1976) suggests that test administrators attempt to find ways in which the student does learn, ways that can be strengthened through instructional activities.

In sum, it is important to evaluate *all* available information and use that which is most helpful in planning for individual students. Data obtained through both informal and formal evaluations can serve as a guideline in planning remedial programs. Some of the information can be used directly in the teaching process, whereas other information can be used for total program planning. Evaluation data serve as a foundation upon which future successes can be built.

INDIVIDUAL EDUCATION PROGRAMS

The U.S. Congress passed the Education for All Handicapped Children Act (P.L. 94–142), guaranteeing handicapped students the right to a free and appropriate education. Goodman (1976) describes this federal law as the "Bill of Rights for the Handicapped." According to Larsen and Poplin (1980), P.L. 94–142 stipulates essentially that school districts and other public agencies are no longer able to exclude handicapped pupils simply because they exhibit problems too severe to be handled in the school setting, they are judged to be ineducable, or appropriate programs have not been developed.

As one of the requirements of P.L. 94–142, an individualized education program (IEP) must be developed and maintained for each handicapped pupil. The basic rationale underlying the development of an IEP is the implicit need for a comprehensive plan to systematically provide each handicapped student with an education appropriate to her unique needs. According to Larsen and Poplin (1980), each IEP must achieve the following: (1) direct educational planning and programming, (2) some degree of accountability, and (3) adequate communication within the school and between home and school. Bateman and Herr (1981) believe that the IEP is the key to ensuring that a handicapped student is provided a free and appropriate public education.

Federal regulations mandate the general participants who are to be involved in the development or revision of an IEP. These individuals include (1) a representative of the public agency, other than the student's teacher, who is qualified to provide or supervise special education services; (2) the student's teacher(s); (3) one or both parents; (4) the student, when appropriate; and (5) other individuals at the discretion of the parent(s) or education agency. For a handicapped student evaluated for the first time, a member of the evaluation team or an individual knowledgeable about the evaluation results for that student must also attend the IEP meeting. In addition, P.L. 94–142 clearly specifies that the IEP for each student must include the following components.

□ *A statement of the child's present level of educational performance.* Standardized assessment instruments are generally administered to determine what subject/content areas are appropriate for the student and what the student's general level of performance is within each area. This information is usually sufficient for use in establishing annual educational goals for the student.

□ *A statement of annual goals, including short-term instructional objectives.* Setting annual goals usually serves to direct the long-term education of the student in self-help/basic living skills or academics. These goals generally provide a plan for establishing a student's specific educational program. Short-term instructional objectives usually include a stated criterion for mastery (e.g., Tim will maintain eye contact during a conversation with a stranger, 50% of the time when another person is speaking and 50% of the time when he personally is speaking) and constitute specific guidelines for teachers to follow in programming daily instructional activities. Short-term instructional objectives also form the basis for mandated evaluations of student progress.

□ *A statement of the specific special education and related services to be provided to the child and the extent to which the child will be able to participate in regular educational programs.* Under this component the IEP must describe those services within each category which will be provided for the student. The specific special education arrangement (e.g., resource room or self-contained special class) is usually delineated, along with the amount of time to be spent each day or week in the specified setting. The approximate type and amount of related services (e.g., speech therapy or counseling) are also described in the IEP. In addition, the IEP must document the extent to which a student is to participate in regular education programs since, for some handicapped students, the regular classroom is considered the "least restrictive environment."

□ *The projected dates for initiation and anticipated duration of services.* This component demands that educators focus their attention on possible termination of the special educational services, making full educational support through regular education an ultimate goal. Ultimately, the duration of special services will depend on the student's progress in meeting the various educational goals and objectives.

□ *Appropriate objective criteria and evaluation procedures and schedules for determining, on at least an annual basis, whether instructional objectives are being achieved.* In order to determine procedures to use in evaluating goals and objectives, it is important to first determine the behavior(s) that give evidence that the student has mastered the goal or objective. This behavior ultimately becomes the criterion by which the student is evaluated. Larsen and Poplin (1980) recommend standardized instruments for measuring annual goal achievement and teacher-constructed devices and observations for evaluating progress toward short-term instructional objectives. They believe that the establishment of specific schedules, procedures, and criteria for evaluation is the most important component in achieving the accountability of the IEP.

Although the process by which an IEP is developed may differ according to specific school districts, the following steps are generally included: screen students, make appropriate referral, analyze referrral, plan assessment, conduct assessment and analyze results, hold meetings with parents to design the IEP, place student in special education class, develop plan to implement IEP, implement and monitor IEP, review IEP, and continue special education services (Pasanella & Volkmor, 1981).

Federal regulations do not mandate any specific IEP form. Consequently, these forms vary widely in different localities. Figure 3–2 provides one example of an IEP for a hypothetical 12-year-old student.

INSTRUCTIONAL MATERIALS

It has been suggested that if there are significant individual differences in the ways students learn, teachers should use varied approaches in helping them learn (Heilman, Blair, & Rupley, 1981). We believe that there is no one best instructional method or material for students with learning problems. Teachers should be able to handle any number of different learning problems after determining what will work for a particular student. A lack of flexibility in teaching approaches actually contributes to the learning problems of some students.

One of the challenges of regular teaching is adjusting to the individual differences among students. Even more challenging are the differences among students experiencing difficulty in school. Probably the most complex problem confronting the teacher is that of adjusting instruction to accommodate individual differences; it requires a working knowledge of a variety of instructional materials and techniques. It is difficult for some teachers to use more than one teaching method. It is equally difficult to convince some teachers of the merits of a specific approach for a particular student if they are already convinced of the advantages of using a certain approach with all students. Nevertheless, we have found that learning is most often enhanced and teaching is less frustrating when the teacher is flexible in his approach to instruction.

The difficulty of individualizing a program for a few students is frequently mentioned by teachers as an argument against employing a variety of instructional approaches. The ease of using one method with all students is viewed as the corresponding advantage. The obvious flaw in this argument—the extra work entailed in trying to fit a student to materials or techniques not suited to her needs—is rarely considered. That burden is often lightened when teachers match an instructional approach to the learning style of the individual student. Planning for individual pupils suddenly seems to be much less work when students are learning.

Articulate arguments and occasional empirical evidence can be cited in support of certain instructional materials and techniques. Heilman, Blair, and Rupley (1981) report that virtually every method and procedure

Figure 3-2. Example of an Individual Education Program (IEP)

Individual Education Plan (IEP)

Yearly Class Schedule

	Time	Subject	Teacher
1st semester	8:30 - 9:20	math	Franks
	9:30 - 10:20	language arts	Bambara (Resource)
	10:30-11:20	social studies	Bambara
	11:20-12:20	science	Franks
		lunch	
	1:10 - 2:00	art	Shaw
	2:10 - 3:00	P.E.	King
2nd semester	8:30 - 9:20	math	Franks
	9:30 -10:20	language arts	Bambara (Resource)
	10:30-11:20	social studies	Bambara
	11:30-12:20	science	Franks
		lunch	
	1:10	art	Shaw
	2:10 -3:00	P.E.	King

Identification Information

Name: John Doe

School: Beecher Sixth Grade Center

Birthdate: 5-15-65   Grade   6

Parents Name: Mr. and Mrs. William Doe

Address: 1300 Johnson Street

Raleigh, N.C.

Phone: Home   none   Office   932-8161

Continuum of Services

	Hours Per Week
Regular class	20 hours
Resource teacher in regular classroom	6 hours
Resource room	4 hours
Reading specialist	
Speech/language therapist	
Counselor	
Special class	
Transition class	
Others:	

Testing Information

Test Name	Date Admin	Interpretation
PIAT	9-10-86	spell-1.7, math-5.7, read recog-1.2 read comp-N.A., gen info-6.3
test of initial consonants (CRT)	9-11-86	knows 8 out of total-2.0 21 initial consonant sounds
CRT Reading Checklist	9-12-86	oral comprehension - 6th grade reading skills - primary level
Carolina Arith. Inventory (Time)	9-2-86	Level IV
Carolina Arith. Inventory (Number concepts)	9-2-86	Level IV

Checklist

9-1-86	Referral by Louise Borden
9-3-86	Parents informed of rights, permission obtained for evaluation
9-15-86	Evaluation compiled
9-16-86	Parents contacted
9-18-86	Total committee meets and subcommittee assigned
9-28-86	IEP developed by subcommittee
9-30-86	IEP approved by total committee

Committee Members

Teacher   Mrs. Louise Borden

Other LEA representative   Mrs. John Thomas   Mr. William Doe

Parents   Mrs. Mary Franks

Mrs. Joan Bambara

Mrs. Alice King

Date IEP initially approved   9-30-86

Health Information

Vision: good

Hearing: excellent

Physical: good

Other:

SOURCE: From *Developing and Implementing Individualized Education Programs* (pp. 23–25) by A. P. Turnbull, B. B. Strickland, and J. C. Brantley, 1978. Columbus, OH: Charles E. Merrill. Copyright 1978 by Bell and Howell Company. Reprinted by permission.

Figure 3-2 (continued)

Student's Name: John Doe

Subject Area: Reading

Level of Performance:
- can identify 8 of 21 initial consonants.
- can identify a few words at preprimer level.
- can orally comprehend stories from 6th grade books.

Teacher: Mrs. Bambara—resource teacher

Annual Goals:
1. John will successfully complete the primer level of the Bank Street Reading Series.
2. John will recognize and correctly say 90 new sight words.
3. John will master 14 initial consonants.

	September	October	November	December	January
Objectives	Referred	1. Recognize and correctly state the sounds of the initial consonants "b" and "f" 100% of the time. 2. Recognize and correctly say ten new sight words 100% of the time. 3. Complete the first three stories of the primer, reading the material with 50% accuracy.	1. Recognize and correctly state the sounds of the initial consonants "s" and "m" 100% of the time. 2. Recognize and correctly say ten new sight words 100% of the time. 3. Complete the next three stories in the primer, reading the material with 50% accuracy.	1. Correctly recognize and state the sound of the initial consonant "g" 100% of the time. 2. Recognize and correctly say five new sight words 100% of the time. 3. Complete the next story in the primer, reading the material with 50% accuracy.	1. Review and correctly state the sounds of the initial consonants "b," "f," "m," "s," and "g" 100% of the time. 2. Recognize and correctly state the sound of the initial consonant "h" 100% of the time. 3. Review and correctly say 25 previously learned sight words 100% of the time. 4. Recognize and correctly say five new sight words 100% of the time. 5. Review the previously read stories in the primer, reading the material with 60% accuracy.
Agent		resource teacher 1, 2 regular classroom teacher 2, 3	resource teacher 1, 2 regular classroom teacher 2, 3	resource teacher 1, 2 regular classroom teacher 2, 3	resource teacher 1, 2, 3, 4 regular teacher 4, 5
Evaluation		1. informal assessment 2. Criterion Referenced Test (CRT)	1. informal assessment 2. CRT	1. informal assessment 2. CRT	1. informal assessment 2. CRT

SOURCE: From *Developing and Implementing Individualized Education Programs* (pp. 23–25) by A. P. Turnbull, B. B. Strickland, and J. C. Brantley, 1978, Columbus, OH: Charles E. Merrill. Copyright 1978 by Bell and Howell Company. Reprinted by permission.

Figure 3-2 (Continued)

Student's Name: John Doe

Subject Area: Reading

Level of Performance: Can identify 8 of 21 initial consonants.
Can identify a few words at preprimer level.
Can orally comprehend stories from 6th grade books.

Teacher: Mrs. Bambara—resource teacher

Annual Goals:
1. John will successfully complete the primer level of the Bank Street Basal Reading Series.
2. John will recognize and correctly say 90 new sight words.
3. John will master 14 initial consonants.

	February	March	April	May	June
Objectives	1. Recognize and correctly state the sounds of the initial consonants "l" and "d" 100% of the time. 2. Recognize and correctly say 15 new sight words 100% of the time. 3. Complete the next three stories in the primer, reading the material with 60% accuracy and mastering the skills that accompany the stories.	1. Recognize and correctly state the sounds of the initial consonants "r" and "w" 100% of the time. 2. Recognize and correctly say 15 new sight words 100% of the time. 3. Complete the next three stories in the primer, reading the material with 60% accuracy and mastering the skills that accompany the stories.	1. Recognize and correctly state the sounds of the initial consonants "c" and "t" 100% of the time. 2. Recognize and correctly say 15 new sight words 100% of the time. 3. Complete the next three stories in the primer, reading the material with 95% accuracy and mastering the skills that accompany the stories.	1. Recognize and correctly state the sounds of the initial consonants "n" and "y" 100% of the time. 2. Recognize and correctly say 15 new sight words 100% of the time. 3. Complete the next three stories in the primer, reading the material with 95% accuracy and mastering the skills that accompany the stories.	Evaluation
Evaluation Agent	resource teacher 1, 2 regular classroom teacher 2, 3 1. informal assessment 2. Criterion Referenced Test (CRT)	resource teacher 1, 2 regular classroom teacher 2, 3 1. informal assessment 2. CRT	resource teacher 1, 2 regular classroom teacher 2, 3 1. informal assessment 2. CRT	resource teacher 1, 2 regular classroom teacher 2, 3 1. informal assessment 2. CRT	

SOURCE: From *Developing and Implementing Individualized Education Programs* (pp. 23–25) by A. P. Turnbull, B. B. Strickland, and J. C. Brantley, 1978. Columbus, OH: Charles E. Merrill. Copyright 1978 by Bell and Howell Company. Reprinted by permission.

described in the literature has been successful with some students and unsuccessful with others. Even though teachers are likely to become enamored with one method to the exclusion of others, we believe that successful remediation is based upon teacher versatility. Becoming versatile is not an easy task; it requires detailed planning and conscientious study. A particularly difficult aspect of the process is experimenting with different methods and materials. Understandably, some teachers hesitate to experiment for fear of continuing the student's failure. However, the student will often continue to experience difficulty until a successful instructional approach is found. We believe that a variety of teaching methods and materials is absolutely basic to successful remediation.

Selecting Instructional Materials

Some teachers experience difficulty in selecting appropriate materials, which we believe is one of the most important tasks that a teacher performs since successful remediation is often dependent upon the method or material that is used. The following questions, according to Mendell and Gold (1984), can be considered basic guidelines in selecting specific materials.

☐ Is the cost justifiable?
☐ For what age group or developmental level is the material designed?
☐ Does the format promote mastery learning?
☐ Is the material biased?
☐ Is there a correspondence between mastery activities provided by a material and instructional objectives?
☐ Are directions clearly stated?
☐ What kinds of student responses are required?
☐ How much time is needed to use the material?
☐ Is the material motivating for students?
☐ Who is to use this material?
☐ Are special storage requirements needed? (pp. 108–110)

The current proliferation of commercially prepared instructional materials has certainly added to the teacher's material-selection dilemma. It is unfortunate that many advertising gimmicks have helped to sell basically inferior materials; creative packaging has left educators skeptical. We believe that teachers must become aware of packaging and advertising deception and begin to judge a material on its intrinsic value and appropriateness to particular instructional settings. Various models for evaluating instructional materials have been offered by Van Etten and Van Etten (1978) and Wiederholt and McNutt (1977). In addition, Wilson (1982) recommends that curricular, teacher, and student variables be considered in selecting appropriate materials. Table 3–3 lists the items that Wilson includes for each of the three variables.

Information about instructional material can also be obtained from publishers, material resource centers, colleges and universities, and various

Table 3-3
Variables to Be Considered in Material Selection

Curricular Variables	Student Variables	Teacher Variables
Content area	Needs of the student	Method
Specific skills	Current level of	Approach
Theories and tech-	functioning	Time
niques associated	Grouping	Training
with the concepts	Programming	Education
Methodology	Methods	
Modification	Physical, social,	
	and psychological	
	characteristics	

SOURCE: From "Selecting Educational Materials and Resources" by J. Wilson in *Teaching Children with Learning and Behavior Problems* (3rd ed., pp. 410–413) by D. D. Hammill and N. R. Bartel, 1982, Boston-Allyn & Bacon. Copyright 1982 by Allyn & Bacon. Adapted by permission.

retrieval systems. One federally funded retrieval system, the National Instructional Materials Information System, is part of the National Center for Educational Media/Materials for Handicapped in Columbus, Ohio. This system includes abstracts of media and materials appropriate for students with learning problems.

After an analysis of all available information (test results, informal observations, prior use of certain materials, and individual interests), the teacher should be able to list a number of alternative instructional approaches. A variety of factors usually complicate the final material selection: the availability of certain materials, the financial status of the school district, administrative policies of the school district, and teacher preference. Nonetheless, when all these factors have been considered, the final decision rests with the individual teacher.

Adapting Instructional Materials

Our experience suggests that students who have encountered academic difficulties over a long period require some time to adjust to new methods and materials. Learning problems do not disappear immediately. Although flexibility in the use of materials is encouraged, the instructional approach must be given time to succeed.

Many instructional materials need to be adapted for use with the learning handicapped because of complex directions, fast pace, high reading level, boring content, confusing format, or lengthy assignments (Mercer & Mercer, 1985). Some of the adaptations listed by Mandell and Gold (1984) and Lerner (1985) include

□ rewriting material
□ providing study guides

□ allowing students to respond orally rather than in writing
□ tape-recording directions
□ increasing the amount of repetition
□ providing more time for completion of work
□ providing more examples and activities
□ providing glossaries for content areas

We believe that the tendency of some educators to switch materials from year to year can be extremely debilitating for students with learning problems. It is discouraging to examine a cumulative folder and discover the large number of different programs and materials to which a learning handicapped student has been exposed, generally to no avail since many of these students are continuing to experience academic difficulties. Any number of reasons may explain the continuing difficulty, not the least of which may be inappropriate planning for selection of instructional materials.

A number of excellent methods and materials are presently available for use with handicapped learners; many are described in part two. Nonetheless, we believe that there continues to be an acute need for good instructional materials specifically designed for students with learning problems.

Using Microcomputers

The rapid growth in computer technology is essentially a phenomenon of this decade. American schools have witnessed an explosive interest in utilization of microcomputers for many different purposes. In general, Taber (1983) thinks that the microcomputer can assist the teacher in individualizing instruction, extending teacher expertise, and simplifying record keeping and other administrative duties. According to Behrmann (1984), current microcomputer applications in special education fall into three broad categories.

1. *Computer-assisted management* (CAM) is used by school administrators to track and manage personnel and student demographics, to handle statistics for inventory and resource allocation, and to generate reports for state and federal requirements.
2. *Computer-managed instruction* (CMI) is utilized by teachers for data collection, data analysis regarding school achievement, and assistance in writing reports and IEPs.
3. *Computer-assisted instruction* (CAI) is used for direct student instruction. Some of the specific uses of CAI in the classroom are listed in Table 3–4.

Computer-assisted instruction, in particular, seems to hold tremendous promise for the learning handicapped because instructional procedures

Table 3-4
Classifications of Computer-Assisted Instruction

Classification	Use
Drill and practice	To reinforce information learned and for which practice is suggested.
Tutorial	To present information already taught in the classroom but which has to be broken into smaller sequential steps and/or into a lower conceptual level for individual learners.
Simulation	To place a learner in situations that replicate original situations.
Computer-managed instruction	To instruct the learner in subjects through individualized sequencing.
Problem solving	To place the learner in situations to solve problems and to receive appropriate consequences. (Having the learner program as well as run previously developed software falls under this category.)
Assessment/ evaluation	To determine where the learner is regarding a specific objective and for pre- and post-test purposes.
Data retrieval	To provide feedback to the learner as to progress toward objectives, and to analyze data to create individual learning plans.

SOURCE: From "The Microcomputer—Its Applicability to Special Education" by F. M. Taber in *Promising Practices for Exceptional Children: Curriculum Implications* (p. 465) by E. L. Meyen, G. A. Vergason, and R. J. Whelan, 1984, Denver: Love Publishing Company. Copyright 1984 by Love Publishing Company. Reprinted by permission.

recommended for this population are compatible with CAI components. The common components listed by Behrmann (1984) and McDermott and Watkins (1983) include

□ use in either individual or group instruction
□ immediate feedback and reinforcement
□ hierarchical curriculum
□ multisensory presentations
□ self-paced instruction
□ errorless practice
□ performance objectives
□ mastery learning
□ clarity of presentation

Although the use of microcomputers in special education seems promising, several limitations must be mentioned. Lerner (1985) points out that microcomputers are expensive, the student-computer ratio in most schools is low, and the task of increasing computer literacy among teachers poses some difficulty. More importantly, however, research on microcomputers and instruction is limited. According to Williams (1984), the lack of well-designed research is particularly acute in the area of CAI. Stowitschek and Stowitschek (1984) hold that little information is available on how microcomputers can best be applied in the classroom. Specific micro-computer applications in spoken language, reading, written language, math, and study skills are discussed in the appropriate chapters in part two.

ORGANIZING INSTRUCTION

Following the evaluation and selection of instructional materials, teachers face the equally difficult task of organizing and implementing the remedial instruction. Our experience indicates that students with learning problems usually respond favorably to an organized classroom situation with an emphasis on systematic and direct instruction. The unstructured classroom often causes the greatest difficulty for the student with academic problems. Situations in which students do not know what is expected of them often reinforce the behaviors that originally contributed to the learning deficits (Kauffman, 1985). A specific program of organization, therefore, is a primary consideration in planning for remediation.

Instructional Formats

Six basic organizational patterns are available for instructional purposes within a classroom: (1) total group, (2) small group, (3) one-to-one instruc-tion, (4) triads, (5) peer tutoring, and (6) independent seatwork. No particular format is considered best; teachers should consider the flexible use of all formats at some time during their work with handicapped learners.

Total Group. Although the range of skills and attitudes varies considerably in a total group, this instructional arrangement is often effective and quite efficient for some activities. Typically, total group interaction is reserved for lectures, demonstrations, student presentations, field trips, guest speakers, and audiovisual presentations (Tonjes & Zintz, 1981).

Small Group. Students can be grouped into small clusters according to achievement, skill strengths or weaknesses, social needs, and specific interests. Small-group instructional formats usually include four to eight students. As a teaching arrangement this format provides for active student and teacher participation and is often the most effective arrangement for teaching specific skills to students with learning problems. Resource teachers, in particular, find this format efficient for working on the common skill needs of handicapped learners. Carnine and Silbert (1979) point out the effectiveness of small-group instruction and recommend placing students in a semicircle facing the teacher during small-group work.

One-to-One Instruction. This instructional arrangement involves one student working individually with the teacher. One-to-one instruction is used to teach specific skills to learning handicapped students, to clarify directions, or to help students having trouble with seatwork assignments. Mercer and Mercer (1985) point out that one-to-one instruction can take place in 3- to 5-minute segments, an amount of time that is often effective in helping a student understand a concept, receive corrective feedback, or understand directions and still feel motivated to continue working. Students with learning problems probably require a limited amount of one-to-one instruction sometime during each school day.

Triads.   According to Fader (1976), triads are a permanent-type grouping arrangement involving no more than three students in each heterogeneous group. Triads are viewed as helping groups in which students assist each other in answering questions, reviewing work before it is handed to the teacher, and managing the daily routine of schoolwork. This organizational format can provide excellent support for the learning handicapped student in a regular classroom.

Peer Tutoring.   In this instructional arrangement one student who has mastered a specific skill teaches another student under the teacher's supervision. In addition to the obvious benefit of individualizing instruction, peer tutoring seems also to develop responsibility (Allen, 1976) and to help improve attitudes toward school (Feldman, Devin-Sheehan, & Allen, 1976). Additional benefits listed by Jenkins and Jenkins (1981) include an increase in academically engaged minutes, more learning within a single lesson, and more optimum progressions through curriculum sequences for individual learners. Harris and Aldridge (1983) point out that peer tutoring allows the teacher to move ahead with further instruction for those who are ready for it.

Among the many different considerations in implementing a peer tutoring program, Allen (1976) offers the following:

☐ Tutoring session goals and activities must be clearly specified.

☐ Parents should be informed that the tutoring will supplement and not replace teacher instruction.

☐ The tutoring session should not exceed 20 to 30 minutes two or three times per week.

☐ Tutors of the same sex are usually preferred by younger pupils because of mutual interests.

☐ Tutors must have mastered the instructional content before tutoring another student.

Peer tutoring is considered to be ideally suited to the needs of students with learning problems. Gerber and Kauffman (1981) believe that peer tutoring provides educational benefits to both the tutor and tutee. Tutors gain increased responsibilities and self-esteem, whereas tutees are provided additional skill development time. We recommend this instructional format in developing programs for handicapped learners.

Independent Seatwork. Daily classroom activities often include independent seatwork assignments for individual students while teachers work with other pupils within the class. Seatwork assignments usually include worksheets, instructional games, microcomputer activities, and various audiovisual assignments. Independent seatwork is an excellent instructional format for reinforcing the development of previously learned skills. Nonetheless, Mercer and Mercer (1985) caution that students frequently spend too much time completing independent seatwork and that inappropriate materials in this setting can lead to frustration, failure, and the practicing of errors.

Sequential Skill Instruction

An important element in the successful remediation of learning problems is the orderly sequence of skill presentations. Handicapped learners require systematic instruction. Unfortunately, there is a tendency on the part of some educators to neglect the sequences involved in basic academic areas and to emphasize the development of specific isolated skills. The slower paced remedial instruction and the difficulties encountered with specific skills seem to account for this in some remedial settings. Nonetheless, skills must be taught in an integrated, orderly fashion; nothing should be omitted or assumed.

Broad lists of skills and abilities are usually available through curriculum guides, teacher's manuals, and various scope-and-sequence charts. In most instances these charts and guides provide general information concerning the sequence of skills that students should learn at different levels, grades, or ages. Wallace and Larsen (1978) note that charts are usually available by subject area in the teacher's manuals accompanying many basic texts. In addition, many local school districts and state departments of education periodically provide curriculum guides for different subject areas. Although the sequence of certain skills and abilities may differ by grade or age level in various charts and guides, the information serves as an excellent guideline in planning quality programs of remediation.

Program Management

A number of other program management considerations should be taken into account in planning an instructional program for students with academic difficulties. We recommend that students be made aware of the day's plan in terms of what they are expected to complete. The organization of an instructional session should be explained to learning handicapped students. Students should know what they will be doing during a certain session and how the material at hand relates to the particular skill being developed. Setting clear expectations for task completion provides the student with a goal for the day.

Reinforcement can be based on the attainment of specific goals, as suggested in chapter 2. Students should know and see that good work produces appropriate rewards. Students who are succeeding after having failed for a long time need to know that they are doing well. Many times success is self-evident. Nonetheless, it is important that students get some type of overt recognition. Reinforcing events associated with learning provide students with the motivation to do their best (chapters 2 and 7 list appropriate reinforcement techniques).

Otto and Smith (1980) suggest the following guidelines for planning and organizing remedial instruction.

☐ Secure the learner's cooperation
☐ Focus instruction
☐ Take small steps
☐ Reinforce success
☐ Keep learning tasks and materials meaningful
☐ Facilitate remembering
☐ Encourage pupil discovery of relationships
☐ Guard against motivation that is too intense
☐ Provide spaced practice
☐ Build a backlog of success experiences

The teacher working with handicapped learners will reap obvious advantages from a well-organized classroom. The individualization of programs for particular students necessitates concise organization if remedial teaching is to be effective. In fact, the failure of some students to respond to instructional programs can be attributed to a lack of structure in remedial teaching. We believe that a well-organized classroom is a prerequisite to effective instruction in any school; it is even more critical for the student with learning problems.

DIRECTIVE TEACHING

Effective remediation is closely associated with what has been recognized simply as good teaching. Unfortunately, this relationship has been widely misunderstood. It has even been suggested that remediation is based on a set of principles totally different from those adhered to in the regular classroom. Nothing could be more inaccurate. The principles that apply to good teaching should be followed in all classrooms at all levels of instruction. The learning handicapped student should be taught in basically the same manner as the student who is succeeding academically. Any differences are those of degree. The time that is spent teaching a specific skill, the individualization of instruction, and the variability of materials are procedural distinctions brought about by the uniqueness of the learning problem. The teaching that takes place during a remedial session differs little from what usually occurs with so-called "normal" learners.

As soon as the actual teaching program is initiated, it is important for the teacher to focus on the specific behaviors that are being developed (Carnine & Siebert, 1979). There is a tendency on the part of some teachers to neglect those aspects of the learning problem that call for direct remedial action. Teachers are often tempted to devote an inordinate amount of time to peripheral skill development and disregard the actual problem. This situation occurs many times with students who have reading difficulties complicated by perceptual-motor problems. Teachers can easily spend months perfecting the student's skill in walking on the balance beam, while neglecting the deficits in reading. Balance beam walking is a poor substitute for successful reading. In this regard Lovitt (1977) notes that the available data concerning transfer of training do not support the development of proficiency in one skill by instruction in another. On the contrary, students need to be *directly* taught the specific skills they are lacking. They learn to read by reading and to calculate by calculating. Obviously, the more time spent in effectively developing any given skill, the greater the chance that the student will learn that skill.

Furthermore, we view any unique materials, aids, or games used in remedial teaching as temporary devices. These instructional materials should be considered as motivators that help a student overcome a particular difficulty or understand a specific concept (Heilman, Blair, & Rupley, 1981). Lengthy dependency on such aids can serve no useful purpose and will ultimately only hamper a student's chances for success. A teacher must not depend on these materials to do the teaching job. He must realize that the only way a student will learn to read or write or calculate is by being taught to do so. No instructional material can accomplish this for the teacher, and those who say otherwise are merely excusing inappropriate teaching. A conscientious and skillful effort on the part of the teacher is the primary factor in successful remediation.

COMPLEXITY OF LEARNING PROBLEMS

The complex nature of individual learning difficulties is understandable when one considers the complexity of learning and the variety of pressures that affect students. All pupils, at some time, are subjected to school pressures. Most students are able to cope with the frustrations, anxieties, and confusion that can accompany the learning process and suffer little from this encounter. However, the situation is difficult for learning handicapped students; the pressure affecting these students reduces their ability to respond appropriately. Students who remain in such frustrating situations often become increasingly handicapped educationally.

Many students with learning problems are fortunate enough to be recognized and helped. In some cases the slightest alteration of instruction may be enough to move the student along. Other cases may require greater individualization of instruction over a prolonged period of time. Assessment, instructional materials, organization of instruction, reinforcement, and individualization are important considerations in a remedial program. Student progress is sometimes slow and often frustrating. However, we have found that successful remediation makes the entire process worthwhile.

Regular classroom teachers have been led to believe for too long that remediation is the realm of the specialist, and few classroom teachers have been given the opportunity to exhibit their remedial teaching competencies. However, many students with learning problems can and should be handled in the regular classroom by regular classroom teachers. A substantial number of the suggestions presented in this chapter can be easily adapted to regular class instruction; the principles are also applicable to teachers currently involved in remedial programs. Remediation should be the concern of *all* teachers.

SUMMARY

This chapter provides a basis for effective remediation in any educational setting. Many of the instructional methods and materials employed by remedial specialists can be used in the regular classroom. Furthermore, the principles that apply to the remediation of academic difficulties are not limited to a special class but are intended for use in all educational settings.

The initial and ongoing instructional needs of the individual student should serve as the focus of a remedial program. Formal and informal assessment results must be used in planning programs and evaluating program effectiveness. Successful remediation depends on the selection of a wide variety of materials, techniques, and methods tailored to individual needs. Difficulty in overcoming learning problems is directly related to the type of instruction provided. A successful remedial program is based essentially on good teaching.

REFERENCES

Allen, V. L. (1976). *Children as teachers.* New York: Academic Press.

Bateman, B. D., & Herr, C. M. (1981). Law and special education. In J. M. Kauffman and D. P. Hallahan (Eds.), *Handbook of special education.* Englewood Cliffs, NJ: Prentice-Hall.

Behrmann, M. (1984). *Handbook of microcomputers in special education.* San Diego, CA: College-Hill Press.

Bertrand, A., & Cebula, J. P. (1980). *Tests, measurements, and evaluation: A developmental approach.* Reading, MA: Addison-Wesley.

Carnine, D., & Siebert, J. (1979). *Direct instruction reading.* Columbus, OH: Charles E. Merrill.

Cartwright, C. A., & Cartwright, G. P. (1974). *Developing observation skills*. New York: McGraw-Hill.

Ekwall, E. E., & Shanker, J. L. (1983). *Diagnosis and remediation of the disabled reader* (2nd ed.). Boston: Allyn & Bacon.

Fader, D. (1976). *The new hooked on books*. New York: Berkley Medallion Books.

Feldman, R. S., Devin-Sheehan, L., & Allen, V. L. (1976). Children tutoring children: A critical review of research. In V. L. Allen (Ed.), *Children as teachers*. New York: Academic Press.

Gates, A. I., McKillop, A. S., & Horowitz, E. C. (1981). *Gates-McKillop-Horowitz Reading Diagnostic Tests*. New York: Teachers College Press.

Gerber, M., & Kauffman, J. M. (1981). Peer tutoring in academic settings. In P. Strain (Ed.), *Utilization of classroom peers as behavior change agents*. New York: Plenum.

Goodman, L. V. (1976). A bill of rights for the handicapped. *American Education, 12*, 6–8.

Guerin, G. R., & Maier, A. S. (1983). *Informal assessment in education*. Palo Alto, CA: Mayfield.

Harris, J., & Aldridge, J. (1983). 3 for me is better than 2 for you. *Academic Therapy, 18*, 361–365.

Heilman, A. W., Blair, T. R., & Rupley, W. H. (1981). *Principles and practices of teaching reading* (5th ed.). Columbus, OH: Charles E. Merrill.

Jenkins, J. R., & Jenkins, L. M. (1981). *Cross-age and peer tutoring: Help for children with learning problems*. Reston, VA: Council for Exceptional Children.

Kauffman, J. M. (1985). *Characteristics of children's behavior disorders* (3rd ed.). Columbus, OH: Charles E. Merrill.

Larsen, S. C., & Poplin, M. S. (1980). *Methods for educating the handicapped: An individualized education program approach*. Boston: Allyn & Bacon.

Lerner, J. (1985). *Children with learning disabilities: Theories, diagnosis, and teaching strategies* (4th ed.). Boston: Houghton Mifflin.

Lovitt, T. C. (1977). *In spite of my resistance—I've learned from children*. Columbus, OH: Charles E. Merrill.

Mandell, C. J., & Gold, V. (1984). *Teaching handicapped students*. St. Paul, MN: West.

McDermott, P. A., & Watkins, M. W. (1983). Computerized vs. conventional remedial instruction for learning disabled pupils. *Journal of Special Education, 17*, 81–88.

McLoughlin, J. A., & Lewis, R. B. (1986). *Assessing special students* (2nd ed.). Columbus, OH: Charles E. Merrill.

Mehrens, W. A., & Lechmann, I. J. (1978). *Measurement and evaluation in education and psychology.* New York: Holt, Rinehart & Winston.

Mercer, C. D., & Mercer, A. R. (1985). *Teaching students with learning problems* (2nd ed.). Columbus, OH: Charles E. Merrill.

Myers, P. I., & Hammill, D. D. (1982). *Learning disabilities: Basic concepts, assessment practices, and instructional strategies.* Austin, TX: Pro-Ed.

Otto, W., & Smith, R. J. (1980). *Corrective and remedial teaching* (3rd ed.). Boston: Houghton Mifflin.

Pasanella, A. L., & Volkmor, C. B. (1981). *Teaching handicapped students in the mainstream: Coming back or never leaving.* (2nd ed.). Columbus, OH: Charles E. Merrill.

Proger, B. B., & Mann, L. (1973). Criterion-referenced measurement: The world of gray versus black and white. *Journal of Learning Disabilities, 6,* 72–84.

Spache, G. D. (1976). *Diagnosing and correcting reading disabilities.* Boston: Allyn & Bacon.

Stephens, T. (1977). *Teaching skills to children with learning and behavior problems.* Columbus, OH: Charles E. Merrill.

Stowitschek, J. J., & Stowitschek, C. E. (1984). Once more with feeling: The absence of research on teacher use of microcomputers. *Exceptional Education Quarterly, 4*(4), 23–29.

Taber, F. M. (1984). The microcomputer—Its applicability to special education. In E. L. Meyer, G. A. Vergason, & R. J. Whelan, *Promising practices for exceptional children: Curriculum implications.* Denver: Love.

Tonjes, M. J., & Zintz, M. V. (1981). *Teaching reading/thinking/study skills in content classrooms.* Dubuque, IA: William C. Brown.

Van Etlen, C., & Van Etlen, G. (1978). A working model for developing instructional materials for the learning disabled. *Learning Disability Quarterly, 1*(2), 33–42.

Wallace G. (in press). *Assessment: Evaluating students with learning and behavior problems.* Austin, TX: Pro-Ed.

Wallace, G., & Larsen, S. L. (1978) *The educational assessment of learning problems: Testing for teaching.* Boston: Allyn & Bacon.

Wiederholt, J. L., & McNutt, G. (1977). Evaluating materials for handicapped adolescents. *Journal of Learning Disabilities, 10*(3), 132–140.

Williams, R. L. (1984). *Computer-assisted instruction for mildly handicapped students: A need for research.* Unpublished manuscript.

Wilson, J. (1982). Selecting instructional materials and resources. In D. D. Hammill & N. R. Bartel, *Teaching children with learning and behavior problems* (3rd ed.). Boston: Allyn & Bacon.

4

Cognitive Strategy
Training

Students with learning and behavior problems typically show cognitive deficits. Cognitive deficits—deficits in thought processes—seem to be at the heart of many of the academic and social skill problems of children and adults. Students with cognitive deficits do not have strategies for approaching academic tasks or social situations. Instead, they approach these tasks and situations in a disorganized, haphazard way, seemingly without thinking about what they are doing or how others will react to them. Thus, they are unable to perform academically as well as they might or to establish and maintain satisfying interpersonal relationships. In response, educators and psychologists have devised ways of training such students to use cognitive strategies to improve their performance in academic and social areas (Hallahan, 1980; Hallahan, Hall, et al., 1983; Hallahan, Lloyd, Kauffman, & Loper, 1983; Kauffman & Hallahan, 1979; Meichenbaum, 1983; Pressley & Levin, 1983).

Interest in how handicapped and nonhandicapped students respond to academic and social problems has increased dramatically since the mid-1970s. Cognitive and behavioral approaches to psychology have been melded, to some degree, into what has become known as cognitive-behavior modification (see Meichenbaum, 1977, 1980, 1983). Although the term *cognitive-behavior modification* (CBM) means somewhat different things to different people, it generally refers to the use of behavior modification methods (frequent direct measurement of behavior and manipulation of antecedents and consequences) to alter cognitions (thoughts and feeling states) as well as overt behavior. The idea behind CBM is that cognitions partially control behavior and that altering thought processes might therefore be an effective way of modifying overt behavior. Moreover, cognitions are accessible (to others through language and to oneself through conscious awareness and introspection) and can be modified in much the same ways that overt behavior can be controlled. Thus, CBM includes cognitive strategy training—teaching skills in thinking and self-control.

COGNITIVE CHARACTERISTICS

Cognitive strategy training is based on the findings of child development research in several areas: cognitive styles, memory, metacognition, causal attributions, and behavioral self-regulation.

Cognitive Styles

Cognitive style has to do with *how* people think, rather than *what* they think. People are assumed to have different styles of approaching and solving problems, and their styles are assumed to be relatively consistent across different types of problems. Cognitive styles can be described in a variety of ways, but two descriptions have particular relevance for work with handicapped students. These descriptions involve considerations of the extent to which someone is dependent on environmental cues in making perceptual judgments and the extent to which someone is impulsive in making choices. The styles are often referred to as *field-dependence/field-independence* and *impulsivity/reflectivity*.

Field-Dependence/Field-Independence. Someone who exhibits a field-dependent cognitive style is distracted by irrelevant environmental cues when perceptual judgment or interpretation is required. A student who is highly field-dependent, for example, might be unable to separate essential from nonessential information in a reading passage and therefore miss the point or fail to comprehend. A person with a field-independent style, however, is able to separate essential from nonessential information in the perceptual field. The perceptions and interpretations of people with a field-independent style tend to be more accurate than those of people who are field-dependent.

Field-dependence/field-independence has typically been measured with visual-perceptual tasks. For example, students are asked to find geometric figures embedded in a field of distracting, irrelevant lines or to judge a true vertical position when both a rod and the frame surrounding it, which provides a perceptual field for it, have been moved to nonvertical positions. Such testing has generally indicated that learning disabled students perform less capably (i.e., are more field-dependent) than nonhandicapped youngsters (Blackman & Goldstein, 1982).

Impulsivity/Reflectivity. Individuals with an impulsive cognitive style tend to respond quickly and inaccurately to tasks, whereas those with a reflective style tend to take more time and be more accurate. The impulsive person tends to make more careless errors. Impulsivity/reflectivity is typically measured by tests in which the individual must compare a standard figure to each of several (usually six) other figures, all but one of which is different from the standard in some minor detail. The task is to find the matching figure. Research indicates that learning disabled students are generally more impulsive on such tasks than are their nonhandicapped peers (Blackman & Goldstein, 1982; Kauffman, 1985).

Memory

Memory involves holding or storing information mentally for later use. Both short-term and long-term memory have been studied extensively. Short-term memory requires that information be held and retrieved only a few seconds or minutes later. Long-term memory requires retention and retrieval several hours or days later, or even longer. Generally, one must be able to commit information to short-term memory before it can be stored in long-term memory. Thus, short-term memory is of critical importance, particularly in using information for everyday purposes. Someone who has difficulty with short-term memory will certainly have great trouble with most academic tasks and will likely have a hard time with many of the tasks of everyday living (e.g., cooking, cleaning, dressing, getting to and from work, holding a job requiring more than the most menial tasks).

Memory tasks used for research or testing purposes involve information presented via any of the senses, though the material is usually auditory or visual. A short-term memory task using visual material might involve showing a student an array of five pictures for a short time (perhaps 20 seconds), covering the pictures, and then asking her to name the set of pictures. After responding, the student is shown another set of pictures and again asked to recall them after they are covered. This procedure may be repeated for 10 or more trials.

Nonhandicapped children and adults tend to perform rather well on short-term memory tasks, apparently because they employ strategies for remembering. They may, for example, group the pictures categorically in some way that makes them easier to remember (animals, foods, vehicles, shelters). Or they may say the picture names to themselves and rehearse them. Handicapped students, on the other hand, typically do not use spontaneously any strategies for remembering and are usually found to be deficient in short-term memory ability (Swanson, 1979; Tarver, Hallahan, Kauffman, & Ball, 1976; Torgesen & Goldman, 1977). Consequently, they are not able to remember features of academic tasks long enough to perform adequately.

Metacognition

Metacognition is thinking about thinking; it is cognitions about the cognitive process. It involves an awareness of how one goes about solving cognitive problems—how one tries to remember things, to comprehend written passages, or to formulate analogies. It involves both an awareness of the skills needed to perform a cognitive task effectively and an ability to plan an approach to a problem, evaluate ongoing problem-solving activity, check the outcomes, and remediate difficulties. Someone who has a metacognitive deficiency is not able to figure out what to do to improve his performance and, if shown how to use a cognitive strategy on a particular task, is unlikely to use it without constant reminders or for other similar tasks.

Metacognition is usually evaluated by asking students to describe how they would approach a problem (Torgesen, 1979). For example, students might be asked to describe how they would try to remember a friend's phone number or the items their mother asked them to get at the store. They might be asked why they would do what they say they would do or what other strategies they think people could use. Generally, research indicates that handicapped students have more difficulty than nonhandicapped students in describing strategies for remembering and for solving problems. Handicapped students often appear not to have developed metacognitive skills that would be valuable in performing academically and behaving appropriately in social circumstances. They also appear to have deficits in metamemory (Torgesen, 1979), metalistening (Kotsonis & Patterson, 1980), and metacomprehension (Wong, 1982).

Causal Attributions

Causal attributions, in the context of a discussion of learning problems, have to do with what an individual believes is responsible for her success or failure on academic tasks. A person can attribute success or failure to a variety of internal or external causes. Degree of effort is one example of an internal attribution—someone might believe that the primary cause of success or failure on a task is how much effort one puts forth. Someone with an external attribution, on the other hand, might believe that success or failure is determined primarily by factors over which an individual has little control—whether the teacher likes the individual or how much the individual's peers try to distract him. The tendency to attribute the causes of behavior to external or internal factors is sometimes referred to as external or internal *locus of control.*

The differences between external and internal attributions are illustrated by two boys, Lance and Eric, who were diagnosed as hyperactive and were taking a stimulant drug (Ritalin, or methylphenidate).

> Lance, Age 10: Sometimes you won't even listen to yourself when you're telling yourself to not do it. . . . You sometimes forget if you tell yourself, but the Ritalin, it makes you more calmer, and you don't even have to remember anything to tell yourself to be quiet or be calmer.
> Eric, Age 13: [Medication] wouldn't make him do anything, it just helps people. . . . If he *wanted* to do it, the medication could help. *You* have to do it, you know; you can still take a pill and not do it. (Henker, Whalen, & Hinshaw, 1980, p. 22)

Lance clearly attributes the cause of his behavior to Ritalin, an external factor. Eric, on the other hand, attributes his appropriate behavior to something *he* controls, an internal cause. An internal causal attribution (i.e., an internal locus of control) is highly desirable because it is the basis for personal responsibility, a cognitive disposition to assume that one can change one's own behavior to increase the chances of success.

Research indicates that students who have learning problems tend to have external attributions (an external locus of control) and to avoid personal responsibility for their successes and failures (Pearl, Bryan, & Donahue, 1980). They have learned an attitude of helplessness (Seligman, 1975), believing that there is little or nothing they can do to increase their chances of success.

Behavioral Self-Regulation

"Wouldn't it be wonderful if children could be taught to regulate their own behavior! Then they could continuously monitor what they were doing, and could arrange appropriate antecedents and consequences for themselves" (Gelfand & Hartmann, 1984, p. 159). Self-regulation involves a variety of self-control activities—including self-observation or self-monitoring, self-recording, self-evaluation, and self-application of consequences. As students progress through the education system, self-regulation becomes increasingly important to their academic and social success. They are expected to become more independent in their learning and more appropriately self-controlled in their social conduct.

Students with learning and behavior problems typically show deficits in behavioral self-regulation (Hallahan et al., 1985; Kauffman, 1985; Rooney & Hallahan, 1985). They are not able to use their cognitions about behavior and behavioral change to alter their own conduct. Consequently, they lack the strategies of self-control that could help them adapt successfully to the expectations of school, parents, and peers. They may temporarily adopt the cognitive strategies they are given for specific tasks or social circumstances, but they have difficulty applying these strategies to new tasks or to situations outside the classroom.

Cognitive Characteristics of Handicapped Students

Not all handicapped students share all the cognitive deficits that characterize the majority. Thus, it is important to recognize that generalizations are just that—general statements that do not apply to each and every case. However, we have found that research literature supports the assumption that most students with learning and behavior problems tend to exhibit difficulties in certain areas.

1. separating relevant cues or stimuli from irrelevant aspects of their context (i.e., making judgments independent of the environment or field in which stimuli are embedded)
2. reflecting on alternatives before choosing a response
3. using strategies to remember important information, even for a short time
4. analyzing thought processes when faced with a problem-solving situation (i.e., understanding and using strategies to control and evaluate cognitions)
5. attributing successes and failures to appropriate internal factors
6. devising behavioral self-regulation strategies

GENERAL PROCEDURES OF COGNITIVE STRATEGY TRAINING

Cognitive strategy training is designed, quite obviously, to address the strategy deficits just reviewed. Clearly, one would like to help students make use of only relevant environmental cues to solve perceptual tasks, be reflective in responding to tasks, use techniques that facilitate memory, analyze their own thought processes, attribute their successes and failures to the appropriate causes, and regulate their own behavior. Strategy training and other cognitive-behavior modification (CBM) techniques are aimed at one or more of these goals.

Unfortunately, the remediation of cognitive strategy deficits is not so simple as it might appear. Initial successes and promising research results have not yet delineated the keys to helping handicapped students become better thinkers and more fully self-controlled individuals (Billings & Wasik, 1985; Meichenbaum, 1980; O'Leary, 1980; Reeve & Kauffman, in press; Rooney & Hallahan, 1985). In addition, teachers do not always put into practice the theories that they have studied. They may know that their students lack cognitive strategies and may be aware of the theory behind cognitive strategy training yet still may not base their instructional practices on what they know (Swanson, 1984). Nevertheless, even though we do not yet know the specific components of cognitive strategy training that are effective for particular types of problems and students (Gelfand & Hartmann, 1984; Rooney & Hallahan, 1985), progress is being made in devising ways to teach handicapped and remedial students the general strategies that will help them perform and behave more normally. The professional literature on strategy training is growing rapidly (Carnine & Kinder, 1985; Hallahan, 1980; Mastropieri, Scruggs, & Levin, 1985; Meichenbaum, 1983; Pressley & Levin, 1983).

Students with learning and behavior problems have been characterized as inactive, passive, or uninvolved learners (Hallahan et al., 1985). That is, they are typically dependent on external sources of motivation, guidance, and control. They see themselves as failures, helpless in the face of unresolvable problems. Strategy training and other CBM techniques are intended to heighten students' active involvement in learning, to increase their motivation and self-control. Grimes (1981) summarizes a variety of educational procedures that can be used to foster students' independence and self-directed participation in learning (see Table 4–1). We cannot describe here all the procedures that have been devised to encourage students to use cognitive strategies and behavioral self-control. We will, however, briefly describe four such procedures.

Self-Instruction

Self-instruction training involves teaching students who are trying to solve a problem to first ask themselves questions about the nature of the problem, the most effective approach to the task, the relevant stimuli, and the accuracy or quality required in their performance. Next, the students are taught to give themselves instructions regarding performance of the task that will make their cognitions about what they are doing more explicit and will guide their performance of the steps involved in solving the problem. Finally, students are taught to give themselves appropriate feedback and correction or reinforcement. The content of this self-talk varies, depending on the nature of the tasks and the characteristics of the individual student.

Training in self-instruction usually begins with the teacher's modeling or demonstration of appropriate self-talk and proceeds through a sequence of steps leading, eventually, to the student's covert (i.e., silent or internal) self-instruction. Repeated trials—including additional modeling by the teacher, guided practice by the student, and the student's rehearsal of the procedure—are an essential feature of self-instruction training. The training sequence is often approximately as follows:

1. The teacher performs the task while engaging in self-talk aloud—asking questions about the task, giving self-guiding instructions, and making self-evaluations of performance.
2. The student is asked to imitate the teacher's overt (aloud) self-instruction while doing the task.
3. The teacher performs the task, again modeling self-instruction but this time in a whisper.

Table 4-1
Alternative Educational Procedures and Related Student Outcomes

Procedures That Appear to Foster Student Dependency and Failure	*Procedures That Appear to Foster Student Motivation and Self-Control*
Norm-referenced evaluation and grading based on peer comparisons.	Criterion-referenced evaluation and grading.
Teacher use of labels such as *distractible, poor memory, impulsive,* to rationalize child's learning problem.	Realistic teacher expectation of child performance considering child's prerequisite skills and level and amount of information to be learned.
Teacher attitude that child's lack of learning is due to deficits within the child.	Child's lack of learning attributed to use of inappropriate instructional strategies.
Low teacher expectation for child performance.	Teaching of self-instructional strategies of inner speech, memory rehearsal, mnemonics, drill, etc., to enable child to direct own learning.
Achievement testing conducted at end of year to evaluate child's learning.	Direct measurement of skills conducted frequently to measure effectiveness of teaching method and child's learning.
Large-group instruction geared to middle-ability group.	Small group instruction based on child's level and needs.
Instructional content presented in large units of knowledge.	Instructional content presented by the task analysis method with information broken down to manageable steps of learning.
Evaluative feedback very general. Lack of information given in feedback on how to improve performance.	Evaluative feedback specific with demonstration of how to complete problem correctly.
Teacher as sole director of learning experiences.	Child as collaborator in choosing learning experiences, setting goals, charting skills that have been mastered.
Teacher always places the child in the "being helped" role, thus emphasizing his dependent position.	Role reversal where the child as a peer tutor helps another child with the same problem.

SOURCE: From p. 99. "Learned Helplessness and Attribution Theory: Redefining Children's Learning Problems" by L. Grimes, 1981, *Learning Disability Quarterly, 4,* Copyright 1981 by *Learning Disability Quarterly.* Reprinted by permission.

4. The student imitates the teacher's whispered self-instruction.

5. The teacher models covert (silent) self-instruction while doing the task.

6. The student imitates the teacher's covert self-instruction.

An example of a math task requiring a student to match one problem with another just like it and the self-instruction that a teacher might model is shown in Figure 4–1.

Figure 4-1. An Arithmetic Match-to-Sample Item and Possible Self-Instruction

$$
\begin{array}{r}
221 \\
-12 \\
\hline
209
\end{array}
$$

$$
\begin{array}{rr}
221 & 211 \\
-21 & -12 \\
\hline
209 & 209
\end{array}
$$

$$
\begin{array}{rr}
221 & 221 \\
-12 & +12 \\
\hline
901 & 209
\end{array}
$$

$$
\begin{array}{rr}
221 & 221 \\
-12 & -12 \\
\hline
209 & 219
\end{array}
$$

OK, now, what do I have to do? I have to find a problem down here that is just *exactly* the same as this one up here. This is going to be tough, but I just need to relax and get through it. Let's see, now. This problem is 221 minus 12 equals 209. I need to remember to make sure every part of the one I find down here is just the same. I'd better take it one part at a time just to make sure I get it right, because *every* part has to be the same. I know what I'll do, I'll just take it slow, one step at a time, and I'll cross off each one down here if I find something that's different. Because once I find something wrong, I don't have to check that one again because I know it can't be the one. Now, it's got to have 221 at the top. Let's see. This one has 221. But this one has 211 at the top, *not* 221, so it can't be right. So I'll mark it off. This one has 221, and this one, and this one, and this one, so they're OK. Now, it's got to be minus 12. This is minus 21, so it gets marked off. Minus 12 here is OK. Plus 12 can't be it. Minus 12 here is OK and here is OK. Boy, I'm really being careful, and I'm going to get it right. OK. Now I've got to find 209 for the answer. Let's see, 901 is wrong, 209 is right. Looks like I got it now. But I'd better check this other one too. No, 219 is wrong, so it must be this one here. I'm going to double check just to make sure. Up here 221, down here 221. Up here minus 12, down here minus 12. Up here 209, down here 209. Got it. Wow, did I do a great job on *that!*

SOURCE: From *Characteristics of Children's Behavior Disorders* (3rd ed., pp. 201–203) by J. M. Kauffman, 1985, Columbus, OH: Charles E. Merrill. Copyright 1985 by Bell and Howell Company. Reprinted by permission.

An important feature of self-instruction is providing a *coping* model for students. Flawless performance is not characteristic of most activities of most mortals. Students need to be taught that successful performers make mistakes but learn how to cope with them—how to correct them without getting upset or "losing it." Self-recognition of errors and self-correction are vital skills that the teacher should model. For example, in providing self-instruction training related to the task shown in Figure 4–1, the teacher might make an error, accompanied by the following verbalization.

Now I've got to find minus 12. Let's see, minus 12—cross it off. Oops! That *is* minus 12. I'm looking for ones that are *not* minus 12. I almost made a [big] mistake. But I caught it, and I can just erase that line. I'm still OK, because

I'm thinking and being careful. Let's see, plus 12 is *not* minus 12, so I'll cross it off. *Now*, I'm getting it. (Kauffman, 1985, p. 203)

One caution to be emphasized here is the importance of training students on tasks of the type they will actually need to perform. For example, the following steps were used to train a learning disabled boy to use self-instruction to improve his handwriting (Kosiewicz, Hallahan, Lloyd, & Graves, 1982).

1. He said the word to be copied.
2. He said the first syllable of the word.
3. He said the name of each letter in that syllable three times.
4. He named each letter in the syllable as he wrote it.
5. He repeated each of these steps for each remaining syllable in the word.

Training on laboratory or contrived tasks is of little value if the teacher expects improvement on actual academic tasks. The research to date warrants cautious optimism regarding the helpfulness of self-instruction training on actual academic tasks (Hallahan, Hall, et al., 1983; Hallahan et al., 1985).

Self-instruction training has been researched with social-emotional problems as well as academic tasks. Figure 4–2 contains a case illustration for an aggressive student. Such training is clearly experimental, and we will later discuss cautions and guidelines for these procedures.

Self-Monitoring

Self-monitoring involves self-assessment and self-recording. The student must become aware of her behavior as it relates to what is desirable and then keep a record of her performance. Although self-monitoring can be used with a variety of behaviors, most of the research on this technique has been done with on-task behavior. Hallahan and his colleagues at the University of Virginia have conducted extensive research in this area, primarily with learning disabled children (Hallahan, Hall, et al., 1983; Kneedler & Hallahan, 1981). Typically, the procedure has been used during seatwork, when on-task behavior can be clearly defined. Usually, a cassette tape recorder has been used to produce tones (prerecorded to sound at random intervals ranging from 10 to 90 seconds and lasting an average of 45 seconds) that cue the student to self-assess and self-record. The student is instructed to ask himself, when he hears the tone, "Was I paying attention?" Depending on his answer to that question, he checks the appropriate yes or no column on a simple recording form. This procedure has also been used during group work with slight modifications: "Was I paying attention?" is written on the chalkboard, and students use mechanical counters to tally their answers. An example of teacher instructions and training for implementation of the procedure during seatwork is provided

Figure 4-2. Self-Instruction Training for an Aggressive Student

Dave was an 11-year-old Caucasian boy who was referred by a local mental health center to an inpatient psychiatric facility for evaluation and treatment. He was hospitalized because his parents felt they could no longer manage him at home given the severity and frequency of his aggressive behavior. Dave had a 6-year history of aggressive behavior, theft, and truancy. His aggressive acts were often severe. For example, on one occasion, his fighting led to the loss of vision in one eye of one of his classmates at school. At the time of admission, his current teacher feared her own welfare and refused to have him in class because of the physical abuse he inflicted on her. Hospitalization was precipitated in part by Dave's serious stabbing of his younger sister.

Apart from aggressive acts, Dave had a history of theft from stores, including small appliances and games and money from cash registers. Other problems were sporadic over his childhood including encopresis and enuresis, but they were associated with clear episodes of family stress (e.g., separation of the mother and father, death of a grandparent who had lived in the home). Although these problems had continued until his hospitalization, they were viewed as relatively minor in significance given the magnitude and consistency of his aggressive acts and rule breaking.

Upon admission to the hospital, the parents indicated that they would only agree to keep Dave in the home if treatment would have direct impact on his aggressive acts. A twofold treatment approach was recommended in which Dave would receive cognitive therapy and the parents would receive parent management training. The father's frequent altercations with the law and brief incarcerations made him an unlikely candidate to attend treatment. Also, the mother felt that she had already tried everything and could not begin to work in treatment for him.

While in the hospital, Dave received cognitive therapy approximately three times per week for a total of 20 sessions. During treatment, Dave learned and rehearsed problem-solving steps that could be applied in everyday situations (see Spivack, Platt, & Shure, 1976). The steps consisted of training the child to ask the following questions or to make the following statements:

1. What am I supposed to do?
2. I need to look at all of my possibilities.
3. I have to focus in (concentrate).
4. I have to make a choice.
5. How well did I do?

In the early sessions, Dave practiced the steps while working on academic or preacademic tasks, such as deciding what comes next in a series of pictures or what answer might be cor-rect to basic arithmetic problems. In these sessions, learning the steps and responding to each one before proceeding are critical. The specific tasks are not crucial except insofar as they develop use of the problem-solving approach. Training continued with games such as playing checkers or Cat-and-Mouse (a board game utilizing checkers and board).

After the steps were well learned, they were applied to interpersonal situations that were enacted through role-play with the therapist. In each situation, the therapist modeled how the approach was used (as the child) while Dave served as the other person in the situation (e.g., parent or teacher). Dave then enacted the situation while using the steps and receiving prompts, as necessary, to execute the approach correctly.

The situations primarily involved provocative interactions with others in a variety of social situations. The situations included being blamed (justly or unjustly) by teachers for something he had done in class, arguing with siblings or peers, being confronted by the police, and interacting in a variety of situations with others. By the end of treatment, the situations were those that Dave viewed as especially problematic. Also, near the end of treatment, Dave visited his home and spent the weekends with his parents, so he could begin to apply steps to everyday situations outside of the hospital.

The practice weekends impressed the parents who agreed to take Dave home to give him another chance. The mother was explicit with the hospital staff in noting that if he did not control his aggression, he would have to be institutionalized, and they would not want him home again. The parents were fully apprised of the nature of the treatment and the progress that had been made. Also, they were encouraged to help prompt or praise his use of the steps in situations at home.

In the hospital over the course of treatment, Dave made noticeable progress. He frequently avoided arguments and physical fights. He invoked the steps, by his own report and by that of the ward staff, in a variety of situations where he previously would have engaged in fighting. In one instance he was teased by two other boys for his attire. He previously would have beaten both of them, especially since they were smaller than him. Dave mentioned instances such as these with enthusiasm in the treatment sessions and stated (as part of his self-evaluation) that he had done well.

Follow-up contact was continued with the family after Dave was discharged. Up to 8 months after treatment Dave remained in the home and, by his parents anecdotal reports and on objective measures, was doing well.

Figure 4-2 (continued)

Teacher ratings also indicated that his classroom behavior was no longer a problem. By no means was Dave's behavior representative of a model student. His academic performance was average in most subjects, but this was regarded as much better than expected given his checkered history. Also, his problem behaviors were reported as within the range of classroom disruption of other children. Serious aggressive acts were no longer evident, and truancy, not specifically focused on in treatment, had ceased.

Obviously, the success of treatment of this one case would need to be evaluated over a longer term, especially since the prognosis for such children is poor. Moreover, the extent to which treatment accounted for change was not evaluated. Nevertheless, the case illustrates the approach and its application to seriously aggressive children.

SOURCE: From "Aggressive Behavior and Conduct Disorders" by A. E. Kazdin and C. Frame in *The Practice of Child Therapy* (pp. 179–180) by R. J. Morris and T. R. Kratochwill (Eds.), 1983, New York: Pergamon Press. Copyright 1983 by Pergamon Press. Reprinted by permission.

in Figure 4–3. Figure 4–4 shows a recording form used by a teacher of adolescent behavior disordered students who self-monitored several of their inappropriate off-task behaviors during seatwork (talking out without permission, telling off-task stories, humming or singing, and playing with objects). When these students heard the tape recorded tone, they made a slash through the appropriate symbol of any target behavior they had exhibited during the previous interval (McManus, 1985). Partial results of their self-monitoring are shown in Figure 4–5.

Research on self-monitoring has led to some general conclusions (Hallahan, Hall, et al., 1983; Kneedler & Hallahan, 1981).

1. Self-monitoring of on-task behavior, as described by Hallahan and colleagues, typically results in increased on-task behavior.

Figure 4-3. Sample Instructions for Implementing Self-Monitoring of Task Attention

Johnny, you know how paying attention to your work has been a problem for you. You've heard teachers tell you, "Pay attention," "Get to work," "What are you supposed to be doing?" and things like that. Well, today we're going to start something that will help you help yourself pay attention better. First, we have to make sure that you know what paying attention means. This is what I mean by paying attention. (Teacher models sustained attention to task.) And this is what I mean by not paying attention. (Teacher models inattentive behaviors such as glancing around and playing with objects.) Now you tell me if I was paying attention. (Teacher models attentive and inattentive behaviors and requires the student to categorize them.) Okay, now let me show you what we're going to do. While you're working, this tape recorder will be turned on. Every once in a while, you'll hear a little sound like this. (Teacher plays tone on tape.) And, when you hear that sound, quietly ask yourself, "Was I paying attention?" If you answer "Yes," put a check in this box. If you answer "No," put a check in this box. Then go right back to work. When you hear the sound again, ask the question, answer it, mark your answer, and go back to work. Now, let me show you how it works. (Teacher models entire procedure.) Now Johnny, I bet you can do this. Tell me what you're going to do every time you hear a tone. . . .Let's try it. I'll start the tape and you work on these papers. (Teacher observes student's implementation of entire procedure, praises its correct use, and gradually withdraws his/her presence.)

SOURCE: From "Academic Problems" by D. P. Hallahan, J. W. Lloyd, J. M. Kauffman, and A. B. Loper in *The Practice of Child Therapy* (p. 124) by R. J. Morris and T. R. Kratochwill (Eds.), 1983, New York: Pergamon Press. Copyright 1983 by Pergamon Press. Reprinted by permission.

Figure 4-4. Sample Recording Form for Off-Task Behaviors

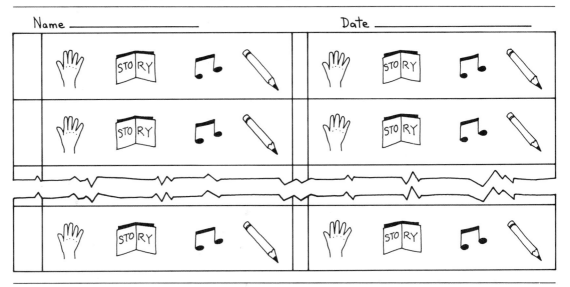

SOURCE: From "Modification of Adolescent Students' Off-Task Behaviors Using Self-Monitoring Procedures" by M. McManus, 1985, unpublished manuscript. Reprinted by permission.

2. Self-monitoring of on-task behavior also tends to result in some increased academic productivity.

3. Improvement in behavior and performance has been found to last for as long as 2.5 months following the end of self-monitoring training (longer follow-up has not yet been tested).

4. The beneficial effects of self-monitoring have been achieved without the use of back-up reinforcers; extrinsic rewards, such as tokens or treats, have been unnecessary.

5. Cues (tones) are a necessary element of the initial training procedure, although students can be weaned from them after initial training. Teacher instruction might follow this sample.

   You've been doing really good work on math lately, don't you think? You've been doing so well that I don't think you need to use the tape recorder to tell you when to mark your card anymore. I think you can do a really good job without hearing the tones and just reminding yourself to record. Today, whenever you think about it, ask yourself the question, "Was I paying attention?" If the answer is yes, say to yourself, "Yes, good job," and mark your answer just as if you'd heard a tone from the tape recorder. If the answer is no, say to yourself, "No, I'd better start paying attention," and mark your card.

6. The self-recording response of students is a necessary element in the initial stages of training, but it, too, can be discontinued after the full procedure has been learned. Teacher instruction might follow this sample.

Figure 4-5. A Record of Off-Task Behavior of Two Behavior Disordered Students

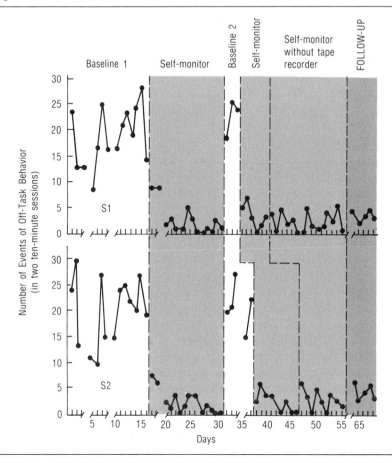

SOURCE: From "Modification of Adolescent Students' Off-Task Behaviors Using Self-Monitoring Procedures" by M. McManus, 1985, unpublished manuscript. Reprinted by permission.

You've been doing a great job on reading, don't you think? You've been doing really well even without the tape recorder. I think you'd be able to pay attention now even without using the self-recording card anymore. Today, I want you to think about whether you're paying attention every once in a while, just like you've been doing. When you think, "Was I paying attention?" and the answer is yes, say to yourself, "Yes, I'm doing a good job." But if the answer is no, then say to yourself, "No, and I'd better start paying attention." The only difference is that now you don't need to mark your answer on the card.

7. Self-recording appears to be more effective when the student assesses her own attentional behavior rather than having the teacher do it. Self-assessment also requires less teacher time.

8. Accuracy in self-monitoring is not critically important. Some students

are in close agreement with the teacher in assessing their on-task behavior; others are not. On- and off-task behavior is sometimes hard to define or discriminate.

9. The cueing tones and other aspects of the procedure are minimally disruptive to other students in the class. After 2 or 3 days other students typically pay no attention to the tones.

Self-monitoring is a relatively simple procedure that has produced good results with a wide variety of students. It is not, however, a procedure that is successful with all students or all problem behaviors.

Memory Strategies

Memory strategies are those designed to help students remember more information and retrieve it more quickly. As noted earlier, students with learning problems often appear not to use the memory strategies that nonhandicapped students devise spontaneously. However, these strategies can be taught to handicapped students, many of whom can then perform memory tasks on a par with their nonhandicapped age peers (Hallahan et al., 1985). Common memory strategies include the following:

- grouping, clustering, or organizing items logically into subclasses (finding common attributes of items and recalling them as subsets)
- rehearsing the recall of information (repeating it to oneself, usually subvocally)
- creating images (trying to visualize the information)
- self-questioning
- paraphrasing (putting the information into one's own language)
- associating (pairing items with other information to be remembered)

Some memory strategies are known as *mnemonics*. A mnemonic strategy involves encoding (or recoding), relating, and retrieving information (Mastropieri, et al, 1985). Recoding requires transformation of the material that is to be learned into a more meaningful form for the individual who wishes to remember it. Relating involves addition to or elaboration of the material so that helpful associations can be formed. Retrieving then requires using the associations to recall the recoded material. One mnemonic strategy that has been used with exceptional students is called the *keyword method* and is described by Mastropieri et al. (1985).

For example, to remember that the Spanish vocabulary word *pato* (pronounced something like "pahtoe") means *duck*, the learner first recodes the unfamiliar word *pato* into an acoustically similar and easily pictured keyword. In this case, a good keyword for *pato* would be *pot*, in that it sounds like a salient part of *pato* and is easily pictured. Second, in the relating stage, the recoded keyword (*pot*) is related to the unfamiliar word's meaning (*duck*) by means of an interactive picture or image. For this example, a good interactive picture or image might be a duck with a pot on its head. Finally, when the learner is asked for the meaning of the word *pato*, a direct systematic retrieval path has been established: The vocabulary word *pato* leads to the keyword *pot*, which in turn leads to the picture of the *pot* on a *duck's* head, which results in the desired definition (*duck*). (p. 39)

Mastropieri et al. (1985) have reviewed literature indicating that the keyword method and related mnemonic techniques are very useful in enhancing the memory of exceptional students. These procedures seem to be limited primarily by teachers' and students' ability to generate creative and workable strategies in each individual case.

Academic Attack Strategies

Students who fail in academic areas often do not know how to attack academic problems. They have not learned a systematic, logical approach to finding solutions. Consequently, they need to be taught just how to go about working math problems or comprehending what they read, for example. Training students to use academic attack strategies requires that the teacher plan three things: (1) the class of tasks to be taught, (2) the specific strategy to be used, and (3) the preskills necessary to use the strategy. Specifying the task class means determining the type of academic problem the student will be given. Examples of task classes are answering all comprehension questions that require recall of a sequence of events, finding entries in an encyclopedia, and solving equations for unknowns. Specifying the strategy means listing, step by step, the plan of action to complete the task. Specifying the preskills involves a task analysis to determine exactly what prior skills must have been learned to use the strategy.

Attack Strategies for Basic Arithmetic. Arithmetic lends itself to the generation of attack strategies because its operations are clearly identifiable and its answers are unambiguously correct or incorrect. Table 4–2 contains a plan for attack strategy training to solve basic multiplication facts. Use of such training not only facilitates performance on the specific problems trained, but also produces generalized improvement on other problems of the same class (Lloyd, Saltzman, & Kauffman, 1981). Training of this type is thus part of effective instructional practice (see Lloyd & Carnine, 1981). However, we caution that students are unlikely to generalize across tasks that are significantly different. "Task-specific strategies appear to have a better chance of being successful than general strategies, at least with regard to academic learning. . . .optimum effects will probably be obtained only when attack strategies for similar types of tasks (e.g., addition and multiplication) include identical steps for the parts of the operation that are identical" (Lloyd, 1980, p. 62).

Attack Strategies for Reading Comprehension. Attack strategies for reading comprehension encourage active involvement of students. They typically involve helping students generate images, descriptions, sum-

Table 4-2
Aspects of Instructional Design for Attack Strategy Training

Task Class for Multiplication Facts

Description: Multiplication of any number (0–10) by any number (0–10).

Examples: $0 \times 6 =$ ___ ; $3 \times 9 =$ ___ ; $7 \times 4 =$ ___ ; $8 \times 8 =$ ___ ; $10 \times 1 =$ ___ .

Objective: Given a page of unordered multiplication problems written in horizontal form with factors from 0 to 10, the student will write the correct products for the problems at the rate of 25 problems correct per minute with no more than 2 errors per minute.

Attack Strategy for Multiplication Facts

Attack Strategy: Count by one number the number of times indicated by the other number.

Steps in Attack Strategy: Examples:

1. Read the problem. $2 \times 5 =$ ___
2. Point to a number that you know how to count by.   Student points to 2
3. Make the number of marks indicated by the other number.   / / / / /
4. Begin counting by the number you know how to count by and count up once for each mark, touching each mark.   "2, 4, . . ."
5. Stop counting when you've touched the last mark.   ". . . 6, 8, 10"
6. Write the last number you said in the answer space. $2 \times 5 =$ <u> 10 </u>

Task Analysis Showing Preskills for Multiplication Attack Strategy

1. Say the numbers 0 to 100.
2. Write the numbers 0 to 100.
3. Name $\times$ and $=$ signs.
4. Make the number of marks indicated by numerals 0 to 10.
5. Count by numbers 1 to 10.
6. End counting-by sequences in various positions.
7. Coordinate counting-by and touching-marks actions.

SOURCE: "Strategy Training: A Structured Approach to Arithmetic Instruction" by D. Cullinan, J. Lloyd, and M. H. Epstein, 1981. From *Exceptional Education Quarterly, 2*(1), pp. 43–44. Copyright 1981 by Pro-Ed. Reprinted by permission.

maries, and questions while they are reading (see Carnine & Kinder, 1985). Wong and Jones (1982) taught learning disabled students to use a self-questioning strategy while reading. Their approach to fostering students' metacomprehension included teaching students to use a particular strategy.

1. Ask yourself, "What am I studying this passage for?"
2. Find the main ideas and underline them.
3. Think of a question about each main idea and write it down.
4. Look back at your questions and mental answers to see how they provide you with more information.

At the secondary level Schumaker, Deshler, Alley, Warner, and Denton (1982) have devised a comprehension strategy they call Multipass. The system requires the student to make multiple passes through the reading material. The passes—called Survey, Size-Up, and Sort-Out—are embedded in a context of highly individualized programming, with heavy emphasis on achieving certain performance goals before moving on to the next stage. The three passes of the multipass system are described in Figure 4–6.

GENERAL GUIDELINES FOR IMPLEMENTING COGNITIVE STRATEGY TRAINING

Procedures falling under the general heading of cognitive strategy training are extremely varied, and the terminology used is inconsistent. Self-regulation, CBM, strategy training, and cognitive training are terms used somewhat interchangeably. More research is needed to confirm the utility of all such procedures; they have been tested experimentally for only about a decade, a brief time in the educational research literature. Also needed is replication of those training programs showing the greatest ini-

Figure 4-6. Three Passes of the Multipass Comprehension Strategy

The purpose of the Survey Pass was to familiarize the student with the main ideas and the organization of the chapter. Thus, this previewing pass required the student to: (a) read the chapter title, (b) read the introductory paragraph, (c) review the chapter's relationship to other adjacent chapters by perusing the table of contents, (d) read the major subtitles of the chapter and notice how the chapter is organized, (e) look at illustrations and read their captions, (f) read the summary paragraph, and (g) paraphrase all the information gained in the process.

The Size-Up Pass was designed to help students gain specific information and facts from a chapter without reading it from beginning to end. This pass required the student to first read each of the questions at the end of the chapter to determine what facts appeared to be the most important to learn. If the student was already able to answer a given question as a result of the Survey Pass, a checkmark . . . was placed next to the question. The student now progressed through the entire chapter following these steps: (a) look for a textual cue (e.g., bold-face print, subtitle, colored print, italics); (b) make the cue into a question (e.g., if the cue was the italicized vocabulary word *conqueror*, the student

asked, "What does the conqueror mean?"; if the cue was the subtitle "The Election of 1848," the student might ask, "Who won the election of 1848?" or "Why was the election of 1848 important?"); (c) skim through the surrounding text to find the answer to the question; and (d) paraphrase the answer to yourself without looking in the book. When the student reached the end of the chapter using these four steps for each textual cue, he/she was required to paraphrase all the facts and ideas he/she could remember about the chapter.

The Sort-Out Pass was included to get students to test themselves over the material presented in the chapter. In this final pass, the student read and answered each question at the end of the chapter. If the student could answer a question immediately, he/she placed a checkmark next to it. If the student was unable to answer the question, however, the answer was sought by (a) thinking in which section of the chapter the answer would most likely be located, (b) skimming through that section for the answer, (c) if the answer was not located, thinking of another relevant section, and (d) skimming that section, and so on until the student could answer the question. A checkmark was then placed next to the question, and the student moved on to answer the next question.

Table 4-3
Some Successful Self-Regulation Training Programs for Replication

References	Clients and Goals	Program	Results
1. Humphrey, Karoly, & Kirschenbaum (1978)	7–9-yr.-olds; increase reading rate and accuracy	Self-reward or response-cost contingencies	Both methods successful, but reward slightly better. Both also decreased disruptive behavior.
2. Brownell, Colletti, Ersner-Herschfield, Herschfield, & Wilson (1977)	8–9-yr.-olds; improve math problem-solving accuracy and persistence	Contingency (no. of points for each correct solution) either self- or externally imposed	Self-imposed enhanced time at task; both increased accuracy, especially stringent standards used.
3. Edgar & Clement (1980)	8–9-yr.-old underachievers	Self- or teacher-controlled reinforcement	Self- more effective than teacher-control, and produced higher achievement test scores.
4. Fantuzzo & Clement (1981)	8–9-yr.-old boys deficient in math and in sustained attention with behavior problems in school	Boys observed a peer self-reinforce for appropriate behavior and were given an opportunity to reinforce themselves.	Produced improved academic and social behavior in observers and in peer models.
5. Ballard & Glynn (1975)	8–11-yr.-olds; increase number of sentences, descriptive and action words, and rated story quality	Post rules and ideas to write about, self-awarded points toward activities time for each action and description word	All targeted behaviors increased, as did non-targeted on-task behaviors.

NOTE: Replications should be confined to clients as similar as possible to those in the original study (e.g., same age, sex, grade, SES). Replication failures frequently stem from attempting treatments which are inappropriate for or unacceptable to another group of children.

SOURCE: From *Child Behavior Analysis and Therapy* (2nd ed., p. 165) by D. M. Gelfand and D. P. Hartmann, 1984, New York: Pergamon Press. © 1984 by Pergamon Press. Reprinted by permission.

tial success. Gelfand and Hartmann (1984) have suggested several programs as particularly appropriate for replication (see Table 4–3).

Gelfand and Hartmann also provide guidelines for attempting self-regulation training. The following are particularly applicable when the desired change involves social-emotional rather than academic behavior.

1. Determine whether the desired goal is developmentally and culturally appropriate for the student.

2. Obtain the cooperation of the student and his caretakers and peers.

3. Do not attempt to use self-regulation procedures to modify long-standing or overly difficult problems unless you are highly experienced in managing such behavior.

4. Try to use naturally occurring methods of self-control (i.e., try to devise self-regulation strategies commonly used by self-controlled individuals, such as covert self-instruction).

5. Identify the student's existing strategies and self-statements, both those that are productive and those that are unproductive.

6. Assess whether the student's existing skills are sufficient to solve the problem.

7. Train the student in self-observation.

8. Reinforce the student for engaging in the desired behavior; gradually transfer control to self-regulation procedures.

9. Assess whether the student is using self-regulation strategies in settings other than the one in which training is provided.

10. Remember that self-regulation is difficult to learn; do not expect miracles.

Meichenbaum (1983) notes that teachers who wish to teach thinking skills to their students must first analyze their own cognitions. He also has suggested 10 guidelines for teaching thinking skills.

1. *Analyze target behaviors* carefully. Determine exactly what it is you wish to teach. Try doing the task yourself and analyze what is involved. Interview students who perform well and students who perform poorly on the task to find out which task strategies distinguish their performances. Observe students performing the task and analyze the reasons for their success and failure.

2. *Listen for students' strategies and emotions* while they are performing the task. Don't teach strategies the student is already using. Listen for indications that the student feels incapable of performing adequately. Teaching a sense of self-efficacy and internal causal attribution is as important as teaching the student to perform.

3. *Select training tasks that are highly similar to those that naturally require the target response* so that training will generalize. Don't waste time training the student to use strategies on tasks that she will not need to continue. Instead, give training that is immediately useful and will continue to be useful because it involves important target tasks.

4. *Collaborate with the student* to generate the training program. Ask the student for advice about how to accomplish the task. Incorporate the student's verbalizations in the strategy training as much as possible.

5. *Train component skills and metacognitive skills* as well. Component skills are needed for performance of the training task, but more general metacognitive skills (e.g., self-questioning, such as "Do I know what I have to do?" and "Is there anything more I need to know before I begin?") are important if the student is to learn a general approach to problem solving.

6. *Give explicit feedback* that shows the student how using the strategy improves performance. Do not merely provide social praise for using the strategy; point out how it leads to improvement.

7. *Generalize the training* by questioning the student about how the strategy or a similar strategy might be used for other tasks.

8. *Give training in multiple settings, with multiple trainers, and with multiple tasks.* Involve other teachers, parents, or peers if possible.

9. *Prevent relapses* by anticipating failures and incorporating them into the training. Provide a coping model who experiences occasional failure but overcomes it.

10. *Terminate training only after a specific criterion has been reached, and provide booster sessions as necessary.* Monitor the student's use of the strategy after training and give additional training on skills that the student does not seem to be using. Remember that teaching thinking skills is a long-term endeavor.

Today, CBM and other cognitive training techniques appear to have reached a transition point (Rooney & Hallahan, 1985). The focus now must not be on changing only visible target responses (although overt behavioral change is important), but on restructuring students' cognitions. Rooney and Hallahan (1985, pp. 48–49) note that to use CBM successfully, the student must be able to do 11 things.

1. recognize the existence of the problem (Friedling & O'Leary, 1979)

2. accept responsibility for his or her behavior within the specific problem context

3. make a personal inventory of the positive and negative behaviors in operation

4. recognize the value of the change on a personal basis and the consequences of not changing (Karoly, 1984)

5. make a decision to implement change (Etzioni, 1982)

6. acquire the specific strategies necessary to accomplish change, for example, goal-setting (Karoly, 1984), self-monitoring of attention (Hallahan, Lloyd, & Stoller, 1982), and self-monitoring of reading (Wong & Jones, 1982)

7. recognize the role of the specific, individual strategies in the context of the overall problem

8. practice the strategies to achieve automatization
9. recognize that task and situation demands vary greatly
10. practice matching acquired strategies with tasks and situations across time, change agents, and settings (Rosenbaum & Drabman, 1979)
11. develop an active, on-going task-strategy assessment approach (Kanfer & Karoly, 1972)

Achieving the promised benefits of cognitive strategy training requires not only that teachers follow the types of guidelines suggested here, but also that they continuously assess the effects of their training. Additional guidelines and assessment questions have been provided by Rooney and Hallahan (1985) and can be found in Table 4–4.

Table 4-4
Guidelines and Assessment Questions for Cognitive Change

---

1. The student should be able to use the strategies independently (O'Leary, 1980): Can the student use the procedure or procedures without cues or assistance? Can the student match the appropriate strategy with the task? Can the student adapt the strategy if necessary?
2. The student should be able to use the strategy spontaneously (O'Leary, 1980): Does the student have to be encouraged to use the appropriate strategy? Does the student accept the strategy as an aid or see it as additional work?
3. The student must be flexible in his or her use of the strategy (Marholin & Steinman, 1977): Does the student assess the situation before using a strategy? Can the student pick out cues in a situation to guide his or her use of strategies? Can the student adapt his or her behavior to different situations? Is the strategy rigidly adhered to even if the situation is inappropriate? Are there spontaneous adaptations to meet the needs of particular situations?
4. The student should use strategies across time (Stokes & Baer, 1977): Does the student use the strategy appropriately during each class period? Does the student use the strategy appropriately throughout the day? Does the student use the strategy only during school time?
5. The student should use the strategy across situations (Stokes & Baer, 1977; Loper & Hallahan, 1982): Does the student's performance vary from situation to situation? Is each strategy tied directly to a teacher, task, or situation? Is there evidence of a spontaneous overlap from one situation to a similar situation? Is there spontaneous transfer to an appropriate but unrelated or dissimilar situation?
6. The student should show an increase in internal locus of control (Meichenbaum, 1983): Does the student attribute success to his or her use of the strategy? Does the student relate success to the difficulty of the task rather than the use of the strategy?
7. The child should show improvement in self-concept (Meichenbaum, 1983): Does the student see himself or herself as an active participant? Does the

student regard himself or herself as a more successful student in general? Does the student seek out new learning situations? In general, does the student conceptualize his or her performance as success oriented or failure oriented? Does the student avoid learning situations or academic tasks?

8. The student should improve in academic performance (Lloyd, 1980): Is there evidence of improvement in academic performance in time on-task, productivity, and/or accuracy? Is there evidence of improvement in the student's grades?

SUMMARY

Students with learning and behavior problems are known to differ from nonhandicapped students in their cognitive skills. They do not seem to use cognitive strategies spontaneously when confronted with problems and thus often do not perform up to their capacity. Specifically, handicapped students tend to show the following cognitive characteristics, which are inimical to success in school: reliance on irrelevant perceptual cues, an impulsive cognitive style, poor short-term memory, lack of metacognitive skills, attribution of success and failure to external causes, and lack of skills in behavioral self-regulation. Cognitive strategy training represents a melding of concepts from cognitive and behavioral psychology. A wide variety of cognitive strategy training techniques have been devised to address the problem characteristics of exceptional students. Numerous terms are used to designate these techniques, including cognitive behavior modification, strategy training, self-regulation training, and metacognitive training. Techniques useful for classroom teachers include at least the following: self-instruction, self-monitoring, memory (and mnemonic) strategy training, and academic attack strategy training.

To date, research on cognitive strategy training techniques is encouraging but does not, in most cases, indicate precisely the training components that are essential or most effective or the students with whom the techniques are likely to be most successful. More research, replication of existing studies, and clinical trials are needed. Meanwhile, teachers should heed the general guidelines for implementation of cognitive strategy training provided by leading researchers. The focus of educators today should be not just on changing observable behavior but also on altering students' thinking about their behavior and academic performance.

REFERENCES

Ballard, K. D., & Glynn, T. (1975). Behavioral self-management in story writing with elementary school children. *Journal of Applied Behavior Analysis, 8,* 387–398.

Billings, D. C., & Wasik, B. H. (1985). Self-instructional training with preschoolers: An attempt to replicate. *Journal of Applied Behavior Analysis, 18,* 61–67.

Blackman, S., & Goldman, K. M. (1982). Cognitive styles and learning disabilities. *Journal of Learning Disabilities, 15,* 106–115.

Bornstein, P., & Quevillon, R. (1976). The effects of a self-instructional package on overactive preschool boys. *Journal of Applied Behavior Analysis, 9,* 179–188.

Brownell, K. D., Colletti, G., Ersner-Hershfield, R., Hershfield, S. M., & Wilson, G. T. (1977). Self-control in school children: Stringency and leniency in self-determined and externally imposed performance standards. *Behavior Therapy, 8,* 442–455.

Carnine, D., & Kinder, D. (1985). Teaching low-performing students to apply generative and schema strategies to narrative and expository material. *Remedial and Special Education, 6*(1), 20–30.

Cullinan, D., Lloyd, J. W., & Epstein, M. H. (1981). Strategy training: A structured approach to arithmetic instruction. *Exceptional Education Quarterly, 2*(1), 41–49.

Edgar, R., & Clement, P. W. (1980). Teacher-controlled and self-controlled reinforcement with under-achieving, black children. *Child Behavior Therapy, 2,* 33–56.

Etzioni, A. (1982). *An immodest agenda.* New York: McGraw-Hill.

Fantuzzo, J. W., & Clement, P. W. (1981). Generalizations of the effects of teacher- and self-administered token reinforcers to nontreated subjects. *Journal of Applied Behavior Analysis, 14,* 435–448.

Friedling, C., & O'Leary, S. G. (1979). Effects of self-instructional training on second- and third-grade hyperactive children: A failure to replicate. *Journal of Applied Behavior Analysis, 12,* 211–219.

Gelfand, D. M., & Hartmann, D. P. (1984). *Child behavior analysis and therapy* (2nd Ed.). New York: Pergamon Press.

Grimes, L. (1981). Learned helplessness and attribution theory: Redefining children's learning problems. *Learning Disability Quarterly, 4,* 91–100.

Hallahan, D. P. (Ed.). (1980). Teaching exceptional children to use cognitive strategies. *Exceptional Education Quarterly, 1*(1), special issue.

Hallahan, D. P., Hall, R. J., Ianna, S. O., Kneedler, R. D., Lloyd, J. W., Loper, A. B., & Reeve, R. E. (1983). Summary of research findings at the University of Virginia Learning Disabilities Research Institute. *Exceptional Education Quarterly, 4*(1), 95–114.

Hallahan, D. P., Kauffman, J. M., & Lloyd, J. W. (1985). *Introduction to learning disabilities* (2nd ed.). Englewood Cliffs, NJ: Prentice-Hall.

Hallahan, D. P., Lloyd, J. W., Kauffman, J. M., & Loper, A. B. (1983). Academic problems. In R. J. Morris & T. R. Kratochwill (Eds.), *The practice of child therapy.* New York: Pergamon Press.

Hallahan, D. P., Lloyd, J. W., & Stoller, L. (1982). *Improving attention with self-monitoring: A manual for teachers.* Charlottesville: University of Virginia Learning Disabilities Research Institute.

Henker, B., Whalen, C. K., & Hinshaw, S. P. (1980). The attributional contexts of cognitive intervention strategies. *Exceptional Education Quarterly, 1*(1), 17–30.

Humphrey, L. L., Karoly, P., & Kirschenbaum, D. S. (1978). Self-management in the classroom: Self-imposed response cost versus self-reward. *Behavior Therapy, 9,* 592–601.

Kanfer, F. H., & Karoly, P. (1972). Self-control: A behavioristic excursion into the lion's den. *Behavior Therapy, 3,* 398–416.

Karoly, P. (1984). Self-management problems in children. In E. J. Mash & L. G. Terdal (Eds.), *Behavioral assessment of childhood disorders.* New York: Guilford Press.

Kauffman, J. M. (1985). *Characteristics of children's behavior disorders* (3rd ed.). Columbus, OH: Charles E. Merrill.

Kauffman, J. M., & Hallahan, D. P. (1979). Learning disability and hyperactivity (with comments on minimal brain dysfunction). In B. B. Lahey & A. E. Kazdin (Eds.), *Advances in clinical child psychology* (Vol. 2). New York: Plenum.

Kazdin, A. E., & Frame, C. (1983). Aggressive behavior and conduct disorder. In R. J. Morris & T. R. Kratochwill (Eds.), *The practice of child therapy.* New York: Pergamon Press.

Kneedler, R. D., & Hallahan, D. P. (1981). Self-monitoring of on-task behavior with learning-disabled children: Current studies and directions. *Exceptional Education Quarterly, 2*(3), 73–82.

Kosiewicz, M. M., Hallahan, D. P., Lloyd, J. W., & Graves, A. W. (1982). Effects of self-instruction and self-correction procedures on handwriting performance. *Learning Disability Quarterly, 5,* 71–78.

Kotsonis, M. E., & Patterson, C. J. (1980). Comprehension-monitoring skills in learning disabled children. *Developmental Psychology, 16,* 541–542.

Lloyd, J. W. (1980). Academic instruction and cognitive behavior modification: The need for attack strategy training. *Exceptional Education Quarterly, 1*(1), 53–63.

Lloyd, J. W., & Carnine, D. (Eds.). (1981). Structured instruction: Effective teaching of essential skills. *Exceptional Education Quarterly, 2*(1), special issue.

Lloyd, J. W., Saltzman, N. J., & Kauffman, J. M. (1981). Predictable generalization in academic learning as a result of preskills and strategy training. *Learning Disability Quarterly, 4*, 203–216.

Loper, A. B., & Hallahan, D. P. (1982). A consideration of the role of generalization in cognitive training. *Topics in Learning and Learning Disabilities, 2*(2), 62–67.

Marholin, D., & Steinman, W. M. (1977). Stimulus control in the classroom as a function of the behavior reinforced. *Journal of Applied Behavior Analysis, 10*, 465–478.

Mastropieri, M. A., Scruggs, T. E., & Levin, J. R. (1985). Maximizing what exceptional students can learn: A review of research on the keyword method and related mnemonic techniques. *Remedial and Special Education, 6*(2), 39–45.

McManus, M. (1985). Modification of adolescent students' off-task behaviors using self-monitoring procedures. Unpublished manuscript.

Meichenbaum, D. (1977). *Cognitive-behavior modification: An integrative approach.* New York: Plenum.

_____ (1980). Cognitive-behavior modification: A promise yet unfulfilled. *Exceptional Education Quarterly, 1*(1), 83–88.

_____ (1983). Teaching thinking: A cognitive-behavioral approach. In *Interdisciplinary voices in learning disabilities and remedial education.* Austin, TX: Pro-Ed.

O'Leary, S. G. (1980). A response to cognitive training. *Exceptional Education Quarterly, 1*(1), 89–94.

Pearl, R., Bryan, T., & Donahue, M. (1980). Learning disabled children's attributions for success and failure. *Learning Disability Quarterly, 3*(1), 3–9.

Pressley, M., & Levin, J. R. (Eds.). (1983). *Cognitive strategy research: Educational applications.* New York: Springer-Verlag.

Reeve, R. E., & Kauffman, J. M. (in press). Learning disabilities. In V. Van Hasselt, M. Hersen, & P. S. Strain (Eds.), *Handbook of developmental and physical disabilities.* New York: Pergamon Press.

Rooney, K. J., & Hallahan, D. P. (1985). Future directions for cognitive behavior modification research: The quest for cognitive change. *Remedial and Special Education, 6*(2), 46–51.

Rosenbaum, M. S., & Drabman, R. S. (1979). Self-control training in the classroom: A review and critique. *Journal of Applied Behavior Analysis, 12*, 467–485.

Schumaker, J. B., Deshler, D. D., Alley, G. R., Warner, M. M., & Denton, P. H. (1982). Multipass: A learning strategy for improving reading comprehension. *Learning Disability Quarterly, 5*, 295–304.

Seligman, M. E. P. (1975). *Helplessness: On depression, development and death.* San Francisco: Freeman.

Spivack, G., Platt, J. J., & Shure, M. B. (1976). *The problem solving approach to adjustment.* San Francisco: Jossey-Bass.

Stokes, T., & Baer, D. M. (1977). An implicit technology of generalization. *Journal of Applied Behavior Analysis, 10,* 349–367.

Swanson, H. L. (1979). Developmental recall lag in learning disabled children: Perceptual deficit or verbal mediation deficiency? *Journal of Abnormal Child Psychology, 7,* 199–210.

_____ (1984). Does theory guide teaching practice? *Remedial and Special Education, 5*(5), 7–16.

Tarver, S. G., Hallahan, D. P., Kauffman, J. M., & Ball, D. W. (1976). Verbal rehearsal and selective attention in children with learning disabilities: A developmental lag. *Journal of Experimental Child Psychology, 22,* 375–385.

Torgesen, J. K. (1979). Factors related to poor performance in reading disabled children. *Learning Disability Quarterly, 2*(3), 17–23.

Torgesen, J. K., & Goldman, T. (1977). Verbal rehearsal and short-term memory in reading disabled children. *Child Development, 48,* 56–60.

Wong, B. Y. L. (1982). Understanding the learning disabled student's reading problems: Contributions from cognitive psychology. *Topics in Learning and Learning Disabilities, 1*(4), 43–50.

Wong, B. Y. L., & Jones, W. (1982). Increasing metacomprehension in learning disabled and normally achieving students through self-questioning training. *Learning Disability Quarterly, 5,* 228–240.

5

Teaching Competencies

Teaching is an art, developed over the course of human history, that encompasses a wide range of individual styles. Teaching is also a science about which certain conclusions have been reached after decades of empirical research (see Hosford, 1984). The art of teaching is learned primarily through practice and the processes of modeling and mentoring—teachers watching other, more artful teachers and receiving feedback on their own performance, thereby learning many of the subtleties of the art. Little of the art can be conveyed effectively in written form. The science of teaching, however, is more readily described in writing, although practice and feedback are important in learning to apply the science. This chapter will focus on the science of teaching—those aspects of instruction and management that have been the subject of empirical research and have led to general conclusions that can be held with confidence.

Effective remedial or special education requires the teacher's mastery of specific instructional and behavior management skills, grounded in the principles discussed in chapters 2 and 3. The specific competencies that put those principles into effect include the teacher's ability to

1. use assessment information to formulate an initial remedial strategy
2. state general instructional goals and specific task objectives and allocate time to their achievement
3. analyze tasks to pinpoint learning problems
4. present tasks effectively and efficiently to remediate problems
5. provide feedback on task performance
6. structure the learning environment
7. monitor student performance

When students have difficulty in school, their teachers must attempt to diagnose and remediate their behavioral or academic problems. However, teachers must first analyze their own teaching behavior. Our suggestion that teachers are responsible for students' learning implies that remediation of teaching problems must precede remediation of learning problems. Teaching involves constant reevaluation of instructional behavior as well as constant reassessment of pupil performance. The behaviors that comprise teaching are no less open to scrutiny and diagnosis than the behaviors that constitute learning. Teachers must continuously monitor and correct their own behavior if they are to be the most effective. This chapter will discuss remedial teaching competencies needed by all teachers and can be used as a checklist for evaluating teaching problems that might be contributing to a student's learning difficulty.

USE ASSESSMENT INFORMATION TO FORMULATE AN INITIAL REMEDIAL STRATEGY

Assessment information should serve one major purpose: it should provide a basis for remediation. Useful assessment information is of two types:

Type I: general information (including standardized test scores, observational data, and case history material) that gives an overall picture of the student and suggests a beginning point for remediation

Type II: specific information (obtained from a student's responses to remedial teaching) (i.e., the results of direct measurement of the student's performance) that provides the basis for further instruction

Type I information is the concern of this section; the use of Type II information will be discussed later in the chapter.

Use All Available Sources of Relevant Information

To get a complete picture of a student's strengths and weaknesses that will be of maximum use in teaching, no source of useful information should be overlooked. All school personnel, both professional and nonprofessional, should be considered potential sources of observational information about the student's academic and social performance. School records, parents, peers, and community agencies (e.g., church, scouts, family service, welfare) are potential sources of useful data. However, we cannot over-emphasize the fact that the classroom teacher is the best single source of relevant information for teaching a student with learning and behavior problems. The teacher must observe and analyze the student's behavior and academic performance, regardless of the availability of other information (see Englert, 1984; Howell, 1985; Shinn & Marston, 1985). An important consideration in this process of seeking and sharing information is protecting the confidentiality of personal information regarding students.

Adjust Initial Expectations to the Student's Developmental Level

An initial remedial strategy must be consistent with a student's level of development. For example, the teacher must note whether the student's physical development differs from the norm, whether his social behavior is age- and sex-appropriate, whether his academic achievement is within the expected range, and whether the rewards he prefers are characteristic of other students of the same age and sex. Initial remedial activities must fall within the student's physical capacity, degree of socialization, academic ability, and reward preference. The teacher must begin by estimating the student's developmental level and expecting performance consistent with that level.

Eliminate Possible Health and Sensory Factors as Causes

Efficient learning requires that a student be in good health and have properly functioning senses. It is particularly important for the teacher to be alert to indications of general health problems (including problems related to abuse and neglect) and hearing or vision problems that might contribute to learning difficulties. Indications of such problems are described in most introductory special education textbooks. If the teacher has reason to suspect that the student has a health problem or sensory defect, referral must be made to apropriate professionals, who can provide evaluation and treatment. However, the teacher must not use suspected or real health problems or sensory defects as an excuse for failing to develop the best possible remedial teaching program. On the one hand, the teacher must do everything possible to ensure that the student's health and sensory functioning have been properly assessed and that any problems are being addressed; on the other hand, the teacher retains the responsibility to plan a remedial program in spite of the student's condition.

Observe the Methods Through Which the Student Learns Best

Academic learning in any curriculum area normally involves multisensory stimulation and a variety of response modes. The primary channels through which school learning takes place appear to be auditory-vocal and visual-motor. A primary concern of the teacher, then, should be to identify the instructional methods that work best with a given student, regardless of the supposed strengths or weaknesses in modal learning indicated by tests of perceptual or psycholinguistic processes. To know that a student learns spelling words more quickly by tracing them than by hearing them spelled is more useful than to know that she scored high on visual-motor or low on auditory-vocal tasks on a standardized test. From the first moment that a teacher works with a student, he should begin observing the instructional and management methods that work best in teaching specific skills to that individual (Lovitt, 1977).

Integrate Type I Information into an Initial Teaching Strategy

Type I information includes test scores, anecdotal observations, and informal assessment data that are useful in formulating an initial teaching strategy. The value of such a beginning strategy is that it allows the teacher to focus quickly on remedial tasks and teaching methods that have a high probability of success. The integration of Type I information into an initial remedial strategy is illustrated by Ted's case, which follows.

AN INITIAL TEACHING STRATEGY FOR TED

Background Information

Ted is a quiet but friendly 8-year-old who is in the third grade. He has no history of medical problems and shows no indications of sensory defects. He is of average height and weight but appears somewhat uncoordinated in his movements and is rather weak, slow, and clumsy in sports and playground activities compared to his classmates. He is an only child, pampered by his mother and ignored by his father. His mother, a high school graduate, works part-time as a hostess in a restaurant; his father, a college graduate, is a business manager for a branch office of a large corporation. During the past year his parents separated for about 6 months, apparently in anticipation of filing for a divorce. Ted's mother moved into an apartment, and during these months of separation Ted and his father interacted much more. They shared chores around the house, and his father took an active interest in Ted's daily activities. However, now that Ted's mother is living at home again, Ted's father pays almost as little attention to him as before the separation. Ted's comments to his teachers have made it obvious that he admires his father and enjoys doing things with and for him.

Ted is not actively rejected socially by his classmates, nor is he a social isolate. However, he has few close friends, mainly because of his lack of skill in active games and sports. He is considerate of others and good natured but seldom invites social contacts and is not a social leader. He typically chooses adult company rather than play with his peers, and he thrives on praise from adults.

Ted's third grade teacher is concerned about his progress in three areas: reading, motor development, and social development. His progress in arithmetic is satisfactory; in fact, he is ahead of most of his classmates. If given the opportunity, he would spend almost his entire school day working math problems, looking at pictures, or listening to stories. He seems to be a bright child who has no difficulty comprehending what he hears and grasping quantitative relationships. However, oral and silent reading are difficult for him and hinder his progress in other subjects, such as science and social studies. His attitude toward reading is that he'd prefer not to do it—he often dawdles over his reading assignments and complains that the work is too hard. He is not a social failure, but he needs to learn to initiate more social contacts with his peers. His lack of the gross motor skills required in active games and sports seems to be a major hindrance to his social development.

Test Results

Ted was cooperative throughout the testing sessions and appeared interested in the tasks. He was tested in October, when his grade placement was 3.2. On the Slossen Intelligence Test Ted achieved a mental age of 9 years, 8 months (his chronological age was 8 years, 7 months) and an IQ of 113. He was given the Peabody Individual Achievement Test (PIAT) with the following results:

Subtest	Grade Equivalent
Mathematics	4.0
Reading recognition	2.2
Reading comprehension	2.8
Spelling	2.0
General information	4.3
Total test score	3.0

The Key Math Diagnostic Arithmetic Test was given, and his overall grade equivalent score of 3.8 was consistent with his teacher's report and his score on the PIAT. On the Berry-Buktenica Developmental Test of Visual-Motor Integration Ted scored an age-equivalent of 7 years, 4 months, reflecting his lag in skills necessary for achievement in action games and sports. He was given the Woodcock Reading Mastery Test with the following results:

Subtest	Easy Reading Level	Instructional Level	Frustration Level
Letter identification	2.6	3.0	3.6
Word identification	1.8	1.9	2.0
Word attack	1.6	1.8	2.1
Word comprehension	1.9	2.4	2.6
Passage comprehension	1.9	2.2	2.6
Total reading	1.9	2.2	2.5

He was given the Wepman Auditory Discrimination Test and was found to have average auditory discrimination skills.

Informal Observations

Ted's teacher has a well-controlled, highly structured class. Most of the activity in the classroom consists of individual, teacher-directed tasks; most social interaction between children takes place at recess or on the playground, where Ted is at a disadvantage because of his lack of visual-motor skills. Ted's positive social interactions with his peers occur most often during games and activities requiring little visual-motor skill (for instance, checkers and chess, at which he excels). His oral reading is slow and characterized by many hesitations, repetitions, and errors on small words. He fails to recognize many of the words that are part of his speaking vocabulary. He relies primarily on contextual clues in figuring out words and does not appear to use any other word attack skills consistently. When he is given a silent reading task, Ted typically responds in one of two ways: he either hurries through it, making many careless errors in his slap-dash performance; or he dawdles and daydreams, failing to complete the task. He seldom receives praise from his teacher for his performance on reading tasks.

Initial Strategy

First, there appears to be a serious motivational problem in reading. Because he seems to respond well to social praise and attention, social rather than material rewards for appropriate responses should be tried first.

Second, reading tasks should be kept well within his capability (i.e., he should be able to read the material with 95% accuracy), and tasks should be kept short. Praise for correct performance should be given immediately, and a favorite activity (e.g., math or a game of chess) should be scheduled immediately following reading. However, the reading task must be completed correctly before Ted engages in the preferred activity.

Third, Ted should be asked to read for 1 minute each day from the same reader, and careful records should be kept of his errors and his correct reading rate (i.e., words read correctly per minute). Analysis of his performance on these daily probes will reveal the consistency of his errors and indicate what specific skills he is lacking.

Fourth, instruction should be given in phonetic word analysis skills, and drill should be provided on common sight words.

Fifth, an attempt should be made to obtain the assistance of Ted's father by requesting that he listen to Ted read a short passage (specified by the teacher) every evening and praise Ted for his performance.

Sixth, Ted's father should be encouraged to teach him some of the skills useful in organized games and sports (e.g., throwing, catching, and batting a baseball; dribbling and shooting a basketball; swimming).

Seventh, Ted's teacher should be asked to provide small-group activities in which Ted can interact with his peers, and these activities should be ones in which Ted can be highly successful (e.g., projects involving arithmetic problems).

STATE INSTRUCTIONAL GOALS AND SPECIFIC PERFORMANCE OBJECTIVES AND ALLOCATE SUFFICIENT TIME FOR THEM

In using Type I information to initiate a remedial program, a teacher must give careful attention to instructional goals and objectives. Goals and objectives are important because they lead directly to the choice and presentation of instructional tasks. Goals are general or global statements about what students should learn or what their education should accomplish. Goals provide a general orientation or direction for instructional activities; they are important in providing a rationale for teaching particular skills. If the goals of education are not clear, instruction becomes a hodgepodge of activities with no identifiable purpose other than keeping students out of mischief. Objectives are statements about what a student will be able to do under specified circumstances. They include a description of what the student will do, the conditions under which she will do it, and the criteria that will be used to judge her performance (Mager, 1962). Objectives help teachers decide which specific skill to teach and evaluate the extent to which they have taught that skill effectively.

Formulate Appropriate Goals

Goals state the desired outcomes of education and guide the delivery of a curriculum. Some goal statements are extremely general (e.g., "To prepare students for the world of work," "To teach students the importance of good citizenship," or "To help students become competent in basic arithmetic operations"). Obviously, more specific goal statements are needed to guide instructional planning (e.g., "To show tolerance for other people's points of view," "To understand that adjectives describe people, places, and things," or "To tell time"). The teacher must choose goals that are consistent with the student's developmental level and that maximize the chance for integration in mainstream classes.

State Instructional Objectives in Performance Terms

Every remedial teaching lesson should include clearly stated performance objectives. Objectives help the teacher keep sight of the goal of instruction and avoid wasting time and effort on irrelevant activities; they also help the teacher and the student evaluate progress more reliably. Adequate performance objectives include the behavior, the conditions, and the evaluation criteria. The following are examples of adequate performance objectives.

- Given any world map or globe, the student will identify each of the seven continents by tracing its outline.
- Given any printed standard English sentence in which he can read all the words, the student will be able to underline the adjectives with 95% accuracy.
- Given a conversation in the classroom during which someone expresses a differing opinion or belief, the student will show tolerance for the other person's point of view by allowing her to speak and not interrupting or physically attacking her or making sarcastic or derogatory comments.

Like goals, objectives can be made more finite or specific. For example, a performance objective for time telling might be stated as follows: Given any clock or watch face, the student will tell the time shown to the nearest minute. Subobjectives representing successive approximations of telling time to the nearest minute might be stated as

☐ Given a large clock face with arabic numerals, the student will read correctly the o'clock and half-past times for any hour or half hour.
☐ Given such a clock face, the student will count the minutes by 5s, proceeding clockwise from 1 (5) and continuing through 11 (55).
☐ Given such a clock face, the student will tell time to the nearest 5 minutes as _____ minutes after _____ or _____ minutes 'til _____ for any position of the hands.

The teacher's task is to objectify the student's performance and state performance objectives that lead logically toward stated educational goals. Instructional objectives suggest remedial tasks that lead to remediation of the learning problem.

Allocate Time for Accomplishing Goals and Objectives

Goals and objectives are not accomplished by good intentions or by magic. Only if the teacher allocates sufficient time for instruction and practice— and keeps students engaged in appropriate academic activities during the allocated time—will goals and objectives be realized. This may seem to be a common sense or even trivial point, but research has indicated clearly the critical importance of scheduling time for academic instruction and maintaining students' engagement in academic activities (see Berliner, 1984; Rieth, Polsgrove, & Semmel, 1981; Stevens & Rosenshine, 1981).

ANALYZE TASKS TO PINPOINT LEARNING PROBLEMS

Instructional tasks are the essence of remedial teaching. By performing instructional tasks, students move closer to mastery of the skills in which they are deficient. Consequently, no aspect of remedial teaching competence deserves closer attention than the analysis of instructional tasks (see Engelmann & Carnine, 1982). Task analysis is a sequence of evaluation activities that pinpoints the instructional problem and guides the teacher in planning an effective sequence of remedial tasks.

Specify the Task

A task is something to do. It is an observable behavior that completes the phrase "The student will . . . " in an instructional objective. For example, the following are tasks.

☐ point to the red ball
☐ write the lowercase alphabet in manuscript letters
☐ copy a square

□ find the sum of three two-digit numbers
□ stay seated while taking the spelling test

More important than defining a task is consideration of the task in question. The teacher must specify what the student is to do. Otherwise, both the teacher and the student will become confused about what response is expected. Following oral directions is a different task from following written directions. Pointing to the correct object is a different task from naming it. Tasks must be defined precisely before their response requirements can be identified.

Identify the Task's Response Requirements

A task requires a response from a student. Every response can be broken down into a set of sequential subskills or response requirements that are prerequisites for successful task performance. Identifying the response requirements or prerequisite skills for instructional tasks is of primary importance in task analysis. Only when the component responses of a task are known can the student's learning problem (or the teacher's instructional problem) be pinpointed. The teacher must analyze the instructional task by asking, "What are the things the student must do to perform this task successfully? What are the possible ways in which the student could make an error?" For example, when given the oral instruction "Print your name at the top of the paper," the student must be able to

1. interpret (understand) the directions
2. find the top of the paper
3. hold the pencil in writing position
4. print each of the letters in his name
5. print the letters in his name in sequence

Each of these five response requirements is a task in itself. As a task, it can be analyzed in terms of its own response requirements. Whether a response requirement must be further analyzed as a separate subtask depends on the student's performance. Furthermore, the teacher must determine whether the objective is to teach only the specific task in question or to teach a class or range of tasks requiring similar responses (see Engelmann & Carnine, 1982).

Note the Student's Errors

Task analysis requires that the student be directed to perform the task. When the student's task performance breaks down, it is imperative that the teacher pinpoint the difficulty. Thus, if a task is not performed successfully, the teacher must analyze the first response requirement on which the student makes an error. In the example "Print your name at the top of the paper," the teacher must analyze the fourth response requirement if the student has mastered the first three requirements but does not print all the letters in his name correctly. The teacher must note which letters were not properly printed and identify the response requirements for printing those letters. Then the teacher must present those tasks (e.g., "Make the letter A") and note the student's errors on specific response requirements. This process of task presentation and error identification must continue until a task is found that the student can perform without error.

Describe the Learning Problem as a Performance Deficit

Careful analysis of the student's errors indicates what the student has not learned that is essential for successful task performance. The learning problem can then be described as a performance deficiency that can be remediated. What the student should be taught follows logically. To return to the example "Print your name at the top of the paper," if a student named Randy consistently responds to the task by printing **Rnady** at the top of the paper, his performance deficit is that he reverses the order of the letters *a* and *n* in his name. Because he has mastered all the other response requirements for completion of the task, it is obvious that what he must be taught is the correct sequence of letters. If, on the other hand, a student named Sue responds to the task by printing *2d* at the top of the paper, it is clear that the response requirement of forming the letters in her name must be analyzed as a set of separate tasks. If an analysis of the task of printing the letter S shows that Sue does not visually discriminate S from *2* , although she reliably discriminates and copies some other letter forms (e.g., *t* and *o*), her performance deficit (failure to visually discriminate S from *2*) indicates precisely what she must be taught.

Task analysis explicates what is required for performance, what the student can do, what the student cannot do, and what sequence of skills must be taught to remediate the problem (see Engelmann & Carnine, 1982; Howell, 1985; Lovitt, 1977).

PRESENT TASKS TO REMEDIATE THE PROBLEM

The teacher must design and present a sequence of remedial tasks that will help the student overcome her performance deficits. The nature of the tasks themselves and the manner in which they are presented will determine the student's progress in learning.

Organize Tasks for Efficient Presentation

Tasks must be organized so that the child is not distracted or confused. The necessary instructional materials must be arranged so that tasks can be presented in fairly rapid succession and with a minimum of teacher effort. As soon as one task is completed, the next task should be presented, unless the task is to be followed by a break for rest or reinforcement. If the teacher has to search for the needed materials or cannot manipulate the materials efficiently, the student's attention is likely to stray from the task. Unneeded teaching materials and other objects that might attract the student's attention should be removed from the teaching environment. The student's attention can then be focused on the task at hand. The teacher must be in a position to direct the responses and manipulate the teaching materials smoothly; the student should be positioned so that an appropriate response can be made easily. In any remedial teaching situation the teacher must

- select the materials to use in teaching the task(s)
- know how to use the materials
- arrange the task environment for efficient presentation and response
- remove unnecessary materials
- have necessary materials within easy reach
- position the student at an appropriate desk, table, chair, or other work area
- stay within easy reach of the child and the materials

Be Directive

The teacher must assume responsibility for directing the student's attention and responses. To do this effectively, the teacher must establish a pleasant but controlling relationship with the student. The teacher must know exactly what the child is to do and must communicate this information clearly to the child.

Tell, Don't Ask. Teachers should become accustomed to telling students what they are to do in a pleasant but firm manner. Questions should be reserved for situations in which the student has a legitimate choice or is expected to supply a correct answer to a task. The teacher should avoid using questions in situations such as these.

- The teacher wants the student to put together a puzzle: "Let's put the puzzle together, O.K.?"
- The teacher wants the student to read the next paragraph: "Do you want to read the next paragraph?"

If the teacher has determined that the student should or must do these tasks, it would be better to direct the student.

- "Here's a puzzle to put together. Let's see how well you can do it."
- "Now read the next paragraph for me, please."

The student's task and the teacher's expectation must be made unambiguous (see Englemann & Carnine, 1982). Teaching is most effective when the teacher pleasantly but firmly and clearly directs the learning activities.

Questions *are* appropriate when the teacher wants the student to choose one of two or more alternatives, any one of which is acceptable. For example, "Which do you want to do first, reading or arithmetic?" is an appropriate question when either choice is acceptable. "What is Barney doing in this picture?" is another acceptable question for which the teacher can expect a specific answer.

Get the Student's Attention Before Giving Directions. Directions given to a student who is not paying attention are a waste of time and breath. Before presenting a task, the teacher must be sure that the student is looking at and listening to the appropriate stimuli (person and/or material). Thus, before telling a student what he is to do, the teacher may need to command the student's attention: "Look at me," "Listen carefully," "Look at this page." Such conditions as physical proximity and eye contact may be necessary to ensure that the student is attending to the directions. Time and effort spent in ensuring attention to directions are not wasted; on the contrary, they prevent the waste of time and effort on false starts and miscommunication.

Wait for the Student's Response. When the student is paying attention and has been given a direction, the teacher must allow reasonable opportunity to respond appropriately. Some students do not respond immediately and correctly; if the teacher waits patiently, however, they do produce the desired response. Before proceeding with another comment, instruction, or direction, the teacher should give a student at least 5 to 10 seconds to respond.

When the teacher has waited an appropriate interval for a response but the student has not responded, the teacher must take action to help her complete the task correctly. The teacher may do this by repeating and simplifying instructions or by using cues, prompts, and models. Clear, direct instructions or removal of ambiguity from a task is sometimes all that is necessary to remediate an apparent learning problem (Englemann & Carnine, 1982; Lovitt, 1977).

Repeat and Simplify Directions. The teacher must be absolutely certain that the student understands exactly what to do. Otherwise, the reason for the student's failure cannot be determined. If the student does not respond promptly and correctly to directions for performing a task, then the directions should be repeated. Furthermore, the teacher must be sure that the student understands each part of the directions given. For example, if the task directions are "Draw a straight line from the monkey to the house," the teacher must be sure that the student understands what it means to draw a straight line from one object to another and that the student can identify both the monkey and the house. Thus, before assuming that the student cannot perform the task or prompting the student's response, the teacher should repeat the task directions and, if necessary, simplify them. Directions can be simplified by using simpler vocabulary or by breaking them down into smaller, component parts.

Cue Responses.   If a student does not respond to repeated or simplified directions or if he responds before listening to the directions, then the teacher must take further action. The student might respond appropriately if given a cue, which is a signal to the student—"Wait," "Do it now," or "Do it here." The teacher can cue a response with a word, a gesture, or any other visual, auditory, or tactile signal. For example, if a student tends to respond at an inappropriate time, the teacher might call his name, use a hand signal, or touch the student to cue a response at the appropriate time. If the student is attending to the wrong stimuli, the teacher can use a pointing or tapping cue to direct the student's attention and response.

Use Prompts.   If a student does not respond to the teacher's cue, the response may need to be prompted. Prompting means that the teacher physically assists the student in performing the task or adds a detail that emphasizes relevant features of instructional material. For example, if the student cannot perform the task of drawing a square, the teacher might take the student's hand and help her draw the figure (i.e., provide a physical prompt). Occasionally, only a partial physical prompt is needed, as when the teacher helps the student draw only three sides of the square. Prompts can be faded out as the student learns the task. A physical prompt should be faded out by gradually dropping assistance, beginning at the point of completion for many motor tasks. The physical prompt for drawing a square, for example, should be faded in this way.

1. help the student draw all four sides
2. help the student draw only the first three sides
3. help the student draw only the first two sides
4. help the student draw only the first side

b d b d b d b d b d

The manner in which a visual prompt for the b/d discrimination which might be faded over successive presentations is shown here. The goal is to teach the student to respond appropriately by paying attention to the visual prompt in the beginning but relying less and less on the prompt and eventually responding correctly without it. Visual prompts can be external or within the stimulus (an integral part of the stimulus) and can involve critical or noncritical features (see Figure 5–1). Whenever possible,

Figure 5-1. Examples of Visual Prompts

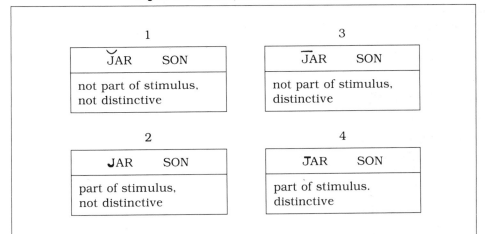

These examples illustrate within-stimulus (part of the stimulus) and extra-stimulus (not part of the stimulus) visual prompts involving distinctive (not shared) and nondistinctive (shared) features. The best prompt is one that uses a within-stimulus distinctive feature (Example 4). Notice that the curved line of the *J* in JAR is not a distinctive feature in this example (JAR/SON discrimination) because it is shared by the curved line of the *S* in SON. The straight line on the top of the *J*, however, is a distinctive feature, because there is no equivalent line in the word SON. The prompts (lines above the letters) in Examples 1 and 3 are extra-stimulus because they are separate from the letters themselves; those in Examples 2 and 4 are intra-stimulus because they are emphasized parts of the letters themselves.

SOURCE: From *Special Education Today*, March, 1984, *1*(2), p. 9. Copyright 1984 by *Special Education Today*. Adapted by permission.

the teacher should use visual prompts that involve both critical features and integral parts of the stimuli to be discriminated (see also Engelmann & Carnine, 1982, chapter 20; Rincover, 1978).

Provide a Model. Students often learn a task more quickly if they have a model to follow. If a student does not make an appropriate response, the teacher may need to demonstrate how to do the task. For example, if the student does not cut on the dotted line or does not clap his hands when told to do so, the teacher should demonstrate the correct response. Instructions such as "Watch me" or "Do it like this" should be given as the teacher models the response. In some cases it might be helpful to have another student provide the model. If the task involves solving problems and writing answers, it might also be helpful to leave an example (a model) of a correctly completed problem on the student's desk for easy reference (Lovitt, 1977).

Present Only Essential Tasks

The student should be given only tasks that are directly related to the concept being taught; irrelevant tasks should be eliminated, and each task should be an essential step in reaching the next performance objective. As suggested in chapter 3, the teacher must teach directly to the problem; that is, the teacher must deliver a curriculum that leads to the desired outcomes (Berliner, 1985). If the objective of instruction is to teach the student to catch a ball, little is to be gained by having the student name pictures. If the teacher wants the student to learn sight words, the student should not be asked to walk on a balance beam or draw circles on the chalkboard or complete other tasks not directly related to naming the sight words in question. Instructional time must be allocated to those activities leading directly to selected instructional goals and objectives.

Present Tasks Sequentially

The sequence in which tasks are presented affects the rate at which students learn. Complex tasks are mastered by sequential learning of many simpler tasks (see Engelmann & Carnine, 1982). The teacher must be aware of the sequential development of academic and social learning so that tasks can be ordered effectively. Furthermore, adequate opportunity for practice of each successive skill is essential so that learning results in mastery of the material.

Maintain a Brisk Pace During Instruction

An effective teacher keeps the lesson moving—tasks are presented in fairly rapid succession (Berliner, 1984). The teacher should wait, if necessary, for the student to respond, but the student should not be kept waiting for the teacher to present the next task. The time during which students are not engaged in academic activity is nonproductive time, and it should be kept to a minimum during periods set aside for instruction. After a student's response the teacher should be prepared to move quickly to the next question so that opportunities to respond occur frequently and speedily. Such a pace requires that the teacher be well prepared, familiar with the instructional materials and the structure and purpose of the lesson.

Provide Ample Opportunity for Practice Until Mastery Is Achieved

Academic progress, particularly for students who have difficulty in learning, is dependent on students' controlled practice until they experience consistent success. After the teacher has presented a task and obtained correct responses, it is important that the student be given work to complete independently, that the teacher remain ready to provide assistance if the student has difficulty, and that the student be given repeated opportunities to practice until he is performing the task consistently with at least 90% accuracy (see Stevens & Rosenshine, 1981).

Teach Students in Small Groups, As Appropriate for the Individual

Remedial and special education must be highly attuned to the individual student. However, students need not be working alone or on tasks of their own choosing. On the contrary, the most effective instruction typically occurs in small groups, with both individual and group responses required (see Berliner, 1984; Stevens & Rosenshine, 1981). Individual work is usually most appropriate for practice sessions, during which the student can complete seatwork independently.

PROVIDE FEEDBACK ON TASK PERFORMANCE

Competence in remedial teaching demands more than merely presenting appropriate tasks. To learn efficiently, students must be informed clearly, immediately, and frequently of the adequacy of their performance. One of the advantages of programmed instruction, microcomputer programs, and other highly structured teaching systems is that they provide such feedback. As discussed in chapter 2, what happens immediately after a response determines to a large extent whether that response is likely to occur again. Teachers who fail to give appropriate feedback on task performance risk eliminating the very responses they are trying to teach.

Give Clear Feedback

Ambiguous feedback on performance is worse than no feedback at all; ambiguity only heightens the student's anxiety and confusion. The teacher's feedback should leave no room for doubt in the student's mind about the correctness of her response. Feedback might include such statements as "That's perfect," "It's all right except for this part right here," "No, that's wrong," or "Yes, it's a bicycle." The teacher should also give explicit feedback that is affective—communicated clearly with smiles, hugs, pats, winks, and a variety of other physical and verbal responses. In addition, extrinsic rewards are necessary for some students.

Give Corrective Feedback

Positive feedback for appropriate performance is corrective: it strengthens correct responses to remedial tasks. When the student gives an incorrect response to a task, the teacher's feedback should tell the student how to improve his performance. "Make this line a little straighter," "You must put the second number right under the first one," and other such remarks go beyond merely telling the student that a particular response is wrong. Feedback can also be corrective in another sense—it helps the student evaluate his own performance accurately. By giving corrective feedback, the teacher provides a model that can be incorporated into the student's self-evaluation. Thus, when feedback is adequately corrective, it reinforces correct responses, eliminates incorrect responses, indicates how task performance can be improved, and provides a model of realistic evaluation.

Give Feedback Immediately

Feedback is usually most effective when it is given during or immediately after performance. When the teacher is continuously observing the student's performance, encouragement and praise or correction can be given while the student is performing the task, as well as immediately after it is completed. In other circumstances the teacher must establish a structure and routine that allow feedback to be given as soon after task completion as possible.

Give Feedback Frequently

Feedback is so vital to learning that very few, if any, responses should go without it, especially in the beginning stages of remediation. Most teachers tend to overestimate the frequency with which they provide feedback and allow the student to make many responses without feedback. This tendency must be corrected if teaching is to be maximally effective. A good rule is to give feedback at almost every opportunity. Feedback should be a consequence for task performance, an essential element in classroom structure.

STRUCTURE THE LEARNING ENVIRONMENT FOR SUCCESS

Chapter 3 suggested that remedial teaching must be highly organized. Such organization results in an environment that is structured for learning, and a highly structured environment has been found to be helpful in teaching both high-achieving and low-achieving students (Berliner, 1984; Rieth et al., 1981). Structure includes classroom expectations, rules, routines, and consequences for misbehavior—in short, it sets the social-emotional climate of the classroom. In a well-structured classroom expectations are clear, rules are simple, routines are dependable, and consequences are consistent. Such a structure creates an atmosphere that is conducive to learning and good teacher-pupil relationships.

Expect Good Behavior and Performance

Teachers can communicate their expectations for students in many ways. A pleasant, positive, but businesslike attitude toward academic work is important. The atmosphere of the classroom, including the teacher's demeanor, should communicate to students, "I expect you to behave appropriately and complete your academic work with a high degree of accuracy, and I will be pleased when you do so." Students should be able to expect that their school and classroom will be safe, orderly, and academically focused.

Keep the Rules Simple

Rules for behavior need to be kept short and simple, as discussed in chapter 2. This suggestion applies to all classroom rules, including those covering academic responses and routines. The teacher should determine which rules and routines are essential for efficient classroom operation and should concentrate on making them work. Rules governing movement about the room, talking in turn, and completing assigned tasks should not be complicated. Likewise, routines for distributing and collecting materials, preparing to leave the room, and following a schedule of activities should be clear and simple. When the structure of the classroom is elaborate, students are likely to become confused about what is expected, required, tolerated, and prohibited.

Build Rewards into the Structure

Adults, including teachers, often tend to assume that appropriate performance and behavior are their own rewards (Strain, Lambert, Kerr, Stagg, & Lenkner, 1983). For many students with learning and behavior problems—and probably for most other students as well—this is not the case. A good classroom structure emphasizes explicit positive consequences for cooperative, productive behavior. The teacher must arrange rewards for good performance as an integral part of the structure, scheduling positive consequences for appropriate academic responses and conduct. The consequences need not be extrinsic rewards, such as food or trinkets, although such rewards might be necessary for some students. The teacher must develop competence in finding meaningful consequences for individual students and in helping students learn to work for more mature rewards (i.e., for social praise and attention rather than food or trinkets or for intrinsic rewards related to successful performance rather than praise from others).

Adhere Firmly and Consistently to the Structure

Rewards are effective only when they are kept in the proper relationship to performance. The teacher must be firm and consistent in providing rewards only after appropriate responses are made. The reward-now-perform-later plea of students must be resisted. Likewise, if the structure established by the teacher calls for an aversive consequence for certain behavior, the teacher must not allow that behavior to go unpunished (see Kauffman, 1985; Kerr & Nelson, 1983; and Polsgrove, 1983, for discussion of the uses and misuses of punishment). The primary aspects of a well-structured classroom environment are clear directions, firm expectations, and consistent follow-through in applying consequences (Haring & Phillips, 1962). However, consistency does not mean rigidity. Some circumstances require that routines be varied or that rules be broken. Nonetheless, if classroom rules and routines are varied at the whim of either the teacher or the students, learning cannot be optimal.

Develop a Good Teacher-Pupil Relationship

Good teacher-pupil relationships are based on mutual respect and trust. Many students with learning and behavior problems neither respect nor trust teachers. It is the teacher's responsibility to show respect for students as individuals and to demonstrate reasonable trust in them in spite of a lack of reciprocal regard. Students are most apt to learn respect if their teacher's behavior is fair, consistent, and task-centered. An effective teacher need not become a confidant of the students; lasting confidence grows out of a history of predictable interactions. The teacher can develop a sound and productive relationship with students in a variety of ways.

1. demonstrating concern for individuals by gearing teaching to specific needs
2. remediating learning problems through skillful instruction
3. making learning enjoyable by exciting interest and providing rewards for appropriate performance
4. remaining confident in students' ability to learn
5. being cheerful, pleasant, and fair but firm, consistent, and predictable in interactions with pupils

MONITOR STUDENT PERFORMANCE AND KEEP USEFUL RECORDS

Monitoring student performance and keeping records of progress are essential features of effective teaching (see Berliner, 1984; Fuchs & Fuchs, 1984; Lovitt, 1977, 1981; Wesson, Skiba, Sevcik, King, & Deno, 1984). Monitoring progress means checking frequently to see that students are on task and completing their work correctly. This process requires the teacher to move about the room, interacting frequently with students (giving feedback, prompting, helping). Good record keeping is important in evaluating and planning instruction. Accurate, objective records serve several purposes.

1. They provide feedback to the teacher regarding the adequacy of instruction (by indicating the rate and accuracy of student responses to the curriculum).
2. They simplify communication with other teachers and with parents (by conveying precisely and succinctly how the student is performing).
3. They provide a guide to future instruction (by indicating when a student should move on to new tasks or should repeat previous tasks).

Keep a Log of Teaching Activities

A teacher's log should provide a brief, narrative account of the instructional tasks presented, the materials used, each student's responses to the tasks, and the teacher's evaluation of the outcome (see chapter 3). Many teachers find a card file system particularly useful as a log. It is important to date each entry so that the log becomes a chronology of instruction. Anecdotal records of the student's social-interpersonal behavior should also be entered in the log so that the relationship between academic and social learning can be observed. Entries in the log, including the teacher's evaluation of instruction, must be kept accurate and objective if the log is to serve its intended purpose. Any record of subjective impressions and feelings should be kept as a separate set of notes. The log should summarize the teacher's instructional activities so that each student's educational experience can be documented for parents and other professionals and for IEP and evaluation conferences.

Measure and Chart the Student's Progress

The student's progress in learning specific skills or social behaviors should be measured frequently (see Lovitt, 1981; Wesson et al., 1984). Technically adequate measurement—frequent (at least several times per week) but brief samples of the student's performance on curriculum tasks—is invaluable in making instructional decisions. Plotting the student's performance on a graph can be exciting and motivating for both the student and the teacher. The visual feedback from a graph is more immediate and understandable than the information obtained from written reports or summary tables. Whenever possible, students should be encouraged to maintain their own graphs, since the graphing itself is often a reinforcing activity.

Test What You Teach

Tests that are not based on the curriculum are of little value in assessing what has been taught. Many norm-referenced tests contain a high percentage of items to which a student may never have been exposed. If the purpose of testing is to assess what has been learned from instruction, the tests must present items of a type that has been taught (Berliner, 1985; see also Resnick & Resnick, 1985). Thus, the teacher who wants to measure the effects of instruction must either teach the types of tasks known to comprise the test or construct a test based on the types of items that have already been taught.

SUMMARY

Successful remedial teaching, whether accomplished by regular or special education teachers, requires specific teaching competencies. These scientifically based competencies must be applied artfully to the solution of students' learning difficulties. The competencies involve making an initial assessment, setting goals and objectives, analyzing tasks, presenting tasks, giving feedback, structuring the learning environment, and monitoring and measuring student progress. Mastery of these skills enables the teacher to provide an environment in which a student can learn both academic skills and appropriate social behavior.

REFERENCES

Berliner, D. (1984). The half-full glass: A review of research on teaching. In P. L. Hosford (Ed.), *Using what we know about teaching.* Alexandria, VA: Association for Supervision and Curriculum Development.

_____. (1985, April 26). School improvement research: Its impact on teaching. Presentation at the University of Virginia, Charlottesville.

Engelmann, S., & Carnine, D. (1982). *Theory of instruction: Principles and applications.* New York: Irvington.

Englert, C. S. (1984). Effective direct instruction practices in special education settings. *Remedial and Special Education, 5*(2), 38–47.

Fuchs, L. S., & Fuchs, D. (1984). Criterion-referenced assessment without measurement: How accurate for special education? *Remedial and Special Education, 5*(4), 29–32.

Hosford, P. L. (1984). The art of applying the science of education. In P. L. Hosford (Ed.), *Using what we know about teaching.* Alexandria, VA: Association for Supervision and Curriculum Development.

Howell, K. W. (1985). A task-analysis approach to social behavior. *Remedial and Special Education, 6*(2), 24–30.

Kauffman, J. M. (1985). *Characteristics of children's behavior disorders* (3rd ed.). Columbus, OH: Charles E. Merrill.

Kerr, M. M., & Nelson, C. M. (1983). *Strategies for managing behavior problems in the classroom.* Columbus, OH: Charles E. Merrill.

Lovitt, T. C. (1977). *In spite of my resistance—I've learned from children.* Columbus, OH: Charles E. Merrill.

_____. (1981). Charting academic performances of mildly handicapped youngsters. In J. M. Kauffman & D. P. Hallahan (Eds.), *Handbook of special education.* Englewood Cliffs, NJ: Prentice-Hall.

Mager, R. F. (1962). *Preparing instructional objectives.* Palo Alto, CA: Fearon.

Polsgrove, L. (Ed.). (1983). Aversive control in the classroom. *Exceptional Education Quarterly, 3*(4), special issue.

Resnick, D. P., & Resnick, L. B. (1985). Standards, curriculum, and performance: A historical and comparative perspective. *Educational Researcher, 14*(4), 5–20.

Rieth, H. J., Polsgrove, L., & Semmel, M. I. (1981). Instructional variables that make a difference: Attention to task and beyond. *Exceptional Education Quarterly, 2*(3), 61–71.

Rincover, A. (1978). Variables affecting stimulus fading and discriminative responding in psychotic children. *Journal of Abnormal Psychology, 87,* 541–553.

Shinn, M., & Marston, D. (1985). Differentiating mildly handicapped, low-achieving, and regular education students: A curriculum-based approach. *Remedial and Special Education, 6*(2), 31–38.

Stevens, R., & Rosenshine, B. (1981). Advances in research on teaching. *Exceptional Education Quarterly, 2*(1), 1–9.

Strain, P. S., Lambert, D. L., Kerr, M. M., Stagg, V., & Lenkner, D. A. (1983). Naturalistic assessment of children's compliance to teachers' requests and consequences for compliance. *Journal of Applied Behavior Analysis, 16*, 243–249.

Wesson, C., Skiba, R., Sevcik, B., King, R. P., & Deno, S. (1984). The effects of technically adequate instructional data on achievement. *Remedial and Special Education, 5*(5), 17–22.

6

Early Intervention

Early intervention in special education has two major goals. The first is to identify high-risk children and develop intervention procedures that preclude or greatly reduce the probability that such children will encounter significant difficulties in learning. The second is to use therapeutic teaching methods that minimize existing problems, provide solutions to problems, or prevent complications. Although the first goal is the ultimate goal of special education, the second has been the focus of most special education and related services. Educators have tended to wait for problems to manifest themselves before taking any action—they have been more involved in secondary than in primary prevention.

The value of early identification and prevention, both to individuals and to social institutions, seems obvious. The student and her parents are spared considerable psychological suffering when unnecessary difficulties in learning are avoided. And communities and institutions reap benefits in human and economic resources when learning and behavior problems are prevented. Nevertheless, the implementation of preventive programs in the schools is not universally lauded, nor are the preventive efforts of individual teachers always accepted without controversy (Bower, 1982).

Most people do agree that a major concern of the schools is the prevention of learning problems, and nearly all educators agree that two fundamental principles of prevention are early detection of problems and good teaching. Instruments and procedures designed to assist teachers in early detection of problems are readily available. And agreement apears to be increasing among educators about what constitutes good teaching (see Berliner, 1984; Lloyd & Carnine, 1981). Thus, the possibilities for effective early intervention are improving.

EARLY DETECTION

Studies of the effectiveness of early intervention with handicapped children have yielded promising results (Berrueta-Clement, Schweinhart, Barnett, Epstein, & Weikert, 1984; Frank, 1985). Whether the youngsters involved have been autistic preschoolers (Lovaas, 1982) or preschool-primary children who were aggressive and oppositional to their parents (Strain, Steele, Ellis, & Timm, 1982), the research clearly indicates the value of early identification and intervention. The earlier the intervention in these studies, the greater the benefits to the children involved.

Early detection of learning and behavior problems should be a systematic and continuous effort of all professionals who deal with children and youth. Effective and efficient early identification cannot be accomplished through testing or observation alone; both keen observation of learning and behavior in the everyday environment and the use of screening instruments are needed. We first list the major behavioral indicators of potential problems, then describe several screening instruments that educators may find useful.

Behavioral Indicators of Potential Problems

The problem behaviors listed in this section must be viewed within the broad context of current knowledge of child development. Every child exhibits some inappropriate behaviors. Furthermore, many normal children temporarily exhibit a large number of behaviors characteristic of children with severe learning problems. Maladaptive behavior and academic deficits should be viewed as pathological or handicapping only when demonstrated to a marked extent and over a protracted period of time (Bower, 1982). This does not mean that preventive action should be taken only after a child has shown a severe and chronic learning or behavioral difficulty. However, it does mean that the child will not be considered to have a serious problem on the basis of an isolated incident or a temporary condition. It also means that the child's behavior must be judged in terms of developmental norms and the demands of his particular school environment.

Only major categories of problem behavior are outlined here. Behavior relevant to preschool and primary age children is stressed because preventive efforts are logically concentrated at that age level.

Indications of Low Self-Esteem or Depression.   Children with academic and/or social learning problems often reveal that they do not feel good about themselves; they feel incompetent, inadequate, and worthless. Depression is now recognized as a serious problem among children and youth, and its manifestations often parallel those seen in adults (Kaslow & Rehm, 1983; Kauffman, 1985). The teacher may suspect that a child has such negative feelings about self or is depressed if she exhibits several of the following characteristics persistently.

1. speaks disparagingly about self; expresses feelings of worthlessness, self-reproach, or excessive or inappropriate guilt
2. is usually sad or unhappy, seldom smiles, cries often or for no apparent reason
3. expresses feelings of hopelessness, does not believe that things will get better
4. demonstrates inability to make everyday decisions
5. cannot concentrate
6. cannot seem to experience pleasure or joy
7. speaks of or attempts suicide or self-injury
8. has sleep difficulties (is either not able to sleep or sleeps excessively)
9. has appetite disturbances (chronically overeats or eats too little) or weight problems (markedly overweight or underweight)
10. is excessively active or lethargic
11. is chronically tired, has no energy
12. is typically unwilling to attempt new or difficult tasks
13. is unrealistically fearful of new situations
14. is excessively shy and withdrawn
15. lacks appropriate self-reliance, often says "I can't"
16. shows excessive concern over acceptance by others
17. demonstrates inability to accept errors or correct mistakes
18. shows extreme negative reaction to minor failures
19. has a slovenly, unkempt appearance
20. is unable to evaluate behavior realistically, brags excessively or denigrates accomplishments

Disturbed Relations with Peers.   A child with learning or behavior problems is often a social misfit in the classroom. Problems in peer relations may be indicated if the child consistently

1. has no close friends or chums in the peer group
2. is avoided by other children in games and activities
3. hits, bites, kicks, or otherwise physically assaults peers

4. is incessantly teasing or teased by others
5. belittles accomplishments of others
6. seeks company of much older or younger children
7. withdraws from group activities

Inappropriate Relationships with Teachers, Parents, and Other Authority Figures. A constructive relationship with authority is often a special problem for children with problems in school. Adults who are responsible for a child are often in a quandary when he frequently

1. refuses reasonable requests
2. defies direct commands
3. disobeys classroom rules
4. encourages peers to disrupt the class or defy adults
5. strikes, bites, kicks, or otherwise attempts to injure adults
6. runs away from school or home or leaves the classroom without permission
7. steals
8. lies
9. manipulates adults for personal advantage
10. is overprotected, seldom allowed to enter new age-appropriate situations alone or to take reasonable risks
11. is overindulged, "spoiled" by being given noncontingent or excessive rewards

Other Signs of Social-Emotional Problems. In addition to maladaptive behavior related specifically to self, peers, and authority, the child with problems at school may exhibit a variety of other inappropriate responses. The teacher may observe that the child frequently

1. exhibits behavior inappropriate to the context (e.g., laughs when someone is hurt, interprets figures of speech literally)
2. is overly suspicious or jealous of others
3. complains of physical symptoms, pains, or fears in mildly stressful situations; complains of every little hurt
4. is in constant motion; compulsively manipulates objects, moves about the room excessively
5. engages in repetitive, stereotyped motor behavior, such as tics, nail-biting, thumb-sucking, or rocking
6. talks excessively, frequently talks without permission or interrupts conversations
7. explains inappropriate behavior by rationalization or intellectualization

8. does not seem to learn from experience, does not improve with usual disciplinary measures
9. acts impulsively and shows poor judgment, does not seem to consider or understand the consequences of her behavior
10. fails to learn even though there is no evidence of intellectual, sensory, or health problems
11. makes meaningless or animal noises
12. has not mastered bowel or bladder control
13. shows extreme interest in monsters, war, fighting, or gruesome events
14. eats inedible materials
15. has violent outbursts of temper
16. lacks curiosity
17. daydreams, sits with a vacant expression

Deficits in Speech and Language.   A child's speech and language often betray his emotional status or intellectual or academic competence in unique ways. A teacher may suspect that a child is experiencing social-emotional difficulty and/or a speech or language problem when the child consistently

1. does not speak
2. speaks only when spoken to
3. speaks with inappropriate pitch (voice too high-pitched or too low-pitched for age and sex)
4. speaks with inappropriate volume (voice too loud or too soft)
5. has irritating vocal quality (voice too harsh, hoarse, nasal)
6. speaks with marked dysfluency; stutters, clutters, or otherwise interrupts the flow of speech
7. uses primarily jargon, neologisms, profanity, or other speech inappropriate to the context
8. misarticulates (mispronounces) many words
9. has difficulty learning signs and symbols
10. cannot interpret directions
11. lacks ability to describe persons, places, and things clearly
12. cannot identify an object from its verbal description
13. does not comprehend simple sentences

Disordered Temporal Relationships.   Orientation in time and ability to sequence events are required for adequate social and academic functioning. A child's behavior may indicate a learning problem if she typically

1. cannot tell a story in sequence

2. does not repeat sound patterns in order
3. cannot remember a sequence of events
4. is chronically late
5. is absentminded, forgets important events
6. is unable to plan a sequence of behavior
7. refuses to talk about the past
8. cannot shift readily from one activity to another
9. is easily confused by a change in routine
10. confuses seasons, months, years, days, and other intervals of time after the age at which most children learn these concepts
11. cannot remember basic auditory sequences such as telephone numbers, the alphabet, or nursery rhymes

Difficulties in Auditory and Visual Perception. The child's ability to integrate what he sees and hears in a meaningful way is essential for progress in school. The child may have a serious problem in interpreting visual and auditory stimuli if he consistently

1. attends to irrelevant details
2. cannot organize materials
3. loses place frequently when copying
4. has difficulty cutting, coloring, or pasting
5. does not discriminate differences in size, shape, color, or perspective
6. does not discriminate changes in pitch, loudness, or timbre of sounds
7. has difficulty recognizing common objects when a part is missing
8. has difficulty recognizing sounds made by common objects
9. does not understand words indicating position (e.g., *up, down, above, in*)
10. cannot relate pictures to parts of a story, does not understand the meaning of pictures
11. has difficulty drawing simple geometric shapes (e.g., cannot copy a square, circle, rectangle)
12. is unable to recognize rhymes or give rhyming words
13. makes poorly formed or reversed letters
14. has difficulty drawing corners or angles
15. has difficulty spelling phonetic word units or words
16. makes facial contortions when doing visual tasks

Poor Quantitative Reasoning and Computational Skills. Quantitative reasoning and computational skills are considered basic components of intelligence. They are a vital part of school learning and are necessary for independent functioning in our society. When a child has a learning problem in this area, she often

1. has difficulty with concepts of inequality (e.g., more-less, larger-smaller, heavier-lighter)
2. does not understand one-to-one correspondence
3. is unable to count to a number appropriate for her age
4. has marked difficulty learning basic number facts
5. does not understand the value of coins
6. does not understand place value (cannot regroup for borrowing or carrying)
7. can make necessary computations but is unable to organize information from a story problem
8. relies excessively on finger or bead counting for simple computations

Deficits in Basic Motor Skills. The child's abilities in the area of fine and gross motor skills often are important to his adjustment in school. A problem in motor learning may be suspected if the child typically

1. is unable to balance on one foot
2. has an unsteady, awkward, or unusual gait
3. is unable to throw and catch a ball
4. does not hold a pencil or scissors normally
5. has poor coordination, is clumsy and inaccurate in movement, often accidentally breaks things
6. cannot tie shoes, button or zip clothing
7. avoids physical activities or sports

Screening Instruments

Rating scales, checklists, and other types of tests that formalize or standardize observations often help teachers survey the behavior and achievement of their pupils in specific areas so that learning or behavioral difficulties can be identified. Brief, easily administered tests that have good predictive validity and that sample the skills the child needs to succeed in school are most useful to classroom teachers (see Wallace & Larsen, 1986). Screening devices are not diagnostic tests but are instruments that identify children with a high probability of difficulty in school. (Bower, 1982). Any child whose score on a screening instrument indicates a possible learning or behavior problem *must* be evaluated more thoroughly before any determination of exceptionality can be made.

The number of rating scales, checklists, and observation schedules available to school personnel is vast and growing. Teachers must be careful to select screening devices that meet the needs of particular situations (age level, setting, type of educational program). We include here brief descriptions of several instruments that may be administered by the classroom teacher (see Salvia & Ysseldyke, 1985; Wallace & Larsen, 1986; Ysseldyke & Shinn, 1981; and Zigmond, Vallecorsa, & Silverman, 1983, for further description and discussion of assessment devices). Other tests and scales that might be useful for screening and assessment in specific areas of learning are listed in each of the chapters in part two.

Barclay Classroom Assessment System (BCAS) (Barclay, 1983). This instrument is a screening device for Grades 3 through 6 and is designed to be administered to an entire class of students. Each student completes a multiple choice evaluation booklet, after which the teacher completes a brief checklist on each student's booklet. Administration is estimated to take less than one hour. The booklets are designed to be computer scanned and scored by the publisher. The publisher returns computer-generated reports for the class as a whole and for individual students. The classroom summary report includes referral recommendations for students suspected of having problems in self-confidence, self-control, physical skills, attitudes toward school, peer support, verbal skills, and teacher support. Students who appear to have the best potential as peer tutors are identified, as are those who may have achievement problems and those who may be gifted. Those areas of greatest concern to students in the class are identified. Individual student reports include profiles of behavioral characteristics (e.g., adaptive social skills, introversion, leadership, energy level); comparisons of self, peer, and teacher ratings; and achievement summaries and recommendations for instruction.

Basic School Skills Inventory—Diagnostic (BSSI-D) (Hammill & Leigh, 1983). This test is both norm-referenced and criterion-referenced. It is a readiness test designed for use with children between the ages of 4 years and 6 years, 11 months (6.11). There are 110 test items distributed across six subtests: daily living skills, spoken language, reading, writing, mathematics, and classroom behavior. A screening version of the test (the BSSI-S) is available; it consists of 20 items drawn from the 110 comprising the BSSI-D. The BSSI instruments present a series of precisely stated questions about the child's school-related performance, each followed by a brief explanation that defines and clarifies the performance that should be expected. The tests are administered individually, usually by the classroom teacher, and are helpful in identifying children who are significantly below their peers in the skills sampled and documenting educational progress.

Boehm Test of Basic Concepts (BTBC) (Boehm, 1971). This test is appropriate for use with kindergartners and first and second graders. The test samples 50 specific concepts (e.g., top, over, always, half) in four categories: space, quantity, time, and miscellaneous. The teacher reads instructions aloud (e.g., "Look at the apples. Mark the apple that is whole"), and the children mark a test booklet containing pictures and forms. Administration can be handled with small groups of 8 to 12 children and requires 15 to 20 minutes for kindergarten children. The purposes of the test are to measure children's mastery of concepts considered necessary for achievement in the first years of school and to identify the specific concepts requiring instruction.

Brigance Diagnostic Inventory of Early Development (BDIED) (Brigance, 1978). This is a criterion-referenced instrument designed for use with children from birth to age 7. It can be used to describe the developmental level of a child, identify areas of relative strength and weakness, support decisions regarding further assessment or referral, and provide information relevant to choice of instructional objectives. Use of the instrument may involve observation and parent interviews as well as direct testing. The test includes 98 skill sequences grouped into 11 areas: preambulatory motor skills and behavior, gross motor skills and behavior, fine motor skills and behavior, self-help skills, prespeech, speech and language, general knowledge and comprehension, readiness, basic reading skills, manuscript writing (printing), and math. Also available are the Diagnostic Inventory of Basic Skills (Brigance, 1977), designed for use with children functioning at kindergarten through sixth grade levels, and the Diagnostic Inventory of Essential Skills (Brigance, 1980), intended for use at the secondary school level.

CIRCUS (Educational Testing Service, 1979). This instrument is designed for use with children from prekindergarten through third grade. It provides a large number of subtests that are relatively easy to administer, score, and interpret in terms of norms or specific criteria. Directions and guidelines for interpretation are set forth clearly in the manual. The battery of subtests (grouped according to skills appropriate for the age levels) is designed to be used in diagnosing the instructional needs of individual children. The subtests include skills in prereading, mathematics, listening, general information, productive language, oral reading, writing, and a variety of other areas important for success in school.

Early Screening Inventory (Meisels & Wiske, 1983). This screening device is designed to be administered individually to children 4 to 6 years of age. Administration takes approximately 15 minutes. The test has four sections: (1) initial screening items tap the child's ability to respond to an unstructured drawing task requiring fine motor control; (2) visual-motor/adaptive items examine fine motor control, eye-hand coordination, ability to remember visual sequences, ability to draw visual forms, and ability to reproduce visual three-dimensional structures; (3) language and cognition items assess comprehension and expression, ability to reason, ability to count, and ability to remember auditory sequences; (4) gross motor/body awareness items examine balance, large motor coordination, and ability to imitate body positions from visual cues. Also included as part of the screening kit is a parent questionnaire that inquires about the child's medical, family, and developmental history.

School/Home Observation and Referral System (SHORS) (Evans,

1978). This screening instrument is designed to provide training for teachers, parents, and others who are caretakers of young children. It provides instruction in making referrals to appropriate specialists, communicating information about a child to others, and implementing suggestions or intervention plans devised by specialists. Orientation activities and materials, printed instructions, and record-keeping forms are included. The teacher's guide gives clear directions for setting up observation and referral records. Specific guidelines for each of seven checklists are provided, including a short listing of things to "observe for" and specialists to "refer to." Also included is a discussion of the importance of screening for problems in a given area, more detailed description of what to look for, a method of handling referrals, and the requirements of following up a problem.

Test of Early Reading Ability (TERA) (Reid, Hresko, & Hammill, 1981). This is an individually administered, untimed test for children between the ages of 4 years and 7 years, 11 months (7.11). It can be used to identify those children who are significantly behind their peers in reading and to document progress in a child's learning to read. It consists of 50 items drawn from the following areas: meaning construction (e.g., reading signs and logos), alphabet knowledge (e.g., letter naming), and the conventions of written language (e.g., punctuation and left-right orientation). Each item on the test is scored as pass or fail.

GOOD TEACHING

Our thesis is that teachers must be primarily concerned with instructional and behavior management variables as etiological factors—not with other causes over which they have little or no control. It follows that our major concern in the areas of early intervention and prevention is competent teaching. If teachers are to effective preventive agents, they must commit their professional efforts to refining their teaching skills.

Good teaching implies early identification of learning and behavioral difficulties through observation and testing. It also implies teacher responsibility for children's learning. Without this assumption the onus of school failure falls on children, who should not be required to bear that burden, or on the negative influences of our society, for which no remedy can be expected to affect the crucial years of children's lives.

The health-related disciplines have found that fostering good health practices is the best preventive strategy for most diseases; similarly, educators are discovering that competent classroom instruction is the most effective strategy for preventing the majority of learning and behavior problems. The earliest school-based intervention—and the best preventive measure we can suggest—is application by all teachers of what research supports as effective teaching. We have discussed principles of behavior management, academic remediation, and teaching competencies in previous chapters. We restate here in brief form several principles of good teaching that are supported by recent educational research.

Allocate Time to Learning

Commonsensical as it may seem, one of the most important factors governing how much children learn is how much time their teachers allocate to instruction. Good teachers understand the critical nature of how the school day is divided for various activities, and they make sure that their students' schedules include as much time as possible for the academic curriculum. Particularly when students are having learning problems, there is no justification for letting nonacademic activities consume most of the hours set aside for schooling. Teachers must set priorities for the allocation of time, and good teachers give priority to the academic core curriculum.

Keep Students Engaged in Learning

Not only do good teachers make sure that sufficient time is allocated to instruction in core academic subjects, but they also maintain students' on-task behavior during the time allocated. Students must know what they are to do and how to do it, have frequent opportunities to respond, and get frequent feedback from the teacher. Allocating time to instruction is not enough; a high percentage of that time must involve students in active response to the curriculum.

Provide a High Level of Success for Students

Students learn best when they experience a high rate of success in their assigned tasks. Little or nothing is learned when a student's experiences are primarily failures. Good teaching normally requires that learning tasks match students' abilities so that they experience success at least 80% of the time. If a student has a history of low achievement or school failure, he should be given tasks at which success will be experienced at least 90% of the time. Such a high rate of success can be provided without the student's becoming bored only if the teacher assesses the student's ability accurately, chooses tasks carefully, and provides appropriate feedback on performance. Practice at a high level of success must be maintained until the student has fully mastered the tasks.

Assess What Has Been Learned

Testing and other means of assessment must be directly related to the curriculum if they are to be functional for the teacher and the student (and, ultimately, for educational policy makers). Good teaching requires keeping up with what students are learning (and not learning) so that review and mastery lessons can solidify the skills and knowledge that students have recently acquired and new lessons can fit logically between what students have learned and what they do not yet know. This kind of assessment involves frequent (daily or almost daily) measurement of what the student can do, particularly if the student has learning problems. Frequent, precise measurement and careful record keeping are essential tasks of competent teaching.

Keep the Classroom Structure Firm and Positive

A good teacher has a highly structured classroom in which students know what is expected of them and what they can expect from their teacher. The teacher is directive, firmly in control. But the emphasis is on recognition and praise for appropriate conduct and performance. When the teacher focuses on what children are to do rather than on what they are not to do, the climate of the classroom is conducive to the students' productivity and the teacher's mental health. Such an environment does not require that students' inappropriate responses go without correction or that punishment is always avoided. It does suggest, however, a primary emphasis on positive teacher-pupil interactions; a good teacher is genuinely concerned about the feelings and welfare of students.

SUMMARY

The goals of early intervention are early detection of high-risk children and prevention through therapeutic teaching. Studies of early intervention have yielded promising results. It appears that the earlier intervention can begin for children with learning and behavioral difficulties, the better the ultimate outcome. Early detection of learning and behavior problems requires careful observation to identify potential problem areas of development—low self-esteem or depression, disturbed relations with peers, inappropriate relationship to authority figures (teachers, parents, and other adults), a variety of other social-emotional problems, deficits in speech and language, problems in temporal relationships, difficulties in auditory and visual perception, poor quantitative reasoning or computational skills, and deficits in basic motor skills. A variety of tests, checklists, and other instruments are available to assist teachers in systematizing their observations for screening purposes.

Early intervention and prevention are also accomplished by good teaching—with teaching practices based on instructional and behavior management research. Good teaching involves allocating sufficient time to academic instruction, keeping students actively engaged in learning during the time allocated for instruction, providing a high level of success for students, continuously and precisely assessing what has been learned, and keeping the classroom firmly structured in a positive way.

REFERENCES

Barclay, J. R. (1983). *The Barclay Classroom Assessment System.* Los Angeles: Western Psychological Services.

Berliner, D. (1984). The half-full glass: A review of research on teaching. In P. L. Hosford (Ed.), *Using what we know about teaching.* Alexandria, VA: Association for Supervision and Curriculum Development.

Berrueta-Clement, J. R., Schweinhart, L. J., Barnett, W. S., Epstein, A. S., & Weikert, D. P. (1984). *Changed lives: The effects of the Perry preschool program on youths through age 19* (Monograph No. 8). Ypsilanti, MI: High/Scope Education Research Foundation.

Boehm, A. E. (1971). *Boehm Test of Basic Concepts.* Cleveland: Psychological Corporation.

Bower, E. M. (1982). *Early identification of emotionally handicapped children in school* (3rd ed.). Springfield, IL: Charles C. Thomas.

Brigance, A. (1977). *Brigance Diagnostic Inventory of Basic Skills.* North Billerica, MA: Curriculum Associates.

——— . (1978). *Brigance Diagnostic Inventory of Early Development.* North Billerica, MA: Curriculum Associates.

——— . (1980). *Brigance Diagnostic Inventory of Essential Skills.* North Billerica, MA: Curriculum Associates.

Educational Testing Service. (1979). *CIRCUS.* Princeton, NJ: Author.

Evans, J. S. (1978). *School/Home Observation and Referral System.* New York: CTB/McGraw-Hill.

Frank, M. (Ed.). (1985). *Infant intervention programs: Truths and untruths.* New York: Haworth.

Hammill, D. D., & Leigh, J. E. (1983). *Basic School Skills Inventory— Diagnostic.* Austin, TX: Pro-Ed.

Kaslow, N. J. & Rehm, L. P. (1983). Childhood depression. In R. J. Morris & T. R. Kratochwill (Eds.), *The practice of child therapy.* New York: Pergamon Press.

Kauffman, J. M. (1985). *Characteristics of children's behavior disorders* (3rd ed.). Columbus, OH: Charles E. Merrill.

Keogh, B. K., & Becker, L. D. (1973). Early detection of learning problems: Questions, cautions, and guidelines. *Exceptional Children, 40,* 5–11.

Lloyd, J. W., & Carnine, D. (Eds.). (1981). Structured instruction: Effective teaching of essential skills. *Exceptional Education Quarterly, 2* (1), special issue.

Lovaas, O. I. (1982, September). *An overview of the young autism project.* Paper presented at the annual convention of the American Psychological Association, Washington, DC.

Meisels, S. J., & Wiske, M. S. (1983). *Early Screening Inventory.* New York: Teachers College Press.

Reid, D. K., Hresko, W. P., & Hammill, D. D. (1981). *The Test of Early Reading Ability.* Austin, TX: Pro-Ed.

Salvia, J., & Ysseldyke, J. E. (1985). *Assessment in special and remedial education* (3rd ed.). Boston: Houghton Mifflin.

Strain, P. S., Steele, P., Ellis, T., & Timm, M. (1982). Longterm effects of oppositional child treatment with mothers as therapists and therapist trainers. *Journal of Applied Behavior Analysis, 15,* 163–169.

Wallace, G., & Larsen, S. L. (1986). *Assessment: Evaluating students with learning and behavior problems.* Austin, TX: Pro-Ed.

Ysseldyke, J. E., & Shinn, M. R. (1981). Psychoeducational evaluation. In J. M. Kauffman & D. P. Hallahan (Eds.), *Handbook of special education.* Englewood Cliffs, NJ: Prentice-Hall.

Zigmond, N., Vallecorsa, A., & Silverman, R. (1983). *Assessment for instructional planning in special education.* Englewood Cliffs, NJ: Prentice-Hall.

PART TWO

A Guide to Instructional Activities

Sound principles are needed to guide teaching practice, but sound practice goes far beyond a mere understanding of principles. It is not enough for a teacher to know that behavior that is reinforced is more likely to occur again or that remedial teaching involves continuous assessment of a student's performance. The teacher must know how to reinforce appropriate behavior and how to assess a student's performance. A major purpose of this book is to provide the teacher with an array of specific behavior management and instructional activities that have proven value in the classroom.

Chapter 7 suggests techniques for dealing with social-behavioral problems. Chapters 8 through 12 contain suggested instructional activities for remediating specific learning problems in the areas of spoken language, reading, written language, math, and study skills. Each of the chapters includes a brief statement of the skills required to perform adequately in that area, followed by suggestions for assessment of the student's problems—including observation, informal appraisal techniques, and formal tests. Instructional suggestions are organized by teaching programs and specific teaching activities. The use of the microcomputer in each area is also discussed in each chapter.

We have attempted to organize the teaching activities within each chapter according to the sequential development of skills. However, a full exposition of sequential skill development in any curriculum area goes far beyond the skeletal framework of our chapters. We hope that our outlines of sequential learning provide a beginning point for further study and analysis.

Many teaching activities are intended for use with students who are deficient in basic skills. However, we have also included specific activities for older students within each chapter. The source of some of our remedial activities is our own teaching experience. Many of the activities, however, did not originate with us, and the sources of those suggestions, or of slight variations of them, have been cited wherever possible. In many cases the original sources of tried-and-true activities simply could not be found.

7

Social Behavior

Social-behavioral development is inseparably linked to a student's acquisition of academic skills. Inappropriate behavior seriously limits the student's chances for success at school; conversely, school failure often prompts undesirable behavior. Many students who have learning problems are distinguished by their poor work habits, nonproductivity, uncooperativeness, and lack of social graces (Hallahan, Kauffman, & Lloyd, 1985; Kauffman, 1985; Kerr & Nelson, 1983). Remediation of these students' social-behavioral deficits is as important as remediation of their academic problems. Frequently, it is necessary to establish good work habits and eliminate problem behavior before academic remediation can be accomplished.

The objectives of behavior management should be to prepare the student for academic learning and increase the efficiency and effectiveness of instruction. As suggested in previous chapters, the teacher must deal with work habits and social behavior directly. Teachers must concern themselves with two basic questions.

1. What academic responses (e.g., incomplete work, work refusal, high error rates) prevent the student from learning efficiently?

2. What social-behavioral characteristics (e.g., daydreaming, aggression, talking out) interfere with the student's learning?

Excessively aggressive or shy behavior and poor self-control are problems in school, but they also seriously limit social adjustment and opportunities for education and employment throughout life (Kauffman, 1985). Consequently, intervention to change such characteristics is critical from a developmental perspective.

ASSESSMENT

Much of the assessment of social-behavioral problems requires direct observation of behavior, analysis of the antecedent conditions and contingencies involved, and experienced clinical judgment—none of which is available in the form of standardized tests. Screening instruments are available, however, for identifying potential problems. Screening is only a preliminary step in assessment, designed to identify students with potential problems that require further study.

Screening Instruments

In addition to the screening devices mentioned in chapter 6, the tests included here may be of value to the teacher. Each of these screening devices samples at least three sources of information: teacher, self, and peer or parent ratings. As we mentioned in chapter 5, it is important to obtain as complete a picture as possible of the student's problem early in the assessment process. The objective should be to obtain information about the student's *social ecology*, the microcommunity in which she lives. This involves consideration of much more than classroom behavior.

Child Behavior Checklist (CBCL) (Achenbach & Edelbrock, 1983). The CBCL is actually a group of scales designed to assess social competence and behavior problems. The parent rating scale (the original CBCL) can be used with children aged 4 through 16. The teacher's report form (TRF) is appropriate for boys and girls aged 6 through 16. The direct observation form (DOF) is designed to be used by an experienced observer, who observes the student for 10-minute periods in a classroom or group activity. The youth self-report (YSR) is to be filled out by young people aged 11 through 18 who have a mental age of at least 10 years and fifth grade reading skills (although it can be administered orally.)

Behavior Rating Profile: An Ecological Approach to Behavioral Assessment (BRP) (Brown & Hammill, 1978). The BRP was designed for students in Grades 1 through 7 (ages 6.5 through 13.6). It includes student (peer), teacher, and parent rating scales and a sociogram. The intent is to derive a profile of the student's adjustment in school and at home and to evaluate behavior from a variety of perspectives.

A Process for the Assessment of Effective Student Functioning (Lambert, Hartsough, & Bower, 1979). This screening process parallels the work of Bower (1981), who did extensive studies of maladaptive school behavior beginning in the 1950s. Separate forms are used for primary, elementary, and secondary levels. At each level the student's behavior is evaluated through teacher, self, and peer ratings. The purpose of the process is to select for further study those students who seem likely to be exhibiting troublesome behavior.

Direct Observation

Useful assessment of social-behavioral problems depends primarily on the classroom teacher's direct observation of what the student does and does not do. Chapter 2 presented observation and recording techniques that teachers can use. More detailed discussion of direct observation can be found in a variety of sources (e.g., Gelfand & Hartmann, 1984; Kazdin, 1984; Kerr & Nelson, 1983; Morris, 1985).

Students' problem behavior can be conceptualized in terms of excesses and deficiencies. When the teacher is assessing behavioral excesses, the following questions are pertinent.

1. What does the student do that is maladaptive?
2. How often does he do it under present conditions?
3. What environmental events seem likely to maintain the behavior?
4. How can the events that support the undesirable behavior be eliminated?

Assessment of behavioral deficiencies should address different questions.

1. What do I want the student to do?
2. How often does the student perform the desired behavior under present circumstances?
3. What approximations of the desired behavior can be identified?
4. What reinforcers can be identified that are available to the teacher, parent, or peer?
5. How can reinforcers be provided systematically for approximations of the desired behavior?

The key to management of many behavior problems is finding effective reinforcers for the student. Motivation for improved academic performance and behavioral self-control often depends on identifying what the student is willing to work to obtain and then making those items or events available, contingent upon behavioral improvement. Table 7–1 contains a list of potential reinforcers that provide a beginning point for identifying what is reinforcing for a particular student. Additional lists and suggestions for identifying reinforcers can be found in Gelfand and Hartmann (1984), Madsen and Madsen (1974), and Morris (1985).

Table 7-1.
Some Potential Reinforcers

1. Helping in the cafeteria
2. Assisting the custodian
3. Cleaning the erasers
4. Erasing the chalkboard
5. Using colored chalk
6. Watering the plants
7. Leading the pledge of allegiance
8. Decorating the bulletin board
9. Leading the line to recess or the lunchroom
10. Using a typewriter
11. Running the ditto machine
12. Stapling papers together
13. Feeding the fish or animals
14. Giving a message over the intercom
15. Writing and directing a play
16. Picking up litter on the school grounds
17. Cleaning the teacher's desk
18. Taking the class roll
19. Carrying messages to other teachers
20. Holding the door during a fire drill
21. Serving as secretary for class meetings
22. Raising or lowering the flag
23. Emptying the wastebasket
24. Carrying the wastebasket while other children clean out their desks
25. Distributing and collecting materials
26. Using an overhead projector
27. Operating a slide, filmstrip, or movie projector
28. Recording personal behavior on a graph
29. Writing with a pen or colored pencils
30. Correcting papers
31. Teaching another child
32. Playing checkers, chess, tiddlywinks, or other table games
33. Choosing a game to play
34. Being captain of a team
35. Working with clay
36. Doing "special," "the hardest," or "impossible" teacher-made arithmetic problems
37. Reading the newspaper
38. Reading or drawing a road map
39. Listening to the radio with an earplug
40. Arm wrestling
41. Reading or writing poetry
42. Learning a magic trick
43. Lighting or blowing out a candle
44. Being allowed to move desks
45. Sitting beside a friend
46. Going to the library
47. Helping the librarian
48. Writing to the author of a favorite book
49. Looking at a globe
50. Making or flying a kite
51. Popping corn
52. Making a puppet
53. Carrying the ball or bat to recess
54. Visiting with the principal
55. Making a book
56. Recording time taken to do a task
57. Having a spelling bee
58. Doing a science experiment
59. Telling the teacher when it is time to go to lunch
60. Sharpening the teacher's pencils
61. Opening the teacher's mail
62. Sitting next to the teacher at lunch
63. Doing crossword puzzles or math puzzles
64. Sweeping the floor of the classroom
65. Weighing or measuring various objects in the classroom
66. Reading a wall map
67. Giving a spelling test
68. Adjusting the window shades
69. Sewing
70. Having an arithmetic contest at the chalkboard

ABC Analysis

Adequate assessment requires that the teacher or other observer attend not only to the student's behavioral excesses and deficiencies, but also to exactly what typically happens just prior to and just after the student exhibits a problem behavior. Observation of antecedents and consequences is often referred to in the professional literature as an ABC analysis (see chapter 2). Such an analysis provides the most useful information for managing social-behavioral problems.

An ABC analysis requires consideration of the following: A—the antecedents of the behavior, the events that occur immediately before the behavior and seem to set it off or provide the occasion for it; B—the behavior itself, exactly what it is that the student does, defined precisely enough to be observed and measured reliably; and C—the consequences of the behavior, what happens immediately after the behavior and reinforces it.

First, one must consider exactly what the student does that is a problem: What does she do or say that can be observed and recorded? When did the student last exhibit the behavior? How often does the behavior occur? Does the problem seem to be getting better, worse, or staying about the same?

Second, one must consider the situations in which the behavior occurs: Does it occur in school, at home, or in both settings? If it occurs at school, in what locations or during what activities does it occur? Can particular events be identified that trigger the behavior? Who is usually with the student when she exhibits the behavior?

Third, one must consider what happens as a consequence of the student's behavior. How does the teacher (and/or other adults) usually respond? How do other students respond? Does the student usually get her own way, receive someone's attention (even if it is negative attention), or obtain some other reinforcer?

Finally, one must consider what attempts have been made to modify the behavior: What methods have been tried? For how long, by whom, and with what success has each intervention been implemented? What range of methods can be tried, given the student, other students, adults, and resources in the situation?

After considering these questions, the teacher must observe and record the student's behavior, as discussed in chapter 2. The direct daily measurement of behavior indicates the magnitude of the problem and the degree of success in resolving it.

PROGRAMS

Most social-behavioral skills are learned as part of the everyday interaction of children and youth with each other and adults. No substitute can be found for a well-managed social environment in which naturally occurring social rewards shape and maintain appropriate behavior. When maladaptive behavior is encountered, the most effective approach is to rearrange the demands of the student's everyday world and the reinforcement he receives for particular behaviors. Thus, intervention typically requires that the teacher use basic behavior modification and instructional principles, as discussed in part one, to construct a unique program for the individual student.

There are relatively few instructional materials commercially available that are specifically designed for teaching social skills. Part of the reason for this scarcity is that social skills are difficult to define and measure precisely (Bellack, 1983; Gresham, 1981; Strain, Odom, & McConnell, 1984). Nonetheless, several kits, booklets, and program descriptions focused on teaching compliance, self-control, or understanding of self and others are available. We caution that the materials and programs listed in Table 7–2 vary widely in the extent to which they have been field tested and validated. The teacher should certainly consider packaged programs, but these cannot be adequate substitutes for a contingency management system that is individually tailored (see Walker et al., 1983, for further discussion).

Table 7–2.

Selected Programs Designed to Teach Various Social-Behavioral Skills

---

Self-Management Training

The Self-Control Curriculum

    A small book containing suggested activities for teaching elementary students component skills required for self-control (available from Charles E. Merrill Publishing Company, Columbus, OH)

Teaching Behavioral Self-Control to Students

    A small book describing various self-control strategies (including self-assessment, self-monitoring, and self-reinforcement) and their classroom application for students of all ages (available from Pro-Ed, Austin, TX)

Study Strategies: A Metacognitive Approach

    A kit designed for teaching study skills to students in grades 4 through 12 (available from White Mountain Publishing Company, Rock Springs, WY)

Social Skills Training Programs

The Social Learning Curriculum

    An instructional kit designed for mildly handicapped learners that covers a variety of skills thought to be necessary for independent living and occupational competence (available from Charles E. Merrill Publishing Company, Columbus, OH)

Social Skills in the Classroom

    An extensive curriculum guide indexing 136 different skills, including environmental, interpersonal, self-related, and task-related behaviors (available from Charles E. Merrill Publishing Company, Columbus, OH)

ACCEPTS: A Curriculum for Children's Effective Peer and Teacher Skills (The Walker Social Skills Curriculum)

    A complete social skills curriculum (with optional color videotapes available) for teaching important classroom behavior and peer-to-peer

Table 7-2 *(continued)*

social skills to children in kindergarten through grade six, appropriate for
handicapped and nonhandicapped students (available from Pro-Ed,
Austin, TX)

ASSET: A Social Skills Program for Adolescents
A program including printed materials and videocassettes or films
designed to teach adolescents the following skills through modeling, explanation, discussion, and practice: giving positive and negative feedback, accepting negative feedback, resisting peer pressure, problem
solving, negotiation, following instructions, and conversation (available
from Research Press, Champaign, IL)

Reprogramming Environmental Contingenies for Effective Social Skills
(RECESS)
A behavior management program designed for use with socially negative,
aggressive children in kindergarten through third grade (information
about RECESS as well as other behavior management programs designed
for acting-out behavior, low academic survival skills, and social
withdrawal [CLASS, PASS, and PEERS] available from CORBEH, Clinical
Services Building, Center on Human Development, University of Oregon,
Eugene, OR

Affective Training Programs

Developing Understanding of Self and Others: Revised (DUSO-R)
Instructional kits designed to help elementary youngsters (kindergarten
through grade four) understand and cope with their own and others'
social and emotional behavior (available from American Guidance Service, Circle Pines, MN)

Toward Affective Development (TAD)
An activity-centered instructional kit for use with children in grades
three through six, designed to help students achieve self-awareness and
learn to work with others (available from American Guidance Service,
Circle Pines, MN)

TEACHING ACTIVITIES

Control of Interfering Social-Emotional Behavior
Attendance Problems

1. Have a special treat or activity planned and waiting for the student each
   day when she comes to school.
2. If one parent brings the student to school, arrange to have the other
   parent bring the student until she is able to ride the bus or walk alone.
3. Award every student a star for each day of attendance. Have a party
   on Friday for all who have had perfect attendance during the week.
4. Start a club in the area of greatest interest to the student (science, math,

reading, music). Make participation in weekly meetings contingent upon at least 4 days' attendance since the last meeting.

5. Obtain the parents' cooperation in withholding a reinforcing activity (e.g., watching TV) when the student stays at home.

6. Arrange to have the school principal stop by the classroom each morning to compliment the student on her presence at school.

7. Let students earn the privilege of going to a special monthly party by attending school regularly during the preceding month.

8. Increase positive attention to the student when she is in the classroom. Keep your interaction outside the classroom at a minimum.

9. Tell the student that you will spend 20 minutes working with her on a favorite activity after school (e.g., sewing, painting, cooking) if she comes to class (or does not leave without permission).

Challenging Authority

1. Provide the class with several specific examples of a good attitude. Include examples of obeying commands and complying with teacher instructions. Later, praise the student by commending his good attitude when behavior approximates what is desired.

2. Arrange a time-out area in the room (e.g., an empty corner or an area marked off around a chair). If the student does not obey a direct command within 15 seconds, send him to the time-out area for 5 minutes. After 5 minutes allow the student to leave the time-out area only if he is willing to follow directions. Praise the student when he does obey commands.

3. Ignore the student when he disobeys a direction given to the class. Do not allow him to comply with your next command to the class until the previous command is followed. Compliment the student for obedient behavior whenever he follows your directions.

4. Give a "Do" or "Don't" command clearly and only once. Wait a few seconds for the student to comply. If the student complies with your command, give immediate praise and a small treat (e.g., a raisin, small candy, popcorn). If the student does not comply within a few seconds, give a physical prompt (i.e., use the minimum physical assistance necessary to obtain compliance) and reinforce the student immediately with praise for compliance (Neef, Shafer, Egel, Cataldo, & Parrish, 1983).

5. Whenever the student begins to dispute an assignment or direction, stop all interaction by turning and walking away. If the student begins an assignment or follows a directive without arguing, praise him for not arguing.

Out-of-Seat Behavior

1. Make explicit rules concerning movement about the classroom. Ignore students who do not follow the rule, and frequently praise those who observe the rule. (This same basic strategy of ignoring inappropriate and praising appropriate behavior can be used with a wide variety of inappropriate behavior.)
2. Allow students who have remained in their seats during the work period to play musical chairs, eraser tag, seven-up, or some other game involving movement.
3. Set a timer for varying brief intervals. If the student has remained in her seat during the interval, provide a small reward and praise.
4. Set a timer for varying brief intervals, but hide it from the student's view. Have the student record whether she is in or out of her seat whenever the timer rings.
5. Shuffle a deck of playing cards and let the student select a suit. For each academic task completed during seatwork, allow the student to turn a card face up. If the card turned face up is one of the chosen suit, let the student get out of her seat to get a drink a water, go to the game corner for 5 minutes, or make some other quiet, appropriate movement about the room.
6. Mark off an area of the floor around the student's desk with heavy tape. Make explicit rules about the student's territory and other students' intrusion into her "private space." Reinforce students for compliance with the rules and respecting territorial rights.

Disruptive and Inappropriate Verbalizations

1. For each 30-minute period that the student does not talk out, allow the student to engage in a preferred activity for 5 minutes (e.g., playing with a toy, drawing, looking at magazines). Adjust the interval according to the frequency of talk-outs.
2. When the student talks out or interrupts, do not recognize him in any way. Turn your back or walk away if the student tries to get your attention by tugging at your sleeve or standing in front of you. When the student does obtain your permission to talk or waits his turn to speak, recognize him immediately and offer a compliment on his appropriate behavior.
3. If there are fewer than a certain number of talk-outs during a given period (set the number well within the ability of the students), allow the class a 10-minute break for casual conversation.
4. Move the student's desk away from those to whom he tends to talk.

5. Award a point for each 5-minute period during which the student works without talking. When he has accumulated 10 or more points, allow the points to be exchanged for a certain number of minutes during which he can interview other pupils and tape-record the conversation.

6. Have the student self-record on-task and off-task behavior whenever he hears a tape-recorded tone (Kneedler & Hallahan, 1981). (This same basic self-monitoring, self-recording strategy may be used with a variety of off-task behaviors, including talk-outs, out-of-seats, daydreaming).

7. If the student continues to make excessive noise with an object after he has been warned, take the object away for a specified period of time.

Temper Tantrums and Social Immaturity

1. Call the student by her preferred name (and insist that other children use that name also) only when she is not crying.

2. When the student begins a temper tantrum, immediately send her to a time-out area. Be firm but unemotional in dealing with the student. Allow her to return to regular class activities after 5 minutes, provided she is exhibiting appropriate behavior.

3. Give absolutely no attention to the child during a tantrum. Attend positively to her when her behavior is appropriate.

4. At the beginning of class give the child five colored slips of paper with her name written on each. Take one slip away for each whine, cry, complaint, or other component behavior of tantrums. If the child has slips left at the end of the day, offer praise and allow the child to accumulate the slips as points that can be exchanged for a rewarding activity (e.g., reading to a younger child, being a class monitor). (This same response cost strategy can be used with a wide variety of other inappropriate, immature behaviors, such as thumb-sucking (Lloyd, Kauffman, & Weygant, 1982).

5. During story time stop reading to the child immediately when thumb-sucking or other undesirable behavior occurs. Resume reading immediately when appropriate behavior is exhibited.

Stealing and Property Destruction

1. If the student is caught stealing, require him to make restitution—give back the stolen item plus something else or an equivalent item plus an extra one.

2. Mark all the student's items, perhaps with a marker, and reward him for having only marked items in his possession (Rosen & Rosen, 1983). Reward the student for periods of nonstealing only if you can be absolutely certain that no theft has occurred (see Williams, 1985, for further discussion).

3. Make each instance of stealing result in loss of a privilege or reward, with theft of items of greater value resulting in greater loss.

4. Teach the student a cognitive strategy to use when he is tempted to steal (e.g., "I want this, but I can't just take it because it belongs to _____ . What can I do? I could ask to share it. I could earn the money to buy it, or I could ask _____ to trade it" (McGinnis, Sauerbry, & Nichols, 1985).

Physical Aggression

1. Completely ignore the student who struck another. Go immediately to the student who was struck and give her positive attention, care, and comfort. Give the victim your attention, not the aggressor. (This suggestion is appropriate for managing young children who hit or pinch others but do not seriously harm them.)

2. Arrange a chair in a corner of the room that is away from interesting objects or other children. Each time the child hits, kicks, pinches, or otherwise hurts another, place him immediately and unemotionally in the chair and require that he sit there quietly for 5 minutes. After 5 minutes let the child rejoin the group if his behavior is appropriate.

3. Observe the activity during which the most fighting or other aggression takes place. For each day that no fighting occurs during the chosen activity, allow the student to visit with the principal for 5 minutes. The principal must be willing to chat pleasantly with the student, contingent on the student's good behavior.

4. If aggressive behavior occurs at a high rate during unsupervised play, plan organized games that engage students in directed activity (Murphy, Hutchison, & Bailey, 1983).

5. Provide instruction in cognitive self-control of anger (e.g., stop and count to 10, think of all your choices before you act) (McGinnis et al., 1985).

Teasing and Negative Peer Interaction

1. Do not reprimand the teasing student. Instead, grant the student who is being teased the privilege of helping you for 5 minutes after school (or spending some other time with you) each time teasing occurs without her making a response. (The idea is to remove the fun of the teasing by eliminating the reaction of the target.)

2. When teasing begins, go immediately to the student who is being teased, turn that student away from the teaser, and engage the student in a pleasant conversation before she begins to react to the teasing.

3. Tell the student who teases that he may not tease other students but that you are an appropriate target for teasing.

4. Give a firm, brief, private reprimand for teasing others.

5. Have the teased student record the number of times she does not respond to teasing. Let that student earn a certificate or "medal" for bravery for being teased without responding.

6. For each 10-minute interval during which the student does not bother anyone else in the class, let him spend 1 minute visiting socially with another student during a specified period.

7. Let the student earn the right to sit at a preferred desk or move his desk to a preferred location, contingent on not interrupting or bothering other students.

8. Establish a special 10-minute recess or activity time. Define the negative interactions or disruptive behavior clearly. Each time the negative behavior is exhibited, make a tally mark on the chalkboard. Subtract 1 minute from the 10-minute period for each tally mark.

Social Withdrawal and Rejection

1. If the student seldom talks to peers or the teacher, allow her to record her own voice with a tape recorder. Praise the student for recording and gradually require more and more conversational speech.

2. Give the student praise and a small reward (e.g., a raisin or snack cereal) each time you observe her talking with a peer. Gradually require more speech for the reward.

3. Coach other students to approach the withdrawn student, to establish and maintain (for gradually longer periods of time) conversation or interactive play (see Strain, 1981a, 1981b, for further discussion of involving peers).

4. Arrange for the withdrawn student to work with a peer who is friendly, affectionate, and nonthreatening on a special project for a brief period each day. Coach the peer to ask questions and respond positively to the withdrawn student's comments. When conversation is established between the two, add a third student to the group. Gradually increase the size of the group with which the student interacts.

5. Have the rejected student be the source of rewards or desired materials for peers. For example, assist the rejected student in learning to distribute rewards (e.g., snacks) or materials (e.g., art supplies). Provide supervision that assures positive interaction with peers.

6. Be certain that you interact positively with the rejected student. Find things to compliment in the student's behavior or appearance. Give attention to peers who interact positively and ignore those who show rejection.

7. Provide direct instruction in affectionate behavior. Encourage, but do not require, the child to participate in "games" involving shaking hands, greeting, hugging, and sharing other signs of friendship (Twardosz, Nordquist, Simon, & Botkin, 1983).

Misbehavior Outside the Classroom

1. Arrange to send home a daily report card on the student's lunchroom behavior. The report could state simply whether the student has earned a home reward (e.g., the privilege of staying up later than usual or watching TV longer than usual).
2. Arrange special activities that students can earn by behaving appropriately in the lunchroom, on the bus, on the playground.
3. Have the student observe and record what is happening on the bus. Reward her for the number of words or sentences used to describe what she observed.
4. Have the student self-record problem behavior outside the classroom. Work with the student to devise a self-control procedure to deal with the problem behavior. She might use self-questioning and self-instruction to maintain self-control (e.g., "What can I do when the other kids start teasing me on the bus? Right, I can just pretend like I don't hear it").

Modification of Unproductive Academic Response Problems
Refusal to Begin Tasks

1. Present the student with two or three alternative tasks that require similar skills. Let him choose the preferred task.
2. Ignore comments such as "I don't want to" or "I ain't gonna do this stuff." If the student destroys the work, be prepared to give another identical assignment. Do not allow the student to participate in another activity until he has begun the task. As soon as he has, comment positively on that fact.
3. Require only a small amount of academic work, after which the student is allowed to make the next move in a checker or chess game or complete another step in a preferred activity. Gradually increase the amount of work required to do the preferred activity.
4. Have the student record his own work refusals daily. If the number of refusals is fewer than the day before, allow him to have a special privilege. When work refusals seldom occur, base the reward on the number of days work is not refused.
5. Record the amount of time that elapses before the student gets down to work. Show the student the record and have him take over recording the time. Provide a reward for starting to work sooner than the day before, or allow the student a special privilege or reward based on the number of days he starts to work immediately when the assignment is given.
6. When a task is assigned, set a kitchen timer for 1 minute. If everyone in the class has begun the task when the bell rings, allow the class an

additional 5 minutes of recess time.

7. Have the student begin his work at a special desk where there are fewer distractions. After the first part of the task is completed, allow the student to return to his usual desk.

8. Play "working chairs." Set a timer for variable intervals ranging from 30 seconds to 5 minutes, and place the timer where students cannot see it. Make a rule that any student who is working when the timer goes off can move to the next chair if he wishes.

Failure to Complete Tasks

1. Give the student a sticker or decorative seal for each paper completed and turned in.

2. Have students negotiate and write their own contracts for work to be completed for payment (which may be in the form of any tangible reward or activity that is available and meaningful to the student) (Kelly & Stokes, 1984).

3. Break the task down into smaller units (e.g., assign one row of math problems or one individual problem rather than a page). As the student completes each part of the task, offer praise and assign another small unit. Gradually lengthen the assignments.

4. If you are certain that the task is within the student's capability, do not allow her to engage in any other activity until the task is completed. As soon as it is, praise the student and allow her to engage in a favorite activity. Avoid nagging the student to finish the task. State the contingency positively (e.g., "You may go to recess as soon as you've finished your reading assignment").

5. Allow the student to check her own work as soon as it is finished.

6. Give five points for each completed task. When the student has earned 20 points, allow her to skip the next similar assignment.

7. Make up a daily report card on which you report the number of tasks assigned and the number of tasks completed. At the end of each day send the student to the office with the report card. Arrange to have the principal chat with the student for a few minutes if the report card is better than the one the day before. If it is not better, the principal should not talk with the student.

Difficulty Following Directions or Returning to Tasks

1. Present directions in the form of a code or secret message (e.g., NO EGAP 12 FO RUOY HTAM KOOBKROW OD YLNO EHT TSRIF EERHT SWOR). Challenge the student to demonstrate that he has cracked the code.

2. Simplify the directions. Give each step in the directions separately and praise the student for following each step.

3. Record the directions on a tape recorder. Let the student listen to the directions at the listening station and replay them as many times as necessary.

4. Teach the student the strategy of rehearsal and self-instruction (using self-questioning and repeating directions, such as "What am I supposed to do? I'm supposed to work all the problems on page 46").

5. Write out the directions or have the student write them out, step by step. Have the student keep the written directions handy for repeated reference.

Difficulty Working Independently or Trying New Tasks

1. Break the task into very small work units (e.g., one math problem or operation, one comprehension question). Require the student to complete the first small unit on her own; then provide help on the next unit of work. Alternate short, independently completed tasks with those on which you give some assistance. Gradually require more independent work before giving help. (Make sure the student has the prerequisite skills to do the work independently.)

2. Talk with the student about the need to work independently. Measure the student's height in inches and construct a thermometer graph marked off in inches. For each 10-minute period that she works independently, let her color in 1 inch toward the total height.

3. Assign a very small portion of the new task (e.g., one simple subtraction problem) that must be completed before the student goes on to an old, familiar task (e.g., several addition problems). Gradually increase the ratio of new tasks to familiar tasks.

4. Discuss with the student her unwillingness to attempt new tasks. Make an adventurer badge and explain that she may wear it for a specified period of time after attempting a new task without hesitation or after asking to be given a new task. When five badges are earned, give the student a choice of wearing an explorer's helmet or showing an adventure filmstrip.

5. Make a "Look What I Tried" scrapbook in which is recorded each new task the student has tried. Let the student illustrate each task and take the scrapbook home.

Problems with Accuracy and Neatness

1. If the student's work reaches a predetermined level of accuracy, allow him to be a supervisor and help other students with their work.

2. Have the student verbalize each task as he is doing it. (Verbalization

or self-instruction sometimes improves accuracy or other features of performance but sometimes appears to hinder overall performance. Do not assume that verbalization will be helpful; measure its effect on the student's performance.)

3. Allow students to go to their play areas or interest centers only when their work reaches a reasonable standard of accuracy.

4. Each day compute the percentage correct of the student's assignments, and have the student plot his performance on a graph.

5. Divide the class into two teams. Compute the average percentage of correct completions for each team, and give a special designation to the team with the highest average. Allow the winning team a special privilege.

6. State specific criteria for neatness (e.g., all letters formed on the line, heading in the proper place on the paper, no numerals touching each other). Post papers that approximate the criteria under a heading on the bulletin board. Gradually increase the standard for posting work and add additional criteria.

7. Teach students to judge the neatness of each other's papers using specific criteria.

8. Establish a required level of neatness and accuracy for the student's completed work. Praise the student for meeting the criterion and allow him to engage in a favorite activity immediately after reaching the criterion. Set the criterion slightly above the student's usual level of performance, and gradually require a higher level of neatness.

9. If the student improves the neatness of his work, allow him to be your "secretary" or assistant. Dictate messages for the student to write (e.g., complimentary comments on the work or behavior of other pupils, notes to the principal or other teachers, letters or forms ordering materials, or a complimentary note to his own parents).

10. Allow the student to use a pen (perhaps a special pen or marker) only after he meets the stated standard of neatness.

11. When the student makes an error, require him to practice the correct response several times in succession before going on (Singh, Singh, & Winston, 1984).

Nonparticipation in Group Discussion

1. Ask several class members to give positive feedback (e.g., smiles, complimentary comments) to the student whenever she makes a response in class. It is important that the class members be taken into your confidence and that they be liked by the student who seldom responds.

2. If a student responds well in the presence of one other pupil, plan activities in which she has ample opportunity to do so. Then add a sec-

ond peer to the group, later a third, and so on until the group approximates the entire class.

3. Begin by asking the student simple questions in group discussion, requiring only a yes or no answer. When a one-word response is firmly established, gradually require longer responses.

4. Have the student self-record the number of times she volunteers an answer in class, and plot the results on a graph.

5. Assist the student in being a group leader and gradually turn leadership over to her.

Activities Appropriate for Older Students

Many of the activities listed in the preceding sections can be adapted for older students; and many of the following activities can be used, with appropriate adaptations, with younger students. The basic principles of teaching social-behavioral skills apply without regard for students' ages. The teacher must be careful, however, to arrange contingencies and use consequences that are developmentally appropriate for the individual student.

1. Find a person in the community who is able and willing to provide an activity (e.g., riding horses and helping out around the stables or working at a service station) contingent on the student's attending school.

2. Write a contingency contract specifying the rewarding activities the younger person can earn by attending school regularly and behaving appropriately.

3. If the student argues with you and you are certain that your judgment is correct, tell him only once what to do (or what answer is correct). Do not respond in any way to protestations or complaints that you are wrong or unreasonable. However, remember that you can make errors and give the student the benefit of the doubt if an issue is unclear.

4. If off-task questions or changes in the topic fall below an agreed-upon level for several days, allow the class a "free" Friday, when they may discuss anything they wish or engage in any appropriate behavior of their choice for 30 minutes.

5. If the student defaces school property or the personal property of others, require that he clean or repair not only what was damaged but some additional items as well.

6. Get students involved in decorating and sprucing up the classroom (or school). Provide rewards for acts that help keep the room (or building) clean and neat or that indicate personal pride in the classroom (or school) environment.

7. For the rejected student provide direct training in behaviors that will make him more socially acceptable (e.g., grooming, personal care, appropriate social responses).

8. Teach the student a self-talk strategy that will help him tolerate teasing without responding (e.g., "What they're saying doesn't really matter. I'd better just let it go, because if I react and they see I'm getting upset, they'll just do it more. If I just act like they're not saying those things, it won't be any fun for them to tease me anymore").

9. Provide models of appropriate behavior and rehearse with the student how to behave in particular circumstances. Role-play problem situations and effective ways of dealing with them.

10. Teach the student specific skills important in functioning in a group (e.g., listening to others, contributing suggestions, offering help, receiving feedback). Role-play these skills and discuss his progress in using them.

REFERENCES

Achenbach, T. M., & Edelbrock, C. (1983). *Manual for the child behavior checklist and revised child behavior profile.* Burlington, VT: University Associates in Psychiatry.

Bellack, A. S. (1983). Recurrent problems in the behavioral assessment of social skills. *Behaviour Research and Therapy, 21,* 29–41.

Bower, E. M. (1981). *Early identification of emotionally handicapped children in school* (3rd ed.). Springfield, IL: Charles C. Thomas.

Brown, L. L., & Hammill, D. D. (1978). *The behavior rating profile: An ecological approach to behavioral assessment.* Austin, TX: Pro-Ed.

Gelfand, D. M., & Hartmann, D. P. (1984). *Child behavior analysis and therapy* (2nd ed.). New York: Pergamon Press.

Gresham, F. M. (1981). Social skills training with handicapped children: A review. *Review of Educational Research, 51,* 139–176.

Hallahan, D. P., Kauffman, J. M., & Lloyd, J. W. (1985). *Introduction to learning disabilities* (2nd ed.). Englewood Cliffs, NJ: Prentice-Hall.

Kauffman, J. M. (1985). *Characteristics of children's behavior disorders* (3rd ed.). Columbus, OH: Charles E. Merrill.

Kazdin, A. E. (1984). *Behavior modification in applied settings* (3rd ed.). Homewood, IL: Dorsey Press.

Kelly, M. L., & Stokes, T. F. (1984). Student-teacher contracting with goal setting for maintenance. *Behavior Modification, 8,* 223–244.

Kerr, M. M., & Nelson, C. M. (1983). *Strategies for managing behavior problems in the classroom.* Columbus, OH: Charles E. Merrill.

Kneedler, R. D., & Hallahan, D. P. (1981). Self-monitoring of on-task behavior with learning-disabled children: Current studies and directions. *Exceptional Education Quarterly, 2* (3), 73–82.

Lambert, N. M., Hartsough, C. S., & Bower, E. M. (1979). *A process for the assessment of effective student functioning: Administration and use manual.* Monterey, CA: Publishers Test Service.

Lloyd, J. W., Kauffman, J. M., & Weygant, A. D. (1982). Effects of response cost on thumbsucking and related behaviors in the classroom. *Educational Psychology, 2,* 167–173.

Madsen, C. H., & Madsen, C. K. *Teaching/discipline* (2nd ed.). Boston: Allyn & Bacon.

McGinnis, E., Sauerbry, L., & Nichols, P. (1985). Skillstreaming: Teaching social skills to children with behavior disorders. *Teaching Exceptional Children, 17,* 160–167.

Morris, R. J. (1985). *Behavior modification with exceptional children.* Glenview, IL: Scott, Foresman.

Murphy, H. A., Hutchison, J. M., & Bailey, J. S. (1983). Behavioral school psychology goes outdoors: The effect of organized games on playground aggression. *Journal of Applied Behavior Analysis, 16,* 29–35.

Neef, N. A., Shafer, M. S., Egel, A., Cataldo, M. F., & Parrish, J. M. (1983). The class specific effects of compliance training with ''do'' and ''don't'' requests: Analogue analysis and classroom application. *Journal of Applied Behavior Analysis, 16,* 81–99.

Rosen, H. S., & Rosen, L. A. (1983). Eliminating stealing: Use of stimulus control with an elementary student. *Behavior Modification, 7,* 56–63.

Singh, N. N., Singh, J., & Winton, A. S. W. (1984). Positive practice overcorrection of oral reading errors. *Behavior Modification, 8,* 23–37.

Strain, P. S. (Ed.). (1981a). Peer relations of exceptional children and youth. *Exceptional Education Quarterly, 1* (4), special issue.

_____. (1981b). *The utilization of classroom peers as behavior change agents.* New York: Plenum.

Strain, P. S., Odom, S. L., & McConnell, S. (1984). Promoting social reciprocity of exceptional children: Identification, target behavior selection, and intervention. *Remedial and Special Education, 5* (1), 21–28.

Twardosz, S., Nordquist, V. M., Simon, R., & Botkin, D. (1983). The effect of group affection activities on the interaction of socially isolate children. *Analysis and Intervention in Developmental Disabilities, 3,* 311–338.

Walker, H. M., McConnell, S., Walker, J. L., Clarke, J. Y., Todis, B., Cohen, G., & Rankin, R. (1983). Initial analysis of the ACCEPTS curriculum: Efficacy of instructional and behavior management procedures for improving the social adjustment of handicapped children. *Analysis and Intervention in Developmental Disabilities, 3,* 105–127.

Williams, R. L. M. (1985). Children's stealing: A review of theft-control procedures. *Remedial and Special Education, 6* (2), 17–23.

8

Spoken Language

Language serves as an essential prerequisite to all phases of academic achievement. Language development is often viewed in the broad context of acquiring skills in listening, speaking, reading, and writing. Each successive skill is built on the firm foundation of preceding abilities. It is usually expected, for example, that an individual will acquire adequate listening skills prior to developing speech (Wallace & McLoughlin, 1979). Figure 8-1 illustrates the developmental hierarchy that leads to language proficiency. The first level in this model involves the acquisition of an internal language system. The second level involves associations between auditory symbols and experience that result in comprehension of spoken words (auditory receptive language). Auditory expressive language—speaking—is demonstrated at the third level. Finally, the development of reading (visual receptive language) is followed by writing printed words (visual expressive language).

Deficits in spoken language can be very complex. Some students require specialized remediation by highly trained therapists. Nevertheless, the development of spoken language skills must be recognized as an important goal for the classroom teacher. It is our belief that teachers can and should endeavor to identify, assess, and remedy the majority of language problems evidenced in the classroom.

ASSESSMENT

The degree of competency that a student develops in spoken language skills often influences later academic achievement. Consequently, Wallace and Larsen (1978) suggest that the educator must be prepared to assess components of spoken language, if a student is exhibiting school-related problems, to determine whether deficiencies in this area are contributing to academic difficulties.

Most of the many available spoken language assessment techniques can be categorized as either formal or informal. The particular purpose for assessment helps to determine which approach should be used with individual students. Mercer and Mercer (1985), for example, note that formal measures are frequently used in determining a student's language development level, whereas informal measures are best in determining specific teaching objectives. Nonetheless, both types of tests can be used for most spoken language problems.

Figure 8-1. Developmental Hierarchy of an Individual's Language System

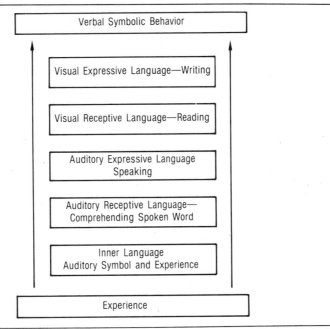

SOURCE: From *Psychology of Deafness* (p. 232) by H. R. Myklebust, 1964, New York: Grune & Stratton. Copyright 1964 by Grune & Stratton. Reprinted by permission.

Formal Tests

There are many different types of published language tests currently available. Some are considered to be comprehensive tests of language ability; others measure only specific components of linguistic performance. In addition, some formal tests appraise various correlates of language functioning, such as cognitive and perceptual ability. Wallace and Larsen (1978) point out that these tests share the following common characteristics: specific directions for administering and scoring the tests, a set of fixed items designed to measure an aspect of spoken language behavior, and norms that permit comparison of an individual's score with the scores of others who have taken the test. Many of the published language tests discussed in this section require specialized clinical training for proper administration and interpretation.

Test for Auditory Comprehension of Language (TACL) (Carrow, 1973). The TACL is designed to be used with children aged 3 years, 11 months to 6 years, 11 months. The test measures oral language comprehension without requiring language expression from the child. The test consists of 101 reproductions of line drawings that represent categories that can be designated by form classes and function words, morphological construction, grammatical categories, and syntactical structures. Percentile ranks are provided for individual test scores. Although norms are available for only the English version, the TACL can be administered in Spanish.

Auditory Discrimination Test (Wepman, 1973). This test is designed to measure the auditory discrimination ability of children from 5 to 8 years of age. Forty pairs of words are presented to the child, who must indicate whether the words are the same or different. In the 30 different-word pairs, the differing phoneme is in the medial position for vowels and in the initial and/or final position for consonants. Because of the limited technical information accompanying the test, it is usually recommended as an informal measure of auditory skills.

Developmental Sentence Analysis (DSA) (Lee, 1974). The DSA is a method for obtaining a detailed and readily quantified, scored evaluation of a child's use of standard English grammatical rules. The child's spontaneous speech in conversation with an adult is analyzed in two separate DSA procedures. The section on developmental sentence types classifies presentence phrases and indicates whether grammatical structure is developing in an orderly manner. The section on developmental sentences is designed to analyze the grammatical structures found in complete sentences. Specific directions for scoring syntactical development are provided in both procedures. Of all the tests available to assess syntactical structure, Wallace and Larsen (1978) consider the DSA to be the most comprehensive and thorough.

The Houston Test for Language Development (Crabtree, 1963). This test measures the language development of children from 6 months through 6 years of age. The first part of the test is intended for very young children (6 months to 3 years) and consists of a checklist that must be completed by an adult. This portion of the test includes vocabulary, sound articulation, gestures, and grammatical usage.

The second part of the test is designed for children from 3 to 6 years of age. It requires the eliciting of spontaneous speech and includes vocabulary, syntax, auditory judgments, and self-identity. Even though the standardization data of the test are minimal, test results can provide an informal estimate of a child's language developments.

Illinois Test of Psycholinguistic Abilities (ITPA) (Kirk, McCarthy, & Kirk, 1968). The ITPA is an individually administered diagnostic test designed for children from 2 years, 4 months to 10 years, 3 months. The test measures psycholinguistic ability in three dimensions: levels of organization (representational and automatic); psycholinguistic processes (reception, organization, and expression); and channels of communication (auditory-vocal and visual-motor modalities). Ten subtests and two supplementary tests constitute the entire ITPA, which has been criticized for not giving specific language proficiency information (Wiederholt, 1978). The test does provide a notion of a child's general perceptual and mental abilities.

Northwestern Syntax Screening Test (Lee, 1969). This is an individually administered test designed to estimate a child's receptive and expressive level of syntactic development. Normative data are provided for children from 3 years, 11 months to 7 years, 11 months of age. Receptive development is measured by having the child select the most appropriate of four pictures related to a sentence spoken by the administrator. The expressive items require the child to repeat sentences spoken by the administrator while the administrator points to various pictures. The accompanying manual provides procedures for interpretation of scores.

Peabody Picture Vocabulary Test—Revised (PPVT) (Dunn & Dunn, 1981). Single-word receptive vocabulary is measured in this widely used test, intended for individuals between 2½ and 40 years of age. The administrator provides an oral stimulus word and a series of plates containing four pictures. The individual is asked to select the picture that best represents the stimulus word. The PPVT also provides an IQ on the basis of the results; however, we believe the test is best used as a measure of receptive vocabulary. Two-thirds of the items in the revised edition of the test are new; as a receptive vocabulary measure, it is extremely useful.

Test of Adolescent Language (TOAL) (Hammill, Braun, Larsen, & Wiederholt, 1980). The TOAL is designed to measure the spoken and written language of students in Grades 6 through 12. The test consists of eight subtests assessing the vocabulary (semantics) and grammar (syntax) used in listening, speaking, reading, and writing. The test can be used to identify spoken and written language problems, to specify areas in need of intervention, and to make meaningful comparisons between language and cognitive abilities, between language abilities and academic achievement, and among the different kinds of language measured. The TOAL is one of the few published measures of adolescent spoken language skills.

Test of Language Development—Primary (TOLD-P) (Newcomer & Hammill, 1982). The TOLD-P is a highly standardized test of language functioning intended for children from 4 years to 8 years, 11 months. The test consists of five subtests (Picture Vocabulary, Oral Vocabulary, Grammatic Understanding, Sentence Imitation, and Grammatic Completion) and two supplementary tests (Word Discrimination and Word Articulation). The entire test can generally be administered in approximately 40 minutes. A child's performance on the test will reveal individual strengths and weaknesses and will further identify the specific skill areas requiring additional assessment and remediation.

The TOLD-I (intermediate) is designed for students from 8 years, 6 months to 12 years, 11 months. It has five subtests that measure different components of spoken language. Both generals and characteristics assess the understanding and meaningful use of spoken words. Sentence Combining, Word Ordering, and Grammatic Comprehension assess differing aspects of grammar. An accompanying manual provides clear directions for administration, scoring, and interpretation of scores.

Utah Test of Language Development (Mecham, Jex, & Jones, 1967). This instrument is designed to measure the expressive and receptive verbal language skills of children from 1 to 15 years of age. Test items include naming common pictures, repeating digits, copying designs, giving word meanings, and reading. The results serve as a useful checklist of normal language development and can be translated into language-age equivalents. The test is probably best used as an estimate of a child's language development.

Informal Techniques

Procedures for informal assessment of spoken language skills have been widely recommended for some time. Spradlin (1967), for example, feels that informal observations of spoken language skills often provide information that can be obtained in no other way. Long-term, daily interactions with a student provide an educator ample opportunity to observe all facets of a student's spoken language development. It is our belief that an educator must include informal appraisal procedures in any assessment process that is to gain useful data relevant to a student's spoken language skills. Two widely used informal procedures are discussed in the following paragraphs.

Case History. A case history of a student with spoken language problems often yields pertinent data. Otto and Smith (1980), for example, suggest that home factors may contribute to a student's difficulty in some cases; in other situations resources in the home may be useful in overcoming the problem. The primary purpose of a case history is to obtain insight into an individual's language development. Case history information can be obtained from interviews with a student's parents, parental completion of a case history form, or even conversation with the student herself. Questions should always be directed at securing information that relates to the observed language difficulty. The following questions are among those recommended by Wallace and Larsen (1978).

□ When did the child speak her first words?

□ Does the child have a history of upper respiratory infections that caused hearing problems?

□ Were there severe emotional upsets in the home during the first few years of the child's life?

□ Do siblings also evidence language problems?

□ Has the child's language problem been evaluated previously?

□ When did the parents notice that something was wrong?

□ Were there long periods in the child's life during which no language was used?

□ At what level is the child's social relationship with peers, siblings, and parents? (p. 263)

Language Samples.   Analyzing a student's spontaneous language, as reflected in a speech sample, has several advantages over other methods of sampling language behavior. According to Wiig and Semel (1984), this method places fewer constraints on the student than do structured language tests. Students may produce syntactic structures in spontaneous speech that are not evident in elicited language samples. In addition, language samples provide evidence of the student's productive language capacity in interpersonal interactions in natural settings. Such samples can be considered to be highly valid.

In securing spontaneous language samples, informal conversation appears to be the preferred method (Atkins & Cartwright, 1982). From age 6 through adulthood, Wiig and Semel (1984) consider elicitation with imperatives (e.g., "Tell me all about . . .") to be the second most preferred method. In no cases should students be forced to speak. When students are hesitant, it may be necessary to devote some time to building effective relationships with them so that they will feel comfortable enough to speak. Wallace and Larsen (1978) point out that the creative use of such stimulus materials as toys, picture books, fruit, musical instruments, and small animals can help elicit language from some students.

As soon as a spontaneous language sample has been elicited, analysis can follow any one of a number of different procedures. The Developmental Sentence Analysis (Lee, 1974), described earlier in this chapter, is one widely used approach. Another method evaluates the average length of the student's spontaneous utterances (mean length of utterances) and provides an indirect estimate of early syntactic growth. These and other methods are discussed in Wiig and Semel (1984) and Wallace (in press).

PROGRAMS

A variety of instructional approaches are available to develop the spoken language skills of handicapped learners. According to Polloway and Smith (1982), instructional programs can be based on commercial materials, an individually designed program, or, most often, a combination of both. We have found the following teaching guidelines to be practical and effective in planning and evaluating instructional programs for students with language problems.

☐ Work with the child at his own level of speech and language, rather than by using words suggested by methods and word lists.

☐ Allow the child to say what he is attempting to say by not being too specific or demanding.

☐ Translate gestures into simple concrete words.

☐ Allow the child to show you what he means if he is unable to express his ideas verbally.

☐ Always give a child the feeling that you are interested in what he is attempting to say.

☐ Attempt to eliminate gestures which substitute for understanding verbal commands.

☐ Work from the concrete to the abstract.

☐ Capitalize on the child's strengths.

☐ Utilize manipulative objects initially in working with a child who has limited speech.

☐ Use stimuli natural to each child's own environment.

☐ Keep careful records of a child's progress. (Wood, 1969, pp. 51–52)

Psycholinguistic Programs

A number of available commercial programs are based on the clinical model of the Illinois Test of Psycholinguistic Abilities (ITPA) (Kirk, McCarthy, & Kirk, 1968). This model attributes language acquisition skills to the following psychological factors: (1) two levels of mental organization, including the representational (meaningful) and the automatic (nonmeaningful); (2) three representational processes (reception, association, and expression) and two automatic mental processes (memory and closure) and (3) two sensory channels, auditory-vocal and visual-motor.

The MWM Program for Developing Language Abilities (Minskoff, Wiseman, & Minskoff, 1975) is a psycholinguistically based language program. It is available on two levels: one for children 5 to 7 years of age and one for students 7 to 10 years of age. Each level contains tasks in auditory reception, visual reception, auditory association, visual association, verbal expression, manual expression, auditory sequential memory, visual sequential memory, grammatic closure, auditory closure, visual closure, and sound blending. The program consists of a comprehensive teacher's manual, an inventory of language abilities, and numerous teaching materials including workbooks, puzzles, and tape recordings.

Another psycholinguistically based language program is Game Oriented Activities for Learning Language Development (GOAL) (Karnes, 1972). It is designed for children with mental ages of 3 through 5. GOAL consists of 337 sequential model lessons classified according to ITPA subtest areas and designed to develop and remediate language skills, social skills, and problem-solving abilities. GOAL lessons include a variety of puzzles, games, templates, and picture cards.

Programs designed to remedy psycholinguistic disorders have been seriously questioned by a number of writers (Hammill & Larsen, 1974; Newcomer & Hammill, 1976). Hammill and Larsen (1974) reviewed 38 studies that attempted to train children in psycholinguistic skills using ITPA as the criterion for measurement. Hammill and Larsen concluded that the effectiveness of psycholinguistic training had not been definitely demonstrated. Approximately two-thirds of the studies were then reexamined by Lund, Foster, and McCall-Perez (1978), who indicated that some of the original 38 studies had been inaccurately reported, inappropriately categorized, and/or misinterpreted. Hammill and Larsen (1978) responded to these changes and essentially reaffirmed their position that psycholinguistic training remains invalidated. More recently, Kavale (1981) reported some evidence of effectiveness when he investigated psycholinguistic training.

The lack of any clear-cut experimental data verifying psycholinguistic approaches leads us to strongly question the use of training programs based on the psycholinguistic model. We believe that the burden of documenting their value rests with those who produce them and/or advocate their use. Before teachers make decisions regarding these teaching procedures, they should become familiar with the positions of professionals both advocating and criticizing these approaches.

Task-Analysis Programs

According to Wiig and Semel (1984), the objective of task-analysis approaches is to increase the complexity of meaning (semantics), structure (morphology and syntax), or function (pragmatics) of the language input-output that the child can handle. The Peabody Language Development Kits (Dunn, Horton, & Smith, 1982) were initially influenced by the ITPA model but are considered to be quite different from other approaches related to the test. The kits provide remediation procedures based on a semantic-linguistic approach (Wiig & Semel, 1984), and each stresses overall language development rather than particular psycholinguistic processes. All four kits offer an array of activities emphasizing reception, expression, and conceptualization. The kits are intended for use with preschool and primary age children or older students with language difficulties. Three of the kits contain 180 lessons apiece, and one kit consists of 360 lessons; the lessons do not require reading or writing, nor is any seatwork involved. The kits can be used by classroom teachers without specialized language training; specific lesson plans are included with each individual kit.

The Fokes Sentence Builder (Fokes, 1976) teaches verbal expression, comprehension, and sentence construction. Students create grammatically correct sentences by selecting cards from color-coded boxes representing five categories of words: *who, what, is doing, which,* and *where.* The program was originally developed for use with children whose language development is delayed, but it can also be used with students whose language development is normal. The Fokes Sentence Builder contains more than 200 picture cards with drawings of people, animals, and common objects. An accompanying guide explains how to build declarative sentences, questions, and negative sentences in the present, past, and future tenses.

Behavioral Oriented Programs

Most behaviorally oriented language programs seek to modify and change existing overt language and communication behaviors. The DISTAR language program (Engelmann & Osborn, 1976) is one such approach. This highly structured and organized program was developed to teach language concepts and skills to educationally disadvantaged children with conceptual problems. Daily lesson plans provide the teacher with explicit directions for implementing precise techniques. The program is based on small, sequential steps with continual repetition, feedback, and reinforcement. Language I focuses on the language of instruction and takes a child from the identification of familiar objects to the description and classification of those objects. Children are also taught concepts for logical reasoning such as *before-after, some,* and *only.* Language analysis is emphasized in Language II through work in opposites, synonyms, analogies, and questioning skills. Lessons also involve classification, function, absurdity, and problem solving. The major focus of Language III is the analysis of both spoken and written sentences. The skills developed are designed to lay a foundation for communication skills, particularly written communication. The teaching materials in this program include a teacher's guide, spiral-bound presentation books, storybooks, color books, and take-home exercises that reinforce concepts taught in the daily lessons and evaluate the skills acquired.

The Monterey Language Program (Gray & Ryan, 1972) is a behaviorally oriented program intended for students with severe language disorders. The program consists of a highly structured series of tasks, presentation techniques, and evaluation guidelines. Imitation, prompts, and reinforcement are used throughout the program. The program progresses from basic to more advanced language skills. In an evaluation of the Monterey program, Matheny and Panagos (1978) found the phonological and syntactic components to be effective with students with multiple linguistic problems.

Microcomputers

During the past few years American schools have witnessed rapid growth in computer technology. In 1982, for example, Blaschke (1982) reported that there were more than 150,000 microcomputers in public schools. Stowitschek and Stowitschek (1984) reported that over 90% of the resource teachers and 66% of the regular classroom teachers responding to their survey had access to microcomputers. Clearly, microcomputer technology is a rapidly growing phenomenon within our schools (Williams, 1984), yet research on computers in instruction is inconclusive. Stowitschek and Stowitschek (1984) point out further that little information is available on how microcomputers can best be applied in the classroom.

Microcomputers have been utilized for a limited number of purposes in spoken language development. Hummel and Balcom (1984) suggest the use of word processing programs for teaching multiple meanings of words. Turkel and Podell (1984) discuss instruction of the Logo programming language. In addition, Cartwright and Hall (1974) report the use of a computer-aided method for developing language in eight nonspeaking handicapped students. In this study the pupils interacted with a computer programmed to play both word and number games. Following several weeks of investigation, the authors reported that the students improved linguistically.

Although preliminary results of some limited studies offer minimal support for the positive effect of microcomputers on spoken language performance, we see the need for increased empirical documentation before microcomputers are widely used in spoken language remediation. We would encourage additional research and study of the many and varied issues arising from the application of computer technology to instruction of students handicapped in spoken language.

TEACHING ACTIVITIES

Discrimination of Speech/Language Sounds

1. Present isolated speech sounds to the student. Ask the student to listen for a specific sound, such as /m/. Present a sequence of sounds (e.g., /m/, /p/, /t/, /s/, /m/, /v/, /k/, /m/, /n/, /s/, /m/) and ask the student to raise his hand each time he hears the /m/ sound.

2. Introduce pairs of sounds (e.g., /m/ and /b/) and ask the student to tell whether the sounds are same or different. The student can respond by shaking his head, raising his hand, or using any other agreed-upon cue.

3. Have the student listen for a particular sound at the beginning of words

read aloud. Present words that are phonetically different at first; eventually present words with more similar beginning sounds. Final and medial sounds can be introduced in the same way.

4. Introduce blends, graphs, and vowel sounds through a procedure similar to that in the preceding activity. The sequence should progress from isolated speech sounds to sounds within words.

5. Provide picture clues and objects for the student who needs additional help in associating speech sounds with letters and words.

6. Give the student a picture that contains many objects, such as an advertisement. Ask the student to point to an object that begins with the same sound as a stimulus sound you provide. This procedure can also be used for final sounds, rhyming, and blends.

7. Lerner (1985) suggests having the student pronounce the name of an object by separating it into individual phonemes (e.g., "Pick up the p-ĕ-n").

8. Provide students with experiences in listening for rhyming words. Prepare a worksheet with pictures of different objects. Ask students to circle the picture that completes a given sentence and rhymes with another word in that sentence. For example, read "The man was holding a _____" and use worksheet pictures of a dog, fan, book, and baby.

9. Play bingo with students who recognize some letter sounds; use initial consonants or other speech sounds for the bingo squares. Call out different words and have the students cover appropriate squares.

10. Pronounce words and ask students to indicate the number of syllables in each by holding up the appropriate number of fingers or clapping or tapping out the number of syllables.

Producing Speech Sounds

1. Pronounce the following sounds and ask the student to repeat each: /m/, /p/, /b/, /k/, /g/, /n/, /t/, /d/, /l/, and /r/.

2. Johnson and Myklebust (1967) recommend taking an inventory of mouth movements and phonemes the student can produce. These sounds can be used to make the student aware of movements and sounds.

3. Encourage the use of any vocal utterances that have some meaning to the student in order to provide a process of communication and motivate her to learn more symbolic language. Gradually require vocal productions that more closely approximate the sounds of words or parts of words.

4. Begin training by looking into a mirror with the student and slowly articulating various sounds in isolation. Have the student imitate your tongue and lip movements. According to Eisenson (1972), the first

isolated sounds should include /m/, /p/, /b/, /k/, /g/, /n/, /t/, /d/, /l/, and /r/.

5. Place the student's hand on your throat or face as you make sounds so that she can feel the movements. Then have the student place her hand on her own throat.

6. Manually guide the student's tongue or lips to produce certain sounds if she is unable to imitate a sound by observation. A tongue depressor can be used for appropriate tongue movements.

7. Provide students with verbal clues if they are needed. For example, Johnson and Myklebust (1967) suggest that you "close your lips and hum" for /m/ or "bite your lip and blow but do not use your voice" for /f/ (p. 128).

8. Have the student practice various tongue and mouth movements such as opening the mouth wide, placing the tongue behind the teeth, and moving the lips to a whistling position.

9. Provide pictures of the tongue and mouth positions that are used for particular sounds. Hold the picture up to a mirror and have the student imitate the position.

10. Have the student close her eyes while making certain sounds so that visual memory is used to recall the movements for particular sounds (Eisenson, 1972).

11. Gradually blend known sounds together as the student progresses in learning isolated sounds. Provide consonant-vowel and consonant-vowel-consonant combinations. Use many of the same procedures suggested in the preceding activities.

Understanding Words

1. Place three or four objects before the student and ask him to point to the one that you name. If the student is able to correctly point to an object, encourage him to say its name.

2. Johnson and Myklebust (1967) advise that only meaningful words should be taught and that words are meaningful only "when the individual has the experience with which they are to be associated" (p. 87).

3. Begin training by working with real objects or pictures. Give the student a chance to feel and play with the object. Say the name of the object a number of times while the student has the object or picture before him.

4. Have the student match an object, such as a banana, with a picture of that object or match similar objects or pictures.

5. Have the student match an object to another object that is basically different in form and features but belongs to a similar category. For example, ask the student what one does with a lock and let him select the "matching" object from a nail, key, and cork (Eisenson, 1972). As

the student progresses, have him match pictures instead of objects.

6. Have the student classify words into categories (e.g., people, food, animals) by sorting pictures and words into groups.

7. Teach more abstract words, such as verbs, by having the student perform the activity. Jumping, walking, and other actions can be repeated until the student understands the meaning of the word.

8. Have the student clap for various reasons when being read to: for example, "Clap for every word that describes something," "Clap for every person's name," or "Clap for every word that rhymes with _____ ."

9. Have the student follow simple directions: for example, "Give me the book," "Stand next to the door," "Show me the paper," "Jump up and down."

10. Have the student match actual noises with the objects that produce those noises. Eisenson (1972) suggests using telephone rings, the vacuum cleaner whir, drum beats, bell clangs, or toy animals that approximate the sounds of the live animals.

11. Teach descriptive words by providing the student with a variety of pictures and having him pick the happy boy, the sad clown, the dirty towel.

12. Provide the student with contrasting sets of experiences to teach the attributes of objects (e.g., hot and cold water, rough and smooth stones, little and big animals) (Lerner, 1985).

13. Present pairs of objects (e.g., a guitar and a violin, a ruler and a tape measure) and point out the similarities and differences. Provide opportunities for the student to use the objects.

Understanding Sentences

1. Have the student respond yes or no in the following questions (Bush & Giles, 1977): "Do flowers grow?" "Do dogs bark?" "Do rabbits hop?" "Do you have four ears?"

2. Gradually add verbs to nouns (e.g., "throw ball," "eat candy") and adjectives to nouns (e.g., "a small truck," "a sad girl") by having the pupil choose the correct picture or perform the appropriate action (Eisenson, 1972).

3. Read a short sentence to the student and ask her a series of questions about the sentence (e.g., "Jean and Jeff go to the ocean and mountains during the summer. Do Jean and Jeff go to the mountains during the winter? Do Jean and Jeff go to the ocean during the summer?"). The student can respond by shaking her head or merely saying yes or no.

4. As the student progresses, read longer and more detailed sentences and paragraphs. Questions can be provided before the reading occurs to enable the student to listen for specific answers.

5. Read a list of sentences to the student and have her sit with her thumbs up. When the student hears a sentence that tells how, she puts her thumbs down (e.g., "The boys run fast," "Virgil eats slowly," "Joyce looks pretty"). Sentences that tell when, where, and who can also be used (Wagner, Hosier, & Blackman, 1970).

6. Prepare a worksheet with various drawings. Ask the student to follow specific directions (e.g., "Draw a circle around the truck," "Put an X on the little girl," "Draw a line under the house").

7. Ask questions that require comparisons (e.g., "Who wears dresses, boys or girls?" "Who shaves every morning, mother or father?" "Who barks, a rabbit or a dog?" "Who puts out fires, a police officer or a fire fighter?").

8. Johnson and Myklebust (1967) suggest preparing a worksheet with a series of pictures and reading sentences that vary in difficulty according to individual needs. Ask the student to follow a specific direction after hearing the sentence (e.g., "Mother bought some apples at the store. Circle what mother bought at the store").

9. Pass objects out to each student in the class. Ask students to stand if they have the object that is described (e.g., "Stand if you have the animal that meows," "Stand if you have the object that cuts meat," "Stand if you have the toy truck that delivers milk").

10. Provide a signal to cue a student to listen for directions that will be given (e.g., flick the lights, play a few notes on the piano, hold your arm over your head, say "Listen"). Use one particular signal consistently for a group of students.

11. Lerner (1985) suggests having the pupil listen to a sentence and supply the correct word (e.g., "I am thinking of a word that tells us what you eat soup with").

12. Zigmond and Cicci (1968) recommend having the student select the word in a sentence that does not make sense (e.g., "It snows during the summer," "We drink milk out of a book," "We use a ball to write").

13. Read a poem or story with obvious missing words. Have the student supply the missing parts (e.g., "Chuck built a snowman with _____ . He used a carrot for the _____ and coal for the snowman's _____ . When the sun came out, the snowman _____ ").

14. Read a short sentence to the student (e.g., "The sun was very bright"). Have the student draw a picture illustrating the dictated sentence.

15. Play charades and ask the student to act out a role, such as a swimmer diving into the water or a carpenter hammering a nail (Bush & Giles, 1977), or have the student guess the role being acted out.

Formulating Words and Sentences

1. Provide the student with familiar objects to name—fruit, clothes, toys,

and so on. Say the words and have the student repeat them.

2. Work on classifying pictures into categories (animals, furniture, food).

3. Facilitate word recall by teaching word association through pairs of words (e.g., hard-soft, salt-pepper, hot-cold). Pictures can be used to supplement the words (Johnson & Myklebust, 1967).

4. Build known words into sentences by using repeated phrases (e.g., "This is a dog," "This is a chair," "This is a boy," "This is a book").

5. Bereiter and Engelmann (1966) expand on repeated phrases by asking questions (e.g., "Is this a book?") and by adding second-order statements (e.g., "This book is red"). They also introduce negative statements (e.g., "This is not a book").

6. Prepare a series of sentences with key words missing. Read the sentences to the student and ask him to supply the key words (e.g., "A dog makes noise by _____ ," "Bicycles have _____ wheels," "We have _____ fingers").

7. Expand on the show-and-tell period by asking the student specific questions about an object brought from home.

8. Prepare a grab bag of familiar objects. Have the student choose one object and describe it in as much detail as possible. Permit other students to guess the object being described.

9. Have the students paint pictures. Ask particular students to describe their pictures to the rest of the class.

10. Have students repeat familiar nursery rhymes along with a record. Eventually have the students recite the rhymes without the record.

11. Use play telephones, tape recorders, or walkie-talkies to focus the student's attention on using words and sentences as a means of communication.

12. Provide puppets for the student to use during free play and more structured periods.

13. Show a picture to the student and ask him to describe what is happening in the picture. Direct questions, specific to a particular picture, can also be asked. Have the student tell what went on before the picture was taken, and what happened afterward.

14. Provide the student with a set of sequence pictures or a comic strip cut into frames. Ask him to tell the story by describing the sequence of events.

15. Smith (1974), emphasizes verbal fluency by having the student respond to questions for which nearly any response is acceptable (e.g., "What would happen if we didn't have electricity?").

16. Give students practice in using articles and prepositions by providing them with certain key words (e.g., *house, boy, door*) and having them build a sentence around these words.

17. Karnes (1968) recommends questions and statements like "Tell me

how . . .," "Why do we . . .," or "Tell me where . . ." (e.g., "Tell me how . . . you tie your shoes/you play kickball/your father washes the car").

18. Gather a number of kitchen utensils or tools. Have a student describe the use of one utensil or tool without gestures.

Listening Comprehension

1. Play Simon Says and have the student perform motor tasks that gradually become more complex as she progresses.

2. Give the student step-by-step directions for folding a piece of paper to make a certain number of squares or rectangles, or provide precut geometric shapes and direct the student step-by-step to assemble an ice cream cone or a balloon (Karnes, 1968).

3. Call students to reading groups or dismiss students for recess or lunch by using row numbers, clothing colors, first-name initials, or other specific directions.

4. Ask a particular student to repeat directions that were given to a class or a reading group. This procedure can be an effective check before the student proceeds with an assignment.

5. Have two children play Master and Robot by appointing one student the master, who gives directions to the other student, the robot (e.g., go to the blackboard, draw a circle, turn around, sit in your chair). Have the pupils change places after a period of time (Wagner, Hosier, & Blackman, 1970).

6. Provide each of the students with a piece of paper. Direct them to complete various activities on the paper (e.g., "Draw a circle in the upper right-hand corner of the paper," "Make a triangle in the lower left-hand corner of the paper," "Write the number 7 in the circle," "Make a square in the middle of the paper"). Tape-record the directions for students to follow by themselves, using earphones.

7. Provide students with a series of directions to a specified place in the school building (e.g., "Go out the door and turn left. Walk straight down the hall and take your first right. At the gymnasium, turn left. Go through the first door on your right").

8. Read directions for making a kite, baking cookies, or building a model. Have the students perform the activity by following the step-by-step directions.

9. Prepare a series of direction cards for students who can read. Allow them to continue choosing cards from a pile as long as they are able to follow the commands. The cards might say, "Go to the library table and find a brown book," "Hop over to the door, turn around, and skip to the window," or "Pass out pencils and math workbooks to all the children in the first three rows."

Receptive Language Activities for Older Students

1. Wagner, Hosier, and Blackman (1970) recommend reading several statements to students and asking them to decide whether a statement is fact or opinion (e.g., "George Washington was our first president," "Thomas Jefferson was our greatest president," "There were eight dogs in Tom's boat").

2. Prepare a worksheet with a list of words. Describe a word and direct the student to place a number before that word (e.g., "Write the number 1 before the word that tells us it is the cold time of the year," "Write the number 2 before the word that describes a fruit that is long and yellow").

3. Read a list of statements and ask the student to tell whether the statements are true or false (e.g., "Elephants can fly in the air," "We swim during the summertime," "We run with our hands").

4. Have one student stand at the front of the room while the students sitting at their seats describe a classmate in the room. The student in front must guess the other student's identity from the descriptions provided (Wagner, Hosier, & Blackman, 1970). The clues might include, "He has freckles," "He rides a bike to school," or "He is wearing a blue shirt."

5. Smith (1967) suggests reading a short paragraph containing several words that have similar meanings. Ask the student to pick out the words that mean the same thing (e.g., "Soon the little man came to a small dining room. He peered through the tiny door and saw a lovely petite room all set up with miniature furniture. There were even minute dishes on the dining room table") (p. 88).

6. Have students arrange scrambled oral sentences in the correct order without using pencil or paper.

7. Read a short story and stop periodically, asking the student to predict what will happen next.

8. Read a list of nouns that belong in a particular category (furniture, fruits, animals). Direct the student to call "Stop" when a noun is read that does not belong in the specified category (e.g., chair, desk, man, couch, table, apple, . . .).

9. Read a series of analogies to the student and have him complete each sentence (e.g., "A banana is to an apple as squash is to _____," "A boy is to a girl as a _____ is to a woman," "A ring is to a _____ as a bracelet is to a wrist").

10. Read a series of three words to the student and have him choose the two words that are related (e.g., dog, cat, apple; chair, table, knife; milk, stone, water).

11. Bush and Giles (1977) suggest asking questions like these to develop logical relationships: "Does a bird have wings?" "Do you read with

your ears?" "Would you go to a grocery store to see a movie?" "Do you lick an ice cream cone with your knees?"

12. After reading a story, ask the student specific questions that require interpretation and imagination. For example, ask the student to imagine that he was the hero. Would he have acted differently? What would have happened if the story had taken place in a different country, season, or century?

13. Use simple riddles to describe familiar people, places, animals. Ask the student to use the description to guess the identity. Have him think of riddles to ask other students.

14. Ask the student to list all the things that he can think of that have wheels, that are smaller than an ant, or that have hair (Smith, 1974).

Linguistic Patterns

1. Prepare a series of sentences with missing words. Read these to the student and have her supply the omitted words (e.g., "We went _____ the store," "The boat is _____ the water," "The plane is _____ the sky," "This is John's jacket. It belongs to _____ ," "Last summer we _____ to the beach"). Plurals, adjectives, prepositions, and other forms can be emphasized with this activity.

2. Use choral speaking to emphasize correct language usage. Bryan (1971) lists over 100 original verses that can be used in the primary grades.

3. Display a picture in front of the student and describe the picture in a sentence (e.g., "This boy is running"). Have the student repeat the sentence. Then omit certain words for the student to insert as the sentence is repeated.

4. Provide the student with two different sized tin cans, a red poker chip, and a white poker chip. Place the red chip in the large can and ask the student, "Is the red chip in the large can?" Gradually have the student verbalize different situations. Vary the manipulations and questions, or verbalize incorrect statements and let the student catch your errors (Karnes, 1968).

5. Have the student repeat words and sentences emphasizing plurals, verb tense, and other constructions, using the Language Master (an adaptation of a tape recorder that plays and records specially perpared cards). As the student progresses, let her use a regular tape recorder to make statements about pictures and objects.

6. Provide the student with pictures showing single and multiple units of different objects. Ask the student to point to the girl in one picture or the girls in another picture. Eventually, have the student make statements about the pictures, such as "The girls are playing ball" (Karnes, 1968).

7. Wedemeyer and Cejka (1970) recommend preparing small cards with nouns, verbs, and adjectives written on them. Group the noun cards on one ring, the verbs on a second, and the adjectives on a third. Attach the rings to a folded cardboard stand so that the cards can be flipped over easily. Then have the student form appropriate sentences (e.g., rabbits/are/soft).

8. Provide phrases (e.g., the big dog, to the mountains, under the house). Have the student build a sentence using the phrases in standard syntactical form.

9. Correct grammar and syntax errors by providing the student with the appropriate usage. Tell the student, "Say it the way I do," or "This is the way you say it in school."

10. Encourage the student to respond in sentences. Incorporate a one-word response into a sentence, and have the student repeat the entire sentence. Groups of students can also repeat particular sentences together.

11. Provide pictures that illustrate the past, present, and future tense of verbs. A sequence with an individual about to do something, doing something, and completing that same act can be described and discussed (Johnson & Myklebust, 1967).

12. Give the student an eraser and instruct her to place it in various locations. Have her describe each new position (e.g. "The eraser is on my head," "The eraser is in the desk," "The eraser is under the chair").

13. Use the flannel board to illustrate sentences that require an oral response. Stress plurals, prepositions, and other syntactical structures. Permit the student to create flannel board situations and verbally describe them.

14. On the chalkboard write a sentence that has its words in an incorrect order, and have the student arrange the words correctly. Flash cards containing single words can also be arranged to form sentences.

15. Bush and Giles (1977) suggest reading a series of sentences to the student, each with a missing word, and having the student supply the correct form (e.g., "I have many dresses, but I have only one blue _____ ," "Yesterday we played ball, and today we will _____ ball," "I like to jump rope; but after I have been _____ for a while, I get tired").

Expressive Language Activities for Older Students

1. Have students build individual lists of words from one common root, such as *ball* or *man*. Assign a point for each word. The pupil with the most points wins the game.

2. Have students list possible synonyms for particular words, such as *car*, *baby*, and *day* (Smith, 1967).

3. Play hangman with students guessing letters to fill in the missing blends of various words. For each incorrect letter guessed, additional body parts are drawn until the loser is "hanged."

4. Ask the student to name all the objects in a room or a picture during a specified time limit. Keep a graph to note improvement (Lerner, 1985).

5. Write any 10 letters on the board and have students compose a 10-word telegram using those letters as the initial letters of the 10 words. Vary the activity by specifying the nature of the telegram (Platts, 1970).

6. Stop periodically while reading a story and have a student supply a word that fits into the context of the sentence.

7. Provide the student with a sentence (e.g., "It rained hard last night"). Ask the student to express the same meaning in as many different ways as possible.

8. Read a story to the student and have him retell it to another student. Encourage him to use his own words.

9. Introduce a word-of-the-day and encourage students to use it throughout the day.

10. Provide students with a word that has multiple meanings, such as *run*. Have the pupils, in turn, use the word in a sentence, employing as many different meanings as possible.

REFERENCES

Atkins, C. P., & Cartwright, L. R. (1982). Preferred language elicitation procedure used in five age categories. *ASHA, 24,* 321–323.

Bereiter, C., & Engelmann, S. (1966). *Teaching disadvantaged children in the preschool.* Englewood Cliffs, NJ: Prentice-Hall.

Blaschke, C. L. (1982). Microcomputers in special education: Trends and projections. *Journal of Special Education, 5*(4), 25–27.

Bryan, R. (1971). *When children speak.* Novato, CA: Academic Therapy Publications.

Bush, W. J., & Giles, M. T. (1977). *Aids to psycholinguistic teaching.* Columbus, OH: Charles E. Merrill.

Carrow, E. (1973). *Test for Auditory Comprehension of Language.* Austin, TX: Learning Concepts.

Cartwright, G. P., & Hall, K. A. (1974). A review of computer uses in special education. In L. Maan & Sabatino, *The second review of special education* (pp. 307–350). Philadelphia: JSE Press.

Crabtree,, M. (1963). *The Houston Test for Language Development.* Houston, TX: Houston Test Company.

Dunn, L. M., & Dunn, L. M. (1981). *Peabody Picture Vocabulary Test—Revised.* Circle Pines, MN: American Guidance Service.

Dunn, L. M., Horton, K. B., & Smith, J. O. (1982). *Peabody language development kits.* Circle Pines, MN: American Guidance Service.

Eisenson, J. (1972). *Aphasia in children.* New York: Harper & Row.

Engelmann, S., & Osborn, J. (1976). *DISTAR language.* Chicago: Science Research Associates.

Fokes, J. (1976). *Fokes Sentence Builder.* New York: Teaching Resource Corporation.

Gray, B.. B., & Ryan, B. P. (1972). *Monterey Language Program (programmed conditioning for language).* Palo Alto, CA: Monterey Language Systems.

Hammill, D. D., Brown, V. L., Larsen, S. C., & Wiederholt, J. L. (1980). *Test of Adolescent Language.* Austin, TX: Pro-Ed.

Hammill, D. D., & Larsen, S. C. (1974). The effectiveness of psycholinguistic training. *Exceptional Children, 41,* 5–15.

————. (1978). The effectiveness of psycholinguistic training: A reaffirmation of position. *Exceptional Children, 44,* 402–414.

Hammill, D. D., & Newcomer, P. L. (1982). *Test of Language Development—Intermediate.* Austin, TX: Pro-Ed.

Hummel, J. W., & Balcom, F. W. (1984). Microcomputers: Not just a place for practice. *Journal of Learning Disabilities, 17,* 432–434.

Johnson, D. J., & Myklebust, H. R. (1967). *Learning disabilities: Educational principles and practices.* New York: Grune & Stratton.

Karnes, M. B. (1968). *Helping young children develop language skills.* Reston, VA: Council for Exceptional Children.

————. (1972). *Game oriented activities for learning.* Springfield, MA: Milton Bradley.

Kavale, K. (1981). Functions of the Illinois Test of Psycholinguistic Abilities (ITPA): Are they trainable? *Exceptional Children, 47* (7), 496–510.

Kirk, S., McCarthy, J., & Kirk, W. (1968). *Illinois Test of Psycholinguistic Abilities.* Urbana: University of Illinois Press.

Lee, L. (1969). *Northwestern Syntax Screening Test.* Evanston, IL: Northwestern University Press.

————. (1974). *Developmental Sentence Analysis.* Evanston, IL: Northwestern University Press.

Lerner, J. (1985). *Children with learning disabilities: Theories, diagnosis, and teaching strategies* (4th ed.). Boston: Houghton Mifflin.

Lund, K. A., Foster, G. E., & McCall-Perez, F. C. (1978). The effectiveness of psycholinguistic training: A reevaluation. *Exceptional Children, 44,* 310–319.

Matheny, N., & Panagos, J. (1978). Comparing the effects of articulation and syntax programs on syntax and articulation improvement. *Language, Speech, and Hearing Services in Schools, 9*(1), 57–61.

Mecham, M., Jex, J. L., & Jones, J. D. (1967). *Utah Test of Language Development.* Salt Lake City, UT: Communication Research Association.

Mercer, C. D., & Mercer, A. R. (1985). *Teaching students with learning problems* (2nd ed.). Columbus, OH: Charles E. Merrill.

Minskoft, E. H., Wiseman, D. E., & Minskoft, G. (1975). *The MWM Program for Developing Language Abilities.* Ridgefield, NJ: Educational Performance Associates.

Newcomer, P., & Hammill, D. D. (1976). *Psycholinguistics in the schools.* Columbus, OH: Charles E. Merrill.

_____. (1982). *Test of Language Development—Primary.* Austin, TX: Pro-Ed.

Otto, W., & Smith, R. J. (1980). *Corrective and remedial teaching* (3rd ed.). Boston: Houghton Mifflin.

Platts, M.E. (1970). *Anchor: A handbook of vocabulary discovery techniques for the classroom teacher.* Stevensville, MI: Educational Service.

Polloway, E. A., & Smith, J. E. (1982). *Teaching language skills to exceptional learners.* Denver: Love.

Smith, J. A. (1967). *Creative teaching of the language arts in the elementary school.* Boston: Allyn & Bacon.

Smith, R. M. (1974). *Clinical teaching: Methods of instruction for the retarded* (2nd ed.). New York: McGraw-Hill.

Spradlin, J. E. (1967). Procedures for evaluating processes associated with receptive and expressive language. In R. Schiefelbusch, R. Copeland, & J. Smith (Eds.), *Language and mental retardation.* New York: Holt, Rinehart & Winston.

Stowitschek, J. J., & Stowitschek, C. E. (1984). Once more with feeling: The absence of research on teacher use of microcomputers. *Exceptional Education Quarterly, 4*(4), 23–29.

Turkel, S. B., & Podell, D. M. (1984). Computer assisted learning for mildly handicapped students. *Teaching Exceptional Children, 16,* 258–262.

Wagner, G., Hosier, M., & Blackman, M. (1970). *Listening games: Building listening skills with instructional games.* New York: Teachers.

Wallace, G., & Larsen, S. L. (1978). *The educational assessment of learning problems: Testing for teaching.* Boston: Allyn & Bacon.

Wallace, G. (in press). *Assessment: Evaluating students with learning and behavior problems.* Austin, TX: Pro-Ed.

Wallace, G., & McLoughlin, J. A. (1979). *Learning disabilities: Concepts and characteristics.* Columbus, OH: Charles E. Merrill.

Wedemeyer, A., & Cejka, J. (1970). *Creative ideas for teaching exceptional children.* Denver: Love.

Wepman, J. M. (1973). *Auditory Discrimination Test.* Chicago: Language Research Associates.

Wiederholt, J. L. (1978). A review of the Illinois Test of Psycholinguistic Abilities. In O. K. Buros (Ed.), *Eighth mental measurement yearbook.* Highland Park, NJ: Gryphon.

Wiig, E. H., & Semel, E. (1984). *Language assessment and intervention for the learning disabled* (2nd ed.). Columbus, OH: Charles E. Merrill.

Williams, R. L. (1984). *Computer-assisted instruction for mildly handicapped students: A need for research.* Unpublished manuscript.

Wood, N. (1969). *Verbal learning.* Belmont, CA: Fearon.

Zigmond, N. K., & Cicci, R. (1968). *Auditory learning.* San Rafael, CA: Dimensions.

9

Reading

Learning to read is considered by many to be the most important skill taught in our schools. Educators regard successful reading as the most significant common denominator of adequate achievement in many areas of the curriculum. Nonetheless, millions of students experience difficulty in reading. Harris and Sipay (1980) estimate that approximately 10 to 15% of the general school population have reading disabilities. Polloway and Smith (1982) point out that reading difficulties are not isolated problems but can affect other curricular areas as well as personal, social, and behavioral adjustment.

The skills involved in learning to read adequately are many and varied. Generally, these skills are classified as either word recognition or comprehension skills. Word recognition skills are needed to decode printed letters and to match letters and words with sounds; comprehension skills are needed to understand the meaning of what is read (Lerner, 1985). Students with reading handicaps typically experience difficulty with both types of skills. It is important for educators to be aware of specific reading deficits in order to plan for appropriate methods and materials to alleviate the reading problem.

ASSESSMENT

A wide variety of assessment procedures are available for appraising various reading difficulties. In most cases the method used to collect data concerning a student's reading problem depends on the specific information that is required. Wallace and Larsen (1978) note, for example, that information concerning the reading level of an entire class is best obtained from a group reading achievement test. On the other hand, detailed information about a particular student's skills might be best obtained from an individual diagnostic reading test or an informal teacher-constructed measure.

Selection of available assessment procedures depends on the particular difficulties experienced by the pupil, the availability of specialized services, and the educator's ability to use diagnostic tools (Wilson, 1977). Regardless of the procedure selected, both regular and special educators must come to understand the student's reading problem. Some of the assessment techniques that help to accomplish this task are discussed in the following sections.

Formal Tests

Formal assessment techniques refer to those formally developed reading tests that are commercially available. According to Wallace (in press), most formal reading tests are norm-referenced, although there are some commercially published criterion-referenced tests. Among the various types of formal tests, diagnostic reading tests provide detailed information concerning a student's skills and abilities in various areas of reading. Generally, these tests include subtests measuring word recognition, word analysis, comprehension, and related components of general reading skills (e.g., auditory discrimination, sound blending). The following paragraphs describe five individually administered diagnostic reading batteries that we believe provide instructionally useful information. In addition, Table 9–1 lists a number of other reading tests designed to provide a concentrated appraisal of a specific reading skill area.

Diagnostic Reading Scales (DRS) (Spache, 1981). This edition of the DRS is an expanded and revised set of individually administered tests for evaluation of oral and silent reading abilities and auditory comprehension. The test battery consists of 3 word recognition lists, 2 sets of 11 graded reading selections, and 12 supplementary word analysis and phonics tests. The word lists function as a pretest for the reading selections, which are used to determine the student's instructional, independent, and potential reading levels. The supplementary tests are intended to reveal the student's ability to recognize and use letter sounds and symbols and common syllables and to synthesize word parts into words.

The DRS is standardized for students functioning at first through seventh grade levels. The word lists sample preprimer through fifth grade vocabulary; the readings include primer through seventh grade reading

Table 9-1
Published Tests of Specific Reading Skills

Test	Grade Level	Reading Skills
Gilmore Oral Reading Test (Gilmore & Gilmore, 1968)	1–8	Accuracy, comprehension, and rate of oral reading
Gray Oral Reading Tests (Gray & Robinson, 1967)	1–college	Speed and accuracy of oral reading, specific error classification
McCullough Word Analysis Tests (McCullough, 1963)	4–6	Identifying initial blends and digraphs, using phonetic discrimination, matching letters to vowel sounds, sounding whole words, interpreting phonetic symbols, dividing words into syllables, and identifying root words in affixed forms
Test of Reading Comprehension (Brown, Hammill, & Wiederholt, 1978)	2–12	General vocabulary, syntactic similarities, paragraph reading, sentence sequencing, and more specific vocabulary needed to read in content areas

material. The entire battery takes approximately 60 minutes to administer. We believe that the 1981 edition of the DRS is a significantly improved version of the test.

Durrell Analysis of Reading Difficulty (Durrell & Catterson, 1980). This battery consists of a series of subtests: Oral Reading, Silent Reading, Listening Comprehension, Word Recognition and Word Analysis, Listening Vocabulary, Pronunciation of Word Elements, Spelling, Visual Memory of Words, Auditory Analysis of Words and Elements, and Prereading Phonics Abilities Inventories. The tests are designed primarily for students at nonreading through sixth grade reading levels. Grade level scores are provided, along with many excellent suggestions for organizing remedial instruction. A checklist of instructional needs follows each subtest and helps focus the teacher's attention on specific reading deficits identified in the test and the classroom. Depending on the number of subtests used, the test can take 30 to 90 minutes to administer.

Gates-McKillop-Horowitz Reading Diagnostic Tests (Gates, McKillop, & Horowitz, 1981). This battery is a revision of the Gates-McKillop Reading Diagnostic Tests (Gates & McKillop, 1962). The tests are designed for individual administration to students in Grades 1 through 6. It is possible, however, to use selected tests with older pupils who have reading difficulties. Administration time ranges from 30 to 60 minutes. The complete battery is composed of subtests: Oral Reading, Reading Sentences, Words—Flash, Words—Untimed, Syllabication, Recognizing and Blending

Common Word Parts, Reading Words, Giving Letter Sounds, Naming Capital Letters, Naming Lowercase Letters, Recognizing the Visual Forms of Sounds—Vowels, Auditory Blending, Auditory Discrimination, Spelling, and an Informal Writing Sample. Minimal technical information is provided with this test, yet it is widely used. Despite the omission of a reading comprehension subtest, the depth and variety of reading skills that the test does appraise are viewed as definite advantages.

Stanford Diagnostic Reading Test (Karlsen, Madden, & Gardner, 1974, 1977). This is a group-administered reading test that is both norm-referenced and criterion-referenced. The test is available on four levels (identified by color) and may be used with students in Grades 1 through 12. The various levels include measures of Auditory Vocabulary, Auditory Discrimination, Phonetic Analysis, Structural Analysis, Word Reading, Reading Comprehension, and Rate. The test yields norm-referenced scores of percentile ranks, stanines, grade equivalents, and scaled scores. Criterion-referenced scores, called progress indicators, are also available. They help to determine whether students have mastered specific skills at various stages of the reading process. The test is recognized as a well-standardized and reliable group test of reading skills.

Woodcock Reading Mastery Tests (Woodcock, 1973). The five subtests comprising this battery include Letter Identification, Word Identification, Word Attack, Word Comprehension, and Passage Comprehension. There are two versions of this test specifically designed for students from kindergarten to Grade 12. Results are combined to provide a composite index of overall reading skill. Traditional grade scores and age equivalents are also available. The mastery scale is intended to predict the child's relative success with reading tasks of varying difficulty.

Informal Methods

Numerous informal assessment procedures are available for appraising the reading skills of handicapped learners. Informal methods are widely used because most are inexpensive, flexible, and easily administered. In addition, Farr (1969) points out that informal methods can be reliable and valid measures of reading, despite the lack of normative data, since more samples of reading behavior are likely to be taken.

Observations. As noted earlier, various observational techniques can provide valuable diagnostic information. Observational procedures are often used to confirm the findings of both formal and informal tests; at other times observations are used to study certain skills and behaviors not covered by formal tests. The classroom setting provides an opportunity to clearly observe the characteristic behavior of an individual student in many different instructional situations. Oral reading, silent reading, group discussion of reading material, seatwork activity, and selection of library books are but a few of the situations in which teachers can informally obtain diagnostic data.

The teacher can use observation to answer a variety of questions.

☐ What word analysis skills does the child utilize?

☐ How extensive is the child's sight vocabulary?

☐ What *consistent* word analysis errors are made by the child?

☐ Does the child depend upon one analysis skill (e.g., sounding words out)?

☐ Are particular words or parts of words consistently distorted or omitted?

☐ Does the child read too fast, too slow, or word by word?

☐ Are factual questions answered correctly?

☐ Is the child able to answer comprehension questions requiring inferential and critical reading ability? (Wallace & McLoughlin, 1979, p. 163)

Most teachers usually find it helpful to have some type of systematic recording of observations. Checklists, for example, can be used to note difficulties readily and to monitor student progress in reading. A number of the diagnostic reading tests described earlier in this chapter (e.g., Durrell Analysis of Reading Difficulty and the Gates-McKillop-Horowitz Reading Diagnostic Tests) include checklists that can be used in observing various reading behaviors. A sample observational checklist is shown in Figure 9–1.

Informal Reading Inventories. An informal reading inventory, commonly referred to as an IRI, consists of a series of carefully graded reading passages appropriate for reading levels from preprimer through eighth grade. The IRI is widely used among educators for informally determining a student's general reading level. Although many educators develop their own IRIs, some teachers have found it convenient to use commercially prepared inventories (see Table 9–2).

Table 9-2
Commercial Reading Inventories

Inventory	Publisher
Analytical Reading Inventory	Charles E. Merrill
Classroom Reading Inventory	William C. Brown
Diagnostic Reading Inventory	Kendall/Hunt
Ekwall Reading Inventory	Allyn & Bacon
Informal Reading Assessment	Rand McNally
Reading Miscue Inventory	Macmillan
Sucher-Allred Reading Placement Inventory	Economy

Figure 9-1. Reading Assessment Checklist

NAME _____

GRADE _____

TEACHER _____

SCHOOL _____

	1st Check	2nd Check	3rd Check		
1				Word-by-word reading	
2				Incorrect phrasing	
3				Poor pronunciation	
4				Omissions	
5				Repetitions	
6				Inversions or reversals	
7				Insertions	
8				Substitutions	Oral Reading
9				Basic sight words not known	
10				Sight vocabulary not up to grade level	
11				Guesses at words	
12				Consonant sounds not known	
13				Vowel sounds not known	
14				Vowel pairs and/or consonant clusters not known (digraphs, diphthongs, blends)	
15				Lacks desirable structural analysis (Morphology)	
16				Unable to use context clues	
17				Contractions not known	
18				Comprehension inadequate	Oral Silent
19				Vocabulary inadequate	
20				Unaided recall scanty	
21				Response poorly organized	
22				Unable to locate information	
23				Inability to skim	Study Skills
24				Inability to adjust rate to difficulty of material	
25				Low rate of speed	
26				High rate at expense of accuracy	
27				Voicing-lip movement	
28				Lacks knowledge of the alphabet	Other Abilities
29				Written recall limited by spelling ability	
30				Undeveloped dictionary skills	

D—Difficulty recognized
P—Pupil progressing
N—No longer has difficulty

The items listed above represent the most common difficulties encountered by pupils in the reading program. Following each numbered item are spaces for notation of that specific difficulty. This may be done at intervals of several months. One might use a check to indicate difficulty recognized or the following letters to represent more accurate appraisal:

SOURCE: From *Locating and Correcting Reading Difficulties* (4th ed., p. 6) by E. E. Ekwall, 1985, Columbus, OH: Charles E. Merrill. Copyright 1985 by Bell & Howell Company. Reprinted by permission.

According to Hammill and Bartel (1982), the directions for developing an IRI include

1. Selection of a standard basal series
   a. Any series that goes from preprimer to the sixth grade level may be used.
   b. Materials that the child has not previously used should be included.
2. Selection of passages from the basal reader
   a. Choose a selection that makes a complete story.
   b. Choose selections of about 50 words at the preprimer level; 100 words at the primer, first, and second levels; and 100–150 words at the upper levels.
   c. Choose two selections at each level: plan to use one for oral reading and one for silent reading, and take the selection from the middle of the book.
3. Construction of questions
   a. Build five questions for each selection at the preprimer level; six questions for each selection at primer, first, and second levels; and ten questions from each selection at level three and above.
   b. Avoid yes and no questions.
   c. Include a vocabulary in the questions at the same level as the vocabulary in the selections.
   d. Construct three kinds of questions at each level in about the following percentages: factual, 40 percent; inferential, 40 percent; vocabulary, 20 percent.
4. Construction and preparation of test
   a. Cut and mount the selection on oaktag, *or*
   b. Note the pages in the book, print the questions on separate cards, and have the child read the selections from the test itself. (p. 52)

Two major types of information can generally be obtained from an IRI. Quantitative information expressed in grade equivalent scores indicates the reader's *independent* reading level (reading with understanding and ease without assistance), *instructional* reading level (reading with understanding under teacher guidance), and *frustration* level (reading material that is too difficult). Qualitative information concerns the reader's word recognition and comprehension skills (Burns & Roe, 1980).

Specific reading difficulties are usually determined by analyzing the pupil's IRI performance. Most marking systems for recording oral reading errors emphasize the actual number of these errors. An alternative method for recording and analyzing oral reading in a systematic fashion is called the *reading miscue* procedure. According to Goodman (1973), a miscue is an actual, observed response in oral reading that does not match the expected outcome. The emphasis is placed on the nature of the miscue rather than on the number of errors. The focus of miscue analysis is on how the student's responses affect the actual meaning of a sentence or passage. This assessment technique is presented in the Reading Miscue Inventory (Goodman & Burke, 1972). It contains reading passages and scoring sheets to be used in miscue analysis. The instrument analyzes miscues according to graphic, syntactic, and semantic characteristics.

Cloze Procedure. The cloze procedure is an informal assessment technique used to estimate the readability level of reading materials or a pupil's instructional reading level. The procedure involves deleting every nth word from a reading passage (starting with the second sentence) and replacing it with a blank line. Students are then expected to read the passage and attempt to fill in the blanks with the correct words for the context of the sentences. Figure 9–2 shows an example of the cloze procedure. The specific steps for designing a cloze test are listed below.

1. Randomly select a minimum of two reading passages of approximately 250 words in length from each graded reading selection to be assessed. Reading passages should begin a new paragraph.
2. Delete every fifth word from the passage starting with the second sentence and replace the deleted words with lines of equal length.
3. Duplicate the passages. In individual administration pupils can simply say the word. In group administration students are instructed to fill in the missing words.

Figure 9-2. Cloze Procedure

Why Live in a City?

R. Boyce and P. Bacon

People live in cities for different reasons. Sometimes the kinds of (*work*) people want to do (*can*) only be done in (*a*) city. Whether or not (*they*) like city life, they (*must*) work there. Usually people (*live*) in cities because they (*like*) city life. Some people (*do*) not have to work (*in*) cities. They have jobs (*they*) could do anywhere. Your (*teacher*) is a person like (*this*). What other kinds of (*work*) can be done anywhere?

(*Some*) city people do not (*work*). They may be too (*old*) to work. These people (*live*) in cities because they (*can*) find help or go (*places*) easily and quickly. Most (*people*) live in cities because (*there*) is always something interesting (*to*) do or see. They (*can*) choose from many things. (*They*) can shop in different (*kinds*) of stores. They can (*eat*) fancy food in fine (*restaurants*) or hot dogs at (*an*) outdoor stand. They can (*go*) to theaters and zoos. (*What*) other interesting places are (*in*) cities?

The most important (*thing*) that cities have which (*the*) country does not have (*is*) many people. Why would (*one*) prefer to be around (*many*) people?

SOURCE: From *Making Choices*, Reader I (Merrill Linguistic Reading Program, p. 106) by W. Otto, M. Rudolph, R. Smith, & R. Wilson, 1975, Columbus, OH: Charles E. Merrill. Copyright 1975 by Bell & Howell Company. Adapted by permission.

Although the cloze procedure has limited usefulness as a diagnostic technique, Harris and Sipay (1980) point out that (1) the procedure is easier and quicker to construct, administer, score, and interpret than an IRI; (2) it requires less expertise; (3) it can be group administered; (4) it provides a good measurement of ability to use semantic and syntactic clues; and (5) research findings regarding its reliability and validity for pupils over age 8 are impressive.

Teacher-Constructed Tests. Another informal assessment method for appraising a student's reading skills is the teacher-constructed test. According to Wallace and McLoughlin (1979), these tests can be used to measure the effects of various instructional programs, to screen for general levels of achievement, to assess specific skills, or to supplement standardized reading tests. Teacher-constructed tests can be designed to measure almost any specific reading skill. Word analysis and word recognition skills, in particular, are ideally suited to the objective format typically used in informal tests.

Teacher-constructed tests can be patterned after published tests and workbook exercises. The sequence of steps in constructing an informal test are described by Otto (1973).

1. Decide exactly what information is desired and what observable behavior is involved.
2. Devise new test items, materials, or situations to sample the behavior to be evaluated, or adapt existing ones.
3. Keep a record of the student's behavior or responses.
4. Analyze the information obtained.
5. Judge how the information fits the total picture and how well it answers the target questions.

METHODS AND MATERIALS

A vast number of methods and materials are available for use with students experiencing reading difficulties. Some of the reading approaches discussed in this section are developmental, whereas others are basically remedial.

Developmental Approaches

Many reading approaches used with the learning handicapped are essentially developmental methods and materials that have been adapted for students with reading problems. Developmental reading approaches, according to Mercer and Mercer (1985), emphasize sequential instruction on a daily basis and are usually programmed according to a normative pattern of reading growth. Basal readers are probably the best known and most widely used developmental reading approach. Table 9–3 summarizes some of the various developmental approaches that are used with reading handicapped students.

Table 9-3
Developmental Reading Approaches

Type of Approach	Where Available	Advantages/Disadvantages/Special Comments
Complete Basals. These usually consist of reading texts, teacher's manual, and supplementary materials such as workbooks. They are often sequenced in a series from K to Grade 6 or 8. The instructional approach is one of introducing a controlled sight vocabulary coupled with an analytic phonics emphasis.	Holt, Rinehart and Winston Ginn 720 Series Scott, Foresman Harcourt, Brace, Jovanovich American Book Company Houghton Mifflin Rand-McNally MacMillan Harper and Row Allyn and Bacon Laidlaw	1. Lend themselves well to the 3-reading-group arrangement; less well to individualizing 2. Content usually designed for the "typical" child; often not appealing to inner-city children or rural children 3. Generally well-sequenced and comprehensive; attend to most aspects of developmental reading 4. Most have complete pupil packets of supplementary materials, saving teacher searching time 5. Sufficiently detailed and integrated that successful use is possible for a teacher lacking in confidence or experience
Synthetic Phonics Basals. Similar to above in some ways, but emphasis is on mastering component phonics skills, then putting together into words.	Open Court Reading Program Lippincott's Basic Reader Series Distar Reading Swirl Community Skills Program (SW Regional Laboratory)	1–5. Same as above. 6. Evidence is that a synthetic approach to word attack is rarely utilized by good readers.
Linguistic Phonemic Approaches. Vocabulary that is used is highly controlled and conforms to the sound patterns of English (e.g., Nan, Dan,	Let's Read (Bloomfield) SRA Basic Reading Series Merrill Linguistic Readers Programmed Reading (Webster, McGraw-Hill)	1. Content and usage in stories (especially early ones) sometimes contrived because of controlled vocabulary

Table 9-3 *(continued)*

Type of Approach	*Where Available*	*Advantages/Disadvantages/Special Comments*
man, fan, ran, etc.). Most programs contain children's texts, teacher manual and supplementary materials.	SRA Lift-Off to Reading Palo Alto Program (Harcourt, Brace, Jovanovich)	2. Same as for Complete Basals
Individualized Reading. Each child reads materials of own choice and at own rate. Word recognition and comprehension skills are taught as individual children need them. Monitoring of progress is done through individual teacher conferences. Careful record-keeping is necessary.	Trade books of many different types, topics, and levels	1. Children are interested in content 2. Promotes good habits of selection of reading materials 3. Need an extensive collection of books from which to choose 4. Teacher needs comprehensive knowledge of reading skills to make sure all are covered 5. Required record-keeping can be cumbersome
Diagnostic-Prescriptive Programs. These consist of entry-testing and exit-testing of skills related to specific skills. Students who pass entry test go on to other needed areas. Reading objectives fully stated.	*Print* Wisconsin Design for Reading Skill (National Computer Systems) Fountain Valley Reading Support System (Richard Zweig) Ransom Program (Addison-Wesley) *Non-Print, Computer Assisted* Stanford University Project Harcourt Brace CAI Remedial Reading Program	1. Skills are usually well sequenced 2. Pupils work at own pace 3. Learning may be boring, repetitive, or mechanistic 4. Provide for on-going assessment and feedback 5. De-emphasize the language basis of reading (interaction and communication with other people) 6. Only those skills that lend themselves to the format are taught

Table 9-3 (continued)

Type of Approach	Where Available	Advantages/Disadvantages/Special Comments
Language Experience Approach. Based on teacher recording of child's narrated experiences. These stories become basis for reading. May be based on level of group or individual child. Stories are collected and made into a "book."	Teacher-made materials	1. Relationship to child's experience is explicit 2. Firmly establishes reading as a language/communicative act 3. Provides no systematic skill development (left up to the teacher to improvise) 4. Can become reinforcing only at child's existing level, rather than pushing him or her on 5. Highly adaptable to pupils with unique needs and backgrounds

SOURCE: From *Teaching Children with Learning and Behavior Problems* (3rd ed., pp. 74–75) by D. H. Hammill and N. R. Bartel, 1982, Boston: Allyn & Bacon. Copyright 1982 by Allyn & Bacon. Reprinted by permission.

Developmental reading approaches can be adapted for an individual pupil or for a group of students with similar reading problems. Some of the adaptations listed by Lerner (1985) include

- increasing the amount of repetition
- providing more time for the completion of work
- giving more examples or activities
- providing more review
- introducing the work more slowly
- expanding background information
- using different standard books and materials

Remedial Approaches

Remedial methods and materials are also used with students experiencing reading difficulties. Most of the remedial approaches discussed in this section were specifically designed for use with the reading disabled student.

High Interest/Low Vocabulary Materials. Students with reading problems are often frustrated with developmental reading materials because books geared to their interest level are beyond their reading ability (Mercer

Table 9-4
High Interest/Easy-to-Read Materials

Titles	Reading Grade Level	Interest Grade Level	Publisher
Action Kits	2–6	7–12	Scholastic Magazine
Breakthrough Series	1–8	6–12	Allyn & Bacon
Cowboy Sam Series	pp*–3	1–6	Benefic Press
Dan Frontier Series	pp–4	pp–6	Benefic Press
Deep Sea Adventure Series	1.8–5	3–10	Addison-Wesley
Galaxy 5	2	4–12	Children's Press
Laura Brewster Mysteries	3	4–12	Children's Press
Morgan Bay Mysteries	2–4	4–11	Addison-Wesley
Pacemaker Series	2–3	5–12	Fearson
Pal Paperbacks	1–5	5–12	Xerox Education Publications
Profiles: A Collection of Short Biographies	3–4	7–12	Globe
Racing Wheels Series	2–4	4–12	Benefic Press
Reading for Concept Series	3–8	5–12	McGraw-Hill
Reader's Digest Skill Builders	1–4	2–5	Reader's Digest Service
Rock 'n Pop Stars	4	4–12	Children's Press
Sailor Jack Series	pp–3	1–6	Benefic Press
Sports Mystery Series	2–4	4–9	Benefic Press
Sports Profiles	5	4–11	Raintree
Venture Series	4–6.5	7–12	Follett

*Preprimer

& Mercer, 1985). Therefore, books that are designed to be of high interest yet at an easier reading level are an appealing alternative for older students with reading difficulties. As noted in Table 9–4, many different books of this type are available through numerous publishers.

Multisensory Methods. Reading approaches that are labeled multisensory usually attempt to teach reading skills through kinesthetic and tactile stimulation, along with the visual and auditory modalities. Two methods of teaching reading that emphasize a multisensory approach are the Fernald method (Fernald, 1943) and the Gillingham-Stillman method (Gillingham & Stillman, 1966). The Fernald approach incorporates four stages wherein the student progresses from word recognition to extensive reading of books and other materials. This technique utilizes tracing as a method of learning whole words.

In stage one the student selects a word she would like to learn, and that word is written or printed in large letters by the teacher. The student traces the word with her finger and is instructed to say each syllable of the word as it is traced. The student repeats this process as often as necessary until the word can be written as a unit from memory. Next, the student is encouraged to incorporate the word into a story. The story is usually typed for the student by the teacher. Each new word that the student learns is placed on a card and alphabetically filed by the student. These words are frequently utilized in stories.

Stage two is basically identical to stage one except that tracing is eliminated. The student learns words she has dictated and uses these words in stories. In stage three words are no longer written on cards. The student learns dictated words and uses these words in stories, which usually increase in length during this stage. The fourth stage encourages the student to learn new words by generalizing from words already known, to survey a reading passage before reading, and to apply previously learned skills.

The Gillingham-Stillman approach, based on the work of Orton (1937), is another multisensory technique for teaching specific reading skills. According to Wallace and McLoughlin (1979), the Gillingham-Stillman method emphasizes individual letters. Students are taught letter sounds, visual symbols, and various linkages through tracing, copying, and writing particular letters. Phonetic drill cards and short stories are considered crucial parts of the program. Considerable emphasis is also placed on spelling, dictionary skills, syllabication, and rules for both phonics and written language. Individual letters are introduced by the teacher through established procedures.

1. A small card with one letter printed on it is exposed to the student, and the name of the letter is spoken by the teacher. The name of the letter is then repeated by the student.

2. As soon as the name of the letter is mastered, its sound is made by the teacher and repeated by the student. The original card is then exposed and the teacher asks, "What does this letter say?" The student is expected to give the sound.

3. Without the card exposed, the teacher makes the sound represented by the letter and says, "Tell me the name of the letter that has this sound." The student is expected to give the name of the letter.

4. The letter is carefully written by the teacher, and its form is explained to the student. That letter is then traced by the student, copied, written from memory, and then written again without looking at the previously written letters.

5. Finally, the teacher makes the sound and instructs the student to "write the letter that has this sound."

Edmark. The Edmark Reading Program (Bijou, 1977) was developed as a sight-word acquisition program for handicapped students. Students are taught 150 sight words through 227 lessons: (1) prereading lessons that train the student on the match-to-sample format, (2) word recognition lessons of one to two words per lesson, (3) lessons that teach the student to follow printed directions, (4) lessons in matching pictures to phrases, and (5) lessons in a storybook in which the student reads 16 stories orally. Polloway and Smith (1982) note that the purpose is based on the assumption that word analysis can be taught after a student develops a sight vocabulary.

Programmed Reading. Most programmed reading materials are designed to teach reading skills through a concisely organized and sequential approach. In reading, most programmed instruction takes the form of workbooks. Short learning units, called frames, require the student to be actively involved in the reading process by responding to each frame and immediately checking the correctness of the response. Students are usually encouraged to complete the material at their own pace. Wallace and McLoughlin (1979) point out that programmed reading materials offer a different format from the one to which most readers are accustomed. This departure from tradition has proven to be a motivating factor for some students; however, other students do not have the skills required to use self-pacing programmed formats. Among the available programmed approaches, Programmed Reading (Webster/McGraw-Hill) and the Sullivan Reading Program (Behavioral Reading Laboratories) are widely used with the reading disabled.

Remedial Reading Drills. These reading drills (Hegge, Kirk, & Kirk, 1955) were initially designed for mentally retarded students, but they have been primarily used with reading disabled students. The program consists of lists of words emphasizing specific sounds and combinations of letters. The student is intended to use various lists to learn to blend various sounds. A multisensory approach is suggested throughout the program. The use of drills with reading disabled students helps to reinforce many sound-symbol relationships.

Neurological Impress Method. The neurological impress method (Heckelman, 1969; Longford, Slade, & Barnett, 1974) was originally developed for students with severe reading difficulties. This approach uses a system of unison reading, whereby the student and the teacher read aloud simultaneously at a rapid rate. The disabled reader is placed slightly to the front of the teacher, with the student and the teacher holding the book jointly. As the student and the teacher read the materials in unison, the teacher's voice is directed into the student's ear at close range. The student is also encouraged to slide his finger along the line, following the words as they are being spoken. One goal of this method is to cover as many pages of reading material as possible in the allotted reading time. Specific word analysis and comprehensive skills are not taught in this program.

New Alphabets. Some approaches to beginning reading instruction have modified the traditional 26-letter alphabet in order to assure a regular correspondence between sound and symbol and to eliminate multiple spellings of the same sound. The initial teaching alphabet (i.t.a.), the best known of the new alphabets, includes a 44-character alphabet composed of 24 letters from the conventional Roman alphabet (*q* and *x* are eliminated) and 20 additional letters. Some of the new letters resemble Roman letters joined together. This system uses lowercase letters and encourages the use of writing throughout the program.

The i.t.a. system was designed as a change in medium and not a change in method. Consequently, transition to traditional orthography is usually recommended at the end of first grade or the beginning of second grade. Because i.t.a. is designed for beginning reading, it is not used extensively with disabled readers. Woodcock (1967) reports that the approach is no more effective than other reading methods.

Reading Mastery: DISTAR.   The Reading Mastery: DISTAR Reading Program (Engelmann & Bruner, 1984) is a highly structured, fast-paced, and intensive program of reading instruction that emphasizes decoding skills. Students are taught sequencing skills through symbol-action games. Blending exercises are designed to teach the synthetic relationships of sounds and words. Students are taught to blend by the say-it-fast technique, whereas spelling words by sounds teaches the reverse procedure. Students receive continuous positive reinforcement throughout the program. Their mastery of various skills is appraised through criterion-referenced tests. Special lessons are available for skills that have not been mastered. Although published research evidence is minimal, many educators report positive results from using this program with reading disabled students.

The SRA Corrective Reading Program (Engelmann, Becker, Hanner, & Johnson, 1980) is based on DISTAR concepts and is intended for students in Grades 4 through 12. This particular program is divided into decoding and comprehension sections, each with 340 lessons. Lessons include teacher-directed activities, independent work, and assessment materials. Student contracts and progress charts also accompany the program. Lessons last approximately 35 to 40 minutes and include a built-in reinforcement system.

Microcomputers

The rapid growth in the use of microcomputers within American classrooms is actually a phenomenon of the 1980s that holds promise for improving the quality of educational services for all students in our schools. Microcomputer applications for the reading disabled, according to Sapona (1985), are similar to those for nondisabled students. These applications include programs for drill and practice of skills and presentation of information in a tutorial format. However, most studies suggest that microcomputers are used primarily for drill and practice activities. Becker (1983), for example, found that the most common microcomputer application among elementary schools in his nationwide survey was drill and practice activities.

Using the microcomputer for the drill and practice of reading skills is partly a response to the unique presentational ability of the microcomputer. Torgesen and Young (1983) point out that microcomputers can present material and require responses in a manner that is unavailable in more traditional teaching methods. A number of studies have suggested that the use of the microcomputer for drill activities may be more interesting to students, particularly when the software is in a gamelike format (Schiffman, Tobin, & Buchanan, 1982; Chaffin, Maxwell, & Thompson, 1982). Lerner (1985) believes that students with learning problems enjoy practicing reading skills with the microcomputer for a variety of reasons.

1. It provides individual instruction.
2. It provides nonthreatening feedback and corrective procedures immediately and continually.
3. It has infinite patience, providing the opportunity for as much drill and repetition as the student needs and wants.
4. It can provide large amounts of skills-oriented practice.

On the other hand, we believe that it is important to point out that, at the present time, there is no empirical evidence of the effect that microcomputer use for drill and practice activities has on the academic achievement of the reading disabled (Sapona, 1985). Furthermore, most educational computer software is considered to be of less than acceptable quality. We recommend the selective use of microcomputers with the reading handicapped until computer software is vastly improved and a good amount of sound research is conducted.

TEACHING ACTIVITIES

Readiness

1. Display a number of buttons of different sizes (or nails, blocks, pieces of the same color paper) in front of the pupil. Instruct her to match the buttons according to size or shape.
2. Place a number of objects (cup, pencil, ruler, block, eraser, nail) in front of the child. Display a duplicate of one of the objects and ask the child to pick up the similar object. Include only three or four objects initially. As time progresses and the child improves in this skill, increase the number of objects.
3. Instruct the student to match pictures of objects with the actual objects. Variations of this activity could include allowing the pupil to cut pictures from magazines to match actual objects or matching pictures to pictures.

4. Give students various shapes of macaroni to sort. Initially, the student can group the macaroni pieces according to shape and place them in small boxes. Later, the macaroni can be colored so that it can be sorted according to shape and color.

5. Show the child a picture with missing parts. Direct her to draw in the part that is omitted. Examples might include a tree without a trunk, a cup with a missing handle, faces with various parts missing (nose, ear, eye), a child without a shoe, a house without a door. Require the child to draw parts that match the sample drawing. Gradually make the missing parts less obvious.

6. Display three triangles and one square. Ask the student to identify the shape that is unlike the others. Various geometric shapes can be included. As the student progresses, increase the number of shapes to be discriminated. Shapes of different colors can be used after the student learns color discriminations.

7. Encourage the pupil to become aware of sizes and shapes. Cut out different sizes of squares, circles, triangles. Explain that a square is still a square even though it is smaller or larger than others. This activity can be extended by having the student find all of the square shapes in the room or all of the circle shapes in a magazine.

8. Describe an object that is familiar to the pupil (e.g., "I am thinking of something that is round, bounces up and down, and is needed to play certain games"). Ask the student to identify that object in one of four pictures that are presented to her. Actual objects can be used also.

9. Have the student complete dot-to-dot pictures of familiar objects or animals. Gradually increase the detail of the pictures, and ask the student to describe them.

10. Present the student with different arrangements of blocks, geometric shapes, familiar objects. Ask her to choose the one arrangement that is different from the others and to explain why. For example,

11. Have the student trace words and letters in or on any of the following media: finger paint, salt, sandpaper, felt, instant pudding, clay, or wet sand.

12. Write a number of letters on the chalkboard. While the students' eyes are closed, erase one letter. When the students open their eyes, ask them to identify the missing letter. Words can also be used for this activity.

13. Allow students to view a pegboard design, marble board, or bead design for a short period of time, and then ask them to duplicate the design.

Students working in pairs can also construct their own designs.

14. Encourage students to use a toy telephone to learn the telephone numbers of their friends.

Visual Discrimination

1. Present rows of four- or five-letter cut-outs to the student. Ask him to circle the same two letters in each row.

2. Have the pupil match capital and lowercase letters: *Aa, Mm, Pp, Bb.*

3. Play letter bingo with small groups of students. Cards with different letters printed on them are passed to the students. As the teacher or another student calls out various letters, each student covers these letters on his card. The first student to fill his card is the winner.

4. Have the student trace various letter templates and stencils.

5. Let the pupil use the typewriter to find specific letters. He can be instructed to find certain letters in a given amount of time.

6. Present letters of varying size to the student, and ask him to find matching letters. For example, a large $\mathcal{M}$ can be presented with a very small *M*, along with a medium size lowercase *m*.

7. Pictures that closely correspond to the shapes of individual letters can be presented with those letters as a memory device. For example, a wiggly snake $\mathcal{U}\!\!\!\sim$ can be presented with the letter *S*; a telephone pole, with the letter *T*; a wheel, with the letter *O*.

8. Present students with partially completed letters and ask them to identify and/or complete them. For example,

9. Show the pupil the alphabet with specific letters omitted. Ask him to fill in the missing letters (e.g., ab __ d __ fgh __ __ k __ m). Increase the number of missing letters as the student progresses.

10. Tape an individual alphabet to the student's desk to provide a quick reference and guide.

11. Dot-to-dot pictures can use letters instead of numbers. The teacher can provide instructions: "Draw a line to the letter *p*, now a straight line over to the letter *s*, down to the letter *b*." This activity can also be planned so that the lines are drawn in alphabetical sequence.

Auditory Discrimination

1. Read a word, such as *fat*. Ask the student to repeat the word. Then read a list of words and have the student clap when she hears a word that rhymes with the stimulus word.

2. Select two different noise makers, such as a bell and a drum. Stand behind the pupil and ring the bell. Ask the student to point to the ob-

ject used to make the sound. Gradually increase the number and similarity of sounds that can be discriminated.

3. With the aid of a tape recorder, ask the student to identify common sounds, such as those made by an airplane, a car, various animals, and household appliances. These sounds can gradually be changed to the voices of familiar people.

4. In working with the sounds of letters, focus initially on grossly different sounds, such as /m/ and /p/, /s/ and /b/, or /a/ and /v/. Gradually work into the finer discriminations, such as /b/ and /f/ or /m/ and /n/.

5. Associate a sound with a picture or a real object. The following pictures or items are helpful to most students (Russell & Karp, 1938).

apple	jacks	sack
boat	kite	tail
cat	lamp	umbrella
duck	mouse	vest
egg	nest	wagon
fox	orange	xylophone
goat	pail	yard
house	queen	zebra
ice cream	rooster	

6. Write sounds on large pieces of paper and place them on the floor. Say a word beginning (or ending) with a specific sound, and have the student walk to the sound she has heard.

7. Give the student a box containing a number of different toy objects, such as boats, cars, plastic dishes, chalk, pencils, and erasers. Ask the student to select all the objects that begin with, for instance, the /p/ sound. Gradually introduce five or six boxes that emphasize different sounds.

8. Let the class listen to commercial records that teach auditory awareness of sounds.

9. Provide the student with a number of different pictures. Direct her to match pictures of objects with rhyming names. This activity can be varied by duplicating pictures for seatwork.

10. Give the student a list of rhyming words and direct her to circle the parts of the words that are alike. This activity checks student awareness of the fact that many rhyming words have parts that are spelled similarly.

11. Give the student a list of words and ask her to circle all those that rhyme with a given stimulus word. This activity can be varied by giving the student a list of words and instructing her to supply a word that rhymes with each.

12. Read a sentence with a word omitted (e.g., "We play baseball with a ball and _____ "). Instruct the student to change the omitted word

to one that rhymes with it. (Acceptable responses for this example include *cat, mat, fat,* and *sat.)*

13. Give the student two cards numbered one and two. Instruct her to listen for a specific sound as you say a word. She should indicate whether she heard it at the beginning or end of the word by holding up card number one or card number two.

14. Say a word such as *sad* and require the pupil to provide a word that rhymes with it but has a different initial consonant.

15. Ask the student to say all the words she knows that begin with a specific sound.

16. Make up nonsense sentences using the same letter at the beginning of each word (e.g., "Bad Bill bit blueberries" or "Holy Harry has hot hands").

17. Provide the student with a number of individual oak tag cards with one sound on each. Instruct the student to listen carefully to a series of words and hold up the letter she hears at the beginning (or end) of each word.

18. Instruct the student to classify a number of pictures according to initial or final sounds. Appropriately labeled boxes are helpful for this activity. Have the student place pictures with the beginning /s/ sound in one box, the beginning /f/ sound in another, and so on.

19. Give each pupil the same number of oak tag cards, each with a word written on it. Ask for all the cards that begin or end with a certain sound or rhyme with a certain word (e.g., all the cards that end with the same sound as *bag*). Continue to ask questions until each student's pile of cards is depleted.

Sound Blending

1. Ask the student to blend specific sounds to a given list of phonograms (e.g., blending the /p/ sound to *at, in, it, an*).

2. Ask the student to blend different consonants to a specific word family. For example, he might blend initial consonants to the *in* family— *pin, fin, tin.*

3. Call out words that have the same blend in either the initial or final position. Let the student tell where he hears the blend (e.g., *chip, chum, charge; search, patch, march*).

4. After the student knows specific sounds, give him three- to five-letter nonsense syllables. Ask him to blend the sounds. The syllables can become progressively longer as the student improves in this ability.

5. Provide the student with a picture of a specific object, such as a block. Below the picture appears the name of the object, spelled without a particular consonant blend, such as _____ _____ ock. Have the student supply the missing blend, either writing it in or saying it.

6. Have the student draw a word from a box containing words with initial blends. The student must pronounce the word he chooses and give another word that begins with the same blend.

7. Print words with blends on oak tag and cut each word after the blend. Mix up a number of word parts and have the student sort them correctly. Gradually increase the number of words as the student succeeds with this task.

8. Make two concentric circles, one with blends and the other with phonograms. Have students rotate the circle and read the words. Circles for initial consonants can also be made.

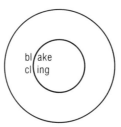

9. Give each student a large piece of paper with a blend written on it. Write a phonogram on the chalkboard and ask the students to make a word with their blend and the phonogram on the board.

10. Prepare a series of three stimulus words. Pronounce one of the words in each series. Have the children underline the word you pronounce. For example,

blue	black	drum	plain	dress
blow	plank	dear	plant	dire
brake	blank	drink	party	drive

Reversals

1. Present students with a stimulus word and four choices from which to choose the matching word. For example,

pot	otp	top	tip	pot
lap	pal	pil	lap	alp
war	row	war	raw	awr

2. Have the student make an association for letters that are reversed. For example, a student with a freckle on the left hand could remember that a *d* points in that direction. Likewise, a student who wears a ring on one of the fingers on the right hand could associate the ring with the direction of the letter *b*.

3. Print frequently reversed letters on oak tag strips. These letters should also be outlined on tracing paper. Let the student match the tracing paper letter with the oak tag strip by placing the tracing paper over the letter.

4. Give the student words with missing letters accompanied by matching pictures. This exercise can emphasize frequently reversed letters. For example,

5. Instruct the pupil to trace specific letters on sandpaper or in salt trays. Be sure that the student says the name of the letter as he traces it.

6. Describe a letter (e.g., "I am thinking of a letter that is a straight line up and down and another line straight across"). Have the student find that letter among three or four placed in front of him, and ask him to name it.

7. Place words that are frequently reversed on flash cards and use them for periodic drills. Arrow cues can be added for help. For example,

SAW	DOG	NET	TAR
→	→	→	→

8. Place words on flash cards and present them to the student by covering up all but the first letter. Slowly uncover additional letters until the student correctly pronounces the word. This activity emphasizes left-to-right orientation. An overhead projector can also be used.

Structural Analysis

1. Provide the student with a list of words and direct her to circle the root (graphemic base) in each word; for example, *singing*, *jumps*, *ended*. This activity can be applied to prefixes and suffixes.

2. Provide the pupil with a variety of root words on oak tag strips and an envelope of endings that can be added to these root words. Ask the student to make as many words as she can.

3. Give the student a series of sentences in which certain words are missing prefixes or suffixes. Have the student complete each sentence. For example,
   a. Mary walk _____ to the store each morning.
   b. She is _____ sure of the correct street.
   c. They are play _____ in the yard.
   d. He did not _____ connect the refrigerator.

4. For older students give a root word and the meaning of a new word. Ask them to write the new word (e.g., *read,* "to read again," *reread*).

5. Under two columns list words that can be made into compound words. Leave a third column blank so that the student can supply the compound word.

Column A	Column B	Column C
base	ball	_____
cow	boy	_____
light	house	_____

6. The preceding activity can be varied by leaving blank either Column A or Column B in addition to Column C. Another variation could place a drawing in either of the first two columns.

Column A	Column B	Column C
_____	_____	_____
base		_____
	boy	_____
light		_____

7. Use the words in the preceding exercises in random order. Ask the student to put together as many compound words as she can (e.g., *ball, house, flash, boy, base, light, cow, boat*).

8. Prepare a paragraph with missing parts of compound words. Ask the student to supply the missing parts, for example,

> John and Tom play base*(ball)* or *(basket)*ball every after*(noon)* on the *(play)*ground. *(Some)*times they also play *(horse)*shoes or play in the sand*(box).* In the winter they build *(snow)*men and make snow*(balls).*

9. Students can make their own compound words. Have them define each word they make.

10. Letters or parts of words can be color cued for memory. For example, in the word *raining, -ing* can be color coded red.

Sight Words

1. Prepare a tape recording of the most common sight words. Have the student listen to the tape through earphones and follow a work-

sheet. The voice on the tape says, "Number 1 is *guess*, number 2 is *could*, ..." To test a student, give him a word list without numbers and let him mark the worksheet. In this case the voice says, "Put the number 1 in front of *guess*; put the number 2 in front of *could*; . . . ."

2. Write five sight words on the chalkboard. Read each one aloud and ask the student to close his eyes. Erase a word and ask, "What is missing?" Continue until all the words are erased. Next, ask the pupil to remember the five original words, and write them again on the board. See whether he can read the entire list.

3. Use the Language Master, which can play and record special cards, to teach new words or review those previously taught. Use the blank cards to program the most persistently miscalled words.

4. Duplicate a sheet with groups of words that are similar in configuration. Direct the pupil to circle the word you read. For example,

a.	<u>at</u>	is	it	in
b.	see	saw	<u>sea</u>	sip

Record the stimulus words if you want the student to use a tape recorder with this activity.

5. Picture dictionaries can be helpful in learning words and associating meanings. Encourage students to make their own dictionaries with either magazine pictures or their own illustrations.

6. Within a group of assorted words written on tag board, write all difficult sight words in red to alert the student that he must recall the word by memory.

7. With sight words on cards, a student can review words previously learned by placing the words he knows in a "friends" pile and the troublesome words in an "enemies" pile. Students can work in pairs.

8. Draw a baseball diamond on the chalkboard. Place sight words printed on flash cards on the chalk ledge. Label the words "single," "double," "homerun," and so on. Groups of students can play baseball by reading the words. This activity can also be adapted to football, fishing, or mountain climbing.

9. Tracing can be beneficial for students with poor visual memories. The student should say the word as he traces it—in the air, on the chalkboard, in salt trays, on large pieces of paper.

10. Pairs of words can be presented to students to facilitate memory. Examples include *salt* and *pepper, bread* and *butter, black* and *white, hot* and *cold.*

11. Have the pupil find a match for a stimulus word in a list of visually similar words, such as those illustrated here.

bed	bid	bad	bud	dab	bed
hop	hip	hop	bop	hup	dip
run	run	rat	fun	sun	nun

This activity can be varied by calling out the stimulus word.

12. Label objects around the room and periodically review these labels with the students. Mix the labels and have a pupil put them in the proper place.

13. Print letters or words on removable gummed labels, and place them on the squares of a checkerboard. Let students play checkers but require them to name the letter or word before they make a move.

14. Provide students with scrambled words and ask them to arrange the letters correctly. For example, present *cat* as *atc* and *bag* as *agb*.

15. Some basic sight words are listed here (Ekwall, 1976). Incorporate them into your teaching activities.

Preprimer

a	do	here	look	put	two
and	down	him	make	run	water
are	eat	his	my	said	we
away	for	house	no	the	what
be	get	I	not	then	where
big	go	in	of	this	who
but	good	it	oh	three	will
can	has	know	one	to	you
come	have	like	play	too	your
did	her	little			

Primer

about	came	help	on	some	up
after	could	how	other	something	us
all	day	is	over	stop	very
am	find	jump	ran	take	want
an	fly	let	red	that	was
around	from	man	ride	them	way
as	funny	may	sat	there	went
back	give	me	saw	they	when
blue	green	mother	see	time	would
by	had	now	she	tree	yes
call	he	old	so		

Reader 1

again	buy	girl	Mrs.	rabbit	think
any	children	got	much	read	thought
ask	cold	happy	must	shall	took
at	color	high	name	side	under

ate	cry	if	never	sleep	walk
ball	dog	into	new	soon	well
been	door	just	night	stand	were
before	far	laugh	or	tell	white
began	fast	light	out	than	why
better	father	long	party	thank	with
black	five	more	please	their	work
boy	four	morning	pretty	these	yellow
brown	fun	Mr.	pull		

Reader 2

always	end	grow	live	place	ten
another	enough	hand	made	right	thing
because	even	hard	many	round	those
best	every	head	men	say	together
book	eye	hold	near	school	told
both	fall	home	next	should	until
box	first	hot	once	show	wait
bring	found	hurt	only	sit	warm
carry	friend	keep	open	six	which
clean	full	kind	out	start	while
cut	gave	last	own	still	wish
does	going	left	pick	sure	year
each					

Reader 2

dear	most	present	sing	today	use
done	off	seem	small	try	wash
drink	people	seven	such	turn	write

Reader 3

also	draw	goes	its	leave	upon
don't	eight	grand	king	myself	

Reading Comprehension Activities for Older Students

1. Have students read untitled stories. When they complete each story, have them write an appropriate title.

2. Be sure that material to be read is worth the pupil's effort to read it. In addition, it should not be at too difficult a level for the student.

3. Give the students a series of written true/false statements to answer (e.g., cats have three legs, a square has four sides, triangles have five sides).

4. Give the students a series of absurd short stories to read. Ask them to find the absurdity (e.g., "The students put on their bathing suits. They collected their towels and snowballs to take swimming").

5. Have students read newspaper articles from which the headlines have been deleted. Then have them select the correct headlines from a group arranged on your desk.

6. After the students have read a story, print a list of phrases on the chalkboard, only some of which are related to the story. Ask the students to choose those that pertain to the reading selection.

7. Point out devices used by authors to emphasize certain passages: chapter titles, subheadings, italics, indentions.

8. Discuss with the students a story they have read and list the main ideas. Select students to illustrate specific story events with drawings. The story can then be retold by rolling the drawings in sequence on a makeshift TV screen or overhead projector.

9. After they have read a story, ask the students a number of questions that require them to remember details (e.g., "What grade did Ann fail?" "Who gave Peter the black eye?" "How much did the car cost?").

10. Ask the students to compose a telegram repeating the events of a story or of a certain part of a story. Limit the telegram to a specific number of words.

11. Distribute a worksheet with three or four sentences reflecting a sequence of events in a story. Have the students arrange the sentences in proper order.

12. Ask students to read a stimulus sentence and four multiple-choice responses. Have them select the correct responses. To ensure precise reading, have more than one correct response. For example,

    Mary and John are eight-year-old twins in the third grade at Smith School.
    a. John is one year older than Mary.
    b. John and Mary go to the same school.
    c. John and Mary were probably born in the same year.
    d. Mary and John do not have any other brothers and sisters.

13. Encourage students to indicate exactly when in a particular story they first knew it was sad or funny.

14. Let one pupil take the role of a character in a story that the class has read. The rest of the class should try to guess the identity of the character, using clues given to them by the impersonator.

15. Have students read a story on how to do some activity (e.g., build a kite, make soap, or bake a cake). Ask them to perform the activity in proper sequence.

16. Distribute specific instructions on paper slips (e.g., "Put all the books in the library corner in order" or "Pass out a yellow piece of paper to each girl in the room"). Ask students to carry out the instructions.

17. Tape-record advertisements heard on radio and television, and have students discuss the merits of certain statements (Ekwall, 1985).

18. Stop periodically while reading a story aloud, and ask students to predict the outcome.

19. Encourage pupils to discuss why they liked or disliked certain characters in a story.

20. Have students indicate whether a sentence is fact or opinion (e.g., Virginia is the best state in the country for fishing. Susan is 43 years old. Ronald Reagan was elected president of the United States. Pepperoni pizza is too spicy, April is the fourth month). Discuss particular responses.

21. Have students compare two editorials on the same subject (Lerner, 1985).

22. Ask students to predict what a story will be about on the basis of chapter headings or illustrations.

23. Have students read a story on a controversial issue. Discuss the pros and cons of the author's particular viewpoint.

REFERENCES

Becker, H. J. (1983). How schools use microcomputers. *Classroom Computer Learning, 4*(2), 41–44.

Bijou, S. W. (1977). *Edmark Reading Program.* Bellevue, WA: Edmark.

Brown, V. L., Hammill, D. D., & Wiederholt, J. L. (1978). *Test of Reading Comprehension.* Austin, TX: Pro-Ed.

Burns, P. C., & Roe, B. D. (1980). *Informal reading assessment.* Chicago: Rand McNally.

Chaffin, J. D., Maxwell, B., & Thompson, B. (1982). ARC-ED curriculum: The application of video game formats to educational software. *Exceptional Children, 49,* 173–178.

Durrell, D. D., & Catterson, J. H. (1980). *Durrell Analysis of Reading Difficulty* (3rd ed.). New York: Harcourt Brace Jovanovich.

Ekwall, E. E. (1976). *Diagnosis and remediation of the disabled reader.* Boston: Allyn & Bacon.

————. (1985). *Locating and correcting reading difficulties* (4th ed.). Columbus, OH: Charles E. Merrill.

Ekwall, E. E., & Shanker, J. L. (1983). *Diagnosis and remediation of the disabled reader* (2nd ed.). Boston: Allyn & Bacon.

Engelmann, S., Becker, W., Hanner, S., & Johnson, G. (1980). *Corrective reading program.* Chicago: Science Research Associates.

Engelmann, S., & Bruner, E. (1984). *Distar reading.* Chicago: Science Research Associates.

Farr, R. (1969). *Reading: What can be measured?* Newark, DE: International Reading Association.

Fernald, G. M. (1943). *Remedial techniques in basic school subjects.* New York: McGraw-Hill.

Gates, A. I., & McKillop, A. S. (1962). *Gates-McKillop Reading Diagnostic Tests.* New York: Columbia University, Teachers College Press, Bureau of Publications.

Gates, A. I., McKillop, A. S., & Horowitz, E. C. (1981). *Gates-McKillop-Horowitz Reading Diagnostic Tests.* New York: Teachers College Press.

Gillingham, A., & Stillman, B. (1966). *Remedial training for children with specific difficulty in reading, spelling, and penmanship* (7th ed.). Cambridge, MA: Educators Publishing Service.

Gilmore, J. V., & Gilmore, E. C. (1968). *Gilmore Oral Reading Test.* New York: Harcourt Brace Jovanovich.

Goodman, K. S. (1973). Miscues: Windows on reading. In K. S. Goodman (Ed.), *Miscue analysis.* Urbana, IL: Eric Clearinghouse.

Goodman, Y. M., & Burke, C. I. (1972). *Reading miscue inventory: Manual procedures for diagnosis and remediation.* New York: Macmillan.

Gray, W. S., & Robinson, H. H. (Eds.). (1967). *Gray Oral Reading Test.* Indianapolis, IN: Bobbs-Merrill.

Hammill, D. D., & Bartel, N. R. (1982). *Teaching children with learning and behavior problems* (3rd ed.). Boston: Allyn & Bacon.

Harris, A., & Sipay, E. R. (1980). *How to increase your reading ability* (7th ed.). New York: Longman.

Heckleman, R. G. (1969). The neurological impress method of remedial reading instruction. *Academic Therapy, 4,* 277–282.

Hegge, T. G., Kirk, S. A., & Kirk, W. D. (1955). *Remedial reading drills.* Ann Arbor, MI: George Wahr.

Karlsen, B., Madden, R., & Gardner, E. F. (1974, 1977). *Stanford Diagnostic Reading Tests.* New York: Harcourt Brace Jovanovich.

Lerner, J. (1985). *Children with learning disabilities: Theories, diagnosis, and teaching strategies* (4th ed.). Boston: Houghton Mifflin.

Longford, K., Slade, K., & Barnett, A. (1974). An explanation of impress techniques in remedial reading. *Academic Therapy, 9,* 309–319.

McCullough, C. M. (1963). *McCullough Word-Analysis Test.* Boston: Ginn.

Mercer, C. D., & Mercer, A. R. (1985). *Teaching students with learning problems* (2nd ed.). Columbus, OH: Charles E. Merrill.

Orton, S. (1937). *Reading, writing, and speech problems in children.* New York: Norton.

Otto, W. (1973). Evaluating instruments for assessing needs and growth in reading. In W. H. MacGinitie (Ed.), *Assessment problems in reading.* Newark, DE: International Reading Association.

Polloway, E. A., & Smith, J. E. (1982). *Teaching language skills to exceptional learners.* Denver: Love.

Russell, D. H., & Karp, E. E. (1938). *Reading aids through the grades.* New York: Teachers College Press.

Sapona, R. H. (1985). *Writing productivity of learning disabled students: The effects of using a word processing program.* Unpublished doctoral dissertation, University of Virginia.

Schiffman, G., Tobin, D., & Buchanan, B. (1982). Microcomputer instruction for the learning disabled. *Journal of Learning Disabilities, 15,* 557–559.

Spache, G. D. (1981). *Diagnostic Reading Scales.* Monterey, CA: CIB/McGraw-Hill.

Torgesen, J. K., & Young, K. A. (1983). Priorities for the use of microcomputers with learning disabled children. *Journal of Learning Disabilities, 16,* 234–237.

Wallace, G., & Larsen, S. L. (1978). *The educational assessment of learning problems: Testing for teaching.* Boston: Allyn & Bacon.

————. (1986). *Assessment: Evaluating students with learning and behavior problems.* Austin, TX: Pro-Ed.

Wallace, G., & McLoughlin, J. A. (1979). *Learning disabilities: Concepts and characteristics.* Columbus, OH: Charles E. Merrill.

Wilson, R. M. (1977). *Diagnostic and remedial reading for classroom and clinic* (3rd ed.). Columbus, OH: Charles E. Merrill.

Woodcock, R. (1967). *The Peabody-Chicago-Detroit reading project—A report of second year results.* Nashville, TN: George Peabody College.

Woodcock, R. W. (1973). *Woodcock Reading Mastery Tests.* Circle Pines, MN: American Guidance Service.

10

Written Language

Written language is one of the highest forms of communication. In the hierarchy of language abilities, it is the last to be learned. Most individuals develop skills in listening, speaking, and reading before they develop writing skills. According to Johnson and Myklebust (1967), difficulties in any of these other language areas will certainly interfere with the acquisition of written language skills.

Learning handicapped students usually encounter many different types of written language problems. According to Weiner (1980), their work is often characterized by graphic imperfections (erasures, pencil pressure marks, size and spacing irregularities), misspellings (phonetic spelling, letter or syllable omissions), grammatical errors, and semantic errors. In general, difficulties occur most frequently in handwriting, spelling, and written expressions. A listing of the general competencies required for each of these areas is shown in Table 10–1. Many of these competencies are discussed in this chapter.

Table 10-1
General Competencies for Written Language

Prerequisite Skills for Handwriting

Able to touch, reach, grasp, and release objects
Able to distinguish similarities and differences in objects and designs
Has established handedness

Handwriting Skills

Grasps writing utensil
Moves writing utensil up/down
Moves writing utensil left to right
Moves writing utensil in a circular manner
Copies letters
Copies own name in manuscript form
Writes own name in manuscript form
Copies words and sentences in manuscript form
Copies manuscript from far-point
Copies letters and words in cursive writing
Copies sentences in cursive writing
Copies cursive from far-point

Spelling Skills

Recognizes letters of the alphabet
Recognizes words
Says words that can be recognized
Recognizes similarities and differences in words
Differentiates between different sounds in words
Associates certain sounds (phonemes) with symbols or letters
Spells phonetically regular words
Spells phonetically irregular words
Generates rules for spelling various words and word problems
Uses correctly spelled words in written compositions

Written Expression Skills

Writes phrases and sentences
Begins sentences with a capital letter
Ends sentences with correct punctuation
Uses proper punctuation
Demonstrates simple rules for sentence structure
Writes complete paragraphs
Writes notes and letters
Expresses creative ideas in writing
Uses writing as a functional means of communication

SOURCE: From *Strategies for Teaching Retarded and Special Needs Learners* (3rd ed., p. 266) by E.A. Polloway, J. S. Payne, J. R. Patton, and R. A. Payne, 1985, Columbus, OH: Charles E. Merrill. Copyright 1985 by Bell & Howell Company. Reprinted by permission.

HANDWRITING

Handwriting is considered the most concrete of the communication skills because it can be directly observed, evaluated, and preserved (Lerner, 1985). Handwriting is indispensable for most written expression. Regardless of how well organized a written passage may be, it will not convey a thought adequately unless it is presented in a legible fashion (Wallace & Larsen, 1978).

Handwriting difficulties, sometimes referred to as dysgraphia, can be related to a number of contributing factors. In addition to poor motor skills, some students are hampered by directionality confusion or poor visual memory. Motivational difficulties and inadequate instruction can also contribute to handwriting problems. Among the more specific handwriting difficulties, Mercer and Mercer (1985) list slowness, incorrect directionality of letters and numbers, too much or too little slant, spacing difficulty, messiness, inability to stay on a horizontal line, illegible letters, too much or too little pencil pressure, and mirror writing.

Some teachers of learning handicapped students have persistently questioned whether to concentrate on manuscript (printed) or cursive writing with these students. Polloway, Payne, Patton, and Payne (1985) suggest that traditional rationales for using manuscript have pointed to its similarity to book print, the relative ease of letter formation, and the benefit of not confusing students with a second writing form. Those who advocate the use of cursive usually argue that this form of writing has a natural rhythm, social status, speed, and fewer spacing and reversal problems because cursive letters are written as units. Our experience suggests that students with learning problems generally are more confident if they utilize the writing form of their peers. Therefore, we recommend that most learning handicapped students use the same form of writing being used in their individual classrooms.

Handwriting Assessment

Direct observation of writing samples in daily work is an excellent informal technique for focusing on specific handwriting problems. Copying exercises, various types of dictation, and creative writing assignments are ideal instructional situations for directly observing a student's handwriting. In attempting to isolate particular handwriting deficits, Wallace and Larsen (1978) suggest that the teacher consider the following: (1) letter formation, (2) spacing, (3) slant, (4) line quality, (5) letter size and alignment, and (6) rate.

In addition to an informal analysis, we usually recommend the use of a general scale to further assess a pupil's handwriting. The Zaner-Bloser (1979) evaluation scale is probably the most comprehensive and commonly used instrument currently available. It provides five specimens of handwriting for each grade level through the eighth grade. The specimens are based on a national sampling of student handwriting. The quality of a particular student's handwriting is determined by comparing a sample of that student's handwriting to the five specimens, which are classified as high, good, medium, fair, or poor. Although the scale is helpful in determining generalities about a student's handwriting, it does not specify particular handwriting deficits.

The Test of Written Language (Hammill & Larsen, 1983) is a norm-referenced test that includes a subtest for assessing cursive writing for students in Grades 3 through 8. A sample of the student's writing is rated against various graded writing samples included in the manual.

SPELLING

The ability to spell has been recognized as a complex and multifaceted process. Hunt, Hadsell, Mannum, and Johnson (1963) suggest that, besides general intelligence, the following four factors greatly affect the ability to spell English words: (1) the ability to spell words that are phonetic; (2) the ability to spell words that involve roots, prefixes, suffixes, and rules for combining; (3) the ability to look at a word and reproduce it later; and (4) the ability to spell the demons.

Spelling is believed to be a more difficult task than reading since the opportunity to draw on peripheral clues is greatly reduced. Lerner (1985) points out that the student may use contextual, structural, or configuration clues in reading whereas in spelling there is no opportunity to draw on such clues in reproducing a word. Consequently, the student who is unable to decode words in reading will almost always perform poorly in spelling as well.

Students with learning problems exhibit many different types of spelling difficulties. Some of the most common error patterns have been listed by Edgington (1968) and Polloway and Smith (1982).

□ additions of unneeded letters
□ omissions of needed letters
□ reflections of a child's mispronunciations
□ reflections of dialectal patterns
□ reversals of whole words
□ reversals of letters
□ phonetic overgeneralizations
□ letter order confusion
□ final consonant changes

Many of these error patterns occur with the words shown in Table 10–2.

Table 10-2
One Hundred Most Commonly Misspelled Words

again	dropped	looked	their
all right	every	many	then
always	February	money	there
an	first	morning	they
and	for	mother	they're
animals	friend	name	things
another	friends	named	thought
around	frightened	off	threw
asked	from	once	through
babies	getting	our	to
beautiful	going	people	together
because	happened	pretty	too
before	hear	received	tried
believe	heard	running	two
bought	here	said	until
came	him	school	very
caught	interesting	some	wanted
children	its	something	went
clothes	it's	sometime	were
coming	jumped	started	when
course	knew	stopped	where
cousin	know	surprise	with
decided	let's	swimming	woman
didn't	like	than	would
different	little	that's	you've

Spelling Assessment

The vast majority of available spelling assessment techniques can be broadly classified as either informal procedures or formal published tests, some of which are standardized. We have found that the various informal techniques provide more usable information regarding a student's specific instructional needs than any of the presently available published tests. According to Wallace and Larsen (1978), an efficient informal assessment procedure should clearly outline the relevant skills a student has or has not mastered, pinpoint patterns of errors, provide direction for systematic remedial instruction, and permit nonsubjective evaluation as the pupil moves from task to task.

One widely used and particularly effective informal procedure is the Informal Spelling Inventory (ISI). The general purpose of the ISI is to determine a student's general spelling level and note specific patterns of spelling errors. In this technique, according to Wallace and McLoughlin (1979), the teacher selects a sample of 15 to 20 words from each basal spelling book of a given spelling series. Words from each list are dictated to students until six consecutive words are missed. A student's achievement level is determined by finding the highest level at which a score of 90 to 100% is obtained. The teaching level is the highest level at which a score of 75 to 89% is obtained. Specific spelling deficits can also be noted by analyzing various spelling errors.

There are few published tests available to assess spelling skills. Spelling subtests, which are part of larger achievement batteries, have not served adequately for specific diagnosis because of their emphasis on grade and age-level scores. From the limited number of published tests in this area, we have chosen to review the more widely used tests.

Gates-Russell Spelling Diagnostic Test (Gates & Russell, 1940). This instrument appraises nine areas: (1) oral spelling, (2) word pronunciation, (3) giving letters for sounds, (4) one-syllable spelling, (5) two-syllable spelling, (6) word reversals, (7) spelling attack, (8) auditory discrimination, and (9) the effectiveness of visual, auditory, kinesthetic, and combined methods of study. Grade scores are provided for each specific subtest. The test can be effectively used as an initial step in observing spelling difficulties (Wallace & Larsen, 1978).

Spellmaster: Spelling, Testing, and Evaluation (Cohen & Abrams, 1974). This diagnostic spelling test measures three categories of words: (1) regular words with uniform phoneme-grapheme correspondence; (2) irregular words that do not follow basic phonological and morphological rules; and (3) homonyms that must be learned in conjunction with their meanings. A scope and sequence chart that includes the specific skills being tested and the grade level where each is usually taught can help the teacher select the initial level for diagnostic testing. Profile charts for individual students and classes are included, along with a helpful chart correlating the phonetic and structural elements being tested with a number of widely used spelling programs.

Test of Written Spelling (Larsen & Hammill, 1976). This test was specifically designed to pinpoint a student's current spelling level as well as to specify the basic types of words with which the pupil is having difficulty. The test involves administering one list of predictable words and a separate list of unpredictable words. Raw scores are translated into a spelling age score, a spelling quotient, and a spelling grade equivalent. The test can be administered to small groups of children. It provides extensive norms with consistently high reliability across grade levels. We believe this test is a valid measure of the written spelling ability of children.

WRITTEN EXPRESSION

In order to become proficient in written expression, an individual must develop skills and abilities in all of the various language arts, including speaking, reading, spelling, handwriting, capitalization, punctuation, word usage, and grammar (Wallace & Larsen, 1978). When one considers the complexities of written expression, it is not surprising to note that many learning handicapped students are unable to utilize the written form of language as an effective means of communication.

Students who experience difficulties in written expression usually encounter problems in the transfer of ideas to written communication; some may make grammar and syntax errors(Myklebust,1965).Other major problem areas for the learning handicapped involve inadequate spoken and written language vocabularies and difficulty with the mechanics of writing (punctuation, capitalization).

Most students with problems in written expression are usually referred for assistance in the upper elementary grades, middle school, and high school, where written expression is more often emphasized in the curriculum. The focus in the early elementary grades is usually on the skills prerequisite to written expression—spoken language, reading, handwriting, and spelling.

Assessment of Written Expression

Techniques for assessment of written expression are usually divided into two broad categories: standardized tests or informal testing procedures. According to Wallace and Larsen (1978), the first step in conducting an informal assessment of written expression entails obtaining a representative sample of the student's written work. Once a writing sample has been secured, Wallace and Larsen suggest an analysis of certain areas.

1. general composition including evidence of purpose, content, and organization as well as sentence and paragraph development
2. appropriate diction (word choice) that permits a clear discussion of the topic selected
3. mastery of the rules that underlie the use of capitalization and punctuation
4. quality of handwriting (p. 409)

The usefulness of any informal assessment procedure essentially depends on obtaining representative samples of a student's written work and carefully analyzing them for error patterns.

Three published tests of written expression that provide a comprehensive analysis of skills within this area are currently available for individuals interested in formal assessment procedures.

Picture Story Language Test (Myklebust, 1965).   This test is one of the few available published tests measuring a child's written expression. Following the presentation of a picture, the child is asked to write a story that is judged for productivity, correctness, and meaning. The numbers of words, sentences, and words per sentence are computed for productivity; word usage, word endings, and punctuation are judged for correctness; and story content is appraised for the meaning scale. Scores for the test can be converted into age equivalents and percentiles. The test can also be utilized in informal assessment (Wallace & Larsen, 1978).

Test of Adolescent Language (Hammill, Brown, Larsen, & Wiederholt, 1980). This norm-referenced test is intended for administration to students between the ages of 11.0 and 18.5. Two of the eight subtests require written language. The writing/vocabulary subtest asks the student to read a word and then write a sentence using the word correctly. The writing/grammar subtest asks the student to combine several short sentences into one sentence containing all the same information. In addition to individual scaled scores, the writing subtests combine to provide a writing composite score. Reliability and validity information is considered to be quite good for this test.

Test of Written Language (Hammill & Larsen, 1983). This test is intended to identify students with written language problems in Grades 2 through 8. The test includes subtests in the following seven areas: word usage, style, spelling, thematic maturity, vocabulary, thought units, and handwriting. The test results can be used to identify students with problems in writing, especially composition, and to isolate specific areas of difficulty. Polloway (1984) feels that this test is the most well-designed, diagnostically useful formal instrument presently available for assessing the writing of handicapped students.

COMMERCIAL MATERIALS

A number of commercial programs and materials are available for working with students experiencing written language difficulties. In addition to briefly describing some of these programs and materials, we discuss in this section the use of microcomputers in developing various written language skills. The addresses of all publishers mentioned here are listed following chapter 12.

Handwriting Programs

Handwriting with Write and See (Lyons & Carnahan Educational Publishers). The six books in this series are designed to teach manuscript and cursive writing to students who traditionally have had little interest in legible handwriting. The student progresses from quite simple to more complex writing movements through the use of a fading technique that teaches letter formation. The student writes with a special pen on specially prepared paper, which turns a different color when incorrect letter formations are made. The program can be used with elementary school students. Its individualized and self-pacing components make it ideally suited to the needs of students with handwriting difficulties.

Penskill (Science Research Associates). This program is designed to develop and improve the cursive writing skills of students from fourth grade on. It emphasizes slant, size, spacing of letters and words, alignment, and shape. Practice in number formation is also included. No stylized form is advocated, and the ultimate goal of the program is a legible handwriting that suits each child. Although the program is not designed for students with writing problems, the programming allows the materials to be used individually. Special instructions are also included for the left-handed child.

D'Nealian Handwriting Programs (Scott, Foresman, & Company). This program is designed for children from preschool age through the eighth grade. The basic letter formation, size, slant, and spacing taught for manuscript are similar to those for cursive writing. In fact, simple connective strokes are all that are employed in transferring manuscript letters into the cursive form. Student workbooks and teacher's editions are available for each grade level in the program.

The Writing Road to Reading (William Morrow Publishing). Elements of the English language are taught by combining the teaching of speech, writing, spelling, and reading. Precise techniques for handwriting and accurate pronunciation are taught first in order to teach 70 phonograms. Position and techniques for handwriting are introduced by the teacher, who gives general rules governing the letters. Letters are either tall or short. Manuscript letters involve six different strokes and are formed by using a clock face. Cursive writing is introduced in the middle of the second year. Five connecting strokes are introduced as an adaptation of manuscript writing.

Microcomputers. In the short time since microcomputers have been introduced in our schools, they have become a widely used tool for helping learning handicapped students overcome difficulties in both handwriting and typing. Students learn to use the microcomputer keyboard with the aid of software called typing tutors. Behrmann (1984) points out that all major brands of microcomputers have some type of typing tutor. Some are designed as games for use with younger children or even older students who might require some motivation. Other typing tutors are utilized for drill and practice and are often effective in teaching typing skills to older students.

For the student with severe handwriting problems, the microcomputer has the potential of becoming an indispensable tool for communication. However, we believe that even the mildly handicapped student can effectively utilize the microcomputer as an additional aid in helping to remedy various handwriting problems.

Spelling Programs

Spelling Workbook Series (Educators Publishing Service). The four workbooks that comprise this series are designed for corrective spelling instruction in primary through secondary grades. The primary workbooks emphasize phonic elements of words in context, whereas the intermediate workbook is specifically designed for students with poor visual recall of letters and words. Spelling rules and generalizations are emphasized in the secondary workbook. The program provides a relatively large amount of kinesthetic reinforcement throughout the workbooks.

Spelling (Behavioral Research Laboratories, Inc.). This programmed spelling series employs a linguistic progression of sound-symbol associations tightly controlled for consistency in phoneme-grapheme comparison. Words are taught as vocabulary items so that the student does not need advanced reading skills before beginning the program. The eight levels of the series are intended to be used during the first four elementary grades. The lesson format includes 30 minutes of a teacher-directed presentation and 30 minutes of individual workbook assignments. Audio tapes can also be purchased for individual presentation of the teacher-directed portion of the program.

Spelling Word Power Laboratory (Science Research Associates). This individualized program is intended for use with students through Grade 7. The kit includes a word wheel, record booklet, and check-test cards. The word wheel is used to master specific spelling principles and rules; the record booklet is used for practicing words and principles that were missed; and the check-test cards are used to determine whether the student has mastered a principle well enough to proceed.

Teaching Resources Spelling Series (DLM Teaching Resources). This linguistically based program is designed to meet the needs of students who have failed to progress in traditional spelling programs. The program emphasizes mastery of crucial spelling rules, phonetic patterns, and sight words most frequently misspelled. The program provides extensive drill, repetitions, and regular review. The series consists of student workbooks and teacher's guides for Grades 2 to 4. The workbooks contain 30 lessons designed to be completed within one week. Activities emphasize listening, saying/spelling words aloud, copying, writing, proofreading, and self-correcting.

Working Words in Spelling (Curriculum Associates). This complete spelling program is designed for students in Grades 1 to 8. It consists of eight student books and a teacher's annotated edition for each level. The program includes words used in everyday writing and incorporates the use of derived forms of spelling words. Each lesson involves writing, dictionary skills, word study, a test-study-test procedure, and practice with capitalization, punctuation, word usage, and written expression. The teacher's edition also provides an excellent listing of spelling resource materials for each lesson.

Microcomputers. A number of quite different microcomputer spelling programs have been used successfully with learning handicapped students. Some software programs utilize a game format (hangman, crossword puzzles) to teach various spelling skills. Others teach major spelling principles through the cloze technique, described in chapter 9. Some spelling software programs have a built-in spelling scanner, permitting the student to check for misspelled words. The microcomputer actually locates misspelled words from a predetermined file of common words (Lerner, 1985).

Hasselbring (1982) reports that the Computerized Spelling Remediation Program (CSRP) seems to have excellent potential as a highly powerful yet cost-efficient means of remediating spelling problems in both handicapped and nonhandicapped learners. The CSRP is an interactive program designed to provide the student with imitations and modeling feedback without the need for adult intervention. The program was developed for the Radio Shack TRS–80 Model I microcomputer.

We believe that there are vast possibilities for spelling and microcomputers. Students with learning handicaps seem to respond quite positively to software programs that aim to correct various spelling difficulties. For the present, we recommend additional research in this area and the development of more innovative software programs.

Programs for Written Expression

Think and Write (DLM Teaching Resources). This writing skills program is intended for elementary grade students and consists of five kits. Kit 1 is a teacher-directed kit in which all concepts are taught by the teacher through examples. Writing activities are carried out through dictation. Kits 2 through 5 are student-directed with concepts and skills introduced on teaching cards. Activity cards provide practice and application of the skill or concept that was taught on the teaching card. Skills emphasized in the program include categorizing, classifying, comparing, punctuating, choosing words, using words, editing, proofreading, and rewriting.

Lessons for Better Writing (Curriculum Associates). This writing improvement program is designed for students in Grades 6 to 12. The program consists of a concise text supported by three independent books of duplicating masters for intensive student practice in editing, writing, and word usage. "Better Sentences" contains sentences that the students rewrite, editing as necessary. "Better Writing" focuses on effective student writing for difficult audiences. "Better Words" provides practice in understanding pairs of often confused, related words with subtle distinctions in meaning.

Phelps Sentence Guide Program (Academic Therapy Publications). This writing experience program is intended for use with students having writing difficulties. The program is divided into nine stages, which progress from sentence writing to paragraph and story writing. Sentence structuring is taught through a sentence guide activity in which the student classifies various parts of a sentence (e.g., Who? What? Where?). The visual aid of this guide and the verbal interaction between student and teacher help to make this an excellent program for learning handicapped students.

Microcomputers. Microcomputers and various word processing programs have been an excellent resource tool for both elementary and secondary level students experiencing difficulty with written expression. Word processors electronically store written passages on computer discs or tapes, allowing the writer to easily change any part of the passage. Behrmann (1984) identifies some of the benefits of word processing.

☐ There is no penalty for revising.

☐ It is easy for students to experiment with writing.

☐ Interest in the writing task is maintained.

☐ Editing is simple: spelling, punctuation, and grammar can be changed or checked.

☐ Writing and editing are less time-consuming.

☐ Frustration is minimized.

☐ It is easy to produce perfect copy.

☐ Computerized spelling checkers are available. (p. 96)

We agree with Lerner (1985) that word processing eliminates the task of rewriting or retyping and encourages the important cognitive process of writing. One of the most widely used word processing programs is the Bank Street Writer. This program was developed to meet the writing needs of students in Grades 4 to 12. It consists of three modes, which appear at the top of the screen. The write, edit, and transfer modes allow the student to utilize a number of different functions, including correcting, adding to, and deleting any part of the written passage. Kerchner (1984) believes that the Bank Street Writer can be used whenever written expression is taught; she considers it an important piece of software for any special classroom.

TEACHING ACTIVITIES

Readiness

1. Perform gross body exercises showing direction (e.g., up and down, left and right, forward and backward, out and in). These activities should be done first without writing instruments. For example, direct the child to "raise your right hand *up* in the air," "make large circles with your writing hand *in front of* your body," "bring your arms *in* toward your body," "make long straight lines with your writing hand going from *top* to *bottom*."

2. Use the chalkboard for some of the exercises listed above. For example, direct the child to "make a long line from *left* to *right*," "draw a circle in *toward* your body," "make a line going from *bottom* to *top*."

3. Some children must be taught how to hold a writing utensil. Practicing painting with a paint brush may be helpful. McKenna (1970) also suggests the following finger exercises: finger tapping firmly and rhythmically on a desk; lifting and lowering designated fingers on command; sorting cards; and "playing the piano" on a desk, with hands arched properly and fingers pressing down firmly.

4. Some children may have difficulty remembering how to hold a pencil. Johnson and Myklebust (1967) suggest placing a piece of adhesive tape on the pencil, cutting a small notch in the pencil, or painting the specific area where the fingers should be placed.

5. Use templates of geometric figures for tracing with fingers, chalk, a pencil. Gradually encourage the child to make the figures freehand, using the templates as examples. Templates can be made from oak tag, wood, plastic, foam rubber.

6. Use dot-to-dot figures on the chalkboard or on duplicating paper to teach line sequence. Initially use circles and squares. Gradually include actual letters.

7. Have children trace figures and letters by placing tracing paper over the figures to be duplicated. In the beginning tape or tack the tracing paper to the desk.

8. Direct children to reproduce figures with their fingers in wet sand, salt trays, pudding mixes, or finger paint.

9. Ask children to identify wooden figures or letters while their eyes are closed. If wooden forms are not available, draw letters with your finger on the back of the child's hand or on her back. Children can work in pairs and tally points. Stress particularly difficult figures and letters.

10. Use games that encourage children to learn the common strokes of most letters.

    a. Vertical lines ("Finish building the house.")

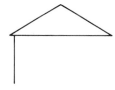

    b. Sharp peaks ("Put a crown on the king's head.")

    c. Wavy lines ("Make some wiggly snakes.")

d. Circles ("Finish the man's face.")

e. Half-circles ("Put the handles on the other cups.")

11. Gradually, direct the children to reproduce different shapes on command.

12. Prepare a worksheet of sample pictures with instructions to follow (e.g., put a line *under* the house, put an X *on* the apple, put a circle *around* the boy).

13. Have the children sort and identify right and left boots, shoes, gloves, hand outlines (Valett, 1967).

14. On paper construct a large map of a town. Have the child guide toy cars on the roads, verbalizing turns and directions. Give the child some specific directions to follow and have her guide the car to its final destination using those directions.

15. Provide a pegboard and a number of different pegs. Give the child specific directions for placing the pegs in the pegboard (e.g., "Put the green peg *above* the blue peg," "Put the red peg to the *left* of the brown peg," "Put the orange peg *below* the yellow peg").

16. Prepare a scrapbook of pictures that illustrate position words, such as *in, out, below, under, on, up,* and *down.* Ask the child to find pictures in magazines that illustrate these words.

17. Ask the child to sort beads according to size, color, or shape. Provide a pattern to duplicate with beads or ask the child to create her own pattern.

18. Provide model clay to manipulate. Ask the child to mold particular objects (e.g., balls or fruits) or have the child create her own figures.

19. Manipulating tools or kitchen utensils provides fine motor practice. Have the children use screw drivers, hammers, wrenches, egg beaters, spoons, and cutlery in a variety of situations.

Manuscript Writing

1. Use boxes to help teach correct forms for beginning letters. All of the basic vertical and horizontal letters can be taught with boxes. As the child progresses, gradually fade out the boxes.

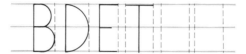

2. Use masking tape as a tactile clue for margins and different letter placements. Place a section of masking tape along the left side of the paper to provide the child with a clue for directionality. Use smaller pieces of tape for specific letter directions.

3. Use arrow clues for specific letters. For example,

4. Place a little green dot at the starting position for the letter stroke and a small red dot at the termination point. For example,

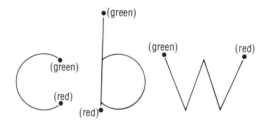

5. Teach the basic strokes for most letters sequentially. For example, teach the letter ✝ as two separate strokes: │ and ─ . Likewise, teach ⓱ as │ and ⌐ . Eventually, encourage the child to join the basic strokes together.

6. Teach letters with easier strokes first. The following letters are considered the least difficult for children to learn: c, i, l, o, t, v.

7. Tape an individual alphabet to the child's desk. Ditto the alphabet or parts of it at the top of the child's seatwork papers.

8. Use clean, lined paper for children with aligning and spacing difficulties. Also, use paper with color-coded lines or different colored ditto masters.

9. Introduce capital letters in familiar words, such as the child's name, his city or state. Employ the same techniques used for teaching lowercase letters (boxes, color cues, masking tape).

10. Teach children to "talk out" strokes in making specific letters. For example,

⌒ —short line down, back up, around, and down

W —slant down, slant up, slant down, slant up

i —short line, dot

† —tall line down, short line across near top

11. For children with spacing difficulties, use plastic, wooden, felt, or oak tag letters. Instruct them to match the spacing in given words. Likewise, provide words with improper spacing and instruct the children to space the letters properly.

Cursive Writing

1. Do not teach cursive writing to students who are still having difficulty with manuscript writing. In all likelihood such students will also experience difficulty or failure with cursive writing.
2. Devise games for student practice of various cursive strokes. For example,

Stringing the beads

Making waves

Making curly hair

Lassoing the horses

3. Use dot-to-dot or dash-to-dash letters to informally assess readiness for cursive writing. Gradually fade out the dots or dashes, allowing the child to make the complete letter independently. Judge the accuracy of the last letter.

4. Demonstrate the similarity between manuscript and cursive writing by making cursive letters over the corresponding manuscript letters.

   Use a different colored pencil or a felt-tipped pen for the cursive letter.

5. Make any of the previous strokes on ditto paper and have the child trace over them with her finger, pencil, crayon.

6. Teach letters with similar movement patterns sequentially. The following four groups contain similar strokes: (1) *a, c, d, g, o;* (2) *b, h, f, k, l, e;* (3) *i, j, p, r, s, t, u, w;* (4) *m, n, v, x, y, z.*

7. In the beginning stages of cursive writing, give above-the-line and below-the-line stops to cue letter formation (e.g., where to stop a loop). Use colored dots, short lines, or masking tape.

8. Place a heavy (possibly weighted) bracelet or wristband on the wrist of a child who has difficulty keeping his wrist in the proper position on the desk.

9. Break cursive letter strokes into steps and teach sequentially. For example, teach the letter *f* as a three-step combination of the four strokes shown here on the left.

10. Have children with spacing difficulties work with cursive letters cut from oak tag or wood. Direct them to match the spacing in a number of given words or join letters to spell words given verbally by the teacher.

11. Use verbal cues in teaching cursive writing. Teach letters with similar strokes in sequence so that the child can more easily follow the cues. For example, use the *a* strokes in teaching the *g* strokes: "First come around like the *a*, then go up, ..."

Handwriting Activities for Left-Handed Students

1. Observe whether the child uses the correct bear-left position and keeps her arm parallel with the edge of the paper. Use the following activities to correct any problems.

2. Tape the student's paper to her desk in the correct position as a reminder in the beginning stages of handwriting.

3. Use the commercially available writing frame (a wire guide attached to the pencil) to teach left-handers (and right-handers, too) the correct hand position for writing.

4. Encourage practice with paint brushes, chalk, crayons, and magic markers to correct the hooked-wrist position that many left-handers use. Constantly reinforce the proper holding of all writing utensils.

5. The left-hander's writing should be slightly sloped to the left, even though it appears to be somewhat backhanded. Provide appropriate examples for left-handed children to follow: left-handed teachers, older left-handed students, and left-handed children in the same classroom with exemplary work and patterns.

6. Provide special equipment, such as left-handed scissors and left-handed desk chairs, whenever possible.

7. Trembly (1970) reports that a Southpaw Club was organized for left-handers in one school. Children in the group pooled their ideas and experiences; the boys in the club even organized a baseball team and challenged a group of right-handers.

8. The Plunkett (1954) writing exercises are a commercial aid for left-handers, offering a sequentially developed program.

Spelling Activities for Younger Students

1. Analyze the type of spelling errors that a child is making to identify the specific letter(s) prompting difficulty. Ask the child to write specific letters of the alphabet from dictation. Also, pronounce different letter sounds and ask the child to write the appropriate letter symbols. Use the results of these activities in formulating a remedial program.

2. Ask the child to "write the letter that the word *ball* begins with" or "write the letter that *cup* ends with and so on.

3. Ask the child to complete missing words by filling in the omitted letter(s) (e.g., "They like to (s)ing song(s)," "Mary (s)at on the (s)ixth chair," "The dog(s) were very (s)ick"). Vary this activity by concentrating on specific letters in the initial, medial, or final positions.

4. Provide the child with a sheet of letters with similar configurations. Name a letter and direct the child to circle it on his sheet. As the child progresses, ask him to write the letters from dictation. Still later, ask the child to write the letter that comes after a particular letter in the alphabet.

5. Strengthen the revisualization of specific letters by having the child trace the letters in various media, such as clay, salt, and sand. Provide tactile exercises with sandpaper, felt, or wooden letters.

6. Provide the child with letter cut-outs and ask him to spell certain words by arranging the letters in correct sequence. Emphasize specific letters.

7. Print difficult words on flash cards for periodic student review. Print especially troublesome letters in red, to signal caution and to focus the child's attention.

8. Show a letter to the child for a short period of time; then have him select that letter from a group of four letters written on a worksheet. As the child improves in this activity, shorten the exposure time, expose multiple letters, gradually add words, or ask the child to write the exposed letter(s). A tachistoscope (or an index card with a "window" cut out) is useful here, but flash cards are adequate.

9. Ask the child to write letters that have been verbally described (e.g., "Write the letter that looks like a wiggly snake" or "Write the letter that looks like a small circle". Eventually, spell words in this manner, and ask other children to describe the letters verbally.

10. Assign memory clues for particularly troublesome letters. Include only a minimum number of letters so that the clues do not become as difficult to remember as the letters. Associations provided by the child himself are much more effective than teacher-assigned clues. One child we know remembered *i* with an upward-pointing arrow ↑ and *a* with a circular arrow ↻ .

11. Trace words on the back of the child's hand or on his back, just as you traced letters. The child must remember the visual image of each letter until the word is completed. Then have him write the word on the chalkboard or on paper. Use two- or three-letter words at first.

12. Cover up an entire word. Gradually expose each successive letter until the child can guess the correct word. Give letter clues, such as "The next letter comes after *m* in the alphabet."

13. Use the Language Master as a visual/auditory/kinesthetic reinforcement for the child. Use whole words, spelling each word letter by letter. Have the child trace the word on the card after it has gone through the recorder.

14. Assign children in the room different letters, blends, endings. Call on a child to spell a word by selecting the fewest children with the correct letters or groups of letters. For example, the word *jumping* should be spelled by choosing the one child with *ing* rather than the three separate children with *i*, *n*, and *g*. Encourage the children to look for the easiest way to spell a word (Arena, 1968).

15. Tape an individual alphabet chart on each child's desk to help with revisualization.

16. Introduce a word family, such as *at.* Ask the children to list words in that family. Make this activity more specific by directing the children to add certain letters, blends, or endings and then pronounce each word.

17. Present sentences containing words with missing letters, words with mixed-up letters, and words portrayed by pictures. Ask the children to complete the sentences. For example,

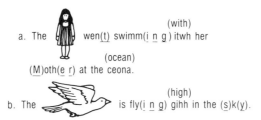

                                                   (with)

  a. The   wen(t) swimm(i n g) itwh her

                    (ocean)

(M)oth(e r) at the ceona.

                              (high)

  b. The   is fly(i n g) gihh in the (s)k(y).

Spelling Activities for Older Students

1. Write a difficult word on the chalkboard and ask the students to study the word for a few seconds. Then erase the word and ask them to write it from memory. Underline or circle difficult parts of the word as a memory device.

2. Provide the students with a word, such as *tablecloth.* Ask them to write as many words as possible beginning with *t* or *l* (or any other letter), using only the letters in *tablecloth.* Students can compete to write the most words. Variations of this activity include using letters in other positions or writing three-letter words only.

3. Provide students with sets of four words and ask them to circle the correctly spelled version of each word (e.g., *mega, gmae, game, gaem; talbe, table, taebl, tabel; bread, braed, brdae, bader).*

4. Make crossword puzzles of particularly difficult words. Encourage other students to make the puzzles.

5. Present configurations of specific words to a student and ask her to match a given set of words with the configurations.

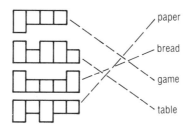

6. As a pupil progresses with the preceding activity, ask her to identify similar configurations in other words. Also, present four-word groups to the student and ask her to circle the two words with similar configurations (e.g., come, ball, park, talk).

7. Make a file box of difficult spelling words. Have the student copy the words correctly onto a set of flash cards and periodically review them. Encourage the student to study the cards by writing the words from memory on the back of the cards or on a piece of paper. Add and delete words as time progresses.

8. Ask the student to circle all the little words contained within a list of longer words (e.g., *friend, follow, report, oral, hand, easy*). This activity often serves as a recall device for spelling the longer words.

9. Encourage associative relationships in spelling. Some associations may be peculiar, but they may serve as meaningful memory devices for individual students nonetheless. Individual associations can often be the most effective method for revisualizing certain words.

10. Play spelling baseball. Divide the class into two teams. Batters must correctly pronounce and spell a given word. When they do, they move to first base; movement around the bases parallels that of regular baseball. The field can be made up of specific areas in the classroom or can be drawn on the board so that students stay in their seats (Polloway, Payne, Patton, & Payne, 1985).

Vocabulary Development

1. Provide a student with a colorful and descriptive illustration or picture. Have him tell a story about the picture (Zigmond, 1976).

2. Give students a word, such as *run*, and ask them to list as many words as they can that are similar in meaning (e.g., *rush, scat, race, hurry, dash*). Encourage the students to keep these words in their notebooks and use them for reference when they are writing stories.

3. Play word tennis with two teams of pupils. The first person on one team says a word, such as *happy.* Synonyms are then provided by successive team members on alternating teams until one member can no longer think of a synonym. Scoring variations include tallying points for each side for each correct synonym and subtracting points each time a team fails to provide a synonym.

4. Give a student a word with multiple meanings and ask him to write sentences using the different meanings. Afterwards, discuss the different meanings with the student. Examples of some appropriate words include *hit, run, show, bat, fan, fly, watch,* and *file.*

5. Give the student a list of meanings and a second list of words to match with those meanings. To make the activity more challenging, choose unusual meanings.

Word Meanings	Words to Choose from
a wispy puff of color in the sky	juice
mostly liquid, and sometimes good to drink	humid
sticky and moist	cloud

6. Provide the pupil with a list of general categories and a large number of words to classify. For example, categories such as transportation, food, and music might be used. Words to be classified might include *tugboat, drum, soup, rocket, feet, orchestra, sandwich,* and *singer.* Require the student to make finer discriminations as he progresses. Eventually, supply only the categories and have the student provide the examples in each category.

7. Ask several questions that can be answered by either selecting the correct word or responding affirmatively or negatively (e.g., "Does the spendthrift or the thrifty man save his money?" "Are the jagged rocks harder to climb than the slick, rounded rocks?" "Is the senior citizen an oldster?").

8. Have students invent new words by blending two familiar words and providing definitions for the new words. For example, *squabbit* might be a cross between a squirrel and a rabbit, and *glup* might be a glass and cup combination.

9. Have students find specific words in a story to answer specific questions (e.g., "Find the word in the third paragraph that describes the size of the town in which Tom lived" or "Find the expression on page 36 that tells you that Jane was sad").

10. Have students keep unusual or colorful words in a special notebook or a special place on the bulletin board (e.g., *argy-bargy,* which is a Scotch expression meaning "argument or controversy"). Encourage students to use these words in their written assignments.

11. Provide students with input experiences such as field trips, stories to read, discussion periods, and oral language activities. A variety of such experiences should stimulate ideas for written expression.

Syntax and Grammar Activities

1. Provide the student with sentences with grammar, usage, and/or syntax errors to be corrected. Initially, concentrate on one type of error; gradually progress to multiple error types. Underline sentence errors during the beginning stages of this activity.

> Mary have two apples.
> John in the morning has breakfast.
> She were running down the path.
> Girls plays with dolls.

2. Vary the preceding exercise by working on a specific skill, such as plurals, and leaving a blank for the student to supply the correct form. Students can also be given a choice between two words for the correct answer.

> Susan and Jane (play, plays) together each day.
> He (run, runs) to school.
> They (like, likes) to ride bikes.
> The children played many (game, games).

3. Provide the pupil with a set of scrambled flash cards that match a sentence that you verbalize. Ask the student to place the cards in the order of your sentence. A tape recorder can be used for this activity.

4. Provide students with a list of words for which they must furnish the past tense form; for example, *come (came), go (gone), run (ran), see (saw)*.

5. Expand the preceding activity into sentences for which students are asked to provide the correct verb form.

> He <u>play</u> with me yesterday.
> After he <u>jump</u>, John hurt his finger.
> Yesterday, Sally <u>ride</u> her horse).

6. Have the students write one-minute group stories. Allow each pupil in a group, in succession, to write on the chalkboard for one minute. Each student continues the original story line, with the last student in each group writing a conclusion (Platts, Marguerite, & Shumaker, 1960).

7. Provide students with a story containing incorrect syntax, grammar, and usage; ask them to rewrite the story correctly.

8. Have the students complete sentences with missing words.

> She _____ two teeth missing.
> Barbara thinks it is _____ hot.
> Give me the _____ shoe.
> To _____ is he talking?

Written Expression

1. For individuals experiencing difficulty in expressing their thoughts in writing, supply specific instructions, activities, and exercises. These students respond to structured assignments that tell them exactly what to do. As the pupil progresses, decrease the structure gradually.

2. Give the student a list of words and ask her to write a short story using those words.

3. Give the student an uncluttered picture of a specific object (or the actual object) and ask her to write its name. Gradually add action and description until a sentence develops.

4. Give each student an action picture, such as a stock car race. Instruct each pupil to write a one-sentence description of what is happening in the picture.

5. Read an exciting story to the class, omitting the ending. Have students write their own endings.

6. Have a student use a tape recorder to dictate a story on a specific topic. Type the story onto paper, leaving key words blank. Ask the student to read the story and complete the sentences. Students can verify their work by replaying the original tape.

7. Provide the student with a number of different sentences. Ask her to rewrite each sentence, saying the same thing in a different way. Examples might include (1) the circus is an exciting place to visit, (2) it rained very hard last night, (3) she looked pretty in her new pink dress.

8. Provide the pupil with a list of words and a paragraph with missing words. Ask her to complete the paragraph by inserting the words appropriately.

        stories   play   rained   pictures

    radio   broken   house   games   mother

Today it _____ all day. We had to stay in the _____

to _____ . The television was _____ , so we listened to

the _____ for a while. We also played some _____ and

painted some _____ . The best part was when _____

read us some _____ .

9. Encourage the class to keep a daily diary. Initially, let the class write the daily entries as a group. Eventually permit individual students to write the entries. Ultimately, let each pupil keep her own diary.

10. Ask each student to write a sentence summarizing a story that was read to her, a film that she viewed, a record that was played for her, or a story that she read. Gradually increase the length of the summary or abstract.

REFERENCES

Arena, J. I. (1968). *Building spelling skills in dyslexic children.* San Rafael, CA: Academic Therapy Publications.

Behrmann, M. (1984). *Handbook of microcomputers in special education.* San Diego, CA: College Hill Press.

Cohen, C., & Abrams, R. (1974). *Spellmaster.* Exeter, NH: Learnco.

Edgington, R. (1968). But he spelled them right this morning. In J. I. Arena (Ed.), *Building spelling skills in dyslexic children* (pp. 23–24). Novato, CA: Academic Therapy Publications.

Gates, A., & Russell, D. (1940). *Gates-Russell Spelling Diagnostic Test.* New York: Columbia University, Teachers College, Bureau of Publications.

Hammill, D. D., Brown, V. L., Larsen, S. L., & Wiederholt, J. L. (1980). *Test of Adolescent Language.* Austin, TX: Pro-Ed.

Hammill, D. D., & Larsen, S. L. (1983). *Test of Written Language.* Austin, TX: Pro-Ed.

Hasselbring, T. S. (1982). Remediating spelling problems of learning handicapped students through use of microcomputers. *Educational Technology, 22,* 31–32.

Hunt, B., Hadsell, A., Hannum, J., & Johnson, H. W. (1963). The elements of spelling ability. *Elementary School Journal, 63,* 342–349.

Johnson, D. J., & Myklebust, H. R. (1967). *Learning disabilities: Educational principles and practices.* New York: Grune & Stratton.

Kerchner, L. B. (1984). Software reviews. *Learning Disability Quarterly, 1,* 201–202.

Larsen, S. L., & Hammill, D. D. (1976). *Test of Written Spelling.* Austin, TX: Pro-Ed.

Lerner, J. (1985). *Children with learning disabilities: Theories, diagnosis, and teaching strategies* (4th ed.). Boston: Houghton Mifflin.

McKenna, A. R. (1970). Some notes on the teaching of handwriting. In J. I. Arena (Ed.). *Building handwriting skills in dyslexic children.* San Rafael, CA: Academic Therapy Publications.

Mercer, C. D., & Mercer, A. R. (1985). *Teaching students with learning problems* (2nd ed.). Columbus, OH: Charles E. Merrill.

Myklebust, H. R. (1965). *Picture Story Language Test: The development and disorders of written language* (Vol. 1). New York: Grune & Stratton.

Platts, M. E., Marguerite, S. R., & Shumaker, E. (1970). *Suggested activities to motivate the teaching of the language arts.* Stevensville, MI: Educational Service.

Plunkett, M. A. (1954). *A writing manual for the left-handed.* Cambridge, MA: Educators Publishing Service.

Polloway, E. A. (1984). Review of *Test of Written Language.* In J. V. Mitchell (Ed.), *Ninth mental measurements yearbook.* Lincoln, NB: Buros Institute of Mental Measurements.

Polloway, E. A., Payne, J. S., Patton, J. R., & Payne, R. A. (1985). *Strategies for teaching retarded and special needs learners* (3rd ed.). Columbus, OH: Charles E. Merrill.

Polloway, E. A., & Smith, J. E. (1982). *Teaching language skills to exceptional learners.* Denver: Love.

Trembly, D. (1970). Should your child write with the left hand? In J. I. Arena (Ed.), *Building handwriting skills in dyslexic children.* San Rafael, CA: Academic Therapy Publications.

Valett, R. E. (1967). *The remediation of learning disabilities.* Palo Alto, CA: Fearon.

Wallace, G., & Larsen, S. L. (1978). *The educational assessment of learning problems: Testing for teaching.* Boston: Allyn & Bacon.

Wallace, G. (in press). *Assessment: Evaluating students with learning and behavior problems.* Austin, TX: Pro-Ed.

Wallace, G., & McLoughlin, J. A. (1979). *Learning disabilities: Concepts and characteristics.* Columbus, OH: Charles E. Merrill.

Wiener, E. (1980). Diagnostic evaluation of writing skills. *Journal of Learning Disabilities, 13*(1), 48–53.

Zaner-Bloser. (1979). *Evaluation Scale.* Columbus, OH: Author.

Zigmond, N. (1976). *Teaching children with special needs.* Dubuque, IA: Gorsuch Scarisbrick.

11

Mathematics

The difficulties encountered by students with learning problems in mathematics have received increased attention over the past few years. Today, successful performance in mathematics is considered fundamental to school success. Furthermore, math skill is being increasingly recognized as important and necessary for independent daily living.

According to Wallace and Larsen (1978), many handicapped learners have difficulty learning mathematics, and students experiencing math problems can be found at all age levels. During preschool and the primary grades many children have trouble matching or sorting objects, differentiating various sizes, and understanding the language of mathematics. During the elementary grades the student with math difficulties most likely encounters problems with computational skills. Problems with measurement, fractions, percentages, and decimals can also be experienced during the elementary grades. Math difficulties among secondary level students are not necessarily different from those of younger pupils. On the contrary, Wallace and McLoughlin (1979) point out that many students have problems in mathematics at the secondary level because of inadequate foundational skills.

Because learning problems in math are often connected to other academic difficulties, it is frequently necessary to investigate related deficits. Difficulties in discrimination, memory, comprehension, and handwriting can affect achievement in mathematics as well as other academic areas.

ASSESSMENT

Although recent activity in this area has resulted in the development of a number of math tests, mathematics has not been as thoroughly studied or researched in regard to handicapped learners as have other academic areas. Among the available assessment measures of math achievement, most can be classified as formal methods or informal procedures.

Formal Tests

Most general achievement tests measure a student's skills in various achievement areas (e.g., reading, math). These tests are intended to provide an overall measure of achievement in each academic area, not an intense analysis of a student's abilities. Therefore, achievement tests are generally not recommended for diagnostic purposes. Five of the more commonly used achievement tests with math sections are listed in Table 11–1.

Table 11-1
General Achievement Tests with Math Sections

Name of Test	Grade Level	Math Skills Evaluated
California Achievement Tests (CTB/McGraw-Hill, 1977, 1978)	K–12	Computation, concepts, and application
Metropolitan Achievement Tests (Prescott, Balow, Hogan, & Farr, 1978)	K–12	Numeration, geometry and measurement, problem solving, and operations
Peabody Individual Achievement Test (Dunn & Markwardt, 1970)	K–12	Matching skills through trigonometry concepts
SRA Achievement Series (Naslund, Thorpe, & Lefever, 1978)	K–12	Concepts, computation, and problem solving
Stanford Achievement Test (Madden, Gardner, Rudman, Karlsen, & Merwin, 1973)	1.5–9.5	Concepts, computation, and application
Wide Range Achievement Test (Jastak & Jastak, 1978)	Preschool to adulthood	Counting, number symbols, oral problems, and written computations

Criterion-referenced tests are usually designed to ensure that the behavorial objectives of a curriculum, a sequence of instruction, or an entire course of study have been assessed (Schminke, Maertens, & Arnold, 1978). Most criterion-referenced test items are keyed to predetermined, specifically stated behaviors. Table 11–2 provides a brief summary of some criterion-referenced math measures.

Another type of formal math measure is the diagnostic test. Generally, these batteries include multiple subtests that assess specific math skills. Diagnostic math tests usually provide helpful information for planning an instructional program for a learning handicapped student. Several diagnostic math tests are summarized here.

Key Math Diagnostic Arithmetic Test (Connolly, Nachtman, & Pritchett, 1976). This is an individually administered diagnostic arithmetic test for children in preschool through Grade 6, with no upper limits for remedial use. Key Math is comprised of 14 subtests organized into three areas: content (Numeration, Fractions, and Geometry/Symbols), operations (Addition, Subtraction, Multiplication, Division, Mental Computation, and Numerical Reasoning), and applications (Word Problems, Missing Elements, Money, Measurement, and Time). The test requires little reading or writing ability and can be administered in 20 to 30 minutes. Results include a grade equivalent score based on the total test performance, along with a diagnostic profile depicting the student's relative performance in the 14 skill areas. A metric supplement is also available to assess a child's understanding of metric measurement.

Stanford Diagnostic Mathematics Test (Beatty, Madden, Gardner, & Karlsen, 1976). This group-administered battery consists of four levels (appropriate for Grades 1 to 12) with two parallel forms at each level.

Table 11-2
Criterion-Referenced Math Tests

Name of Test	Math Skills Evaluated
Criterion Test of Basic Skills (Lundell, Brown, & Evans, 1976)	Numbers and numeral skills, basic operations, money, measurement, time telling, symbol operations, fractions, decimals, and percents
Diagnostic Test of Arithmetic Strategies (Ginsburg & Mathews, 1984)	Basic arithmetic operations
Diagnostic Tests and Self-Helps in Arithmetic (Brueckner, 1955)	Operations with whole numbers, common fractions, decimal fractions, percents, and measures
Wisconsin Design for Math Skill Development (Armenia, Kamp, McDonald, & VonKuster, 1975)	Numeration/place value, basic operations, fractions, geometry, measurement, money, time, and graphs

Although the subtest content varies by level, each of the four levels covers the number system and numeration, computation, and applications. In addition to total test scores, grade equivalents, percentile ranks, and a program indicator score are available for all subtests. A program indicator score indicates whether students have reached performance levels necessary for progress in specific skill sequences.

Test of Early Mathematics Ability (TEMA) (Ginsburg & Baroody, 1983). The TEMA is an individually administered test that measures the mathematics performance of children between the ages of 4.0 and 8.11. This 50-item test was designed to measure both informal mathematics and formal mathematics. *Informal mathematics* items include concepts of relative magnitude (the ability to judge which of two spoken numbers is larger or to judge relative distances on a mental number line), counting skills, and calculational skills. *Formal mathematics* items include knowledge of conventions (the ability to read and write numbers), number facts, calculational skills, and base 10 concepts. Testing time is generally less than 20 minutes. Performance is reported in terms of a math quotient, percentiles, and math ages. Although the test is norm-referenced, the results can be interpreted in a criterion-referenced fashion.

Test of Mathematical Abilities (TOMA) (Brown & McEntire, 1984). The TOMA was designed to provide information about two major skill areas, story problems and computation, and related information about attitude, vocabulary, and general cultural application. The test includes five subtests and can be used with students in Grades 3 through 12. The TOMA provides a standard score for each subtest, percentiles, and quotients that incorporate standard scores for all administered subtests. This test should be of special interest to those concerned with the relationship of language and cognition to mathematics, as well as to those who are interested in the relationship of attitudes to mathematics achievement.

Informal Techniques

Since many formal math tests yield little usable teaching information, informal assessment procedures are frequently used in identifying and analyzing a student's strengths and weaknesses in mathematics (Wallace & Larsen, 1978). We have found that observational techniques, oral interviews, error analysis, and teacher-constructed tests are among the best and most commonly used informal assessment procedures in math.

Observation. Frequent observations of a student during written assignments, chalkboard work, and oral discussions provide useful information for specifying particular math problems and planning an instructional program. The chalkboard has the additional advantage of allowing a teacher to observe the work of several students simultaneously. The use of some type of standard system for both gathering and recording observational data is recommended. Math observations are often recorded with checklists, rating scales, and anecdotal records. Wallace and Larsen (1978) note that checklists, in particular, result in more precise math observations since a great deal of information can be recorded rapidly. In addition, checklists allow the observer to focus on specific mathematical skills or behaviors.

Oral Interviews. In this informal approach the student is usually asked to describe aloud the steps that were involved in solving a particular math problem. The student actually reworks the problem orally, while the teacher listens and questions in order to determine misunderstandings and incorrect procedures. Ginsburg (1982) believes that the interview is the single most important alternative to standardized tests in mathematics because it provides insight into a student's mathematical thinking. Hammill and Bartel (1982) suggest the following guidelines for conducting an oral interview.

1. *Select one problem at a time.* The selected problem should be sequentially prior to others in a task analysis. For example, an addition problem should be cleared up prior to a multiplication difficulty.
2. *Begin with the easiest problem first.* This will give the student a sense of confidence.
3. *Tape or keep a written record of the interview.*
4. *The child simultaneously solves the problem in written form and "explains" what he is doing orally.*
5. *The child must be left free to solve the problem in his own way without a hint that he is doing something wrong.*
6. *Avoid hurrying the pupil.* The interview may last from 15 to 45 minutes. (pp. 118–119)

Error Analysis. Teacher analysis of a student's written work is another informal assessment procedure. Wallace and McLoughlin (1979) suggest than an analysis of a pupil's completed written assignment usually pinpoints specific difficulties the student is encountering with particular math concepts. A pattern of errors often emerges when various written assignments are closely examined. Moran (1978) points out that error patterns in math performance are of at least three major types, individually or in combination.

1. *Inadequate facts*: Using a correct operation and a sound strategy, the student applies inaccurate addition, subtraction, or multiplication facts. This is probably the most frequent type of error.
2. *Incorrect operation*: Using accurate facts, the learner subtracts rather than adding or divides instead of multiplying.
3. *Ineffective strategy*: Using the proper operation and accurate facts, the learner applies steps out of sequence, skips steps, or applies a tactic which does not always result in a correct outcome. Errors in this category are considered more serious because they arise from misunderstanding or a misapplication of algorithms. (pp. 58–59)

Informal Teacher-Constructed Tests. Informal teacher-made measures of math ability are considered to be well suited to the specificity of math difficulties. Most teacher-constructed tests measure a specific math skill since this type of informal test provides more exacting information for the teacher. In addition to providing instructionally relevant data, Wallace and Larsen (1978) believe that teacher-constructed tests help to identify problems, determine levels of understanding, and monitor student progress over a period of time. A number of excellent suggestions for constructing informal tests are provided by Reisman (1978) and Wallace and Larsen (1978).

PROGRAMS

For the learning handicapped student, as well as for every other student, proper instruction in math should consist of the amount of direct instruction necessary for the student to learn the task, the amount of practice time required for student mastery, and the kind of reinforcement needed to develop and maintain the desired behavior (Haring & Bateman, 1977). In addition, Otto and Smith (1980) offer the following principles for remedial math teaching.

1. Write specific objectives to deal with specific problems.
2. Arrange regular practice sessions.
3. Provide immediate and positive feedback during practice sessions.
4. Reinforce appropriate responses.
5. Provide for practice under speeded conditions.
6. Provide for concrete learning experiences.
7. Reteach the skills that have not been well established.
8. Provide practice in the applications of number facts to new and different situations.
9. Keep an accurate record of error levels and response rates.
10. Structure organizational routines.
11. Encourage pupils to set goals, to suggest changes in the organizational routine, and to ask questions.
12. Plan for games and play activities.
13. Match the task activities to the level of competence of the child.
14. Arrange regular practice sessions with hand calculators.
15. Diagnose errors regularly. (pp. 441–444).

During the past few years many published materials and programs have become available for teaching math to students with learning problems. This section will describe some of the current approaches.

Commercial Math Programs

The most frequently employed approach to teaching math is the use of a basal text (Polloway, Payne, Patton, & Payne, 1985). Some of the most commonly used basal math series are listed in Table 11–3.

Table 11-3
Basal Math Series

Title	Publisher
Essentials of Math	Ginn
Growth in Mathematics	Harcourt Brace
Individual Math Improvement Series	Bobbs-Merrill
Math for Individual Achievement	Houghton Mifflin
Mathematics Around Us	Scott, Foresman
Mathematics in Our World	Heath
Modern School Math: Structure and Use	Houghton Mifflin
Skillseekers	Addison-Wesley
SRA Mathematics Program	Science Research Associates

Most students with learning problems require some type of adaptation to basal math textbooks because of their specific academic deficits. Manipulative materials, repetition, and color are equally emphasized in many math programs for the learning handicapped. Some of the specialized commercial materials used with these students are briefly described here.

Computational Arithmetic Program (Pro-Ed Publishers). This program is designed to be used with groups or individual students in Grades 1 through 6 who need to become proficient in the basic computational skills of addition, subtraction, multiplication, and division. The program includes 314 sequenced worksheets for teaching whole number computations. The teacher's manual includes placement methods, charting and analysis of pupil performance, and ways to evaluate student progress.

Corrective Math Programs (Science Research Associates). This series is a remedial program intended for use with students in Grade 3 through adulthood. Corrective Math is a structured program that includes a systematic sequence of skill development in the four basic operations. Materials included with the program are a teacher's guide, student books, placement tests, preskill tests, and a series of mastery tests. Daily lessons include a specific teacher-directed activity and some independent seatwork for the student. The program also includes a built-in point system for students.

Cuisenaire Rods (Cuisenaire Company). The Cuisenaire rods are a set of over 200 color-coded rods, which were primarily designed to teach an understanding of the basic structure of mathematics. The rods vary in length, and each rod is systematically associated with a different number. The rods are commonly used in the primary grades for all basic arithmetic processes and with older students experiencing severe arithmetic difficulties. The emphasis in using the rods is on meaning and discovery. The combined visual, tactile, and auditory modes make the rods most appropriate as a supplementary aid for students with learning handicaps.

DISTAR Arithmetic (Science Research Associates). This is a highly directive beginning arithmetic program with carefully structured lessons intended for small groups of students. The ordered sequence of steps is designed to develop understanding of basic arithmetic skills through active student participation. The program includes counting, algebra, addition and subtraction, story problems, and counting by various numbers. Immediate feedback and repetition are an integral part of the program. The materials are primarily designed for primary age children, although the program can be easily adapted for older students. The teacher's manual is highly specific and well organized.

Project Math (Educational Development Corporation). This curriculum was designed to present a mathematics instructional program to students through the sixth grade. One goal of the curriculum was to develop a means for the nonreader to demonstrate proficiency in math without being impeded by the lack of reading ability.

The program consists of a Mathematics Concept Inventory that was developed to screen and place the learner. The instructional program includes four kits, each of which covers approximately 1½ grade levels. Each kit contains a Multiple Option Curriculum, which provides the instructor with four alternative ways for the learner to demonstrate proficiency. Six mathematical strands (geometry, patterns, sets, numbers and operations, measurement, and fractions) form the basis of the content. Verbal problem solving is treated from an informational processing perspective, and instructional activities are distinguished from those contained in the Multiple Option Curriculum (Cawley, 1977). Project Math also includes a series of miniunits called LABS, which are actually mathematically based activities used to structure experiences to facilitate the development of social skills and behaviors. Some of the topics include calculators, telephones, and metrics.

Structural Arithmetic (Houghton Mifflin). This is a complete mathematics program intended for use with students in kindergarten through third grade. However, the materials can be easily adapted for older students with arithmetic difficulties. The program includes a number of manipulatable materials, including number markers, unit box with unit blocks, pattern board, and groups of cubes. The student is expected to gain insight into number relationships and basic arithmetic operations by experimenting with the materials. Roman numerals, fractions, measurement, and monetary values are also included. The well-organized teacher's manual provides a number of excellent suggestions for individualization, enrichment, and assessment.

Microcomputers

During the past few years there has been rapid growth in the use of the microcomputer with the learning handicapped student. In addition to the tremendous promise that the microcomputer holds for educational programming, McDermott and Walkins (1983) point out that the teaching techniques often recommended for use with the learning handicapped are compatible with computer-assisted instruction, which features individualized pairing and programming, frequent and immediate feedback, hierarchical curriculum, outcomes stated as performance objectives, mastery learning, clarity of presentation, motivation, multisensory learning format, and personalized instruction. Microcomputers seem to be a particularly logical match for mathematics because the structure of math can be sequenced and programmed for systematic instruction (Kirk & Chalfant, 1984). In fact, Lerner (1985) points out that computer education in the schools is often part of the mathematics curriculum and the microcomputer is often located in the math lab.

Computer software programs in math are available for both skill instruction and various drill and practice activities. The microcomputer can provide self-correcting feedback so that the student does not practice errors. Mercer and Mercer (1985) report that some software programs present game-playing situations, whereas others effectively use animation and sound effects to maintain student interest.

One of the few reported research studies investigating the efficacy of computer-assisted instruction in teaching math to learning handicapped students was conducted by Trifiletti, Frith, and Armstrong (1984). In their study learning disabled students ranging in age from 9.3 to 15.2 were randomly assigned to either a computer group or a traditional instruction group. All students received the same amount of time for math instruction in both groups. Results indicated that the microcomputer approach was more efficient in math instruction than the teacher-directed approach.

Even though microcomputers seem to hold great potential for teaching math to the learning handicapped, little research has been conducted to determine the best application of the technology. We agree with Williams (1984) that the increased use of microcomputers in American classrooms increases the need for serious research to address the many issues arising from the application of this technology to instruction of handicapped learners.

TEACHING ACTIVITIES

Readiness

1. Cut different sized circles, squares, triangles, and rectangles from oak tag, felt, or wood. Have the child match the cut-out pieces with the correct spaces.
2. Provide the child with different sized buttons, pencils, nails, or paper strips. Be sure that the objects are identical except in size. Ask the child to arrange the objects in order by size, beginning with the smallest and working toward the largest.

3. Ask the children to find all the circular objects within the room. Contests can be held to see which child finds the greatest number of objects. Rectangular, triangular, and square shapes can be found also.

4. Provide the children with a number of different sized containers and lids. Instruct them to fit the lids to the containers. Use a stopwatch to time individuals. Keep graphs to check progress.

5. Provide worksheets with rows of three to four similar geometric designs and one that is different.

Ask the children to mark the different shape in each row. Use size discrimination also by directing the children to mark the smallest or largest design in each row.

Use varying quantities also to check number discrimination.

6. Ask the children to put together simple jigsaw puzzles with additional pieces. Eventually use more complex puzzles with additional pieces.

7. Provide experience in relating the size of an object to an area in which it is placed by asking the child to match index cards of various sizes to different sized envelopes. (Johnson & Myklebust, 1967).

8. Give the child a set of different sized block cubes. Ask her to find all the blocks that are the same size as the one that you choose from the pile. Extend this activity to include size discrimination by asking the child to match the cubes to outlines on paper. Vary this activity to teach shape discrimination by using blocks differing in form.

9. Provide the child with an assortment of different lengths of rope. Ask her to select the rope that seems closest in length to a dimension of a given object in the classroom (Behrmann & Millman, 1971).

10. Cut different shapes from felt and have the child arrange them in a particular order (e.g., smallest to largest) on the flannel board. This activity provides the child with the opportunity to feel and trace with her fingers the outline of the shape.

Classification and Grouping

1. Prepare several series of cards showing various numbers of graphic symbols.

Have the child organize the cards in piles according to number.

2. Make children aware of groups by pointing out that similar things form a group. Show pictures or point out groups of animals, fruit, people. Permit younger children to cut out pictures from magazines and group them according to similarities.

3. As the children progress in their grouping ability, ask them to group objects according to more precise criteria involving combinations of color, size, shape, quantity.

4. Provide a variety of simple pictures or drawings that vary in the number of objects shown. Ask the children to sort the pictures according to the number of objects they contain.

5. Ask a child to arrange pegs or blocks in various groupings. Instruct him to arrange 6 blocks in 3 groups of 2, for example, or 12 blocks in 4 groups of 3. Eventually, ask the child to arrange all the different groupings for a certain number.

6. Prepare a series of cards that show different groupings of symbols for various numbers. Ask the child to organize the cards in piles, according to the number of symbols on the cards. For instance, the pile of fives would include all of the following:

7. Provide simple addition and subtraction statements, such as $5 + 2 = 7$, and ask the child to illustrate them with symbols. Also, provide symbol statements and ask the child to write the appropriate numerical statements.

8. Johnson and Myklebust (1967) recommend cutting strips of paper into pieces 1-inch wide, varying in length from 1 to 10 inches. Ask the child which strip is the longest, shortest, and so on. Demonstrate the many ways two or more strips can be grouped to equal a longer strip.

9. Use egg cartons to demonstrate how groups are made up of individual members. Cut the cartons into different-sized sections and place them together to show the different ways the number 12 can be visualized (e.g., 6 and 6, 4 and 8).

10. Use Cuisenaire rods for grouping work. Ask the child to group the rods according to size or color.

11. Platts (1964) suggests preparing a worksheet similar to the example that follows. Ask the child to circle groups of dots as directed.

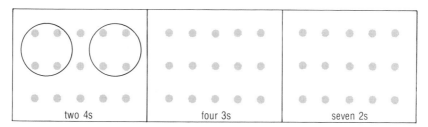

| two 4s | four 3s | seven 2s |

One-to-One Correspondence

1. Place six chips or raisins in a row and ask a child to make another row with the same number of chips or raisins; or ask the child to pass a paper to each boy or girl in the room.
2. Provide the student with a pegboard design to duplicate. Give her the exact number of pegs to arrange so that her design will match precisely.
3. Provide a worksheet with several pictures of the same object, each missing the same part. Require the student to finish each incomplete picture; for example, placing a tail on each dog or a roof on each house.
4. Ask the child to make a tally mark for each time a bell is rung, a note is played on the piano, hands are clapped, or a beat is heard on a drum.
5. Provide a worksheet that requires matching similar sets of objects on a page. Have the child draw a line between boxes that contain the same number of objects. Eventually ask the child to match a numeral (such as 5) with a picture (of perhaps five kites).
6. Smith (1974) suggests practical activities that enhance one-to-one correspondence: playing games of musical chairs, setting a table for the number of children in the class or the family members at home, or checking to see whether enough glasses of milk are available for class members.
7. Provide individual children with a stack of chips or toothpicks. Ask each child to match the given numeral that you draw on the chalkboard. Many children can participate individually in this activity at their desks.
8. Discuss examples of one-to-one correspondence with the children. Ask them to provide suggestions. Examples might include one person, one nose; one elephant, one trunk; one dog, one tail; one hand, one thumb.
9. Ask students numerical questions and require them to provide an answer by showing the correct number of beads on a counting frame (e.g., "How many fingers on your hand?" "How many windows in our room?" "How many jars of paint on the easel?" "How many children with glasses?" "How many chairs in the front of the room?").

Counting

1. Have the student make a motor response as he counts. Have him count pegs as they are placed in the pegboard or beads as they are put on

a string. This activity is especially helpful for the child who skips numbers while counting.

2. Let the student use an abacus. The abacus provides him with a device to manipulate and a visual image as he is counting.

3. Have the child establish the counting principle through motor activities such as clapping four times, jumping two times, or tapping on the table three times (Lerner, 1985).

4. Ask the student to count the number of students in the room when morning attendance is taken or to count aloud rather slowly and deliberately to "see how long it takes the students to get ready for recess."

5. Provide a worksheet with certain quantities of objects pictured (e.g., four balls, six lollipops, two houses). Below each group of objects write the numerals from 1 to 5 or 1 to 10. Ask the student to circle the correct number for each group. Include several groups of objects on each worksheet.

6. Write the numbers from 1 to 20 on a worksheet. Include one number twice. Ask the student to circle all the numbers from 1 to 20 and find the extra number. Various adaptations include writing more than one number twice and extending the sequence beyond 20 (Platts, 1964).

7. Have the student close his eyes and listen to the beats of a drum as he concentrates on counting. Eventually, ask him to make a mark on paper for each sound he hears (Johnson & Myklebust, 1967).

8. Have the student complete a dot-to-dot puzzle numbered in sequence. Gradually extend the sequence of numbers and use more detailed pictures.

9. Attach number lines to the top of each student's desk to provide a constant point of reference. Place longer number lines extending to larger numbers at the top of the chalkboard or on the floor. A shorter number line looks like this:

10. Provide a worksheet with blank spaces before or after individual numbers. Ask the student to fill in the missing numbers (e.g., _____ 7, _____ 13, 19 _____). Eventually, instruct the student to fill in the missing numbers in a series (e.g., 23, _____ , _____ , 26, 27, _____ , 29, _____ , _____ , 32).

Place Value

1. Prepare a worksheet with three columns. The right column should be labeled *Ones;* the middle column, *Tens;* and the left column, *Hundreds.*

Provide the student with numbers such as 130, 28, 497, 5, 17. Instruct her to place each numeral in the correct column on the paper.

2. Cut 30 squares of tagboard and number each card from 0 to 9, making three cards for each number. Write *ones* under each number in one set, *tens* under each number in the second set, and *hundreds* under each number in the third set. Distribute one card to each child in the room. Call out particular numbers, such as 238, and have those students holding the cards needed to form that number come to the front of the room and arrange themselves in the proper order to form that number (Platts, 1964).

3. Prepare a series of cards similar to the example that follows, and ask the student to figure out the number on the front of the card. The back of each card can correctly identify the number.

Front		Back
Tens	Ones	
///	/////	35

4. The abacus is an excellent aid in showing that position determines the numerical value of symbols. Ask students to represent specific numbers by moving the appropriate numbers of beads.

5. Smith (1974) suggests using a place-value box as part of the instruction in simple addition and subtraction. Use a small box with three equal-size compartments, each labeled *Ones, Tens,* or *Hundreds* (from right to left) and each containing sticks such as tongue depressors. Instruct students to add to or remove sticks from the various compartments as they add or subtract.

6. Prepare a set of cards numbered from 0 to 9. Screw three cup hooks into a board and write the words *Hundreds, Tens,* or *Ones* over the hooks (left to right). Call out a number and have the student place the appropriate cards on the hooks corresponding in place value (Wedemeyer & Cejka, 1970).

7. Make a statement such as "I am thinking of a number that is two tens and four ones." Ask students to write the number on the chalkboard or on a worksheet. Eventually add the hundreds place and let students make up the statements.

8. Ask students questions such as "What place does the 5 represent in 352?" or "How do you write a numeral with a 7 in the hundreds place?"

9. Demonstrate the idea of number bases with sticks or papers tied together and placed as ones or tens. For example, represent 37 with three bundles of "tens" sticks on the left and seven "ones" sticks on the right. Let

students practice making bundles with popsicle sticks and representing different numbers.

Computational Activities for Younger Students

1. Use your fingers to show various addition and subtraction problems. Hold up a certain number of fingers and add or subtract another number of fingers.

2. Provide the student with many concrete experiences in learning to add or subtract. Use sticks, paper clips, buttons, raisins. The objects can be used to form groupings for the more difficult combinations.

3. Give the student auditory clues by clapping out the addition or subtraction operation. Gradually let the student do his own clapping. Adaptations include foot tapping, jumping, or hand tapping on the desk.

4. Prepare a worksheet that illustrates number problems. Use dots, circles, lines, and so on for the number groups. Have the student fill in the correct numerals.

5. Wagner, Hosier, and Gilloey (1964) suggest using an addition ferris wheel to reinforce addition facts. Draw a large circle with numbers written around it on the chalkboard. Place one number in the middle of the circle and ask students to see how quickly they can go around the "ferris wheel" by adding the middle number to each number on the outside of the circle. This activity can easily be adapted for basic subtraction, multiplication, and division facts.

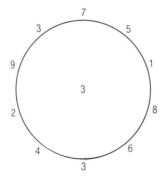

6. Provide each student with a card having a number from 1 to 20 written on it. Call out various combinations, such as 7 + 5 or 2 × 4. The child with the correct answer holds up his card. Gradually add higher numbers to the cards. Eventually, give children more than one card to hold.

7. Use flash cards of basic combinations in addition, subtraction,

multiplication, and division to develop quicker recognition of the combinations. Let students work individually, in pairs, or in groups, either writing or calling out the answers.

8. Adapt games such as those illustrated here for practice with number combinations using addition, subtraction, multiplication, or division. Instruct students to supply the correct answer after landing on a space or before marking or moving to a particular space, otherwise following the regular rules of the game.

Hop scotch

7	8	4
− 2	− 3	− 2
9	6	5
− 5	− 1	− 3
8	1	7
− 6	− 0	− 5

Climbing the ladder

8 × 5
7 × 3
2 × 4
6 × 1
5 × 5
3 × 7

Tic-tac-toe

7 + 5	9 + 4	5 + 3
8 + 3	4 + 8	3 + 7
2 + 1	5 + 6	7 + 2

9. Prepare approximately 40 cards with a number between 1 and 10 written on each card. Place the cards face down and have the student turn up two cards. Direct the student to add, subtract, or multiply the two cards (Wedemeyer & Cejka, 1970).

10. Prepare a number-sentence worksheet leaving different components blank. Ask the student to supply the missing number.

$$6 + \square = 13$$
$$\square \times 7 = 56$$
$$7 - \square = 2$$

11. Prepare a worksheet with several rows of figures. Ask the student to circle any two numbers in sequence that add up to a specific number, such as 12 (Platts, 1964).

4 5 9 6 6 3 4 5 7
9 6 5 7 3 4 8 6 2
3 9 1 5 6 4 8 4 7

12. Play bingo with small groups of students, using cards with a number in each space. Read different number problems, such as 5 + 6, 7 − 3, 6 × 2. Instruct the children to cover any space containing an appropriate answer.

13. Use a number line to demonstrate fundamental operations. For example, teach 3 + 5 by starting at three and jumping five places to eight.

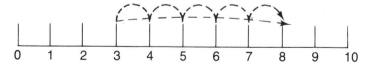

0   1   2   3   4   5   6   7   8   9   10

14. Prepare a division worksheet with illustrated number problems. Have the child supply the corresponding numerical statement.

$$\underline{\quad} \div \underline{\quad} = \underline{\quad}$$

15. Prepare a worksheet with columns of boxes. Write a number in the bottom box of each column, as illustrated here. Ask the student to write in each box a different combination that adds up to the number at the bottom. Use subtraction facts as well as addition for this activity.

Computational Activities for Older Students

1. Use a tachistoscope to measure a student's rate of recognition of number facts. Lerner and Vaver (1970) suggest placing number facts on transparencies, cutting them into strips, and inserting them into a filmstrip projector. The projector can thus be used as a tachistoscope, exposing the selected facts for the desired length of time.

2. Have students use dice to practice addition, subtraction, and multiplication facts, writing or calling out the various answers. Let students continue throwing the dice until they respond incorrectly. Points can be accumulated for each successful answer.

3. Record number facts with answers on a tape recorder. Ask students to write or say the answer before they hear it on the tape. This activity can be administered individually or in groups.

4. Provide students with a variety of long-division problems. Ask them to find just the first number in the quotient. As a variation, provide them with the first number and ask them to show that it is correct.

5. Spitzer (1961) suggests providing a variety of orally presented division questions, such as "12 can be divided into how many 4s?" "24 divided by 6 is how many?" "How many 2s equal 12?"

6. Duplicate or have each student make a multiplication chart. Explain its usage and encourage students to use it freely.

1	2	3	4	5	6	7	8	9	10
2	4	6	8	10	12	14	16	18	20
3	6	9	12	15	18	21	24	27	30
4	8	12	16	20	24	28	32	36	40
5	10	15	20	25	30	35	40	45	50
6	12	18	24	30	36	42	48	54	60
7	14	21	28	35	42	49	56	63	70
8	16	24	32	40	48	56	64	72	80
9	18	27	36	45	54	63	72	81	90
10	20	30	40	50	60	70	80	90	100

7. Provide students with preceding-fact clues for specific combinations; for example, "If 3 + 7 = 10, then what is 3 + 8?" Adapt this activity for subtraction, multiplication, or division facts.

8. Use shade-in math puzzles. Instruct students to shade in the puzzle parts containing numbers divisible by 2, for example, or numbers that are multiples of 3. The shaded puzzle parts form a picture (Polloway, Payne, Patton, & Payne, 1985).

9. Arrange playing cards by suit in sequential order by number, assigning all cards a numerical value. Direct students to add and subtract various card combinations (Lerner, 1985).

10. Use calculators for drill and for checking responses. The National Council of Teachers of Mathematics (1976) has suggested several benefits of calculator instruction. It

    a. assists in helping the student become a wise consumer
    b. reinforces basic number facts and properties of the four operations
    c. develops understanding of selected algorithms through repeated operations
    d. serves as a check on computations
    e. promotes independence in problem solving
    f. solves problems that are normally too time-consuming to be computed by hand

Fractions

1. Let younger students color in fractional components of various geometric shapes.

color 1/2

color 1/4

color 1/3

color 2/5

2. Begin instruction with halves, followed by quarters and eighths. Provide students with familiar pictures that are cut in half, and ask the students to put the halves together. This procedure can also be used with foods, such as fruits, sandwiches, and cookies.

3. Illustrate the importance of parts to a whole by providing pictures with obvious missing parts. Have students find each missing part.

4. Let students manipulate flannel board fractional cut-outs and paper plates divided into fractional parts of different colors in order to better understand fractions.

5. Prepare a worksheet with a different number of circles in each of several boxes on the page. Ask the students to split each circle in the first box into halves, each circle in the second box into thirds, and so on. Let younger students color the parts of the circles.

6. Smith (1974) suggests using charts similar to those shown here to illustrate the relationship of fractional parts to the whole.

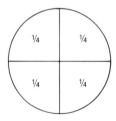

7. Provide each student with a worksheet on which circles or squares have been divided and shaded. Follow each figure with a box in which the student is to write the appropriate fraction for the shaded part (Engelmann, 1969).

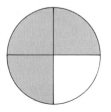 

8. Gradually introduce assignments requiring students to work with fractions without visual clues. Have students discriminate fractional quantities, choosing the largest and smallest quantities from a given list of fractions.

9. Prepare a worksheet comprised of rows of fractions and ask students to circle the two equivalent fractions in each line.

<u>1/3</u>   1/4   3/6   4/5   <u>2/6</u>   7/8

<u>1/2</u>   1/3   <u>4/8</u>   6/7   2/3   4/5

1/9   <u>1/5</u>   1/3   <u>2/10</u>   4/5   2/3

10. Use fraction number lines to introduce students to relative quantities—fractions that are less than, equal to, or greater than one whole. Encourage the students to count forward and backward on the number line.

11. Use the measurements in simple recipes to reinforce fractional components. Have students do the measuring for cookies, pancakes, or cakes to be baked.

Telling Time

1. Prepare a worksheet with a number of clock faces. Instruct the students to draw in the hands of the clock to show various times, which can be given aloud or written under the faces.

2. Provide students with real clocks or teacher-made (or pupil-made) clocks. Clocks can be commercially purchased through most school supply companies or inexpensively made by attaching cardboard hands to paper plates.

3. Use individual clocks for group activities. Ask students a variety of time-related questions and have them set their individual clocks (e.g., "What time does school begin?" "What time do we eat lunch at school?" "What time does school end for the day?" "What time do you go to bed?").

4. Lerner (1985) suggests the following sequence for teaching time: the hour, the half hour, the quarter hour, five-minute intervals, before and after the hour, minute intervals, and seconds.

5. Teach different hand positions on the clock by having students stand with their own hands and arms pointed straight up. Instruct them to represent various times that you call out by moving their hands and arms accordingly (Behrmann & Millman, 1971).

6. Prepare a series of cards with a time written on the front of each card and a clock face showing that time on the back. Direct students to use the cards individually by setting their own clocks with the time on the front and checking their work against the clock face on the back (Platts, 1964).

7. Ask students to perform activities that can be timed (e.g., "How long will it take Margaret to take these papers to the office?" "Let's see how long it will take us to clean up our desks," "We may all go outside for 5 minutes," "We have 3 minutes to finish the arithmetic paper," "How long did it take you to read this story?").

8. Provide the students with TV, plane, or train schedules; ask them questions based upon those schedules. Relate the schedules to the clock and have students find the various times on the clock.

9. Have each student make up an individual time schedule or log of her day, including activities such as getting up, catching the bus, going to recess, eating lunch, going home, eating dinner, and going to bed.

10. Show students pictures (e.g., someone getting out of bed, a child eating lunch) and ask them to set their clocks at the times indicated by the pictures. Take into account individual differences.

Money

1. Prepare a worksheet with coin denominations in separate boxes. Instruct the students to draw a line between boxes that equal the same amount of money (e.g., five pennies equal one nickel, two dimes and one nickel equal one quarter).

2. Provide real money whenever possible to teach money values. Purchase realistic rubber stamp reproductions of actual U.S. coins to use at other times.

3. Platts (1964) suggests preparing a worksheet with problems similar to those listed here and asking students to choose the greater amount and find the sum.

> Quarter + nickel + dime OR two quarters
> Dollar OR nickel + three quarters
> Seven dimes OR three quarters
> Quarter + dime + half dollar OR three quarters
> Three dimes + nickel + quarter OR half dollar
> + nickel

4. Show students combinations of coins and ask them to total the amounts. Use actual coins pasted to cards whenever possible.

5. Set up a grocery store in the classroom with empty boxes and cans of food. Price each item and allow students to be the storekeeper, cashier, and shoppers, using real or play money to conduct business.

Adaptations of this activity include holding several priced items before the class and asking them to find the total cost.

6. Paste pictures of objects (food, toys, and clothes) on cards and label each with a price. Flash the cards to individual students and ask them to write down the change they would receive from a certain amount of money.

7. Give students a certain amount of money and ask them to purchase as many different items as possible with the available money. The student who is able to buy the greatest number of different items without exceeding his supply of money wins the game.

8. Arrange with the cafeteria manager to have certain students act as cashier for specified periods of time. Let other students collect and total milk or bus money.

9. Provide actual or play restaurant menus. Ask the students to order a meal and total the cost. Instruct more advanced students to add tax and tip.

10. Give students newspaper grocery advertisements. Ask students to do the weekly "shopping" for their families and total the cost of their groceries (Platts, 1964).

11. If a token reinforcement system is being used in the classroom, take advantage of its many opportunities to teach monetary concepts in the exchange of tokens for reinforcers (see chapter 2). Make play currency and use it instead of tokens. A currency-based token economy teaches many arithmetic skills directly, including monetary value.

Arithmetic Terms and Signs

1. Prepare a worksheet with missing math signs. Ask the students to fill them in.

$$6 \underline{\hspace{1cm}} 3 = 3$$
$$1 \underline{\hspace{1cm}} 2 = 3$$
$$2 \underline{\hspace{1cm}} 4 = 6$$
$$1 + 1 \underline{\hspace{1cm}} 2$$
$$7 \underline{\hspace{1cm}} 5 = 2$$

2. Promote understanding of the terms *longer* and *shorter* by drawing lines of various lengths on the chalkboard and asking the students to make them longer or shorter. Also, direct students to sort various objects, such as sticks, into piles of longer or shorter items (Wagner et al., 1964).

3. Use number lines to develop vocabulary such as *before, after, between, larger than, smaller than,* and *the same as.* Permit students to refer to the number lines in answering the questions (e.g., What number comes just *before* 7? What number comes just *after* 13? What number comes *between* 6 and 8?).

4. Use auditory stimulation to develop the concepts of *more* and *less* by clapping the number of letters in each student's name. Ask whether *T-i-m* has more claps than *C-h-r-i-s* or whether *M-i-s-s-y* has fewer claps than *J-i-m* (Behrmann & Millman, 1971).

5. Provide students with different colored beads on a string and ask them specific questions (e.g., "Are there *more* blue beads than red beads?" "Are there *fewer* yellow beads than black beads?" "Which color has the *same* number of beads as red?").

6. Prepare a worksheet similar to the example shown here for use with a number line.

	(Check the correct answer)			
	Larger than	Smaller than	The same as	
2 + 2 is				3 + 1
5 + 1 is				3 + 3
17 is				71
3 + 1 is				1 + 3
6 + 2 is				4 + 5

7. Give students a set of cards numbered from 1 to 10. Instruct them to turn up one card and ask whether that number comes before or after a number that you choose at random. Also, use *more* or *less* and *smaller than* or *larger than* for this activity.

8. Give students practice in reading arithmetic problems without working them. Have the students read $2 + 2 = 4$ or $5 - 3 = 2$ with the emphasis on the operational signs (Johnson & Myklebust, 1967).

9. Print operational signs on flash cards. Let the students practice with the cards every day. Add kinesthetic clues by cutting the signs out of sandpaper and pasting them on the cards.

10. Provide color cues for operational signs to call attention to the signs. Also, draw circles or boxes around the signs to enable pupils to attend more closely to the signs.

Problem-Solving Activities for Older Students

1. Present story problems orally and direct the pupils to solve them without using pencil or paper. Students are thus required to listen closely to the presentation. Allow students who successfully arrive at the answer to explain the process they used.

2. Have the students read story problems and decide on the mathematical operation required to solve the problem, without actually doing the computation. Encourage them to discuss why a specific mathematical operation is required for a particular problem.

3. Discuss word clues in story problems that indicate mathematical operations. Make students more aware of these key words by underlining or circling them on seatwork papers. Some word clues include *altogether, left, remain, and, lost.*

4. Ask students to write the correct number sentence for a story problem prior to working out the answer. This process helps pupils to see numerical relationships.

> *Story problem:* The football team had 45 members, and 1/5 of them were seniors. How many students were seniors?
>
> *Number sentence:* 45 ÷ 1/5 = _____

5. Provide story problems that require a one-step solution. Keep the length of the sentences short and include only essential vocabulary during beginning instruction in problem solving.

6. Johnson and Myklebust (1967) suggest using sentences that emphasize "logic and rational thought" rather than rote memorization (p. 270). Practice sentences of this type might include the following true or false statements: "John, who is 38 inches tall, is shorter than Bill, who is 3 feet tall"; "I will have to wait for 14 more days if my cousin is visiting me in 2 weeks"; "There are spaces for one dozen, or 14, more cars."

7. Visually represent the numerical amounts presented in a story problem. For example, in problems involving money actually provide students with the appropriate amount of real or play money.

8. Encourage students to use analogous problems with easier numbers to solve more difficult story problems.

9. Permit students to make up their own story problems involving specific operations, such as addition or subtraction. Require other students in the class to solve the problems or let students provide the answers to their own problems.

10. Orally analyze the steps that are required to solve a particular problem. Spitzer (1961) lists the following procedures to be used in problem analysis and recommends analyzing only one or two steps at a time.

    a. What is given,
    b. What is asked,
    c. What operation or operations to use,
    d. An estimate of the answer,
    e. The solution, and
    f. A check of the answer. (p. 256)

11. Diagram or illustrate story problems on the chalkboard. Discuss each part of the illustration. Then allow pupils to illustrate selected story problems.

12. Mercer and Mercer (1985) suggest having students locate a job advertised in the newspaper and use the salary quoted to compute net pay.

Also, have students compute living expenses by using newspaper ads, apartment rental ads, car ads, and catalogs.

REFERENCES

Armenia, J. W., Kamp, D. A., McDonald, D. H., & Von Kuster, L. (1975). *Wisconsin Design for Math Skill Development.* Minneapolis, MN: National Computer Systems.

Beatty, L. S., Madden, R., Gardner, E., & Karlsen, B. *Stanford Diagnostic Mathematics Test.* New York: Harcourt Brace Jovanovich.

Behrmann, P., & Millman, J. (1971). *How many spoons make a family?* Novato, CA: Academic Therapy Publications.

Brown, V. L., & McEntire, E. (1984). *Test of Mathematical Abilities.* Austin, TX: Pro-Ed.

Brueckner, L. J. (1955). *Diagnostic tests and self-helps in arithmetic.* Monterey, CA: CTB/McGraw-Hill.

Cawley, J. F. (1977). Curriculum: One perspective for special education. In R. D. Kneedler & S. G. Tarver (Eds.), *Changing perspectives in special education.* Columbus, OH: Charles E. Merrill.

Connolly, A. J., Nachtman, W., & Pritchett, E. M. (1976). *Key Math Diagnostic Arithmetic Test.* Circle Pines, MN: American Guidance Service.

CTB/McGraw-Hill. (1977, 1978). *California Achievement Tests.* Monterey, CA: Author.

Dunn, L. M., & Markwardt, F. C. (1970). *Peabody Individual Achievement Test.* Circle Pines, MN: American Guidance Service.

Englemann, S. (1969). *Preventing failure in the primary grades.* Chicago: Science Research Associates.

Ginsburg, H. (1982). *Children's arithmetic: How they learn it and how they teach it.* Austin, TX: Pro-Ed.

Ginsburg, H. P., & Baroody, A. J. (1983). *The Test of Early Mathematics Ability.* Austin, TX: Pro-Ed.

Ginsburg, H. P., & Mathews, S. (1984). *Diagnostic Test of Arithmetic Strategies.* Austin, TX: Pro-Ed.

Hammill, D. D., & Bartel, N. R. (1982). *Teaching children with learning and behavior problems.* Boston: Allyn & Bacon.

Haring, N. G., & Bateman, B. (1977). *Teaching the learning disabled child.* Englewood Cliffs, NJ: Prentice-Hall.

Jastak, J. F., & Jastak, S. K. (1978). *The Wide Range Achievement Test.* Wilmington, DE: Jastak Associates.

Johnson, D. J., & Myklebust, H. R. (1967). *Learning disabilities: Educational principles and practices.* New York: Grune & Stratton.

Kirk, S. A., & Chalfort, J. C. (1984). *Academic and developmental learning disabilities.* Denver: Love.

Lerner, J. (1985). *Children with learning disabilities: Theories, diagnosis, and teaching strategies* (4th ed.). Boston: Houghton Mifflin.

Lerner, J. W., & Vaver, G. (1970). Filmstrips in learning. *Academic Therapy, 5,* 320–324.

Lundell, K., Brown, W., & Evans, V. (1976). *Criterion Test of Basic Skills.* Novato, CA: Academic Therapy Publications.

Madden, R., Gardner, E. F., Rudman, H. C., Karlsen, B., & Merwin, J. C. (1973). *Stanford Achievement Test.* New York: Harcourt Brace Jovanovich.

McDermott, P. A., & Watkins, M. W. (1983). Computerized vs. conventional remedial instruction for learning disabled pupils. *Journal of Special Education, 17,* 81–88.

Mercer, C. D., & Mercer, A. R. (1985). *Teaching students with learning problems* (2nd ed.). Columbus, OH: Charles E. Merrill.

Moran, M. R. (1978). *Assessment of the exceptional learner in the regular classroom.* Denver: Love.

Naslund, R. A., Thorpe, L. P., & Lefever, D. W. (1978). *SRA Achievement Series.* Chicago: Science Research Associates.

National Council of Teachers of Mathematics. (1976). Minicalculators in the schools. *Arithmetic Teacher, 23,* 72–74.

Otto, W., & Smith, R. J. (1980). *Corrective and remedial teaching* (3rd ed.). Boston: Houghton Mifflin.

Platts, M. E. (1964). *Plus.* Stevensville, MI: Educational Service.

Polloway, E. A., Payne, J. S., Patton, J. R., & Payne, R. A. (1985). *Strategies for teaching retarded and special needs learners* (3rd ed.). Columbus, OH: Charles E. Merrill.

Prescott, G. A., Balow, I. H., Hogan, T. P., & Farr, R. C. (1978). *Metropolitan Achievement Tests.* New York: Psychological Corporation.

Reisman, F. K. (1978). *A guide to the diagnostic teaching of arithmetic* (2nd ed.). Columbus, OH: Charles E. Merrill.

Schminke, C. W., Maertens, N., & Arnold, W. (1978). *Teaching the child mathematics* (2nd ed.). New York: Holt, Rinehart & Winston.

Smith, R. M. (1974). *Clinical teaching: Methods of instruction for the retarded.* New York: McGraw-Hill.

Spitzer, H. F. (1961). *The teaching of arithmetic.* Boston: Houghton Mifflin.

Trifiletti, J. J., Frith, G. H., & Armstrong, S. (1984). Microcomputers versus resource rooms for LD students: A preliminary investigation of the effects on math skills. *Learning Quarterly, 1,* 69–76.

Wagner, G., Hosier, M., & Gilloey, L. (1964). *Arithmetic games and activities.* Darien, CT: Teachers.

Wallace, G. (in press). *Assessment: Evaluating students with learning and behavior problems.* Austin, TX: Pro-Ed.

Wallace, G., & McLoughlin, J. A. (1979). *Learning disabilities: Concepts and characteristics.* Columbus, OH: Charles E. Merrill.

Wedemeyer, A., & Cejka, J. (1970). *Creative ideas for teaching exceptional children.* Denver: Love.

Williams, R. L. (1984). *Computer-assisted instruction for mildly handicapped students: A need for research.* Unpublished manuscript.

12

Study Skills

Most educators agree that a major objective of education is to help students become independent learners. According to Tonjes and Zintz (1981), guiding students in the use of appropriate study skills, or techniques for mastering school subjects, usually facilitates their becoming independent learners. Unfortunately, knowing how to study efficiently does not come naturally to most students (Deese & Deese, 1979). Many potentially good students are deficient in basic study skills.

Study skills encompass the tools students use to absorb the material that they are to learn (Lock, 1981). Such skills are usually considered to include those competencies associated with acquiring, recording, organizing, synthesizing, remembering, and using information and ideas encountered in the classroom (Devine, 1981). More specifically, they include listening, reading, note-taking, library usage, test taking, oral and written reports, graphic aids, and time management.

According to Lock (1981), most study skills are needed when students are not under the direct guidance of their teacher (e.g., during homework assignments, library research, preparing for tests). Consequently, most material about how to study is directed at adolescent and older students.

Nonetheless, efficient study skills can be developed during the elementary grades and reinforced as pupils progress through school.

ASSESSMENT

There are few available instruments for evaluating knowledge and use of various study skills. Of the tests that are available, most can be classified as either formal instruments or informal assessment techniques.

Formal Tests

Study skills are often included as a subtest in general achievement batteries. Most achievement tests are norm-referenced, standardized tests that allow comparison of the performance of individual pupils, classes, grades, schools, and school districts throughout the country. Such tests do not usually provide detailed information concerning a pupil's specific skill strengths and weaknesses. The small number of items used to measure each skill area simply do not provide enough data to properly appraise specific skills. The following are among those general achievement batteries with study skills subtests.

☐ California Achievement Test (CTB/McGraw-Hill)

☐ Iowa Test of Basic Skills (Riverside)

☐ SRA Achievement Series (Science Research Associates)

☐ Tests of Achievement and Proficiency (Riverside)

In addition to general achievement tests, a limited number of published tests are available that directly and specifically assess just study skills. Some of these tests are listed in Table 12–1. Most of these tests are quite limited in scope and measure only a few of the many study skills.

Informal Assessment Techniques

Informal appraisal measures are frequently the primary approach to the evaluation of study skills. Informal tests are most often utilized to pinpoint problems or to evaluate readiness for planned instruction. Since informal measures are directly related to classroom instruction, they can often provide specific information concerning study skills. Polloway and Smith (1982) suggest that informal techniques, when used appropriately, provide for direct conversion of results into remedial activities. Informal tests can be designed to measure almost any specific study skill. Ekwall and Shanker (1983) have identified certain study skills and related methods of informal assessment.

1. *Using library card index.* Use questions such as "How many cards have a listing for the book *World War Two Airplanes*?" "What does the Author Card include?" "What does the Subject Card include?" "What is the call number of the book *Hitler*?"

Table 12-1
Published Study Skills Tests

Name of Test	Grade Level	Study Skills Evaluated
Study Attitudes and Methods Survey (Michael, Michael, & Zimmerman, 1972)	HS and college	Academic interest, academic drive, study methods, study anxiety, manipulation, and alienation toward authority
Study Skills Test: McGraw-Hill Basic Skills System (Raygor, 1970)	11–14	Problem solving, underlining, library information, study skills information, and inventory of study habits and attitudes
Survey of Study Habits and Attitudes (Brown & Holtzman, 1967)	7–12 12–14	Study habits and attitudes
The Cornell Learning and Study Skills Inventory (Pauk & Cassell, 1970)	7–13 13–16	Goal orientation, activity structure, scholarly skills, lecture mastery, textbook mastery, examination mastery, and self-mastery
Wisconsin Tests of Reading Skill Development: Study Skills (Stewart, Kamm, Allen, & Sols, 1972)	K–7	Skills necessary for locating, interpreting, and using maps, graphs, tables, and reference materials

2. *Learning to take notes.* Play a short tape recording of a lecture or radio program on a subject in which the students are interested and ask them to take notes.

3. *Using index.* Using students' textbooks, ask questions such as "On what page would you find information on the topic of polar bears?" (pp. 209–210)

In most cases informal tests of various study skills can be constructed by using the students' textbook or workbook exercises as guides. However, teachers must be careful to include a sufficient number of test items to adequately measure the study skill. We believe that informal tests must be precisely planned, administered, and interpreted if the results are to hold any meaning for the teacher.

MATERIALS

The development of various study skills has been part of the curriculum in both developmental and remedial reading classes and has often been included in special lessons and units. According to Devine (1981), much of this instruction is disorganized, unsystematic, and lacking in focus. He believes that many teachers fail to explain and demonstrate to students how to read an assignment; how to deal with new vocabulary; how to listen to various presentations; how to take notes, outline, review, participate in discussions; or how to take a test. This section will present a number of effective study methods and a listing of some commercial materials for developing study skills.

Study Methods

A number of study methods have been designed to help students read and study assigned materials. Most such methods provide a systematic approach or structure for studying.

SQ3R Method. This approach is probably the best known and most widely used of all study methods. It was developed by Robinson (1961) and is used extensively for social studies and science selections. It involves five separate steps.

1. *Survey.* The entire reading selection is quickly scanned to obtain the general ideas that are developed in the selection. The survey includes headings, subheadings, paragraph topics, graphic aids, and any summary and provides the student with a thorough overview.

2. *Questions.* The reader is expected to formulate questions during this stage. The student turns headings and subheadings into *who, what, where, why,* and *how* questions.

3. *Read.* During this stage the student reads to answer the questions formulated in the previous stage. The reading is considered purposeful because the student is responding to her own questions. Additional questions can be added during this stage.

4. *Recite.* To facilitate understanding and memory, the student periodically attempts to respond to the previously formulated questions without looking at the book or notes. Any errors or omissions are noted at this time.

5. *Review.* Upon completion of the reading assignment, the student immediately reviews the lesson to organize the ideas. While headings and notes are reviewed, the student verifies answers to questions. This stage helps to overcome the tendency to forget material shortly after reading it. Robinson (1961) believes that this study method is not learned simply by reading about it but must be practiced under supervision. SQ3R seems to be a more efficient approach when taught in the context of specific content material.

REAP Method. This approach was developed by Eanet and Manzo (1976) as a strategy for improving reading, thinking, and writing skills. REAP is based on the idea that a student must process information and organize it in a way that is useful to himself as well as to others. The strategy includes four steps.

1. *Read.* The pupil reads to find out what the author is saying.
2. *Encode.* The author's message is rewritten by the student in his own words.
3. *Annotate.* This is a crucial step in the REAP method: the student must differentiate the author's ideas, translate them into his own language, and then summarize the results in writing. The student can use any one of seven forms of annotation. Heuristic annotations consist of quotations from a selection that suggest the essence of the selection and stimulate responses. Summary annotations are brief restatements of the author's main ideas and the relationships between them. Thesis annotations state the author's main theme. Question annotations state significant questions that the student thinks the author is addressing. A critical annotation consists of the author's thesis, the student's reaction to the thesis, and a defense of the student's reaction. Intention annotations include the author's purpose. A motivation annotation consists of the student's perspective on the author's motives.
4. *Ponder.* During this stage the student thinks about the author's message and discusses it with others.

EVOKER Method. This study method was developed by Pauk (1963) for use with prose, poetry, and drama. It includes six steps.

1. *Explore.* The entire selection is read silently in order to gain understanding of the overall message.
2. *Vocabulary.* Key words, unfamiliar people, places, and events are noted and looked up by the student.
3. *Oral reading.* The selection is read aloud by the student during this stage.
4. *Key ideas.* In this step the student determines the theme of the selection, along with key ideas, in order to understand the author's organization.
5. *Evaluation.* Key words and sentences are identified during this stage to facilitate evaluation of the key ideas of the selection.
6. *Recapitulation.* The entire selection is reread in this step.

PANORAMA Method. This study technique consists of eight steps and is divided into three stages, according to Edwards (1973).

Preparatory Stage

1. *Purpose.* The student determines why the material is being read.
2. *Adapting rate to material.* This stage consists of deciding at which rate to read the selection, keeping in mind the need for flexibility within sections.
3. *Need to pose questions.* Headings, subheadings, and cue words are used to formulate questions (See SQ3R).

Intermediate Stage

4. *Overview.* The reading material is surveyed (See SQ3R) to help determine the author's organization.
5. *Read and relate.* During this stage the material is read in terms of a particular purpose, and answers are sought for the previously formulated questions.
6. *Annotate.* The student makes written annotations of main ideas in the book or on a separate piece of paper.

Concluding Stage

7. *Memorize.* Outlines and summaries are utilized to highlight important points. The student also uses acronyms to help remember main points.
8. *Assess.* During this stage the student evaluates her efforts in relation to purpose and retention of the material.

Commercial Materials

Few commercial materials are available for teaching study skills. Four different materials are briefly summarized in this section.

Thirty Lessons in Note-taking (Curriculum Associates). The exercises in this skillbook teach and review the principles of choosing useful information, taking organized notes, summarizing and recording information, and using notes to write a report. Some exercises are completed within the book, whereas others draw on outside experiences.

Learning How to Learn: Teaching Strategies (DLM Teaching Resources). This program is designed for learning handicapped students from junior high level to adulthood. Learning techniques are presented for use in academic, social, and vocational settings. The program includes five resource manuals that focus on skills in studying, reading, writing, listening, and teaching. An implementation guide and 20 black-line masters for duplication are provided with the program.

A Guidebook for Teaching Study Skills and Motivation (Allyn & Bacon). This book offers some new and interesting approaches for developing effective study skills. Included within the book are word-by-word class presentations, informal diagnostic instruments, learning activities, and instruments for evaluating progress. Reproduction pages of actual lessons are included and may be dittoed or photocopied in any quantity. All standard study skills are discussed within the book.

The Outlining Kit (Curriculum Associates). This kit consists of reusable lesson cards that sequentially develop outlining subskills. Activities help students discover the logical relationship of ideas and details incorporated in everyday writing and speaking. Masters for duplication are included for pretests and posttests.

Microcomputers

The use of microcomputers to assist the instructional process is widely accepted today by elementary and secondary schools and colleges and universities (Ekwall, 1985). An increasing number of software programs are becoming available in the particular area of study skills. Some software programs focus on learning to read more effectively in content areas by developing skills in finding the main idea, recalling important facts and details, and acquiring content area vocabulary. A number of other software programs help students in some of the following areas: taking tests, notetaking, outlining, writing research papers, using graphic aids, listening, and increasing reading comprehension.

Although there seem to be a number of excellent possibilities for using microcomputers in developing various study skills, we believe that intensive study is needed to determine computer effectiveness, especially with handicapped learners. Presently, little serious research has been conducted to determine the best applications of computer technology. Consequently, we are somewhat hesitant to wholeheartedly endorse the use of microcomputers in developing study skills. Well-designed research studies should fully address the many issues involved in the application of computer technology to instruction of handicapped learners.

TEACHING ACTIVITIES

Time Management

1. Provide students with an after-school calendar to complete for 1 week. Help students evaluate their use of time by first summarizing how much time is spent studying, sleeping, watching TV, working, talking on the phone, socializing.
2. Encourage students to compare their after-school calendars. Discuss reasons for varying amounts of free time, studying, and so on, referring to actual schedules.
3. Have students construct a semester calendar including test and quiz dates, term paper and project due dates, and athletic and social events.
4. Encourage students to share their methods of organization with other students. Use class presentations or posters for this activity.
5. Thomas (1980) recommends the use of a "study budget" for planning an evening's study time. She suggests writing the schedule on a piece of paper.

Task	Time
Write in journal	7:30 – 8:00
Do geometry problems	8:00 – 8:45
Translate French	8:45 – 9:15
Read literature section	9:15 – 9:45

6. Pauk (1974) suggests the following characteristics of a good schedule.
   □ allotted time for all activities
   □ enough time for studying each subject
   □ efficient use of small segments of free time for study
   □ scheduling study time according to the laws of learning: studying a subject as soon as possible after class with a brief review just before the next class, overlearning by frequent review, and so on
   □ time for relaxation and rewards for diligence
7. Encourage students to set specific time limits for particular projects or assignments. Have them keep track of the time actually spent.
8. Mercer and Mercer (1985) suggest having students prioritize school assignments in the order they should be completed. The rankings should subsequently be reviewed in terms of consequences and time factors. Large tasks can be broken into smaller segments, and all tasks can be value-rated by grouping them according to high, medium, and low value.
9. Organize interested students into how-to-study groups. Use one of the books listed in Table 12–2 as a resource guide.

Table 12-2
How-to-Study Resource Books

Title	Publisher
Best Methods of Study	Barnes and Noble
Effective Study	Harper & Row
How to Read a Book	International Reading Association
How to Read and Study for Success in College	Holt, Rinehart & Winston
How to Study	McGraw-Hill
How to Study	Science Research Associates
How to Study in College	Houghton Mifflin
Productive Reading and Study Skills: A Student's Guide	Kendall/Hunt
Study in Depth	Prentice-Hall

Listening

1. Tonjes and Zintz (1981) suggest that students find out what helps them to be better listeners. They recommend playing a guessing game with the speaker, trying to anticipate his purpose, message, and actions. Other suggestions include maintaining eye contact, watching for visual clues to meaning, and relating what is being said to what is already known.

2. Tell students in advance that there will be at least one factual error in the lecture. Ask students to write down the error(s) at the conclusion of the lecture.

3. Remind students to listen for sequence signals (*first, second, next, plus*) or for concluding ideas (*in sum, therefore, finally, in conclusion*).

4. Stop periodically while reading a story or delivering a lecture, and ask students specific questions about material just presented. Ask students to predict the next sequence in the story or lecture.

5. Have students listen to advertisements and determine how the advertisers are trying to get the listeners to buy their products (Lerner, 1985).

6. To help students follow items in sequence, Devine (1981) suggests listing on the chalkboard before a lecture the five most important points of the talk, out of order. Instruct students to listen for those major points and write them in their correct order before the talk concludes.

7. To assess understanding, ask a student to repeat or paraphrase the directions for a homework assignment.

8. Tonjes and Zintz (1981) recommend the TQLR technique for better listening: tune in, question, listen, and review. Initially, the listener must be ready and alert to what is being said. Next, the student should ask herself what position the speaker will take and then listen attentively for the answer. The student should also ask herself new questions as the talk proceeds. Finally, a mental review at the conclusion of the talk will help the student retain the key points.

9. Lock (1981) suggests that instruction in how to listen and record accurately begin with short lectures. Direct students to write what they believe are the important points of a lecture. Afterward, review the lecture and point out what should be in the students' notes.

10. Instruct students to listen for important content, signaled by pauses or changes in volume or tone.

Note-taking

1. Courtney (1965) presents four principles of note-taking.
   a. Students should write notes in their own words rather than in the author's words.
   b. Students should develop a consistent format when note-taking.

    c. Notes should show when they were taken and from what source.

    d. Notes should be complete and intelligible.

2. Bragstad and Stumpf (1982) suggest that the teacher tape-record a lecture about to be given to a class. While the tape is played to the class, the teacher can take notes on an overhead projector in order to demonstrate effective note-taking techniques.

3. Encourage students to follow the traditional outline format for note-taking.

       I. Main idea
      II. Main idea
         A. Subtopic
         B. Subtopic
            1. Supporting statement
            2. Supporting statement
               a. Clarifying detail
               b. Clarifying detail

4. Encourage students to use a highlighter pen to identify key ideas and supporting facts.

5. Devine (1981) points out that simple how-to-do-it presentations are excellent opportunities for note-taking. Have individual students explain how to repair a flat tire, make fudge, or use a book's index. Direct other students to jot down the important steps presented.

6. Have students with outlining difficulties outline two or three paragraphs rather than an entire passage or chapter. Give students a partially completed outline of a story; have them read the story and then complete the outline (Ekwall, 1985).

7. Give students worksheets containing reading passages and related questions. Ask them to underline the answers to the questions as they find them (Ekwall, 1985).

8. Pauk (1974) suggests the following guidelines for underlining.

    a. Finish reading before marking.

    b. Be selective and underline only what is important.

    c. Make notes in the margins in your own words.

    d. Underline quickly and reread only for review.

    e. Be neat and do not clutter a page.

9. Allot time for some general note-swapping in order for students to see and learn other methods of getting lecture points on paper. Encourage students to share aloud strategies they have utilized (Bragstad & Stumpf, 1982).

10. Encourage the use of a tape recorder in note-taking. Have students prepare tape-recorded notes of a chapter or selection and then share those "notes" with the class (Devine, 1981).

11. Teach students to use abbreviations during note-taking. For example,

. ˙ .	therefore
w/	with
=	equals, is, are
w/o	without
+	and

12. Encourage students to review notes as soon as possible after the completion of class. Suggest that they then add thoughts to blank spaces and highlight important points.

13. Organize a note-taking contest. Award one point for each main idea identified and another for each supporting detail or example. Judges, using an answer key of main ideas and supporting examples, can select the award-winning notes (Devine, 1981).

14. Provide students with a set of inferior notes (e.g., no abbreviations, complete sentences, minor details). Have groups of students perfect the notes by applying effective principles of note-taking (Bragsford & Stumpf, 1982).

15. Encourage students to use their notes during class discussions and exam preparation periods.

16. A two-column system for taking notes is offered by Aaronson (1975). One column is utilized to record the speaker's ideas; the other column is used after the lecture to categorize and summarize major points and ideas.

Test Taking

1. Write two headings on the chalkboard—*Objective* and *Essay*. Have the class pool their hints for taking each kind of test (Bragstad & Stumpf, 1982).

2. Discuss how *clue words* often provide a key to answering certain test questions. For example, in true/false questions extremes such as *none, all, never, always,* and *every* are often false, whereas more moderate expressions with terms such as *many, some, few, rarely, often,* and *usually* are often true (Tonjes & Zintz, 1981). Table 12–3 illustrates a number of clue words for essay questions.

3. Point out the types of a student's consistent test errors by reviewing that student's previous quizzes.

4. Devine (1981) points out that students should prepare special word lists before they take a test because vocabulary and special terminology are important in all school subjects. Have students list all possible words associated with the topic, find definitions, and test one another on the words.

5. For major tests, such as college entrance exams, invite students who

Table 12-3
Clue Words for Essay Questions

Clue Words	Meaning
1. describe define trace discuss examine analyze	Give in words a picture of an idea, a concept, or an object. Give clear, concise definitions. Record careful observation. Give the important ideas and show how they are related.
2. compare and contrast differentiate distinguish	Give likenesses and differences. Show differences between items, groups, or categories.
3. enumerate outline	Use lists, outlines, main and subordinate points, and details.
4. state relate	Write concisely and clearly, connecting ideas or concepts. Use chronology of events or ideas where it applies.
5. prove justify	Use facts, or logic, or cite authorities to justify your thesis.
6. evaluate criticize	Make value judgments but use logic to explain. Criticize, pro or con, the merits of a concept or a theory.
7. review summarize synthesize	Summarize main points concisely, restate judgments or conclusions, integrate arguments from different sources.

SOURCE: From Teaching Reading/Thinking/Study Skills in Content Classrooms (p. 246) by M. J. Tonjes and M. V. Zintz, 1981, Dubuque, IA: William C. Brown. Copyright 1981 by William C. Brown. Reprinted by permission.

have already taken the test to describe the experience from their perspective.

6. Since most students have not been taught how to study for tests, review these general guidelines with the class.
   □ Organize all relevant material (notes, books, old exams).
   □ Identify general process goals.
   □ Review notes.
   □ Review worksheets.
   □ Review old exams.
   □ Construct and respond to sample questions.
7. Mercer and Mercer (1985) recommend the following steps in all test taking.
   □ Review the entire test.
   □ Know the time allotted for taking the test.

□ Know the value of specific questions.
□ Follow the directions very carefully.
□ Notice key words in instructions and questions.
□ Reread directions and questions.
□ Go through the test and answer questions you are sure of first.
□ Place a checkmark beside questions you need to return to later.
□ Return to questions that have been checked.
□ Mark an X at the bottom of each completed page.
□ Review all questions. (p. 475)

8. Encourage students to use notes to predict essay questions and then practice writing responses to their questions (Bragstad & Stumpf, 1982).

9. For essay exams encourage students to jot down on the test sheet any facts and formulas that have been memorized and specific points pertaining to each question.

10. Roe, Stoodt, and Burns (1983) suggest the following useful hints for studying for essay tests.

□ Expect questions that cover the most important topics in the course.
□ Expect questions that are broad in scope.
□ Prepare sample questions and respond to them.
□ Responses should include main ideas accompanied by supporting details.

11. Mercer and Mercer (1985) offer guidelines for answering multiple-choice questions.

□ Know how many answers to select.
□ Be aware of the kind of answer you are seeking.
□ Remember the question.
□ Eliminate the obvious wrong answers.
□ Choose the answer that fits best.
□ Be careful in recording the answer.

12. Roe, Stoodt, and Burns (1983) give useful hints for studying for objective tests.

□ Become familiar with important details.
□ Consider the types of questions that have been asked on previous tests, and study for those types.
□ Try preparing mnemonic devices to aid in recalling various lists.
□ Learn helpful definitions.

Library/Textbook Skills

1. Have your class tour the school or public library. Reference librarians are often available for such tours. Be sure to examine the card catalog, reference section, and various indexes and abstracts. Check to find out whether computer searches are available (Carder, Coy, & Rickert, 1979).

2. Have students make posters showing how to use the card catalog, various reference materials, or procedures for checking out and returning library books. Display the best poster in the library.

3. A comprehensive discussion of the skills required to use library resources is available from Burmeister and Stevens (1974). They separate these skills into library organization and reference aids and include a variety of specific skills in each area.

    I. Library organization
       A. Dewey decimal system
       B. Library of Congress system
       C. The card catalog
   II. Reference aids
       A. Periodicals
          1. Indexes to general and nontechnical magazines
             a. *Reader's Guide to Periodical Literature*
             b. Abridged *Reader's Guide to Periodical Literature*
          2. Specialized indexes specific to one field of study or several related fields of study
       B. Books
          1. Bibliographies classified for student interests
          2. Bibliographies classified by content areas
       C. General reference aids
          1. Biographies
          2. Encyclopedias
          3. Almanacs
          4. Atlases
       D. Reviews of audiovisual aids

4. Have students prepare a glossary of library terms and abbreviations. Terms should be defined (e.g., *microfiche, call number, periodical.*) Devine (1981, pp. 216–217) identifies some of the abbreviations and terms often used but seldom learned.

ab.	abridge
anon.	anonymous
bul., bull.	bulletin
c.	copyright
ca.	*circa* or about
cf.	*confer* or compare
ed.	editor
e.g.	*exempli gratia*, or for example
et al.	*et alii* or and others
et seq.	*et sequens* or and the following
f. and ff.	pages following
ibid.	*ibidem* or in the same place
i.e.	*id est* or that is
infra	below
loc. cit.	*loco citato* or in the place cited
ms	manuscript

N.B.	note well
n.d.	no date
n.p.	no place
op. cit.	*opere citato* or in the work cited
p., pp.	page(s)
passim	here and there
pseud.	pseudonym
q.v.	*quod vide* or which see
rev.	revised
seq.	*sequens* or the following page
tr.	translator
v., vid.	*vide* or see
viz.	*videlicet* or that is to say
v., vol.	volume

5. Provide each student with a different card from a library card catalog. Have each explain all of the information on his card to the class or another student. For example, a subject card might include the book's subject, author, title, publisher, and copyright date.

6. Introduce students to the Dewey decimal system (Dewey, 1971) and explain how this classification system is used. Have students find a book in one of the major divisions of this system.

000–099	Generalities
100–199	Philosophy and Psychology
200–299	Religion
300–399	The Social Sciences
400–499	Language
500–599	Pure Sciences
600–699	Technology (Applied Sciences)
700–799	The Arts
800–899	Literature
900–999	General History and Geography

7. Devine (1981) suggests that students create a personal library classification system to replace the Dewey or Library of Congress system. Ask students to provide a justification for their new systems.

8. Give students an assignment to complete using the *Reader's Guide to Periodical Literature.* Have them report back to the class or another student.

9. Have a computer search completed on a specific topic. Explain the printout to students and have them find an article or document included in the printout.

10. Discuss the types of information found in encyclopedias. Give the students exercises in which certain volumes must be located or certain pieces of information must be found by using the letter and/or word guides (Ekwall, 1985).

11. To provide practice in the use of a thesaurus, have students find synonyms for specific words.

12. To provide practice in using a table of contents, ask students to list the topics and subtopics for a specific chapter. Ask students what they expect to learn from the chapter, considering only this information (Thomas, 1980).

13. Ekwall (1985) recommends explaining the purpose of a table of contents, index, and appendix in a book. Ask specific questions about their use (e.g., "What chapter explains how rockets operate?" "What page(s) contain descriptions of different types of rockets?" "Where would you find tables showing the types of rockets operated by various countries?").

Oral and Written Reports

1. Carder, Coy, and Rickert (1979) recommend the following steps in writing a paper.

   □ Select a narrow topic.
   □ Examine the reference materials to locate the sources that are available on the topic.
   □ Read the identified material.
   □ Take notes on cards while reading the selections.
   □ Make an outline from which the paper can be written.
   □ Organize the notecards according to the format of the outline.
   □ Write the paper one section at a time.
   □ Read the paper for cohesiveness and correct format.
   □ Type the final copy. (p. 79)

2. Give an outlining assignment to help students visualize how a particular reading is organized into main ideas and supporting details.

3. To improve the writing of reports, ask students for suggestions on narrowing a broad topic to make it more manageable. Then choose one of the narrowed topics and have students locate sources of information on it in the library. Ask each student to take notes from at least one source and to record bibliographic information. Synthesize the notes into a single outline (Roe, Stoodt, & Burns, 1983).

4. Give assignments in which students must summarize material from longer readings. Writing summaries helps students to concentrate on the major points in a selected reading.

5. Insist that notes for a research paper be kept on index cards that can later be sorted into subtopics. Require bibliographic sources to be included on the index cards.

6. Devine (1981) recommends providing students with opportunities to try different kinds of reporting. He suggests that students prepare three reports on a single topic: one in written form, one to be presented orally, and a third to be presented visually (photo essay, slide-tape). Discuss the advantages and disadvantages of different kinds of reporting.

7. Carefully explain to the students the specific purpose of an oral report. Provide relaxed and nonthreatening settings for all oral reports.

8. Allow some students to tape oral reports or prepare illustrations and audiovisual materials to supplement or substitute for written reports. Allow other students with difficulties to report to classrooms of younger children to avoid the threat of peer criticism (Boland, 1979).

Graphic Aids

1. Discuss with your class why some information is presented graphically. Carder, Coy, and Rickert (1979) identify some of the reasons.
   - Material that is complex in written form may be more easily comprehended graphically.
   - Large abstractions may be reduced to manageable bits of information.
   - Cultural, economic, or geographic differences between or within countries can be shown.
   - Models or systems of operations can be illustrated.

2. Graphic aids are often divided into two major types: (a) maps and (b) charts, diagrams, tables, and graphs.

3. When a map is included within a chapter, ask students specific map-related questions (e.g., "Where is the state capital located?" "Are there any major rivers in the country?" "Where are the airports located?").

4. Teach students to use road maps to estimate distances between locations, find capitals, and locate national monuments.

5. Ekwall (1985) recommends arranging the classroom as a travel bureau during one unit or map study. Have students identify future family trips and then determine places to visit, historical landmarks, and the most efficient travel routes.

6. Ask students to construct a map of an area of interest to the class. Have them draw the map to scale and include a title, directional indicator, and legend (Roe, Stoodt, & Burns, 1983).

7. Have students find textbook examples of the four major types of graphs: picture, circle or pie, bar, and line. Ask students to explain the purposes of the various graphs.

8. Thomas (1980) suggests including a graphic aid question on quizzes to emphasize the importance of various graphic aids.

9. As a practice exercise or for pre- or posttest assessment, Mercer and Mercer (1985) suggest providing students with a map, table, graph, or diagram and asking questions pertaining to the purpose, legend, format, and specific information of the visual aid.

10. Provide students with a descriptive paragraph. Ask them to construct a graphic aid (table, map, graph) concerning some aspect of the information provided.

11. Have students make a diagram of a basketball or football play and present it orally to the class (Mercer & Mercer, 1985).

REFERENCES

Aaronson, S. (1975). Note-taking improvement: A combined auditory, functional, and psychological approach. *Journal of Reading, 19,* 8–12.

Boland, S. S. (1979). Curricular adaptations for mildly handicapped secondary students. *Education Unlimited, 1,* 49–51.

Bragstad, B. J., & Stumpf, S. M. (1982). *A guidebook for teaching study skills and motivation.* Boston: Allyn & Bacon.

Brown, W. F., & Holtzman, W. H. (1967). *Survey of study habits and attitudes.* New York: Psychological Corporation.

Burmeister, L. E., & Stevens, I. J. (1974). Using library resources. In L. E. Burmeister (Ed.), *Reading strategies for secondary school teachers.* Menlo Park, CA: Addison-Wesley.

Carder, M. E., Coy, J. J., & Rickert, C. M. (1979). *Productive reading and study skills: A student's guide.* Dubuque, IA: Kendall/Hunt.

Courtney, B. L. (1965). Organization produced. In H. L. Herber (Ed.), *Developing study skills in secondary schools.* Newark, DE: International Reading Association.

CTB/McGraw-Hill. (1977, 1978). *California Achievement Test.* Monterey, CA: Author.

Deese, J., & Deese, E. K. (1979). *How to study* (3rd ed.). New York: McGraw-Hill.

Devine, T. G. (1981). *Teaching study skills.* Boston: Allyn & Bacon.

Dewey, M. (1971). *Dewey decimal classification and relative index.* Lake Placid, NY: Forest Press.

Eanet, M. G., & Manzo, A. V. (1976). REAP—A strategy for improving reading/writing/study skills. *Journal of Reading, 19,* 647–652.

Edwards, P. (1973). PANORAMA: A study technique. *Journal of Reading, 17,* 132–135.

Ekwall, E. E. (1985). *Locating and correcting reading difficulties* (4th ed.). Columbus, OH: Charles E. Merrill.

Ekwall, E. E., & Shanker, J. L. (1983). *Diagnosis and remediation of the disabled reader* (2nd ed.). Boston: Allyn & Bacon.

Hieronymus, A. N., Lindquist, E. F., & Hoover, H. D. (1982). *Iowa Test of Basic Skills.* Chicago: Riverside.

Lerner, J. (1985). *Learning disabilities: Theories, diagnosis, and teaching strategies.* Boston: Houghton Mifflin.

Lock, C. (1981). *Study skills.* West Lafayette, IN: Kappa Delta Pi.

Mercer, C. D., & Mercer, A. R. (1985). *Teaching students with learning problems* (2nd ed.). Columbus, OH: Charles E. Merrill.

Michael, W. B., Michael, J. J., & Zimmerman, W. S. (1972). *Study attitudes and methods survey.* San Diego, CA: Educational and Industrial Testing Service.

Naslund, R. A., Thorpe, L. P., & Lefever, D. W. (1978). *SRA Achievement Series.* Chicago: Science Research Associates.

Pauk, W. (1963). On scholarship: Advice to high school students. *Reading Teacher, 17,* 73–78.

———. (1974) *How to study in college* (2nd ed.). Boston: Houghton Mifflin.

Pauk, W., & Cassel, R. (1970). *The Cornell Learning and Study Skills Inventory.* Jacksonville, IL: Psychologists and Educators.

Polloway, E. A., & Smith, J. E. (1982). *Teaching language skills to exceptional learners.* Denver: Love.

Raygor, A. L. (1970). *Study Skills Test: McGraw-Hill Basic Skills System.* New York: McGraw-Hill.

Robinson, F. P. (1961). *Effective study* (rev. ed.). New York: Harper & Row.

Roe, B. D., Stoodt, B. D., & Burns, P. C. (1983). *Secondary school reading instruction: The content areas* (2nd ed.). Boston: Houghton Mifflin.

Scennel, D. P. (1978). *Tests of Achievement and Proficiency.* Chicago: Riverside.

Stewart, D. M., Kamm K., Allen, J., & Sols, D. K. (1972). *Wisconsin Tests of Reading Skill Development: Study Skills.* Minneapolis, MN: NCS Interpretive Scoring Systems.

Thomas, E. L. (1980). *Reading aids for every class.* Boston: Allyn & Bacon.

Tonjes, M. J., & Zintz, M. V. (1981). *Teaching reading/thinking/study skills in content classrooms.* Dubuque, IA: William C. Brown.

Sources of Materials

Academic Therapy Publications
20 Commercial Boulevard
Novato, CA 94947

Addison-Wesley Publishing
  Company
2725 Sand Hill Road
Menlo Park, CA 94205

Allyn and Bacon
7 Wells Avenue
Newton, MA 02159

American Book Company
450 West 33rd Street
New York, NY 10001

American Guidance Service
Publishers' Building
Circle Pines, MN 55014

Aspen Systems Corporation
1600 Research Boulevard
Rockville, MD 20850

Behavioral Research Laboratories
P.O. Box 577
Palo Alto, CA 94302

Benefic Press
10300 West Roosevelt Road
Westchester, IL 60153

Bobbs-Merrill Company
4300 West 62nd Street
Indianapolis, IN 46206

William C. Brown Publishers
2460 Kerper Boulevard
P.O. Box 539
Dubuque, IA 52001

California Test Bureau/McGraw-Hill
Del Monte Research Park
Monterey, CA 93940

Children's Press
1224 West Van Buren Street
Chicago, IL 60607

Council for Exceptional Children
1920 Association Drive
Reston, VA 22091

Cuisenaire Company of America
12 Church Street
New Rochelle, NY 10805

Curriculum Associates
5 Esquire Road
North Billerica, MA 01862

Developmental Learning Materials
P.O. Box 4000
One DLM Park
Allen, TX 75002

Economy Company
P.O. Box 25308
1901 North Walnut Street
Oklahoma City, OK 73125

Edmark Corporation
P.O. Box 3903
Bellevue, WA 98009

Educational Performance Associates
600 Broad Avenue
Ridgefield, NJ 07657

Educational Service
P.O. Box 219
Stevensville, MI 49127

Educational Testing Service
Princeton, NJ 08540

Educators Publishing Service
75 Moulton Street
Cambridge, MA 02138

Fearon Publishers
6 Davis Drive
Belmont, CA 94002

Follett Publishing Company
1010 West Washington Boulevard
Chicago, IL 60607

Ginn and Company
191 Spring Street
Lexington, MA 02173

Globe Book Company
50 West 23rd Street
New York, NY 10010

Guidance Associates
1526 Gilpin Avenue
Wilmington, DE 19806

Harcourt Brace Jovanovich
757 Third Avenue
New York, NY 10017

Harper and Row Publishers
10 East 53rd Street
New York, NY 10022

D. C. Heath and Company
125 Spring Street
Lexington, MA 02173

Holt, Rinehart and Winston
383 Madison Avenue
New York, NY 10017

Houghton Mifflin
One Beacon Street
Boston, MA 02107

International Reading Association
800 Barksdale Road
Newark, DE 19711

Jastak Associates
1526 Gilpin Avenue
Wilmington, DE 19806

Kendall/Hunt Publishing Company
2460 Kerper Boulevard
Dubuque, IA 52001

J. B. Lippincott Company
Educational Publishing Division
East Washington Square
Philadelphia, PA 19105

Love Publishing Company
1777 South Bellaire Street
Denver, CO 80222

Lyons and Carnahan
407 East 25th Street
Chicago, IL 60616

Macmillan Publishing Company
866 Third Avenue
New York, NY 10022

McGraw-Hill Book Company
1221 Avenue of the Americas
New York, NY 10020

Charles E. Merrill Publishing
   Company
1300 Alum Creek Drive
Columbus, OH 43216

Milton Bradley Company
74 Park Street
Springfield, MA 01101

William C. Morrow
105 Madison Avenue
New York, NY 10016

National Computer Systems
4401 West 76th Street
Minneapolis, MN 55435

Northwestern University Press
1735 Benson Avenue
Evanston, IL 60201

Open Court Publishing Company
1039 Eighth Street
Box 599
LaSalle, IL 61301

Prentice-Hall
Educational Books Division
Englewood Cliffs, NJ 07632

Pro-Ed
5341 Industrial Oaks Boulevard
Austin, TX 78735

Raintree Publishers Limited
205 West Highland Avenue
Milwaukee, WI 53203

Rand McNally and Company
P.O. Box 7600
Chicago, IL 60680

Reader's Digest Services
Educational Division
Pleasantville, NJ 10570

Research Press
Box 31773
Champaign, IL 61821

Riverside Publishing Company
1919 South Highland Avenue
Lombard, IL 60148

Scholastic Magazine and Book
  Services
50 West 44th Street
New York, NY 10036

Science Research Associates
155 North Wacker Drive
Chicago, IL 60606

Scott, Foresman and Company
1900 East Lake Avenue
Glenview, IL 60025

Teachers College Press
Teachers College, Columbia
  University
1234 Amsterdam Avenue
New York, NY 10027

Teaching Resources
P.O. Box 4000
One DLM Park
Allen, TX 75002

University of Illinois Press
Box 5081, Station A
Champaign, IL 61820

George Wahr Publishing Company
316 State Street
Ann Arbor, MI 41808

Webster/McGraw-Hill
1221 Avenue of the Americas
New York, NY 10020

White Mountain Publishing
  Company
Box 1072
Rock Springs, WY 82902

Xerox Education Publications
245 Long Hill Road
Middletown, CT 06457

Zaner-Bloser Company
2500 West Fifth Avenue
P.O. Box 16764
Columbus, OH 43215

Richard L. Zweig Associates
20800 Beach Boulevard
Huntington Beach, CA 92648

Name Index

Subject Index

Gerald Wallace (standing) graduated from Central Connecticut State University. He earned his M.Ed. degree in remedial reading from the University of Arizona in 1963. After teaching learning disabled elementary students for several years he went on to receive his Ph.D. in special education at the University of Oregon. He taught at the University of Utah and then joined the faculty of the University of Virginia in 1970. He is a past president of the Division for Children with Learning Disabilities (79–80) and has coauthored several publications, including the text *Learning Disabilities: Concepts and Characteristics.* **James M. Kauffman** studied elementary education at Goshen college (B.S.) and Washburn University (M.Ed.). He obtained his Ed.D. degree in special education from the University of Kansas in 1969. He has been a teacher of students in elementary through middle school grades in regular and special public school classes and has worked with emotionally disturbed children at Southard School, the children's division of the Menninger Clinic. At the University of Virginia, where he has been a faculty member since 1970, he has served as chair of the Department of Special Education and associate dean for Research. He has published widely, notably the text *Characteristics of Children's Behavior Disorders.*